HISTORY

OF THE

AMERICAN BIBLE SOCIETY,

FROM ITS

ORGANIZATION TO THE PRESENT TIME.

BY W. P. STRICKLAND,

ONE OF THE SOCIETY'S AGENTS.

WITH AN INTRODUCTION BY REV. N. L. RICE, D.D.,

OF CINCINNATI.

Embellished with a Likeness of the Hon. Elias Boudinot, LL.D.

FIRST PRESIDENT OF THE SOCIETY.

"The Lord gave the word; great was the company of those that published it."—*Psalm* lxviii. 11.

NEW YORK:

HARPER & BROTHERS, PUBLISHERS, 82, CLIFF STREET;

LONDON:

SAMPSON LOW, 169, FLEET STREET.

1850.

TO

THE OFFICERS AND MANAGERS

OF THE

AMERICAN BIBLE SOCIETY,

This Work

IS RESPECTFULLY AND AFFECTIONATELY INSCRIBED.

PREFACE.

The necessity of some such work as the following was suggested to the mind of the author when he entered upon his duties as agent of the American Bible Society several years since.

He found the field of labor in which he had engaged one concerning the nature of which he knew but little. To obtain such information as would qualify him for his work, it therefore became necessary for him to study the policy and operations of the society, as contained in the printed reports, circulars, and letters of instruction issued from the Board from time to time, and embracing a period of many years. He found that, to give a full and intelligible answer in regard to almost any important topic connected with the society, the whole field of its operations must be searched, and the scattered fragments lying here and there must be gathered up and arranged.

In the preparation of each of the thirty-nine chapters, with but few exceptions, the writer has traveled over the entire ground every time, collecting from the reports and collateral documents every important fact connected therewith.

He has made no attempt whatever at embellishment, his object having been to present a plain, unvarnished narrative of facts, as they have occurred in the operations of the society, in consecutive order. How far he has succeeded in this humble attempt is left for the reader to determine.

For assistance in the compilation of the work, the writer acknowledges his indebtedness to the following works: Dr. Spring's Life of Rev. Samuel J. Mills, Horne's Introduction, Townley's Biblical Literature, Buchanan's Researches in Asia, Anderson's Annals of the English Bible, D'Aubigné's Reformation, Edwards's Missionary Gazetteer, Choules's History of Missions, Wyckoff's Bible Question, &c. He also takes pleasure in acknowledging his indebtedness to the Rev. J. C. Brigham, D.D., Corresponding Secretary of the American Bible Society.

SUMMARY OF CONTENTS.

PRINTING, PUBLICATION, AND CIRCULATION OF BIBLES.

BIBLE IN PRISONS.

BIBLE AMONG SEAMEN AND BOATMEN.

BIBLE IN THE ARMY.

BIBLE AMONG THE INDIANS.

BIBLE IN OREGON AND CALIFORNIA.

TRANSLATIONS OF THE BIBLE INTO FOREIGN LANGUAGES.

BIBLE IN CANADA.

BIBLE IN SOUTH AMERICA.

BIBLE IN FRANCE.

BIBLE IN THE CHINESE EMPIRE.

BIBLE IN CEYLON.

APPENDIX.

ANNIVERSARIES—ADDRESSES.

INTRODUCTION.

We live in an eventful age. In a single year changes have taken place in the political and religious condition of the nations of Europe which one would think a half century could not have effected. The wise observer of "the signs of the times" can not fail to recognize, in the revolutions which have occurred, the hand of Him who is "head over all things to the Church;" nor to perceive, from the present aspect of things in Europe, that we have seen but the beginning. Indeed, there has been, especially within the last thirty years or more, a rapid preparation of the world for the millennial day. Every important change in the political world has evidently tended that way; while, through the instrumentality of the Church, in her different branches, a vast moral machinery has been preparing, which, under the Divine blessing, will pour the light of the Gospel upon all nations. By the political changes effected within a few years, the way has been opened for the promulgation of the Gospel in almost every nation on the globe, while the different evangelical denominations have organized their Missionary Boards, and taken their stand side by side in the conflict between light and darkness. At the same time, guided and influenced by the Spirit of God, they have thrown themselves as into one body, that with their united wealth and talents they may place the Bible, without note or comment, in the hands of every individual of our ruined race.

This is a glorious enterprise! Reasoning simply as

philosophers, we can not but conclude that the great cause of human degradation and misery, in all ages, has been human depravity. Men have been sinful, and, therefore, degraded and miserable—"hateful and hating one another." All schemes, therefore, for elevating men and improving their condition, which do not contemplate, as the first and chief thing to be done, their *moral purification*, are unphilosophical and worthless. Society is composed of families, and families of individuals. Improve the moral character of individuals, and families will be virtuous and happy; and the divine declaration will be illustrated and confirmed, that "righteousness exalteth a nation."

But how shall the moral character of men be improved? They must understand their relations, their duties, and the motives which urge and encourage to virtue. Where shall we find a perfect authoritative moral code, with every possible motive to virtue and holy living? In the BIBLE we have such a code. No crime was ever committed which it does not directly or indirectly forbid and condemn; no virtue ever adorned the human character which it does not require and commend; and no motive can be presented in favor of righteousness which is not presented in its fullest power in the Gospel of Christ. With it the man of God is "thoroughly furnished to all good works." Let the authority of the Bible become supreme in every mind, and the ten thousand fountains of human wretchedness, by which this world has become "a vale of tears," will be dried up.

This is not mere *theory*. The history of the world confirms abundantly all we have said. We live in the middle of the *nineteenth century*, in an age considered pre-eminently enlightened, where the arts and sciences are cultivated with astonishing success. Now take a survey of the nations which people our globe.

Carefully inquire into the true condition of the masses of the people, and then answer the two following questions, viz.: 1. Has the world made one step of progress in education, in morals, in the principles of liberty, except so far as it has been brought under the influence, direct or indirect, of Christianity? Is the superstition of India and of China less degrading, and is the moral and social condition of the people a whit better than ten centuries ago? 2. Is not the improvement in the condition of the more enlightened nations precisely in proportion to the extent to which they have been brought under the influence of Christianity in its purity? How else shall we account for the happy condition of Protestant countries as compared with that of France, Spain, Portugal, Italy, Austria, &c.?

The enterprise in which the American Bible Society and her sister societies are engaged, we repeat, is a glorious one. It is so, even if we confine our views of its happy results to the present world. How much more glorious does it appear when we regard the Bible as the clear light given by a merciful God to guide immortal beings to eternal felicity—as "the power of God to salvation to every one that believeth." Without it our origin, our duty, and our destiny are alike involved in impenetrable darkness; and our minds, formed for immortality, are destined to pine in hopeless gloom, and leave the world in despair. In its sacred pages life and immortality are brought to light; and even in the midst of the troubles of this life, we have from God himself the exhortation, "Rejoice evermore."

It is a matter of peculiar interest to see the different denominations of Christians harmoniously uniting in this noble enterprise. False philosophy may, as often it has done, pervert the language of inspiration. Prejudice, and the blending influence of remaining depravity in the Church, may lead to the misinterpretation of its plain teachings. Various causes combining may, for a time, greatly obscure its celestial light. But all are agreed, happily, that it is the lamp to our feet, the light to our path. We may have erred in our interpretation of some portions of it; but, untrammeled by human traditions and by the fiction of church infallibility, we may go again and again to the unerring guide, and there correct previous errors. And as in these latter days the Holy Spirit shall be more abundantly poured upon the Church, and the standard of true piety shall rise higher and higher, the spiritual vision of the servants of God will become clearer, the watchmen on the walls of Zion shall see eye to eye, minor differences will gradually disappear, until the different branches of the Church shall mingle harmoniously together, and she shall "look forth fair as the moon, clear as the sun, and terrible as an army with banners. Then shall the mountain of the Lord's house be established in the top of the mountains, and be exalted above the hills, and all nations shall flow into it."

God in his providence has opened an effectual door in almost every nation for the circulation of the sacred Scriptures. The colporteur in France is no longer in danger of being impressed by the bigoted tools of a corrupt priesthood; even in the states of Italy and in intolerant Austria the way is prepared for putting the Word of God in the hands of the people; and hundreds of thousands of foreigners are annually flocking to the shores of our own happy country, that they may be made acquainted with the pure Word of God.

This is not all. The human mind is excited in a most extraordinary degree. The veil of sanctity is torn from errors whose antiquity shielded them from investigation. Men the world over are waking up from the slumber of ages, and inquiring for *truth.* Romanism, the bitterest and most successful of all the enemies of the Bible, is tottering to its fall. The twelve hundred and sixty years of the reign of anti-Christ are drawing to a close. The pope, lauded for a time as more enlightened and liberal than any of his predecessors, has fled in disguise from his palace, has been deposed as a temporal sovereign by his own children, and now pines in exile! Now is the time for the Church to put forth all her energies, that she may send forth the pure Word of God, as well as the living ministry, to enlighten the nations. It is her wisdom to work when the Lord is working—to hear the noise of a going in the mulberry-trees, and hasten to the conflict.

The author of the following pages has done an important service for the Church. What Christian does not desire to acquaint himself with the history and the success of the efforts which have been made to send the Bible, translated into all languages, to the people of all nations, that they may read, each in his own language, "the wonderful works of God?" It was no small labor to collect and arrange the immense mass of interesting facts which so much enhance the value of the work; and we are sure the author will receive, as he richly deserves, the thanks of every enlightened friend of the cause, and will secure for the work a very extensive circulation. The book, like the enterprise it aims to promote, is in its character *catholic.* Presenting no sectarian dogma, and aiming to build up no party or sect, it will find a welcome in the family library of Christians of all denominations. Filled with important and instructive facts connected with the translation and circulation of the Scriptures, both in our own country and in foreign lands, detailing the labors and success of the different societies co-operating in the glorious work, it will be exceedingly valuable as a book of reference.

Some books, perhaps, require a lengthy and labored introduction to commend them to public favor; but this is not a book of that class. We need only to know its aim, and glance over the table of contents, to be convinced of its value. It is a history (and the *first* history written) of one of the noblest and most philanthropic enterprises ever embarked in by men; and this fact is commendation enough to secure for the work a careful perusal, and a permanent place in the ministerial and family library.

AMERICAN BIBLE SOCIETY.

AMERICAN BIBLE SOCIETY.

CHAPTER I.

CONDITION OF THE COUNTRY PRIOR TO THE ORGANIZATION OF THE SOCIETY.

Before entering upon a narrative of the operations of the American Bible Society, it may not be improper, or foreign to the subject, to take a cursory glance at the condition of the country prior to its organization, and also to notice briefly the efforts that were made to introduce and circulate the Scriptures in the infant colonies of this pilgrim land, and subsequently in the States.

The Puritans having been, by persecution and proscription, "shut up to the faith" of the word of God alone, learned therefrom the true equality of rights, political as well as social and religious, and, fleeing from the land of oppression for conscience' sake, they sought an asylum in this new world. The Bible was the star that guided them across a wintery ocean upward of two hundred years ago; and when they landed upon these shores, and laid the foundations of this great republic, they labored assiduously to incorporate its principles with the elements of government, and diffuse them through all their institutions, civil, literary, and religious. Amid the surrounding darkness of Church and State, and the efforts to abridge ecclesiastical and civil liberty, the Puritans, with their open

Bible, nobly contended for the faith; and Hume himself, who always bore to them a special dislike, has said, "The precious spark of liberty had been kindled, and was preserved by the Puritans alone." They came to this land to make it the land of the Bible and of freedom—to worship God as revelation and conscience might teach.

Seventeen years previous to the landing of the Pilgrims, the translation of the Bible by King James had been made; and the edict by Henry VIII., which restricted its reading to royalty, and barred access to all the rest of mankind, was revoked, and the living oracles were opened to all who could procure them.

The "May Flower" was freighted with the precious legacy of Heaven, and the dim eye of age, together with the flashing eye of youth, caught new fire in poring over its sacred pages, and anon melted at the recital of its messages of mercy and love.

In Mr. Webster's great Bunker Hill oration the following passage occurs:

"It has been said, with very much veracity, that the felicity of the American colonists consisted in their escape from the past. This is true so far as it respects political establishments, but no farther. They brought with them a full portion of all the riches of the past in science, in art, in morals, religion, and literature. *The Bible came with them.* And it is not to be doubted that to the free and universal reading of the Bible is to be ascribed, in that age, that men were indebted for right views of *Civil Liberty.* The Bible is a book which teaches man his own individual responsibility, *his own dignity, and his equality with his fellow-men.*"

The colonists being mostly Christians, as they peopled the country, did, perhaps, all that their limited means would permit to supply the wants of the population with the Bible. As early as the beginning of the last century, laws existed in some of the colonies requiring every family to be furnished with a Bible. This supply continued to be kept up by individual exertion until the meeting of the first Congress in 1777, one year after the declaration of independence. In the early formation of our government, those who looked upon the experiment with jealous eyes anticipated a speedy dissolution, from the fact that it made no provision for the establishment of religion. Although the legislative power of our country is prohibited from making laws prescribing and enforcing the observance of any particular faith or form of worship, yet it is equally powerless in prohibiting the free exercise thereof, while, at the same time, it extends its protecting ægis over the rights of conscience. The government has never been unmindful of the great interests of religion, but has from the beginning adhered to and carried out the language of Washington, that "religion and morality are indispensable supports of political existence and prosperity."

The Congress of 1777 answered a memorial on the subject of Bible destitution in this country by appointing a committee to advise as to the printing an edition of thirty thousand Bibles. The population of the country then was only about three millions, and all the Bibles in the entire *world* at that period did not exceed four millions. Thus it will be seen that its circulation in this and all other countries at that time was exceedingly limited.

The report of the committee appointed by Congress forms one of the brightest epochs in the history of our country, and sheds a clear and steady light over every subsequent eventful period. The public recognition of God in that act was of infinitely greater importance in giving stability to the times, and securing the permanency of our institutions, than all the imposing and formidable array of legal enactments ever made for the establishment of religion.

The committee, finding it difficult to procure the necessary material, such as paper and types, recommended Congress—"the use of the Bible being so universal, and its importance so great—to direct the Committee on Commerce to import, at the *expense* of Congress, twenty thousand English Bibles from Holland, Scotland, or elsewhere, into the different ports of the States of the Union." The report was adopted, and the importation ordered.

In 1781, when, from the existence of the war, an English Bible could not be imported, and no opinion could be formed how long the obstruction might continue, the subject of printing the Bible was again presented to Congress, and it was, on motion, referred to a committee of three.

The committee, after giving the subject a careful investigation, recommended to Congress an edition printed by Robert Aitken, of Philadelphia; whereupon it was "*Resolved*, That the United States, in Congress assembled, highly approve the pious and laudable undertaking of Mr. Aitken, as subservient to the interests of religion; and being satisfied of the care and accuracy of the execution of the work, recommend this edition to the inhabitants of the United States."

How interesting is such a history of the early circulation of the Bible in this country! What moral sublimity in the fact, as it stands imperishably recorded and filed in the national archives! Who, in view of this fact, will call in question the assertion that *this is a Bible nation?* Who will charge the government with indifference to religion, when the *first* Congress of the States assumed all the rights and performed all the duties of a *Bible Society long before such an institution had an existence in the world!* What a standing, withering rebuke this to ecclesiastico-political demagogues, who, imitating the example of a late minister of instruction for France, would expel the Bible from the schools of our land!

The universal circulation and reading of the Scriptures in this country form the foundation upon which rest, as on an immovable basis, our liberty and happiness. Well did De Tocqueville remark (when informed by a superintendent that the Bible was the only text-book in our Sabbath schools), "What an influence this must have upon the destiny of a nation." It is to this fact alone, viz., the universal circulation and unprohibited reading of the Scriptures, that we owe all our distinguishing blessings as a nation. During the infidel revolution in France, at the close of the last century, inquiry was made in the principal book-stores of Paris for a copy of the Bible, but it was not to be found. A similar inquiry was made in Rome of *all* the book establishments of the city, and the invariable reply was, "*E prohibito;*" "*Non est permesso.*" In all Catholic countries it is a condemned and prohibited book. Here it has "free course, and is glorified." Palsied be the hand that would banish it from our schools of instruction! Speechless be the tongue that would utter an anathema against the circulation and reading of the Word of God!

The purest patriots and the most eminent statesmen of our country, from the commencement of our existence as a nation down to the present time, have revered the Bible, and cherished it as the richest legacy of Heaven.

This sentiment is strongly interwoven with the politics of our country, however diversified may be our opinions and variant our political creeds. A single incident will illustrate this point. When it was said by one who occupied a prominent place in the councils of the nation, in speaking of the political creed of a certain candidate for the presidency, that his opinions were as various and contradictory as the teachings of the Bible, one belonging to the same political school indignantly replied, "Let a nation's curse follow the hoary-headed blasphemer to his grave!"

The wrecks of the many nations that lie scattered here and there along the shores of Time afford melancholy proof of the fact, that all who despise the Word of God shall likewise perish. One of the finest Oriental scholars of this or any age, who has devoted his whole life to the acquisition of biblical science, and other studies of a collateral character, has declared, that "in all the Bible there is not one physical, intellectual, or moral error; nothing—absolutely nothing—that infidelity can contradict, or science, in her most enlarged discoveries, rectify."

To all who are impressed with the importance of the Holy Scriptures, no argument is necessary to induce a diligent attention to their oracles as "a light to the feet and a lamp to the path" in this world of doubt and uncertainty; nor does it require any labor to convince those who are thus taught of God the duty of supplying the destitute with the sacred treasure.

This love for the Scriptures, and regard for its divine injunctions, existed in an eminent degree in the hearts of our forefathers; and hence, following the example set by the friends of the cause in England, exhibited in the organization of the *British and Foreign Bible Society*, they organized small local societies in different parts of the United States. These societies were instrumental in accomplishing much good to the immediate vicinities in which they were located, but their operations were necessarily much contracted, and their influence exceedingly limited. Bibles were obtained by these societies from private booksellers at a high price, and many of them were imperfect copies. They labored under these and similar embarrassments in supplying the destitute around them, but no provision was made to send the Word of Life to the destitute abroad. This state of things was felt and deeply deplored by ministers and laymen of the different religious denominations, and they prayed and labored to bring about a better state of things, that the universal brotherhood of man might be made partakers with them of the common salvation.

CHAPTER II.

CAUSES WHICH PREPARED THE WAY FOR THE ORGANIZATION.

In addition to the careful consultation of all the official records of the society, which, in the preparation of this work, have been thoroughly examined, the writer availed himself of the information and reminiscences of some of the remaining few who were members of the Convention which organized the society.

Among this number were the Rev. Dr. Biggs, president of Woodward College, Cincinnati, and Rev. Dr. Beecher, the venerable president of Lane Theological Seminary; the latter being the only surviving officer of that honorable and ever-memorable body, having acted as one of the secretaries.

The Rev. Gardiner Spring, D.D., of New York, the author of two of the most admirably written works on the Bible, entitled "Obligations of the World to the Bible," and "The Bible not of Man," has also kindly furnished us with some incidents connected with the proceedings of the Convention. Dr. Spring took an active part in the proceedings of the Convention, and from that time to the present has devoted the energies of a powerful intellect to the advancement of the Bible cause.

The subject of organizing a national society had been discussed by the friends of the cause from time to time. Ably written articles appeared in many of the leading religious journals of the day in advocacy of the enterprise. Application was also made to some of the oldest and most influential of the then existing auxiliaries to form themselves into a general society, but the time had not yet fully come. A general interest was, however, awakened, and the many seeming difficulties began to give way.

In the year 1814, a correspondent in the "Panoplist and Missionary Magazine" presented a powerful appeal in behalf of the Bible cause, and urged in an impressive manner the importance of the formation of a general Bible Society. He exhibited the biblical wants of the country, and presented facts tending to show conclusively that the few local societies which were in existence could not, in any adequate degree, supply those wants.

He showed, also, the great and essential importance of such an institution in promoting the missionary cause by the translation and printing of the Scriptures in foreign tongues.

Thus the subject continued to be agitated from year to year until 1815, when a plan for the organization of a national society originated with the New Jersey Bible Society, and was sent to the sister societies for concurrence. In 1816 the attention of the Board of Managers of the New York Bible Society was engaged in the plan, and, as the result of their deliberations, the following resolutions were passed:

"1st. *Resolved*, That it is highly desirable to obtain, upon as large a scale as possible, a co-operation of the efforts of the Christian community throughout the United States for the efficient distribution of the Holy Scriptures.

"2d. *Resolved*, That, as a mean for the attainment of this end, it will be expedient to have a convention of delegates from such Bible societies as shall be disposed to concur in this measure, to meet at ——, on the —— day of —— next, for the purpose of considering whether such a co-operation may be effected in a better manner than by the correspondence of the different societies as now established, and if so, that they prepare the draft of a plan for such co-operation, to be submitted to the different societies for their decision.

"3d. *Resolved*, That the secretary transmit the above resolutions to the President of the New Jersey Bible Society, as expressive of the opinion of this board on the measure therein contained, and at the same time signifying the wish of this board that he would exercise his own discretion in bringing the subject before the public."

In pursuance of the above, the Hon. Elias Boudinot, president of the New Jersey Bible Society, published, in the Panoplist and elsewhere, a notice of a general meeting, to be held at the city of New York on the second Wednesday of May, 1816.

The invitation only extended to the different local Bible societies then in existence, and though it was thought at the time it should have included all the friends of the Bible in the country, yet subsequent events fully justified the wisdom of the president in regard to the nature and extent of the call.

The following interesting facts and incidents, in connection with the proceedings of the Convention and the organization of the society, is from the pen of

Dr. Beecher, and kindly furnished by him for this work:

"*Memorandum respecting the Causes which prepared the Way for the establishment of the American Bible Society.*

"The first cause, no doubt, was the existence and prosperous operations of the British and Foreign Bible Society.

"The second was the foreign missionary spirit that was awakened a few years anterior, and the organization of the Foreign Missionary Society.

"The primary agent in this movement, I am well assured, was the *Rev. Samuel J. Mills*, in whose heart the fire of foreign missions first burned for several years.

"In his travels West and South he had the organization of an American Bible Society at heart, and, though a man of little promise in appearance, was distinguished by strong and increasing love to God and man, added to a profound wisdom, indefatigable industry, and unparalleled executive power in the excitement and combination of minds in benevolent organizations.

"It was by personal conversation, I doubt not, with thousands of the most influential men all over our nation, and addressing, when he had opportunity, ecclesiastical bodies, that he had prepared the way for a harmonious concurrence in favor of organization when the Convention met.

"It was a sublime spectacle when the Convention met. Each one had his own mind prepared by an agency which he had scarcely recognized, and of whose ubiquitous influence he had no knowledge. We came to the meeting in great weakness, humility, and prayer, feeling the difficulties in combining all denominations, and feeling every one the necessity of keeping his heart and tongue, and walking very softly, lest a spark of unhallowed fire falling on a train, it should explode. It was a meeting of select hearts, and talents, and influence, and of sublime humility, wisdom, and prayer. We felt that the place was holy where we stood, and that God was there; and our fears were not realized, and our hopes were surpassed exceedingly abundantly, so cordial was our unity. When the vote was put that it was expedient at that time to organize an American Bible Society, there was a moment of exulting, grateful, prayerful silence. There was but one short moment in our proceedings when things seemed to tangle, and some feelings began to rise. At that moment Dr. Mason rose hastily, and said, 'Mr. President,* the Lord Jesus never built a church but what the devil built a chapel close to it; and he is here now, this moment, in this

* Joshua M. Wallace, Esq.

room, with his finger in the ink-horn, not to write your Constitution, but to blot it out.' This sudden address convulsed the Convention with laughter, which in a moment dispelled the storm and revealed a clear sun, which instantly perceiving, he said, 'There! there! he has gone already to his blue brimstone!' "

CHAPTER III.

ORGANIZATION OF THE SOCIETY.

In obedience to the command of our divine Lord and Savior Jesus Christ, requiring the Church to "publish the Gospel to every creature," coupled with the injunction to all to "search the Scriptures," the American Bible Society was instituted. Its primary object was to supply the biblical wants of this widely-extended country, but its benevolence was not designed to be limited to this country alone. The original design was clearly manifested in the language of the first address: "Let it not be supposed that geographical or political limits are to be the limits of the American Bible Society; the designation is meant, not to indicate the restriction of their labor, but the source of its emanation. They will embrace, with thankfulness and pleasure, every opportunity of raying out, by means of the Bible, according to their ability, the light of life and immortality to such parts of the world as are destitute of the blessing and within their reach. In this high vocation they are ambitious to be fellow-workers with those who are fellow-workers with God."

Impressed with such truly catholic principles, the friends of the Bible cause came up to the work, and the 8th of May, 1816, witnessed Christians of almost every denomination, from every part of the United States, assembled in Convention, in the city of New

York, for the purpose of deliberation in reference to the organization of a general society.

The Convention was organized by calling to the chair Joshua M. Wallace, Esq., of Burlington, and the appointment of Rev. Messrs. Romeyn and Beecher secretaries. The following delegates from the different local societies presented their credentials, and were duly admitted to seats:

Bassett, Rev. John, D.D., Bushwick, L. I.
Bayard, Samuel, Princeton, N. J.
Beecher, Rev. Lyman, D.D., *Secretary of the Convention*, Cincinnati, Ohio.
Biggs, Rev. Thomas J., Cincinnati, Ohio.
Blatchford, Rev. Samuel, D.D., Lansingburg, N. Y.
Blythe, Rev. James, D.D., South Hanover, Ind.
Bogart, Rev. David S., New York.
Bradford, Rev. John M., D.D., Albany, N. Y.
Burd, William, St. Louis, Missouri.
Caldwell, John E., New York.
Callender, Levi, Greenville, N. Y.
Chester, Rev. John, D.D., Albany, N. Y.
Clarke, Matthew St. Clair, Washington, D. C.
Cooley, Rev. Eli F., Monmouth, N. J.
Cooper, James, New York.
Day, Orrin, Catskill, N. Y.
Eddy, Thomas, New York.
Ford, Rev. Henry, Elmira, N. Y.
Forrest, Rev. Robert, Roseville, N. Y.
Griscom, John, LL.D., Trenton, N. J.
Hall, Rev. James, D.D., Statesville, N. C.
Henshaw, Rt. Rev. J. P. K., D.D., Providence, R. I.
Hornblower, Joseph C., LL.D., Newark, N. J., Vice President.
Humphrey, Rev. Heman, D.D., Pittsfield, Mass.
Jay, William, Bedford, N. Y., Vice President.
Jones, Rev. David, Holmesburgh, Penn.
Lewis, Rev. Isaac, D.D., Greenwich, Ct.
Linklaen, Gen. John, Cazenovia, N. Y.
M'Dowell, Rev. John, D.D., Philadelphia, Penn.
Mason, Rev. John M., D.D., New York.
Milledoler, Rev. Philip, D.D., New York.
Morse, Rev. Jedediah, D.D., New Haven, Conn.
Mott, Valentine, M.D., New York.

Mulligan, William C., New York.
Murray, John, Jr., New York.
Neil, Rev. William, D.D., Philadelphia, Penn.
Nott, Rev. Eliphalet, D.D., Schenectady, N. Y.
Oliver, Rev. Andrew, Springfield, N. Y.
Platt, Rev. Isaac W., Athens, Penn.
Proudfit, Rev. Alexander, D.D., New York.
Rice, Rev. John H., D.D.
Richards, Rev. James, D.D., Auburn, N. Y.
Romeyn, Rev. John B., D.D., *Sec. of the Convention*, New York
Sands, Joshua, Brooklyn, L. I.
Sayres, Rev. Gilbert, Jamaica, L. I.
Sedgwick, Robert, New York.
Skinner, Ichabod L., Washington, D. C.
Spring, Rev. Samuel, D.D., Newburyport, Mass.
Spring, Rev. Gardiner, D.D., New York.
Swift, Gen. Joseph G., Brooklyn, L. I.
Taylor, Rev. N. W., D.D., New Haven, Conn.
Van Sinderen, Adrian, Brooklyn, L. I.
Vroom, Guysbert B., New York.
Wallace, Joshua M., *Pres. of the Convention*, Burlington, N. J.
Warner, Henry W., New York.
Williams, Rev. John, New York.
Williams, William, Vernon, N. Y.
Wilmur, Rev. Simon, Swedesborough, N. J.
Woodhull, Rev. George S.
Wright, Charles, Flushing, L. I.

It was an auspicious day, pregnant with blessings to this country. The occasion was great, and great were the men, and worthy, that it called together—names illustrious for rare virtues and noble deeds in Church and State. The Bible Society will ever prove an enduring monument to perpetuate their acts. Delegates from twenty-eight local societies participated in the deliberations of that hour. Difficulties, it is true, were anticipated, and some arose; but as they progressed in the spirit of forbearance and mutual concession, they passed away like the mist from the surface of a clear, calm river in the light of the sun. It was the first time the different religious denominations were brought together for concerted action; but they met on the broad platform of the Bible,

"Where names, and sects, and parties fall."

They presented to the world a model of an evangelical alliance, having for its basis the true catholic doctrine—*the Bible*—God's revelation to man, the only and sufficient rule of faith and practice—the right and duty of private interpretation. The great object for which they had assembled was, not to investigate its claims as a rule of faith, or to debate the question of the right of private judgment, but to enter at once upon the work of devising means for its universal circulation, without note or comment, among all nations, of whatever name, or country, or caste, or color, "excluding, by its very nature, all local feelings, party prejudices, and sectarian jealousies." They declared themselves "leagued in that, and that alone, which calls up every hallowed, and puts down every unhallowed principle, the dissemination of the Scriptures in the received versions where they exist, and in the most faithful where they may be required. In such a work, whatever is dignified, kind, venerable, true, has ample scope, while sectarian littleness and rivalries can find no avenue of admission."

The Convention appointed a committee, consisting of Drs. Nott, Mason, Morse, and Blythe, and Messrs. Beecher, Bayard, Wilmer, Wright, Rice, Jones, and Jay, to draft a Constitution, whereupon it adjourned until the following morning.

On the morning of the 11th of May the Convention met agreeably to adjournment; the committee presented the Constitution, which, after having been read in whole, and afterward in paragraphs, and carefully considered, was unanimously adopted, as follows:

CONSTITUTION.

I. This Society shall be known by the name of the *American Bible Society*, of which the sole object shall be to encourage a wider circulation of the Holy Scriptures, without note or comment. The only copies in the English language to be circulated by the Society shall be of the version now in common use.

II. This Society shall add its endeavors to those employed by other societies for circulating the Scriptures throughout the United States and their territories, and shall furnish them with stereotype plates or such other assistance as circumstances may require. This Society shall also, according to its ability, extend its influence to other countries, whether Christian, Mohammedan, or pagan.

III. All Bible Societies shall be allowed to purchase at cost from this Society Bibles for distribution within their own districts. The members of all such Bible Societies as shall agree to place their surplus revenue, after supplying their own districts with Bibles, at the disposal of this Society, shall be entitled to vote in all meetings of the Society, and the officers of such societies shall be *ex-officio* directors of this.*

IV. Each subscriber of three dollars annually shall be a member.

V. Each subscriber of thirty dollars at one time shall be a member for life.

†VI. Each subscriber of fifteen dollars annually shall be a director.

VII. Each subscriber of one hundred and fifty dollars at one time, or who shall, by one additional payment, increase his original subscription to one hundred and fifty dollars, shall be a director for life.

VIII. Directors shall be entitled to attend and vote at all meetings of the Board of Managers.

IX. A Board of Managers shall be appointed to conduct the business of the Society, consisting of thirty-six laymen, of whom twenty-four shall reside in the city of New York or its vicinity. One fourth part of the whole number shall go out of office at the expiration of each year, but shall be re-eligible. Every minister of the Gospel who is a member of the Society shall be entitled to meet and vote with the Board of Managers, and be possessed of the same powers as a manager himself.

The Managers shall appoint all officers, and call special general meetings, and fill such vacancies as may occur, by death or otherwise, in their own board.

X. Each member of the Society shall be entitled, under the direction

* The latter clause of this article was amended by striking out.

† This article was expunged in 1819.

of the Board of Managers, to purchase Bibles and Testaments at the Society's prices, which shall be as low as possible.

XI. The annual meetings of the Society shall be held at New York or Philadelphia, at the option of the Society, on the second Thursday of May in each year, when the Managers shall be chosen, the accounts presented, and the proceedings of the foregoing year reported.

XII. The President, Vice-Presidents, Treasurer, and Secretaries for the time being shall be considered *ex-officio* members of the Board of Managers.

XIII. At the general meetings of the Society, and the meetings of the Managers, the President, or, in his absence, the Vice-President first on the list then present, and in the absence of all the Vice-Presidents, such member as shall be appointed for that purpose, shall preside at the meeting.

XIV. The Managers shall meet on the first Wednesday of each month, or oftener if necessary, at such place in the city of New York as they shall from time to time adjourn to.

XV. The Managers shall have the power of appointing such persons as have rendered essential services to the Society either members for life or directors for life.

XVI. The whole minutes of every meeting shall be signed by the chairman.

*XVII. The President, or, in his absence, the Vice-President first on the list in the city of New York, may, at the written request of six members of the Board, call special meetings of the Board of Managers, causing three days' notice of such meetings to be given.

†XVIII. The Board of Managers may admit to the privileges of an auxiliary any society which was organized, and had commenced the printing, publication, and issuing of the sacred Scriptures before the establishment of this Society, with such relaxation of the terms of admission hereunto prescribed as the said Board, two thirds of the members present consenting, may think proper.

XIX. No alteration shall be made to this Constitution except by the Society at an annual meeting, on the recommendation of the Board of Managers.‡

After the adoption of the Constitution, the Convention proceeded to the election of thirty-six managers, as provided for in the Constitution. These managers were, in accordance with the general principles of the

* This article was added in 1819. † This article was added in 1829.

‡ This is now numbered the XVIth article.

society, selected from the different evangelical denominations co-operating with the American Bible Society. The following were unanimously chosen:

Henry Rutgers,	Ebenezer Burrill,
John Bingham,	Andrew Gifford,
Richard Varick,	George Gosman,
Thomas Farmar,	Thomas Carpenter,
Stephen Van Rensselaer,	Leonard Bleecker,
Samuel Boyd,	John Caldwell,
George Suckley,	Rufus King,
Divie Bethune,	Thomas Stokes,
William Bayard,	Joshua Sands,
Peter M'Cartee,	George Warner,
Thomas Shields,	De Witt Clinton,
Robert Ralston,	John Warder,
John R. B. Rodgers,	Samuel Bayard,
Dr. Peter Wilson,	Duncan P. Campbell,
Jeremiah Evarts,	John Aspinwall,
John Watts, M.D.,	John Murray, Jun.,
Thomas Eddy,	Charles Wright,
William Johnson,	Cornelius Heyer.

They were duly notified of their appointment, and met in the City Hall on the 11th of May, and, in the exercise of the powers granted them by the Constitution, unanimously elected the following as the first officers of the American Bible Society for one year:

President.

Hon. Elias Boudinot, of New Jersey.

Vice-Presidents.

Hon. John Jay, Matthew Clarkson, Esq., Hon. Smith Thompson, } of New York.
Hon. John Langdon, of New Hampshire.
Hon. Caleb Strong, Hon. William Gray, } of Massachusetts.
Hon. John Cotton Smith, of Connecticut.
Hon. Jonas Galusha, of Vermont.
Hon. William Jones, of Rhode Island.
Hon. Isaac Shelby, George Madison, Esq., } of Kentucky.

Hon. WILLIAM TILGHMAN, of Pennsylvania.
Hon. BUSHROD WASHINGTON, } of Virginia.
WILLIAM WIRT, Esq., }
Hon. CHARLES C. PINCKNEY, of South Carolina.
Hon. WILLIAM GASTON, of North Carolina.
Hon. THOMAS WORTHINGTON, of Ohio.
Hon. THOMAS POSEY, of Indiana.
Hon. JAMES BROWN, of Louisiana.
JOHN BOLTON, Esq., of Georgia.
Hon. FELIX GRUNDY, of Tennessee.
ROBERT OLIVER, Esq., of Maryland.
JOSEPH NOURSE, Esq., of the District of Columbia.

Secretary for Foreign Correspondence.
Rev. Dr. J. M. MASON.

Secretary for Domestic Correspondence.
Rev. Dr. J. B. ROMEYN.

Treasurer.
RICHARD VARICK, Esq.

An eloquent and powerful address to the people of the United States, written by Dr. Mason, was reported by the committee, adopted, and published.

We have already quoted from this address, and shall have occasion to recur to its principles frequently in the progress of the work.

In the organization of the society, every subject which came under the review of the delegates composing the Convention received the most frank and full investigation, and the greatest care was taken to exclude whatever had the remotest connection with sectarianism in any of its forms.

The founders of the society, and the first officers elected to manage its concerns, were connected with the leading evangelical churches of the land, such as the Protestant Episcopal Church, the Presbyterian, the Dutch Reformed, the Methodist Episcopal, the Baptist, the Congregational, and the Society of Friends.

The harmony, cordiality, and Christian forbearance which characterized the deliberations and proceedings of the Convention, presented the clearest evidence of the Divine approbation, and a pledge of the Divine blessing upon its future career. Many who had their doubts in regard to the practicability of the plan and its ultimate success, had no sooner witnessed its first movements than they yielded to the conviction that they were in error, and heartily joined with those who had never doubted in cherishing the hope that the institution would ultimately realize its most sanguine expectations.

The managers committed all the interests of the institution to God, believing that he who had "magnified his Word above all his name" would secure the prosperity of an institution which had for its object the circulation of that word throughout the world.

CHAPTER IV.

MANAGERS AND OFFICERS OF THE SOCIETY.

As before stated, the only officers known to the Constitution consist of a *Board of Managers*, composed of thirty-six laymen, every minister of the Gospel who is a member for life being honorary and *ex-officio* members, and also every lay director for life. This board has the power of appointing all the officers of the society, which consist of a *President*, twenty-five *Vice-Presidents*, selected from the different states of the Union, three *Secretaries*, a *Treasurer*, *General Agent* and *Assistant Treasurer*, and also the special and *Standing Committees*, namely, *On Publication and Finance*, *Distribution*, *Agencies*, *Anniversary*, *Versions*, *Legacies*, and *Auditing Committee*.

The board from time to time enacted *By-laws* for their government and that of the society. These rules were collected together from the various reports by a special committee. The board amended them in several particulars, gave them their sanction and adoption. The following are those rules:

BY-LAWS OF THE AMERICAN BIBLE SOCIETY.

ARTICLE I.—*Old Constitution.*

THE several provisions and articles of the Constitution of this Society adopted in the year 1816, and as subsequently amended, are hereby adopted as By-laws of this Society, and shall continue in force as such; and no alteration shall be made in such provisions and articles, nor any By-law be passed by this Society or the Board of Managers thereof, repealing, altering, or impairing the force or effect of any provision or article thereof, except by this Society at an annual meeting on the recommendation of the Board of Managers.

ARTICLE II.—*Tenure of Officers.*

All the officers of this Society shall hold their respective offices during the pleasure of the Board of Managers.

ARTICLE III.—*Election of Officers and Managers.*

Whenever the nomination of an officer or a manager has been referred to a committee to report thereon, such report may be adopted at the same meeting of the Board at which it is made, and such adoption shall be equivalent to an election by ballot. Whenever there is an open nomination of such officer or manager, such nomination shall lie over to a subsequent meeting, when the election shall be made by ballot or otherwise, as the board may then direct.

ARTICLE IV.—*Foreign Versions.*

In appropriating money for translating, printing, or distributing the sacred Scriptures in foreign languages, the Board of Managers shall encourage only such versions as conform in the principles of their translation to the common English version, at least so far that all the religious denominations represented in this Society can consistently use and circulate said versions in their several schools and communities.

ARTICLE V.—*Sale of Books.*

That while the managers of the American Bible Society do not feel at liberty to dictate positive terms on which Auxiliary Societies shall sell books purchased at the General Depository, yet they can not but express their full and unanimous conviction that the interest of the Bible cause will be best promoted by confining the terms of sale to the original cost, together with the expenses incurred in reaching the several places where they are to be reissued.

ARTICLE VI.—*Privileges of Life Members and Directors.*

Each life member of this Society shall be allowed to receive from the Depository annually, for distribution, two copies of the common Minion Bible, or the value thereof in Bibles and Testaments; and each life director shall be allowed to receive annually five copies of the same book, or the value thereof in other books, for the same purpose. An account shall be kept of this class of issues in a separate book, and the amount of such issues shall be presented in the Annual Report.

ARTICLE VII.—*Minutes of Proceedings.*

SECTION 1.—Full and accurate minutes shall be kept of the proceedings of this Society at their annual and other meetings, and of the proceedings of the Board of Managers at their stated monthly and other meetings, which minutes shall be duly recorded in books to be provided for that purpose, and signed by the presiding officers of such meetings respectively. That said minutes shall be kept and recorded by the General Agent of the Society, or, in his absence from any of said meetings, by such person as the meeting shall appoint for that purpose; and such minutes shall be read and approved by the Society and the Board of Managers at their next subsequent meeting.

SECTION 2.—Full and accurate minutes shall be kept of the proceedings of the Committees on Publication and Finance, Versions, Distribution, Agencies, Anniversaries, and Legacies, and shall be duly recorded in books to be provided for that purpose, and signed by the presiding chairman of the said committees respectively. That such minutes shall be kept and recorded by the several officers of this Society, as directed in these By-laws, and in their absence by such persons as the committees shall respectively appoint for that purpose. The minutes of said committees shall be read at the stated meetings of the Board of Managers, and submitted to said board for approval.

ARTICLE VIII.—*Accounts and Books of Accounts.*

SECTION 1.—There shall be kept in double entry a full and complete set of books of account of all the transactions and dealings of this Society, consisting of Ledgers, Journals, and such other books of account as the business and transactions of the Society may require, including a register of life members and directors.

SECTION 2.—The fiscal year of this Society shall commence on the first day of April and terminate on the last day of March, and all accounts with this Society shall be closed and balanced on the last day of March in each year.

SECTION 3.—The books of account of this Society shall be balanced annually, on the last day of March in each year, and a balance sheet and inventory made, showing the funds, property, and effects belonging to this Society on that day, which balance sheet and inventory shall be presented to the Board of Managers at the earliest day practicable, and referred to the Auditing Committee, unless otherwise directed by the board, which committee shall examine the same in detail, and report thereon to said board ; and after being so reported upon, such balance sheet and inventory shall be put on file, and preserved for future use or reference.

SECTION 4.—There shall be kept an account of all expenditures incurred in conducting the business of printing, and at least once in each year the General Agent shall make out and present to the Board of Managers, under the direction of the committee having charge of such business, an estimate showing the cost "per token" of the various kinds of the printing of this Society. And that said Agent at the same time shall present to the Board of Managers a statement showing the price at which the same kinds of printing could be procured by contract from respectable private establishments in the city of New York.

ARTICLE IX.—*Keeping and Deposit of Money.*

The bankable money of this Society shall be deposited daily to the credit of the Treasurer thereof, in the bank designated by the Board of Managers as the one in which the Treasurer shall keep his account, provided the amount on hand exceeds one hundred dollars, and only be drawn therefrom by the official checks of the Treasurer, given in accordance with the warrants of the Committee on Publication and Finance.

ARTICLE X.—*Safe Keeping of Money and Papers.*

The money not deposited, securities, and valuable papers and documents belonging to this Society, shall be kept in a secure and convenient iron safe, and the keys whereof shall be in the sole custody of the General Agent and Assistant Treasurer.

ARTICLE XI.—*Unbankable Money.*

The unbankable money of this Society shall be converted into bankable funds, except when the same can be paid out in the course of business, and under such regulations as may be adopted by the Committee on Publication and Finance.

ARTICLE XII.—*Library.*

There shall continue to be kept a Library of the Society, in which shall be placed and preserved all books not for sale, belonging to the Society, and all manuscripts and other interesting papers which the Society, Board of Managers, committees, or Corresponding Secretary may deem worthy of preservation. There shall also be placed in the Library a copy of the first edition of every book published by the Society, and a copy of every other edition thereof in which material alterations shall have been made in the stereotype plates.

ARTICLE XIII.—*Depository.*

There shall continue to be a Depository, in which shall be placed all the books printed and published by this Society, and completed, ready for sale or use, and in which shall be sold all the books sold at retail by this Society. Full and accurate accounts shall continue to be kept of all books delivered into the Depository and taken therefrom by sale or otherwise, and of all sales made and of all moneys received therefrom; and such accounts shall be balanced monthly, and the results thereof reported to the Committee on Publication and Finance, together with a statement showing the amount of sales in the Depository for cash during the month, and the quantity of each kind of books in the Depository and in sheets at the close of the month, the amount of which sales, and a brief statement of the quantity of Bibles and Testaments on hand in the English language, and also the quantity on hand in all other languages, shall be entered in the minutes of the committee.

ARTICLE XIV.—"*Bible Society Record.*"

There shall be published, as often as once in every two months, a pamphlet called the "Bible Society Record," which shall contain interesting and instructive extracts from the correspondence of the Society, short notices of the proceedings of this Society and its auxiliaries, and a full and complete continuous list of all payments and donations to the Society made and received since the close of such list for the next preceding Record, together with the times when, and the names of the societies, congregations, and persons from whom and through whom such payments and donations were made; and a copy of said Record shall be sent to every payer or donor whose payment or donation is acknowledged in it, and to such other persons and societies as the officers or members of the Board of Managers may designate.

ARTICLE XV.—*Annual Report.*

The several officers of the Society, at the close of the fiscal year thereof, shall prepare and give to the Corresponding Secretary all requisite statements and information relating to their respective departments and business, for the Annual Report of the Society, to enable him to prepare and draw the same.

ARTICLE XVI.—*Contracts.*

SECTION 1.—No contract which shall require an expenditure or outlay of money by this Society exceeding five hundred dollars, shall be made on behalf of the Society without being first approved by the Board of Managers, except for the purchase of materials or other things for use in the current business of the Society.

SECTION 2.—No purchase of property to be permanently held by the Society shall be made except by the direction of the Board of Managers; and no purchase of materials or other things for use in the current business of the Society, exceeding in amount five hundred dollars, shall be made for the Society by the General Agent, or any other officer or Agent thereof, except by direction of the Board of Managers, or under the advice and direction, or with the approval of the committee of the Society charged with that part of the business thereof for which such materials or other things are purchased.

ARTICLE XVII.—*Standing Committees.*

There shall be a standing Committee on Publication and Finance, on Distribution, on Agencies, Versions, Legacies, and Anniversaries, of seven members each, and an Auditing Committee of three members, elected annually at the first meeting of the Board of Managers after the annual meeting of the Society in May in each year.

The Corresponding and Financial Secretaries and the General Agent shall be advisory members *ex-officio* of each of the said standing committees.

ARTICLE XVIII.—*Committee on Publication and Finance.*

This committee shall have charge of the property of this Society, order and direct the necessary repairs of the buildings, authorize and direct the purchase and procurement of the necessary furniture and articles for the offices of the Corresponding and Financial Secretaries, of the General Agent and Assistant Treasurer, and for the Depository and the Library.

This committee shall have charge, in general, of the publications made by the Society, and shall determine the number, quality, and kinds of books to be published, and shall recommend to the board the procuring of stereotype plates when in their judgment they are needed.

This committee shall examine and audit all bills, accounts, and claims, for money or property, upon the Society, and draw warrants on the Treasurer for all payments made by the Society.

This committee shall have charge of all claims and demands due to the Society, and take and direct all necessary and proper measures for their collection and settlement, and shall devise and recommend measures for raising funds.

This committee shall have charge of the business of printing and binding, and of all the manufacturing and mechanical operations of the Society. They shall superintend and direct the procurement of all stereotype plates ordered by the Board of Managers.

All purchases of paper and other materials required in the business of printing and binding, and the other manufacturing and mechanical operations of the Society, shall be made under the advice and direction of, or with the approbation of the committee.

They shall have charge, and superintend and direct the negotiating and making of all contracts relating to the business of printing and binding, and to the other manufacturing and mechanical operations of the Society, subject, however, to the provisions and restrictions contained in the By-laws thereof.

At the first meeting of this committee after the annual election of the standing committees, they shall choose a sub-committee of three members, whose names shall be entered upon their minutes, and who shall have special charge of the business of printing and binding, and of the mechanical and manufacturing operations of the Society, and see that they are conducted with strict regard to economy, and who shall superintend and direct the negotiating and making of all contracts relating to the said business and operations in their charge, subject, however, to the provisions and restrictions in the By-laws. Their proceedings shall be submitted to the Committee on Publication and Finance for approval, and be incorporated in their minutes.

The minutes of the Committee on Publication and Finance shall be kept and recorded by the General Agent, and such committee shall discharge such other duties as the Board of Managers shall direct.

Article XIX.—*Committee on Distribution.*

This committee shall have charge of all grants of books and money both for domestic and foreign distribution; they shall have power to make donations not exceeding two hundred Minion Bibles in common binding, or the value thereof in other books, and shall only recommend all other grants for the approval of the Board of Managers.

This committee shall also have power to establish depositories of books, to an amount not exceeding one thousand dollars, in different sections of the country, as they may deem proper, such books, however, to be sold only for cash.

The General Agent shall keep and record the minutes of their proceedings.

ARTICLE XX.—*Committee on Agencies.*

This committee shall have charge of the entire business of agencies: they shall procure and recommend to the board suitable persons for permanent agents; they shall have power to appoint temporary agents, and to fix the amount of compensation to be allowed them, provided it shall not in any instance exceed ten dollars per week; and they shall also procure, when practicable, delegates to attend the meetings of auxiliary and other societies.

The General Agent shall keep and record the minutes of their proceedings.

ARTICLE XXI.—*Committee on Versions.*

This committee shall have charge of all translations of the Bible published or distributed by the Society, and shall especially examine all new translations thereof presented for the consideration or action of the Society, in respect to their catholicity and fidelity of translation, and shall recommend such as they approve to the patronage of the Society.

The Corresponding Secretary shall keep and record the minutes of their proceedings.

ARTICLE XXII.—*Committee on Legacies.*

This committee shall take charge of and collect all legacies bequeathed to the Society.

The General Agent shall keep and record the minutes of their proceedings.

ARTICLE XXIII.—*Committee on Anniversaries.*

This committee shall have charge of all arrangements for the anniversaries of the Society, and especially shall provide speakers for them, obtain a suitable place for the annual meeting of the Society, and examine and approve the annual report previously to its presentation to the Board of Managers.

The Corresponding Secretary shall keep and record the minutes of their proceedings.

ARTICLE XXIV.—*Auditing Committee.*

This committee shall examine and audit the Treasurer's Report, and the annual balance sheet and inventory of the funds, property, and effects belonging to the Society, and report thereon to the Board of Managers, and shall also examine and audit such other accounts and statements as shall be specially referred to it.

ARTICLE XXV.—*Corresponding Secretary, his Duties.*

There shall be a Corresponding Secretary of this Society. He shall have charge of the Library. He shall, under the direction of the Board of Managers, and of the Committees on Versions, Distribution, and Anniversaries, conduct the foreign and domestic correspondence of the Society in relation to translations of the Holy Scriptures, their distribution and circulation, in relation to the anniversaries of the Society, and the holding of meetings to extend and promote the circulation of the sacred Scriptures. He shall attend such meetings, visit different sections of this country, preach sermons and make addresses as often as time, opportunity, and other paramount duties will permit, and in all ways in his power forward the great work for which the Society was created. He shall draw and prepare the Annual Report of the Society under the direction of the Committee on Anniversaries, and report the same to the Board of Managers for their approval. He shall edit the Record and superintend its publication, and shall make a report monthly to the Board of Managers of his acts and proceedings. He shall also discharge such other duties as shall be directed by the Society or Board of Managers.

Article XXVI.—*Financial Secretary, his Duties.*

There shall be a Financial Secretary of this Society. He shall have charge of the action of this Society connected with the raising of funds, and shall conduct the correspondence of the Society with its auxiliaries, agents, and other persons relating to that subject. He shall, under the direction of the Committee on Agencies, give directions to and correspond with the traveling agents of the Society, and have charge of the matters connected with their agencies. He shall visit the traveling agents of the Society and different sections of the country, attend meetings, preach sermons, and make addresses, whenever time and opportunity will permit, and in all ways in his power promote the interests and forward the object for which this Society was formed, and make a report monthly to the Board of Managers of his acts and proceedings. He shall also discharge such other duties as shall be directed by the Society or Board of Managers.

Article XXVII.—*Treasurer, his Duties.*

There shall be a Treasurer of this Society. He shall keep an account, as Treasurer, with the "Bank of New York," or such other bank as the Board of Managers shall direct, and shall receive and deposit in such bank, to his credit as Treasurer, all moneys paid to him from time to time for or on account of the Society. He shall pay all warrants of the Committee on Publication and Finance for the payment of money, and report to the Board of Managers a monthly statement of his receipts and disbursements for the Society, and of the balance in the treasury. He shall be *ex-officio* a member of the Committee on Legacies.

ARTICLE XXVIII.—*General Agent.*

There shall be a General Agent of this Society, who shall be the Recording Secretary thereof. He shall have the charge and superintendence of all the property and business of the Society, and exercise over the same a vigilant supervision and care. He shall attend to all the business matters, and things of the Society not committed specially to others. He shall arrange and direct the mode of keeping all the accounts and books of account of the Society, and carefully and vigilantly superintend the keeping of the same, and shall make or cause to be made all statements of accounts and inventories directed in and by the By-laws of the Society. He shall examine and recommend to the Committee on Publication and Finance, for audit and payment, or rejection, all bills, accounts, and claims for money or property upon the Society. He shall make all purchases of paper, and other materials and things for use in the current business of the Society, subject, however, to the provisions and restrictions contained in the By-laws thereof. He shall negotiate and settle the terms of all contracts made on behalf of the Society, and report the same for approval to the Board of Managers, or the committee having charge thereof, as the case may be. He shall cause the property, real and personal, of the Society to be insured, and keep the same insured, under the direction of the Committee on Publication and Finance. Certificates of life membership and directorship shall be issued by him. The General Agent shall make, or superintend the making, and shall sign all orders on the Depository for books, and conduct or direct the correspondence respecting the same, and the forwarding of such books to the places and persons for whom they are ordered. He shall give orders for the delivery of paper to the Superintendent of Printing, and see that it, and all other articles and things used in the buisness of the Society, are economically and judiciously used, and that the work done for the Society is well and skillfully performed. He shall report to the Board of Managers monthly a statement of the books issued; and to the Committee on Publication and Finance the accounts and statements connected with the Depository, and the books in it, and in sheets, mentioned and directed in the By-laws of the Society. He shall arrange and cause to be bound up all the correspondence of the Society, and shall place in the library a copy of the first edition of every book printed and published by the Society, and a copy of every other edition in which material alterations shall have been made in the stereotype plates. He shall send, or cause to be sent, a copy of the "Bible Society Record," immediately after its publication, to every Society and the principal officers thereof, and to every congregation and the pastor and principal officers thereof, and to every person and persons from whom or through whom any payment or payments, donation or donations were made or given, and which are mentioned or acknowledged in such Record.

The General Agent shall also discharge such other duties as the Board of Managers shall direct.

ARTICLE XXIX.—*Assistant Treasurer.*

There shall be an Assistant Treasurer of this Society. He shall receive and acknowledge the receipt of all moneys paid or given to the Society, and shall keep full and accurate accounts thereof, and shall deposit every day to the credit of the Treasurer, in the bank with which the Treasurer's account is kept, all moneys and funds of this Society which such bank will receive in deposit at par or for collection, unless said moneys and funds do not exceed in the aggregate on such day, and before closing the bank, the sum of one hundred dollars, and unless the bank shall not on such day be opened for business. The Assistant Treasurer shall attend to the collection and settlement of debts and balances due to the Society from auxiliary and other societies and persons, and conduct the correspondence respecting the same. He shall safely keep all the moneys not in deposit to the credit of the Treasurer, and shall sell or dispose of the uncurrent money of the Society as is directed in the By-laws thereof. He shall make out and furnish to the Corresponding Secretary for each "Bible Society Record" published, for insertion therein, a full and complete continuous list of all payments and donations to the Society made and received since the close of such list for the next preceding Record, together with the times when, and the names of the societies, congregations, and persons from whom or through whom such payments and donations were made. And he shall discharge such other duties as the Board of Managers shall direct.

ARTICLE XXX.—*Depositary.*

There shall be an officer of this Society called a Depositary. He shall, under the direction of the General Agent, have the immediate charge of the Depository, and of the books and other property of the Society in it. He shall, under the like direction, make or attend to the making of all sales of books at retail, and shall fill, or attend to the filling, of all orders for books or other property on the Depository. He shall keep full and accurate accounts of all books and property delivered into the Depository and taken from it, and of all moneys received by him or at the Depository, and shall daily hand over all such moneys to the Assistant Treasurer. He shall make out monthly a full and correct statement of all books and property received into the Depository and taken therefrom during the month, and remaining therein at the end of the month, and of all moneys received by him or at the

Depository, and the amount paid over to the Assistant Treasurer during the same month. This statement he shall present to the General Agent, who shall examine the same, and ascertain its accuracy by comparison with the accounts kept by him or under his supervision.

The Depositary shall discharge such other reasonable duties as may be required of him by the General Agent, any committee of the Society, or the Board of Managers.

Article XXXI.—*Superintendent of Printing.*

The Society shall continue to employ a Superintendent of Printing. He shall, under the direction and advice of the General Agent, and the Committee on Publication and Finance, have the immediate charge of the printing done by the Society, and under the like direction, shall employ and pay all mechanics and laborers engaged in that branch of the business thereof. He shall have the immediate charge of the machinery and building used for printing, and all things connected therewith, and shall keep the same in good order, and see that the printing of the Society is done in the best and most economical manner. He shall advise the General Agent when requested in respect to the purchase of all materials and articles used in printing, and promote and protect the interests of the Society to the extent of his skill and ability.

Article XXXII.—*Proof-reader.*

The Society shall employ a Proof-reader. He shall, under the direction of the Secretaries and General Agent, have charge, and be responsible for the integrity of the text of the English Scriptures printed by or for the Society, and shall see that they are all conformable to the standard copy now in use. He shall examine the printed sheets with minute care, and thus ascertain the state of the stereotype plates, and cause them to be corrected and repaired if necessary. He shall read and correct the proofs of new plates, and see that they are perfectly accurate, or as nearly so as care, skill, and attention can make them.

Article XXXIII.—*Book-keeper, Clerk.*

Section 1.—The Society shall continue to employ a competent Book-keeper, who shall, under the direction of the General Agent, keep the books of account of the Society, and perform such other cognate duties as the General Agent and Assistant Treasurer shall require of him.

Section 2.—The General Agent may employ from time to time a Clerk to assist the General Agent and Assistant Treasurer in the business correspondence of the Society, and in making and copying statements, and doing such other writing and business as the General Agent and Assistant Treasurer shall require.

ARTICLE XXXIV.—*Messenger.*

The Society shall continue to employ a Messenger, who shall, under the direction of the General Agent, lodge in the building, take care of it and of the property of the Society, especially at night, and perform such reasonable duties as shall be required of him by the Corresponding Secretary, Financial Secretary, General Agent, and Assistant Treasurer, any committee of the Society, or the Board of Managers.

ARTICLE XXXV.—*Order of Proceedings and Business.*

The order of proceedings and business of the stated meetings of the Board of Managers shall be as follows, unless otherwise directed by the board:

1st. Open at half past four o'clock, or as soon thereafter as a quorum is present, by reading such a portion of Scripture as the presiding officer may select.

2d. Minutes of the Board of Managers to be read and approved.

3d. Minutes of the Committee on Publication and Finance to be read and approved, and business growing out of them to be disposed of.

4th. The Corresponding Secretary's Report.

5th. The Financial Secretary's Report.

6th. The Treasurer's Report.

7th. The General Agent's Report and Statements.

8th. Minutes of the Committee on Distribution to be read and approved, and business thereon to be disposed of.

9th. Minutes of the Committee on Agencies to be read and approved, and business thereon to be disposed of.

10th. Report of Committee on Versions and Legacies, and minutes of the same.

11th. Reports from special committees.

12th. Unfinished business of previous meetings.

13th. New business.

ARTICLE XXXVI.—*Votes.*

Every member of the Board of Managers may have his vote recorded on any question.

ARTICLE XXXVII.—*By-Laws.*

The Board of Managers shall not make, alter, or amend any By-law, except at the monthly meeting thereof, nor at the same meeting at which such By-law, alteration, or amendment is proposed.

ARTICLE XXXVIII.—*Repealing Act.*

All By-laws and Regulations heretofore passed or adopted by the Board of Managers, and which are inconsistent with the preceding By-laws, are hereby repealed.

Of all the officers first appointed, nineteen in number, including its president, fourteen vice-presidents, three secretaries, and treasurer, not one survives, and not more than two or three of its first managers. "They rest from their labors, and their works follow them."

The society, from the commencement, has used the most scrupulous economy in husbanding all its resources for the purpose of multiplying copies of the Word of Life. It has no permanent funds, and desires to have none. Whatever is received by donation, legacy, or otherwise, is immediately converted into Bibles and Testaments, and put in circulation. All the managers and officers, with the exception of those who devote their exclusive time in the service of the society, such as the Corresponding Secretary, General Secretaries, and General Agent, perform their duties gratuitously.

The following are the present officers and managers of the society:

President.

Hon. Theodore Frelinghuysen, LL.D., New York.

Vice-Presidents.

Hon. Duncan Cameron, Raleigh, N. C.
Hon. David Lawrence Morrill, Goffstown, N. H.
Hon. Charles Marsh, Woodstock, Vt.
Hon. Heman Lincoln, Boston, Mass.
Hon. Robert P. Dunlap, Maine.
Hon. John M'Lean, Justice Supreme Court U. S., Ohio.
Hon. Charles Cotesworth Pinckney, South Carolina.
Thomas Cock, M.D., New York.
Hon. Peter D. Vroom, Trenton, N. J.
Hon. Joseph C. Hornblower, New Jersey.
Isaac Carow, Esq., New York.
John Tappan, Esq., Boston, Mass.
Samuel Rhea, Esq., Blountsville, Tenn.
Hubert Van Wagenen, Esq., Poughkeepsie, N. Y.
Gen. John H. Cocke, Virginia.

Hon. William Jay, Bedford, N. Y.
Hon. John M'Pherson Berrien, Georgia.
Aristarchus Champion, Esq., Rochester, N. Y.
Hon. Allen Trimble, Ohio.
Hon. Luther Bradish, New York.
Freeborn Garretson, Esq., New York.
Charles Chauncey, Esq., Pennsylvania.

Corresponding Secretary.

Rev. John C. Brigham, D.D.

General Secretaries.

Rev. Joseph Holdich, D.D.,
Rev. Samuel Ireneus Prime, D.D.

Treasurer

William Whitlock, Jun., Esq.

General Agent and Assistant Treasurer.

Joseph Hyde, Esq.

Managers.

FIRST CLASS.

Charles N. Talbot,
Pelatiah Perit,
Francis Hall,
Horace Holden,
Thomas L. Servoss,
Richard T. Haines,
James Donaldson,
Silas Holmes,
Wm. H. Aspinwall.

SECOND CLASS.

James Boorman,
Timothy Hedges,
Edward Richardson,
Cornelius Dubois, Jun.,
James Lenox,
Nathaniel Richards,
Benjamin L. Swan,
Frederic T. Peet,
Isaac Wood, M.D.

THIRD CLASS.

George D. Phelps,
William B. Crosby,
James L. Phelps, M.D.,
B. L. Woolley,
G. P. Disosway,
Henry Roosevelt,
A. R. Walsh,
S. S. Howland,
Alfred Edwards.

FOURTH CLASS.

Najah Taylor,
James W. Dominick,
Edward J. Woolsey,
Norman White,
William Forrest,
Anson G. Phelps,
F. S. Winston,
Ralph Mead,
Archibald Russell.

Standing Committees.

PUBLICATION AND FINANCE.

Najah Taylor,
Charles N. Talbot,
B. L. Woolley,
Francis Hall,
F. T. Peet,
Ralph Mead,
A. Robertson Walsh.

DISTRIBUTION.

Rev. Isaac Ferris, D.D.,
James L. Phelps, M.D.,
James W. Dominick,
Timothy Hedges,
Pelatiah Perit,
Rev. G. T. Bedell,
Rev. J. P. Thompson.

AGENCIES.

Rev. Thomas De Witt, D.D.,
William Forrest,
Horace Holden,
F. S. Winston,
Norman White,
Rev. Stephen Martindale,
Rev. J. W. M'Lane.

ANNIVERSARY.

Rev. Stephen H. Tyng, D.D.,
Rev. J. W. Alexander, D.D.,
Rev. Bishop Janes,
William B. Crosby,
Rev. William Adams, D.D.,
Cornelius Du Bois, Jun.,
Rev. M. S. Hutton, D.D.

VERSIONS.

Rev. Gardiner Spring, D.D.,
Rev. T. E. Vermilye, D.D.,
Rev. R. S. Storrs, Jun.,
Rev. George Peck, D.D.,
Rev. Edw. Robinson, D.D.,
Rev. Saml. H. Turner, D.D.
Thomas Cock, M.D.

LEGACIES.

Horace Holden,
Benjamin L. Swan,
Nathaniel Richards,
E. J. Woolsey,
Luther Bradish,
Isaac Wood, M.D.,
Henry Roosevelt.

Auditing Committee.

Anson G. Phelps,
B. L. Woolley,
Gabriel P. Disosway.

CHAPTER V.

AUXILIARY SOCIETIES.

At an early day the managers drew up the following circular, inclosing a plan for auxiliary and branch societies, which they addressed to the ministers and churches of the different religious denominations in the United States:

Circular to the Clergy.

"New York, October, 1816.

"Rev. Sir,—The Managers of the American Bible Society have directed me to send to you a copy of the Constitution of the Society, and of the Address of the Convention which formed it, to the people of the United States.

"Trusting that this national institution will meet with your approbation, they respectfully request that you will do them the favor of reading the said Constitution and Address to your congregation from the pulpit, and adopt such measures as may be deemed necessary by you for securing a congregational collection, to aid them in their labor of love and work of faith.

"The magnitude and catholic nature of the object they conceive will sufficiently apologize for the trouble which they have taken the liberty of giving you in this application.

"I have the honor to be, Rev. Sir, yours respectfully,

"John B. Romeyn, Secretary for Domestic Correspondence."

Circular addressed to Individuals.

"New York, January 8, 1817.

"Sir,—The Managers of the American Bible Society, deeply impressed with a sense of the magnitude of the interest committed to their care, and of the necessity of uniting the efforts of the friends of the institution, in order to procure the necessary funds to enable them to promote that interest, have directed us to address you as one of those friends, and request the favor of your co-operation with such persons of your county as may be willing to aid this great work of Christian charity, in forming an auxiliary society in your county, if there is not one already formed, and also as many Bible Associations in smaller districts as may be convenient. To save trouble, and to facilitate both objects, they subjoin a form of a Constitution for an auxiliary society and for a Bible Association, it being understood that each auxiliary society and association are at liberty to make such alterations in these forms as they may see fit.

"As there may be among your friends and acquaintance some who would be willing to enroll their names among the members or contributors to the American Bible Society, we send herewith the form of a heading for a paper to which such may subscribe, and pay you the amount of their subscription, which you will please to forward, with the list of the subscribers, to Richard Varick, Esq., Treasurer of the American Bible Society.

"We are, respectfully, your obedient servants,

"MATTHEW CLARKSON, Vice-President,

"JOHN B. ROMEYN, Secretary for Dom. Cor."

The following is the Constitution of an

AUXILIARY BIBLE SOCIETY.

I. This Society shall be called the Bible Society of ———, auxiliary to the American Bible Society.

II. The object of the Society shall be to promote the circulation of the Holy Scriptures "without note or comment," and in English those of the commonly received version.

III. All persons contributing any sum to its funds shall be members for one year; those contributing one dollar or more shall receive (if called for within twelve months) a common Bible in return; those contributing fifteen dollars at one time, or twenty dollars at *two* payments, shall be members for life.

IV. All funds not wanted for circulating the Scriptures within the Society's own limits shall be paid over annually to the parent society, to aid distributions among the destitute in other parts of the country and in foreign lands.

V. The officers of the Society shall consist of a President, Vice-President, Secretary, and Treasurer, whose duties shall be such as their respective titles import.

VI. The management of the Society shall be intrusted to an Executive Committee of five (or seven, including the Secretary and Treasurer), which shall appoint its own Chairman and make its own By-laws.

VII. It shall be the duty of this committee to meet frequently on adjournment, or on call of the Chairman, to keep a good supply of books on hand, to appoint local distributors, to see that collections in some way are made annually in every congregation, and that all funds are forwarded early to the parent society, with a statement as to the portion designed for the payment of books and that as a free donation.

VIII. There shall be a general meeting of the Society on ——— of each year, when a full report of their doings shall be presented by the committee (a copy of which shall be furnished the parent society), and when a new election of officers and committee shall take place; should the Society fail of an annual meeting, the same officers and committee shall be continued until an election does occur.

IX. Any Branch Society or Bible Committee formed within the bounds of this auxiliary, by paying over its funds annually, shall receive Bibles and Testaments at cost prices.

X. No alteration shall be made in this Constitution except at an annual meeting, and by consent of two thirds of the members present.

CONSTITUTION OF A BRANCH SOCIETY.

No special plan was proposed for such a society, inasmuch as a few simple rules, such as the constitution of an auxiliary would suggest, would be sufficient, and hence a constitution was not drafted. The Managers make the following suggestions:

"In many parts of the country, counties are divided into separate townships, each of which, should it be deemed advisable, can form a small Branch Bible Society in connection with the county auxiliary. It can adopt a constitution like the one above, with such alterations as the difference of circumstances will suggest. The branch should collect its moneys annually, and pay them over to the county auxiliary some weeks previous to its anniversary. All needed books can be procured through the auxiliary, and kept in a convenient depository. Sometimes a single congregation can resolve itself into a Branch Bible Society, or appoint a Bible Committee of three, who shall collect and forward money and receive books through the county society."

It was before stated that there were several local societies in existence prior to the organization of the national institution. The Philadelphia Bible Society, organized in 1808, was patronized by the most distinguished names. The managers united their efforts to secure the connection of these societies with the general society. In this they were successful. During the first year of its existence, they received official information from eighty-four local societies of their wish and intention to become auxiliary to the parent society, and they were accordingly recognized as such.

It may not be unimportant here to state, that all that is required of auxiliary societies, as a condition of their connection with the parent society, is, that "they shall circulate the Bibles of the common version in the English language, and the surplus funds they may have, after supplying their own wants, shall go into the treasury of the parent society, for the circulation of the Bible among the destitute abroad."

This condition has invariably been adhered to from the beginning. Several Bible societies which had a previous existence signified a desire to become auxiliaries, but upon its being ascertained that there were some things connected with their operations incompatible with the general objects and policy of the society, it was unanimously resolved, in 1819, "that no society could become auxiliary to the parent society until it gave to the board official notice that its sole object is to promote the circulation of the Scriptures without note or comment, and that it will place its surplus revenue, after supplying its own destitute district with the Scriptures, at the disposal of the American Bible Society as long as it shall remain thus connected with it."

An Auxiliary Society Committee was appointed, whose duty it was to devise and suggest to the Board of Managers such measures as in their opinion would promote the establishment and animate the exertions of auxiliaries to the parent society; that in cases in which there shall not be time to receive the direction of the Board of Managers, the said committee shall be authorized to depute one or more persons to attend meetings for the above purposes, and to advise and assist therein, and, in such cases, to defray out of the funds of this society the necessary traveling expenses of the person so deputed; and that authority be given the said committee to open a correspondence with the different parts of the country for the purpose of gaining all necessary information.

The design of this committee was chiefly to obviate the necessity of appointing agents, that from their intimate acquaintance with the auxiliaries, derived through extensive correspondence, they might learn the wants of the various districts of country, and, by the occasional deputation of visitors, secure all the aid and information they might desire. A short time proved the fallacy of relying upon printed circulars and letters of instruction, and the committee recommended the appointment of permanent agents, who should give their time exclusively to this work. From time to time the society had to bewail the dormant condition of the auxiliaries, and their failure from year to year to report their proceedings. Many of them became largely indebted to the parent society for books, and, after many ineffectual efforts to secure payment, the claims were relinquished. In their explorations and distributions, many of them acted without proper judgment and discrimination. Meetings were not held from year to year, Bibles were deposited with individuals here and there all over the county, and, instead of being sold or donated, were laid aside in the garret, or warehouse, or barn, as the case might be, exposed to the weather.

It affords us extreme pleasure, however, to say that these remarks do not apply to a large majority of the auxiliaries, hundreds of which have from the commencement nobly and generously sustained, by their active zeal and liberality, the parent institution, often relieving it from embarrassment, and ever prompt to respond to all its solicitations, and faithful to carry out all its plans of operation.

As powerful allies, many of them have extended their operations beyond their own districts, and have made large donations to aid in printing and circulating the Scriptures in foreign lands. Auxiliaries are indispensable to the existence of the society, for without them but little could be done toward supplying our country with the Bible. They are usually confined to a county, but in several instances embrace entire states.

During the first year of the society's existence, the number of auxiliaries connected with it was eighty-four: this number has been steadily increasing from year to year until the present time. The last report shows that there are about twelve hundred auxiliaries and twenty-five hundred branches, located in all the states and territories of the Union. The officers and members of these societies are composed of the various religious denominations, and invariably embrace the most intelligent and useful portion of the community where they are located. Many, having no connection with any branch of the Church of Christ, yet impressed with the importance of the enterprise, cheerfully engage in it, as productive of the greatest good to man. Indeed, no field can be more inviting, or promissory of more essential good to our country, and one that claims the hearty co-operation of every patriot and philanthropist, than that embraced by the Bible Society.

In the successful prosecution of its work all are interested, and equally interested, for whatever benefits our neighbor necessarily has a reflex influence upon ourselves.

The various auxiliary societies are entitled to purchase Bibles and Testaments of the parent society at five per cent. less than cost. When they are not able to pay in advance for books they are allowed a credit of six or nine months, and when their means are limited, and the destitution great, a donation of plain-bound copies is made to them for gratuitous distribution.

In the resale of books at the depositories of the auxiliaries, the policy of the parent society requires that the common Bibles and Testaments be sold at cost and the amount necessary to cover expenses of carriage, and the better qualities at an advance not exceeding ten per cent.

The Annual Report of the Board of Managers is furnished to auxiliaries gratuitously. One copy is sent by mail to each corresponding secretary communicating his annual reports regularly to the corresponding secretary of the parent society; others are sent when books are ordered.

Each auxiliary receives, also gratuitously, the "Bible Society Record." One copy is also sent to the president, corresponding secretary, and treasurer, and one to the secretary of each branch society. An intimate connection is thus kept up between the auxiliaries and parent society; and when the secretaries are prompt in forwarding their reports, each is kept advised in regard to the operations of the other.

In addition to county auxiliaries, efficient and valuable aid has been rendered to the parent society by similar associations of a somewhat more specific character, such as Female Bible Societies, College Bible Societies, Marine Bible Societies, Young Men's Bible Societies, and Bible Committees. These are located in various parts of the country, and many are actively engaged in promoting the general objects of the society. We might, did our limits permit, review the operations of these societies, and present many interesting facts in relation thereto.

The ladies deserve special notice for the commendable zeal manifested by them in this benevolent enterprise. Much is said about the appropriate sphere of woman. Questions have arisen in regard to the propriety of their engaging in any separate organization. In reference to the organization of a society, the sole object of which is to put the Word of God in the hands of the destitute, no one certainly could exclude woman. This work is peculiarly fitted to her nature, and assorts most beautifully with the character given of devoted females in the days of Christ. To what, we ask, is woman more indebted than the Bible? Rather let me ask what is her condition in those lands where its heavenly light does not shine, and its divine teachings are not known? It is the Bible alone that imparts to her the distinction assigned by her Maker in this world, and points to her more elevated destiny in that which is to come.

The British and Foreign Bible Society acknowledges with gratitude the services of the ladies in the work of distribution, and it is a matter of history that the ladies' associations contribute more to the parent society than all other associations in England.

We must not omit to mention the fact that the very first auxiliary society recognized by the American Bible Society was the "Female Bible Society of New York" in 1816. During the first twenty years of its existence it has paid over to the parent society one thousand dollars per annum. We might mention other honorable instances of efficiency and liberality, but we shall forbear by simply remarking, in regard to this society, "Many daughters have done virtuously, but thou excellest them all."

A mass of the most interesting facts in relation to the destitution in various portions of the country, embracing the cheering results of Bible distribution in the conversion of individuals, families, and neighborhoods, might be gleaned from the various reports, made from time to time to the parent society, which would fill a volume.

CHAPTER VI.

BIBLE HOUSE.

When the Constitution was adopted and the officers elected, there was not one dollar in the treasury. The society had neither Bible House nor Bibles, nor materials for making them. The managers, however, relying upon the goodness of the cause, in humble trust in the God of the Bible, immediately went to work in procuring materials and devising plans for its early publication. Through the liberality of the governors of the New York Hospital and the mayor of the city, they were allowed the use of rooms in which they transacted their business. They were also accommodated by the Historical Society in the New York Institution. Several printers volunteered to publish gratuitously any communications they deemed it necessary to make to the public. The managers procured three sets of stereotype plates in octavo, and three in duodecimo form. Applications for Bibles were made from auxiliaries, which had to be supplied by the New York Bible Society. This society, together with the New York Auxiliary Bible Societies, presented the managers with a complete set of stereotype plates of the duodecimo size and brevier type, and also all the copies in sheets of the French Bible in their possession. A donation of five hundred pounds sterling was received from the British and Foreign Bible Society. A standing committee of five was appointed to take charge of all the property of the society, except the funds in the hands of the treasurer, with power to direct all the affairs and concerns of the society during the recess of the Board of Managers; to enter into all necessary contracts, give orders for the delivery of Bibles, and orders on the treasurer for the payment of money. They had now gotten fairly under way; the first year of their labors had closed; and the success of the institution being no longer problematical, they were excited to renewed energy and perseverance.

One of the first things that engaged the deliberations of the managers was the location of the surplus stereotype plates. On this subject a considerable degree of anxiety was manifested, as some questions of delicacy were involved in its consideration. The managers were fully impressed with the importance of giving every possible aid to the circulation of the Scriptures in distant parts of the country, and they were equally convinced of the necessity of guarding against whatever might excite local embarrassments, and of preserving unimpaired the unity of the national society, and the freedom of its agency through all its ramifications. They adopted certain principles as the basis of their proceedings in regard to this subject. After mature deliberation, in which the policy of the measure was strongly contested, on the ground that, should the society distribute these plates among the auxiliaries, local prejudices might arise affecting, if not in the end destroying, the nationality of the institution, and also on the ground of the risk to be run, and the expensiveness of having two presses established: it was finally determined, as the best that could be done, to send an octavo and duodecimo set to the Kentucky Bible Society, located at Lexington, this society having been promised one of the duodecimo sets previously.

The conditions required on the part of the Kentucky Bible Society were the following:

"The society were to hold the plates as the property

of the American Bible Society, to be removed at the pleasure of the board, whenever they can be more advantageously used elsewhere; and that they print from them, at their own expense, as many Bibles as they think proper for gratuitous distribution or sale within their own district exclusively, rendering to the board a particular account of the number and cost of the Bibles printed and distributed by them. In consideration of the gratuitous use of the plates, they were required to print, bind, and distribute, at the expense of the board, and agreeably to their orders, as many Bibles as they should from time to time direct."

The Kentucky Bible Society acceding to these stipulations, the plates were sent, and they continued to print therefrom until 1822, when it was deemed expedient to have all the printing done at New York. The affairs of the society were carried on, and the several species of their property were kept in a small depository, and, for want of room, in several other places. The value of the property being such, and the continual jeopardy of a large proportion of it; the advanced premium of insurance consequent thereon; the time lost in traveling from place to place, and the labor incurred by this perplexing mode of superintending different parts of the same business, added to the daily increase of all these evils, induced the managers to concentrate their business into a single establishment, either under one roof, or in buildings contiguous to each other. They would have preferred owning a suitable edifice, as insuring greater permanency and a more perfect control; but the amount of funds necessary for such a purpose, and the infant state of the society, did not warrant the undertaking, and they continued to occupy a *hired* house. The managers labored under these embarrassments for some time, and at length the propriety of erecting a Bible House was fully discussed, and resulted in a unanimous agreement, as soon as circumstances would admit, to engage in its erection. In 1822 the corner stone was laid, and the building was finished in the early part of the winter of the same year.

The Bible House embraces fifty feet front upon Nassau street, and extends back thirty feet, when it is contracted to the breadth of thirty feet, and runs seventy feet with that width to Theater Alley, making the whole depth of the building one hundred feet. The basement story contains apartments for the accommodation of the keeper and his family, the large rooms for storing printing paper and other property of the society, and the requisite vaults for fuel.

The first floor of the front building comprises a large room for the agent's office and biblical library, and two smaller ones for the accommodation of the secretaries. The rest of this story, besides the space occupied by stair-cases, being a room of about sixty-two feet by twenty-eight, is devoted to the purpose of a depository for Bibles, and is capable of containing one hundred thousand Bibles, bound and arranged on shelves. On the second story, in front, is the managers' room, which is forty-eight feet long by twenty-eight wide, and sixteen in height, and plainly but neatly furnished.

The second and third stories of the rear building are occupied by the binder, and as a depository for printed sheets. The third story of the front building, with the fourth of the rear, which together form one room, as also the garret, are occupied by the printer to the society.

The ground on which the Bible House stands, with the building, cost twenty-two thousand five hundred dollars, the most of which was obtained by donations from liberal individuals for this specific object.

All the business of the society could now be conducted under one roof. Every record and document necessary to be referred to could easily be obtained, and thus the various committees were furnished with all the facilities required for the prosecution of their work. For eight years the society carried on its operations with regularity and system; but so increasing were the demands of our own and foreign countries for the Bible, that it was found necessary to erect an additional building for purposes of printing. The printing had been carried on in a building located on the opposite side of the street from the Bible House. A lot was procured adjoining the Bible House, and the erection of two additional buildings commenced. They lie north of and adjacent to the Bible House. One of them fronts on Nassau street, and is occupied as a printing office, four stories high, forty-four feet in front and rear, and thirty-four feet in depth. The other is also four stories high, fronting on Theater Alley; it is fifty-six feet in length, and thirty feet in depth, and communicates on each story with the Bible House. The whole establishment, including the old and new buildings, is ninety-four feet in front on Nassau street, and the same in rear on Theater Alley, and, including the Depository, thirty-six feet wide and four stories high, which connects the front and rear, having a depth of one hundred feet, with a court in the center. Under the right wing of the Bible House is a fire-proof vault for the safe keeping of the stereotype plates. The entire building is fire-proof throughout. Sixteen years have elapsed since the erection of these last buildings, and the society has gone on operating with efficiency in every department.

Eight patent steam and twenty-two hand presses are constantly employed, which print daily about two thousand copies of the Bible, the same number being bound and ready for delivery. About two hundred and twenty-two hands are employed in the various departments of printing and binding.

In regard to the printing of Bibles, reference has already been made to the more early operations of the society; we think it proper to embrace under one head all the transactions of the society up to this time, in regard to the kind and qualities of Bibles and Testaments printed and bound at the Bible House.

A set of stereotype plates of the French Bible was received from the British and Foreign Bible Society, in lieu of part of their donation: this, in conjunction with the six sets procured by the society, and the one presented by the New York Bible Society, constituted all they had during the first year of the society's operations. At the end of the third year the managers report that they had in possession eight sets of stereotype plates for the whole Bible, and two sets for the New Testament, in addition to plates for the New Testament in Indian and Spanish. In 1822 the society procured two sets of stereotype plates of the New Testament in the brevier type and the 18mo size. In 1824 a set of stereotype plates was procured for an octavo edition of the New Testament in pica type. In 1833 plates were cast for a modern Greek Testament.

In 1834, two new Bibles, with marginal references, the one a quarto, and the other a royal octavo. In 1835 a new duodecimo reference Bible was printed, adapted to the use of Bible classes and Sabbath schools.

In 1837, a pocket Testament in the German language, in the Spanish language, and one in diamond type, in English, were stereotyped.

In 1838, a new Pica Testament, with the Book of Psalms, in octavo form, was stereotyped, and also a Testament for the blind, by which that large and interesting portion of the community is brought in contact with the Word of God, and by means of which they can now feel after him, and find him to the joy of their hearts.

In 1839 a set of stereotype plates was cast for a new Portuguese Testament.

In 1840, a new English octavo Bible in long primer, and a new duodecimo French Bible in brevier.

A reprint of the Annual Reports of the first twenty-two years of the society's operations was published this year, and bound in one large octavo volume.

In 1841 the managers printed a "Brief View of the Plan of Operations of the American Bible Society," in a small pamphlet, for gratuitous distribution among those who are engaged in promoting the Bible cause. They also printed a "Statement as to the Character of Foreign Versions of the Scriptures patronized by them."

In 1843, the managers, at great expense, had stereotype plates prepared of the entire Bible for the blind.

In 1844 the New Testament was printed in the Ojibwa tongue, for the use of a large tribe of Indians near Lake Superior.

In 1846 the managers prepared plates and issued an 18mo Minion Bible, after a well-known Oxford Bible of that size.

In 1847 two sets of plates were procured for the pocket New Testament.

A new Portuguese Bible, of large duodecimo size, was also printed for the benefit of the numerous Portuguese seamen in our various ports, as well as for the multitudes in Brazil and elsewhere who use that tongue.

In 1848, plates for a new pearl reference Bible, a new nonpareil, or Sunday School Bible, and for a new pocket Testament, were cast.

Also for a Danish Bible, for the use of Norwegian

immigrants; a New Testament, in parallel columns of German and English, for the use of German immigrants who are in need of the Scriptures, and desirous to learn the English language; and one in Dutch and English, for the use of immigrants from Holland, and also New Testaments in the Grebo and Arawack tongues, for those speaking that language in Western Africa and South America. A Testament has been stereotyped for the use of the Choctaws. Thus it will be seen that the American Bible Society has been going forward, as fast as its resources would allow, in making provision for all the wants and demands of the country.

We will add to this a specimen of the types of the Society's Bibles and Testaments, and also a catalogue of the kinds, qualities, and prices of the books on sale at the Depository.

Specimens of the Types of the Society's Bibles and Testaments.

SPANISH.

LONG PRIMER.

10 ¿O si le pidiere un pez, por ventura le dará una serpiente?

11 Pues si vosotros, siendo malos, sabeis dar buenas dádivas á vuestros hijos: ¿cuánto mas vuestro Padre, que está en los cielos, dará bienes á los que se los pidan?

12 Y así todo lo que quereis que los hombres hagan con vosotros, hacedlo tambien vosotros con ellos: porque esta es la Ley y los Profetas.

BOURGEOIS.

13 Entrad por la puerta estrecha: porque ancha es la puerta, y espacioso el camino, que lleva á la perdicion, y muchos son los que entran por él.

14 ¡Qué angosta es la puerta, y qué estrecho el camino, que lleva á la vida: y pocos son, los que atinan con él!

AGATE.

25 Jesus les respondió: Os lo digo, y no me creeis: las obras que yo hago en nombre de mi Padre, estas dan testimonio de mí:

26 Mas vosotros no creeis, porque no sois de mis ovejas.

27 Mis ovejas oyen mi voz: y yo las conozco, y me siguen:

28 Y yo les doy vida eterna, y no perecerán jamas, y ninguno las arrebatará de mi mano.

PORTUGUESE.

BOURGEOIS.

24 Então disse Jesus a seus discipulos: Se alguem quizer vir após mim, negue-se a si mesmo, e tome sobre si sua cruz, e siga-me.

25 Porque qualquer que quizer salvar sua vida, perde-la-ha; porém qualquer que por amor de mim perder sua vida, acha-la-ha.

GERMAN.

BOURGEOIS.

4 Und Gott wird abwischen alle Thränen von ihren Augen; und der Tod wird nicht mehr seyn, noch Leid, noch Geschrey, noch Schmerzen wird mehr seyn; denn das Erste ist vergangen.

5 Und der auf dem Stuhl saß, sprach: Siehe, ich mache alles neu. Und er spricht zu mir: Schreibe; denn diese Worte sind wahrhaftig und gewiß.

NONPAREIL.

1 Richtet nicht, auf daß ihr nicht gerichtet werdet.

2 Denn mit welcherley Gericht ihr richtet, werdet ihr gerichtet werden; und mit welcherley Maas ihr messet, wird euch gemessen werden.

3 Was siehest du aber den Splitter in deines Bruders Auge, und wirst nicht gewahr des Balken in deinem Auge?

4 Oder wie darfst du sagen zu deinem Bruder: Halt, ich will dir den Splitter aus deinem Auge ziehen? und siehe ein Balke ist in deinem Auge.

FRENCH.

BOURGEOIS.

1 Apres cela, je vis un ciel nouveau et une terre nouvelle. Car le premier ciel et la première terre avoient disparu, et la mer n'étoit plus.

2 Et, moi Jean, je vis la ville sainte, la nouvelle Jérusalem qui, venant de Dieu descendoit du ciel, étant parée comme une épouse qui se pare pour son époux.

BREVIER.

17 Ainsi tout arbre qui est bon produit de bons fruits; et tout arbre qui est mauvais produit de mauvais fruits.

18 Un bon arbre ne puet produire de mauvais fruits, et un mauvais arbre ne peut en produire de bons.

AGATE.

15 Après donc qu'ils eurent dîné, Jesus dit à Simon-Pierre: Simon, *fils* de Jean, m'aimez-vous plus que *ne font* ceux-ci? Il lui répondit: Oui, Seigneur, vous savez que je vous aime. Jésus lui dit: Paissez mes agneaux.

16 Il lui demanda de nouveau: Simon, *fils* de Jean, m'aimez-vous? Pierre lui répondit: Oui, Seigneur, vous savez que je vous aime. Jésus lui dit: Paissez mes agneaux.

17 Il lui demanda pour la trosième fois: Simon, *fils* de Jean, m'aimez-vous? Pierre fut touché de ce qu'il lui demandoit pour la troisème fois, M'aimez-vous? Et il lui dit: Seigneur, vous savez toutes choses; vous connoisez que je vous aime. Jésus lui dit: Paissez mes brebis.

Specimens of the Types of the Society's Bibles and Testaments.

PICA.

For God so loved the world, that he gave his only begotten Son, that whosoever believeth in him, should not perish, but have everlasting life. John iii. 16.

SMALL PICA.

And it came to pass, that in the morning watch the LORD looked unto the host of the Egyptians through the pillar of fire and of the cloud, and troubled the host of the Egyptians, Exodus xiv. 24.

LONG PRIMER.

And the anger of the LORD was hot against Israel; and he said, Because that this people hath transgressed my covenant which I commanded their Judges ii. 20.

BOURGEOIS.

And the eyes of them that see shall not be dim, and the ears of them that hear shall hearken.

The heart also of the rash shall understand knowledge, and the tongue of the stammerers shall be ready to speak plainly. Isaiah xxxii. 3, 4.

BREVIER.

Then Shaphan the scribe told the king, saying, Hilkiah the priest hath given me a book. And Shaphan read it before the king.

And it came to pass when the king had heard the words of the law, that he rent his clothes.

And the king commanded Hilkiah, and Ahikam the son of Shaphan, and Abdon the son of Micah, and Shaphan the scribe, and Asaiah a servant of the king's, saying, 2 Chron. xxxiv. 18—20.

MINION.

And ye shall observe this thing for an ordinance to thee and to thy sons for ever.

And it shall come to pass, when ye be come to the land which the LORD will give you, according as he hath promised, that ye shall keep this service. Exodus xii. 24, 25.

NONPARIEL.

A new commandment I give unto you, That ye love one another; as I have loved you, that ye also love one another.

By this shall all *men* know that ye are my disciples, if ye have love one to another. John xiii. 34, 35.

AGATE.

And there were some that had indignation with themselves, and said, Why was this waste of the ointment made?

For it might have been sold for more than three hundred pence, and have been given to the poor. And they murmured against her. Mark xiv. 4, 5.

PEARL AGATE.

And many of them that sleep in the dust of the earth shall awake, some to everlasting life, and some to shame *and* everlasting contempt.

And they that be wise, shall shine as the brightness of the firmament; and they that turn many to righteousness, as the stars for ever and ever. Daniel xii. 2, 3.

PEARL.

He is like a man which built an house, and digged deep, and laid the foundation on a rock: and when the flood arose, the stream beat vehemently upon that house, and could not shake it: for it was founded upon a rock.

But he that heareth and doeth not, is like a man that without a foundation built an house upon the earth, against which the stream did beat vehemently, and immediately it fell, and the ruin of that house was great. Luke vi. 48, 49.

DIAMOND.

When he heard that Jesus was come out of Judea into Galilee, he went unto him, and besought him that he would come down, and heal his son: for he was at the point of death.

Then said Jesus unto him, Except ye see signs and wonders, ye will not believe.

The nobleman saith unto him, Sir, come down ere my child die. John iv. 47, 48, 49.

PRICES OF BIBLES AND TESTAMENTS SOLD BY THE AMERICAN BIBLE SOCIETY, AT THE SOCIETY'S HOUSE, NO. 115 NASSAU STREET, NEW YORK, TO ITS AUXILIARY SOCIETIES, AND TO OTHER SOCIETIES CONTRIBUTING BY DONATIONS TO ITS FUNDS.

The Board of Managers beg leave to state that it is very desirable that orders intended for auxiliaries should be accompanied with payment, it being understood that the moneys are usually collected by auxiliaries previous to their purchasing books. Such is the demand upon the Depository, that long credits prevent the parent institution from receiving the benefit of the discount allowed for prompt payment in the purchase of paper.

DESIGNATING BOOKS BY NUMBER.

☞ *The various descriptions of books may be designated by their numbers. The business will be greatly simplified if orders for books are made by numbers.—So many of No. 1, and so many of No. 2, &c.*

No.	ENGLISH BIBLES.	
	QUARTO.	
1	*Pica*, with references, morocco, gilt	$10 00
2	" calf, gilt	6 00
3	" " embossed	4 25
4	" sheep, lettered, raised bands	2 00
	ROYAL OCTAVO.	
5	*Small Pica*, with references, morocco, gilt	6 00
6	" calf, gilt	3 50
7	" " embossed	2 75
8	" sheep, lettered, raised bands	1 37½
	OCTAVO.	
9	*Long Primer*, morocco, gilt	2 75
10	" calf, gilt	1 75
11	" " embossed	1 37½
12	*Small Pica*, sheep, lettered, raised bands	87½
13	" roan, gilt	1 25
	DUODECIMO.	
14	*Bourgeois* Bible, morocco, gilt	2 25
15	" calf, gilt	1 62½
16	" " embossed	1 25
17	" sheep, lettered, bands	62½
18	*Minion* Bible, calf, embossed	75
19	" sheep, lettered	37½
20	*Nonpareil*, with references, morocco, gilt	2 00
21	" calf, gilt	1 37½
22	" " embossed	1 00
23	" sheep, lettered, raised bands	50
24	" without references, calf, gilt	50
25	" calf, embossed	37½
26	" sheep, lettered	25
	18MO.—POCKET.	
27	*Minion* Bible, morocco, gilt	1 37½
28	" calf, gilt	1 00
29	" roan, gilt	75
30	" sheep, lettered	40
31	*Pearl*, reference, morocco, gilt	1 37½
32	" calf, gilt	1 00
33	" tucks	75
34	" sheep, lettered	37½
	24MO.	
35	*Agate*, pocket, morocco, gilt	1 25
36	" calf, gilt	75
37	" " lettered, embossed	60
38	" sheep, lettered	31¼

No.	32MO.	
39	*Diamond*, morocco, gilt	$1 25
40	" calf, gilt	1 00
41	" tucks	62½
42	" sheep, lettered	40
	ENGLISH TESTAMENTS.	
	OCTAVO.	
43	*Pica*, with Psalms, morocco, gilt	2 00
44	" calf, gilt	1 25
45	" " embossed	1 00
46	" " lettered, raised bands	50
47	" " " without Psalms	37½
	OCTODECIMO.	
48	*Brevier*, Testament and Psalms, morocco, gilt	1 00
49	" calf, embossed	50
50	" sheep, lettered	25
51	" muslin	18¾
52	" Testament, calf, gilt	62½
53	" sheep, lettered	18¾
54	" cloth	12½
55	*Pearl*, reference, tucks	31¼
56	" calf, gilt	31¼
	32MO.	
57	*Pearl*, pocket, calf, gilt edges	25
58	" tucks	25
59	" sheep, lettered	9
60	" glazed muslin, lettered	6¼
	GERMAN.	
61	BIBLES, quarto, sheep	3 50
62	" octavo, calf, embossed	2 00
63	" *Long Primer*, sheep, lettered, raised bands	1 50
64	" duodecimo, *Brevier*, calf, embossed	1 00
65	" sheep, lettered, raised bands	50
66	TESTAMENTS, duodecimo, sheep, lettered	18¾
67	" pocket	37½
68	" 32mo, *Nonpareil*, sheep, lettered	12½
	FRENCH.	
69	BIBLES, quarto, calf, embossed	5 00
70	" duodecimo, *Brevier*, morocco, gilt	2 00
71	" " calf, gilt	1 50
72	" " " embossed	1 00
73	" " sheep, lettered, raised bands	62½

No.		
74	TESTAMENTS, octavo, calf, embossed	$1 00
75	" French and English in parallel columns...	75
76	" French, duodecimo...	18¾
	WELSH.	
77	BIBLES, quarto, calf, plain...........	4 50
78	" octavo, calf, plain	2 00
79	" duodecimo, calf, plain......	50
80	" pocket, calf, plain	1 00
81	TESTAMENTS, octavo, sheep, plain...	62½
82	" duodecimo, sheep, plain..............	25
83	" pocket, sheep, plain..	37½
	SPANISH.	
84	BIBLES, octavo, *Long Primer*, calf, gilt	1 75
85	" sheep, lettered, raised bands.	1 00
86	TESTAMENTS, duodecimo, *Bourgeois*, sheep, lettered.....	18¾
87	Spanish Gospels	6¼
	IRISH.	
88	BIBLES, duodecimo, Roman character	1 50
89	" vernacular character	2 25
90	TESTAMENTS, duodecimo, vernacular character, sheep ...	50
91	" duodecimo, vernacular character, sheep ...	25
92	" Roman character, sheep	50
	CHINESE.	
93	TESTAMENT	1 62½
	RUSSIAN.	
94	TESTAMENT	1 25
	PORTUGUESE.	
95	BIBLES, calf, gilt	1 50
96	" "	1 00
97	" sheep	62
98	TESTAMENTS	25
	DANISH.	
99	BIBLES	2 00
100	TESTAMENTS	50
	SWEDISH.	
101	BIBLES	87
102	TESTAMENTS	30
	ITALIAN.	
103	BIBLES	$2 37½
104	" pocket......................	1 50
105	TESTAMENTS	37½
	ARABIC.	
106	BIBLES	3 37½
107	TESTAMENTS	1 12½
	SYRIAC.	
108	BIBLES	4 50
109	TESTAMENTS	3 37½
110	PSALTERS	50
	POLISH.	
111	BIBLES	2 25
112	TESTAMENTS	37½
	GREEK.	
113	TESTAMENTS	25
	DUTCH.	
114	BIBLES	2 00
115	TESTAMENTS	37½
	HEBREW.	
116	BIBLES	3 00
117	TESTAMENTS	1 50
118	PSALTER	37½
	LATIN.	
119	BIBLES	1 50
	FOR THE BLIND.	
120	BIBLE for the Blind, 8 vols..........	20 00
121	PSALMS for the Blind, 1 vol..........	1 50
	GAELIC.	
122	BIBLES, duodecimo, calf, plain	1 00
123	TESTAMENTS, duodecimo, sheep, plain	31¼
	FINNISH.	
124	TESTAMENTS	75
	INDIAN SCRIPTURES.	
125	NEW TESTAMENT in Ojibwa	75
126	ISAIAH in Mohawk	43
127	EPISTLES OF JOHN in Delaware	8
128	REPRINT OF REPORTS..............	2 00

It will be readily seen, by the specimens of type and the prices of books in the catalogue, that books are far better now than formerly, both in regard to materials and manufacture, and the price has been reduced, in many instances, almost one half, and the higher priced books at least one third. The Minion Bible has been reduced from seventy-three cents to forty-five cents, and the Nonpareil Sunday School Bible is now sold at twenty-five cents per copy, and a well-made New Testament for six and a quarter cents. This reduction is mostly attributable to the improvements in paper-making, and the application of steam power to the business of printing and binding.

CHAPTER VII.

ACTS OF INCORPORATION.

By the following acts of the Legislature of the State of New York, the property of the institution is secure, and all bequests made to it will reach their intended object by adherence to the following form:

"I give and bequeath to the American Bible Society, formed in New York in the year eighteen hundred and sixteen, the sum of —— (or real estate, as the case may be), to be applied to the charitable uses and purposes of said society."

Act of the Legislature of New York in relation to the Society's Property.

The real estate upon which the Society's buildings are situated was conveyed, when purchased by the Society, in fee simple to five individuals as joint tenants, who thereupon executed a declaration of trust, setting forth, among other things, that they held said property in trust for the American Bible Society, and that they, or the survivors of them, would at any time convey said premises as the Board of Managers of said Society should direct. Two of said trustees have deceased, and the survivors being somewhat advanced in years, the board deemed it advisable to have a new conveyance made for the purpose of perpetuating the trust. The laws of this state having been revised since the said deeds of trust were made, and similar trusts, that should thereafter be created, having been declared void, it became a serious question whether the proposed new conveyance would not come within the Revised Statutes, and thus be void. To supersede this question, the board considered it the most prudent course to apply to the Legislature for an act of incorporation, and that, when incorporated, the surviving trustees should convey to the Society as a corporate body. Accordingly, a committee was appointed by the board to make the application. An act of incorporation was drafted and forwarded to the Legislature; but it met with so much opposition, that, at the suggestion of some of the opposers of the bill, a special act was prepared and substituted in its place. This was passed without opposition; and under its provisions the board will be enabled to continue the property in trust according to its original design. The Act is as follows:

An Act to confirm certain Trusts therein mentioned.

[Passed February 21, 1837.]

The people of the State of New York, represented in Senate and Assembly, do enact as follows:

§ 1. The trusts declared in and by two certain deeds or declarations of trust executed by Richard Varick, William W. Woolsey, Samuel Boyd, Benjamin Strong, and John Watts, Jun., the one bearing date on the twenty-eighth day of December, one thousand eight hundred and twenty-one, and recorded in the office of register in and for the city and county of New York, in liber 164 of Conveyances, page 115, and the other bearing date on the first day of May, one thousand eight hundred and twenty-nine, and recorded in the said office in liber 257 of Conveyances, page 226, and relating to certain real estate in the city of New York, purchased for the benefit of a society or association known by the name of the American Bible Society, are hereby confirmed, and it shall be lawful to execute the same and to appoint new trustees in the manner in the said deeds mentioned.

§ 2. This Act shall take effect immediately on its passage.

An Act to Incorporate the American Bible Society.

[Passed March 25, 1841.]

The people of the State of New York, represented in Senate and Assembly, do enact as follows:

§ 1. All such persons as now are or may hereafter become members of the American Bible Society, formed in the city of New York in the year one thousand eight hundred and sixteen, shall be and are hereby constituted a body corporate, by the name of "The American Bible Society," for the purpose of publishing and promoting a general circulation of the Holy Scriptures without note or comment.

§ 2. The nett income of said Society arising from their real estate shall not exceed the sum of five thousand dollars annually.

§ 3. This corporation shall possess the general powers and be subject to the provisions contained in title third of chapter eighteenth of the first part of the Revised Statutes, so far as the same are applicable and have not been repealed.*

* General powers contained in title third of chapter eighteenth of the first part of the Revised Statutes, and given to "The American Bible Society" by the third section of the act incorporating that Society:

1st. To have succession by its corporate name perpetually.

2d. To sue and be sued, complain or defend in any court of law or equity.

§ 4. This Act shall take effect immediately.

§ 5. The Legislature may at any time modify or repeal this Act.

STATE OF NEW YORK, Secretary's Office.

I have compared the preceding with an original act of the Legislature of this state on file in this office, and do certify that the same is a correct transcript therefrom and of the whole of said original.

(L.S.) Given under my hand and the seal of this office, at the city of Albany, the second day of April, in the year of our Lord one thousand eight hundred and forty-one.

ARCH'D. CAMPBELL, Deputy Secretary.

The following proceedings were taken by the society at the next stated annual meeting after the passage of the act of incorporation:

An Ordinance to establish a Board of Managers, and for other Purposes.

The American Bible Society do ordain as follows:

1st. The business of this corporation shall be conducted by a Board of Managers, constituted and appointed in like manner as prescribed by the Constitution under which the American Bible Society acted immediately before its incorporation, in relation to the Board of Managers therein mentioned.

2d. The Managers who were members of the said board at the time of the said incorporation (except those whose time of service has expired), shall continue in office during the terms for which they were respectively elected. And all persons who at the time of such incorporation were officers of the said Society, shall continue to hold their respective offices during the pleasure of the said board.

3d. The Board of Managers shall have power to appoint all officers of the Society, and to allow to such of them as they may think proper a suitable compensation; to purchase and hold such real and personal estate as may be permitted by the charter; to cause to be made and to use a common seal for the corporation, and to make by-laws not inconsistent with the laws of this state; and they shall have such fur-

---

3d. To make and use a common seal, and alter the same at pleasure.

4th. To hold, purchase, and convey such real and personal estate as the purposes of the corporation shall require, not exceeding the amount limited in its charter.

5th. To appoint such subordinate officers and agents as the business of the corporation shall require, and to allow them a suitable compensation.

6th. To make by-laws, not inconsistent with any existing law, for the management of its property and the regulation of its affairs.

ther powers as were given by the said Constitution to the Board of Managers therein mentioned. Ten members of the Board of Managers shall be a sufficient number to form a board for the transaction of business, and every decision of a majority of the persons duly assembled as a board shall be valid.

The Act and Ordinance were severally adopted.

CHAPTER VIII.

PRINTING, PUBLICATION, AND CIRCULATION OF BIBLES.

THE first field, both in regard to order and importance, in the estimation of the society, in reference to occupancy and cultivation, was the *Home Field.*

Its first work was to supply the destitute population of this country with the Holy Scriptures.

During the first year of the society's operations, eleven thousand five hundred and fifty copies of the Bible were printed, and six thousand four hundred and ten copies were sent out from the Depository and distributed all over the country, from Maine to Georgia, and from the Atlantic to the Mississippi, carrying joy and gladness to the destitute in many desolate places.

The first donation made by the board was to the East Tennessee Bible Society, of five hundred Bibles for the destitute in that region.

The society resolved, at a very early period in its history, to distribute no Bibles gratuitously except through the auxiliaries, as the proper media of its benefactions. This wise regulation it has faithfully adhered to until the present time.

The second year closed its labors, and the board were enabled to make the gratifying announcement to the friends and patrons of the institution, that twenty thousand four hundred Bibles had been printed, and seventeen thousand five hundred and ninety-four were issued from the Depository, while one thousand five hundred and twenty-one had been gratuitously distributed by the auxiliaries.

The next year, 1819, the number of books printed was seventy-one thousand three hundred and twenty. The number issued from the Depository was thirty-one thousand one hundred and eighteen. There were also printed, in the Gaelic, Welsh, German, French, and several Indian languages, two thousand four hundred and fifty. The number gratuitously distributed during the year was between four and five thousand.

In 1820 the number of Bibles printed was sixty-four thousand four hundred and eighty-two, and the number issued was forty-one thousand five hundred and thirteen, which, added to those issued in the German, Spanish, Gaelic, French, Welsh, and Indian languages, amounted to ninety-seven thousand one hundred and two. The number gratuitously distributed this year was eighteen thousand six hundred and seventeen.

In 1821 the number of Bibles printed was fifty-nine thousand eight hundred, and the number issued was sixty-eight thousand one hundred and seventy-seven, in eight different languages, of which number thirteen thousand seven hundred and six were gratuitously distributed.

In 1822 the number printed was thirty-six thousand six hundred and twenty-five. This was the year the society removed to the new house. The issues were fifty-four thousand eight hundred and six, in the various languages above enumerated. Of this number twelve thousand nine hundred and twenty-three were gratuitously circulated.

In 1823 the number printed was fifty-three thousand six hundred. Issues, fifty-four thousand eight hundred and five. The number gratuitously distributed this year was twelve thousand three hundred and twenty-five.

In 1824 the number printed was seventy-seven thousand five hundred and seventy-five, and the issues amounted to sixty thousand four hundred and thirty-nine, in the usual languages. Of this number fourteen thousand seven hundred and twenty-nine were gratuitously distributed through the appropriate channels. Two hundred Bibles were donated to the United States army, on the application of an officer of high rank.

In 1825 the number printed was forty-eight thousand five hundred and fifty, and the issues the same year were sixty-three thousand eight hundred and fifty-one. Of the above number nineteen thousand six hundred and twenty-three were distributed gratuitously.

In 1826 the number published was eighty-one thousand, and the issues sixty-seven thousand one hundred and thirty-four. Of this number, in the various languages, in our own country, and the West Indies, Sandwich Islands, Mexico, and South America, there were gratuitously distributed sixteen thousand five hundred and forty-seven.

In 1827, seventy-six thousand seven hundred and thirty-four were printed, and the issues amounted to seventy-one thousand six hundred and twenty-one. Thirteen thousand one hundred and sixty-nine were gratuitously circulated.

1828. There were printed this year one hundred and eighteen thousand seven hundred and fifty, and issued one hundred and thirty-four thousand six hundred and seven. Distributed gratuitously, seven thousand two hundred and sixty.

1829. The number printed was, during this year, three hundred and sixty thousand. Issues, two hundred thousand one hundred and twenty-two. Gratuitously distributed, eight thousand four hundred and sixty-five.

1830. There was printed this year three hundred and eight thousand. Issued, two hundred and thirty-eight thousand five hundred and eighty-three. Distributed gratuitously, fifty thousand three hundred and forty-nine.

In 1831 there were printed two hundred and seventy thousand. Two hundred and forty-two thousand were issued from the Bible House, and thirty-nine thousand were gratuitously distributed.

In 1832 one hundred and fifty-six thousand five hundred were printed, one hundred and fifteen thousand eight hundred and two were issued, and eighteen thousand nine hundred and thirty-one were distributed gratuitously.

1833. This year the financial condition of the society was such as to justify the printing of but few Bibles, and in view of this, the numbers being so unimportant, they were not made a matter of record. The work of distribution, however, was carried on, and the issues amounted to ninety-one thousand one hundred and sixty-eight, and the gratuitous distribution to twelve thousand and seven.

In 1834 the number printed was one hundred and forty-nine thousand three hundred and seventy-five. Issues, one hundred and ten thousand eight hundred and thirty-two. Gratuitous distribution, nineteen thousand and seventy-six.

In 1835 the number printed was thirty-four thousand. Issued, one hundred and twenty-three thousand two hundred and thirty-six. Gratuitous distribution, thirty-three thousand four hundred and eighty-eight.

In 1836 the number printed was one hundred and ninety-four thousand. Issued, two hundred and twenty-one thousand six hundred and ninety-four. Gratuitously distributed, seventy-eight thousand four hundred and eighty-nine.

In 1837 the number printed was two hundred and twenty-eight thousand. Issued, two hundred and six thousand two hundred and forty. Gratuitous distribution, one hundred and forty-six thousand nine hundred.

In 1838 one hundred and forty-two thousand were printed, one hundred and fifty-eight thousand issued, and thirty-four thousand four hundred gratuitously distributed.

In 1839 the number printed was one hundred and fourteen thousand. Issued, one hundred and thirty-four thousand nine hundred and thirty-seven. Gratuitously distributed, eight thousand nine hundred.

In 1840 the number printed was one hundred and thirty-nine thousand. Issued, one hundred and fifty-seven thousand two hundred and sixty-one. Gratuitously distributed, fifteen thousand four hundred.

In 1841 the number printed was one hundred and sixty-six thousand eight hundred and seventy-five. Issued, one hundred and fifty thousand two hundred and two. Gratuitously distributed, nine thousand eight hundred.

In 1842 the number printed was two hundred and seventy-six thousand. The number issued, two hundred and fifty-seven thousand and sixty-seven. The number gratuitously distributed, one hundred and nine thousand two hundred.

In 1843 the number printed was two hundred and twenty thousand. Issued, two hundred and sixteen thousand six hundred and five. Gratuitously distributed, one hundred and eight thousand.

In 1844 the number printed was two hundred and ninety-three thousand. Issued, three hundred and fourteen thousand five hundred and eighty-two. Gratuitously distributed, twenty-three thousand eight hundred.

In 1845 the number was four hundred and seventeen thousand three hundred and fifty. Issued, four hundred and twenty-nine thousand and ninety-two. Gratuitously distributed, forty thousand six hundred and fifty-six.

In 1846 the number was four hundred and eighty-two thousand. Issued, four hundred and eighty-three thousand eight hundred and seventy-three. Gratuitously distributed, forty-seven thousand one hundred and fifty-nine.

In 1847 the number was six hundred and seventy-one thousand five hundred. Issued, six hundred and twenty-seven thousand seven hundred and sixty-four. Gratuitously distributed, sixty-six thousand and ninety-seven.

In 1848 the number printed was *seven hundred and sixty thousand nine hundred.* The number issued was *six hundred and fifty-five thousand and sixty-six.* Gratuitously distributed, *seventy-nine thousand six hundred and seventy-eight.*

We have gleaned the above facts in regard to the publication and distribution of the Bible from the Annual Reports of the society, and we believe that they are in the main correct. They present an interesting table of the society's operations during a period of thirty-two years. Many of the Bibles issued by the society, in foreign languages, have been imported from time to time from Bible depositories in other countries.

From the American Bible Society there have been issued, since its organization to the close of the last year, *five millions eight hundred and sixty thousand, four hundred and ninety-three* copies of Bibles and Testaments. These precious volumes have gone out to disseminate blessings all over our own country, and to shed light in many foreign lands. The society has circulated the Word of God directly in upward of twenty different languages, and assisted in circulating it in upward of fifty other languages. The wants of our home population have been strictly attended to, and the hundreds of thousands of immigrants who annually come to our shores from all parts of the Old World are not forgotten. The German, French, Irish, Italian, Swede, Welshman, Spaniard, Portuguese, Jew, Pole, Arab, Norwegian, and all of every tongue who seek an asylum here, are proffered the Word of Life without money and without price.

Notwithstanding much has been done in supplying our native and foreign population, much yet remains to do. In a population of twenty-two millions, there is, at the least calculation, one million five hundred thousand destitute, and they must be supplied. It can not be that they shall be left to "*perish without the law*" when the Church possesses the means to supply them.

Through its faithful allies, the auxiliaries, the society has sent the Bible into every nook and corner of our land. It has circulated it in every state and territory, in every county, and city, and village. In the Sabbath school and common school, in the college and seminary; in the hotel and asylum, and hospital and prison; among soldiers, and sailors, and slaves; on sea and on land, at home and abroad, every where has it, in its beneficence, sent the Gospel of salvation.

The society does not think it strange that in this work of mercy it has met with opposition, inasmuch as its Divine Author himself was persecuted and crucified.

Its principal opponents are the Roman Catholic priests, who, assuming to dictate to the members of that Church in all matters of faith and practice, prohibit them from reading it, and have gone so far as to burn the Bible in this land of "freedom to worship God."

Political demagogues have been found ready to coalesce with the Roman Catholic Church for the purpose of carrying any measure that Church might adopt with the hope of securing its influence in a political point of view—men who would be willing to sacrifice all that is dear in religious liberty, so that they might, in the end, attain political power. We are happy to be able to state that this language does not apply to any party, much less to the people of this country, who, in the main, are deeply imbued with the spirit of liberty, but to a few whose selfish ambition would lead them to advocate principles favorable to their interests, right or wrong. An effort was made a few years since by a Roman Catholic bishop in one of our large cities to exclude the Bible from the common schools. This same bishop has figured extensively in the political world; and having a face to suit all political phases, at one time you hear him haranguing the multitude in the behalf of oppressed Ireland, the loudest in the cry of "Repeal or blood," but, *tempora mutantur!* and you hear him again lifting his voice in opposition to the patriotic movements of the masses of oppressed Italy.

The citizens of this country must be taxed to educate poor Roman Catholic children in the doctrines of their Church. In other words, the funds, nearly all of which are collected from Protestants, must be divided, and the Roman Catholics must have their proportion in accordance with the number of their children. The common school system of instruction in this country is pernicious; the Bible must be expelled, and all the text-books expurgated; and Roman Catholic teachers must be employed ere this rapacious Church can be satisfied.

When it was said, "This is a Protestant country, and we are willing the children of Roman Catholics shall fare equally with ours," this same bishop openly declared "*it was not.*" He might have been ignorant of the fact that the first Congress printed and circulated the Bible. Had he been as conversant with the history of this country as he is with monkish legends and Latin masses, he certainly would have known the views entertained by the Congress of 1774 in relation to this subject, and their opinion of his Church, when, in an address to the people of Great Britain, they said, "The dominion of Canada is to be extended; their numbers, daily swelling with Catholic immigrants from Europe, may become formidable to us, and reduce the *ancient free Protestant colony* to a state of slavery. Nor can we express our astonishment that a British Parliament should ever consent to establish in that country *a religion that has deluged your island in blood, and dispersed impiety, bigotry, persecution, murder, and rebellion throughout every part of the world.*"

We rejoice that this is a Protestant country, and we do not believe it will ever cease to be a Protestant country so long as the "Word of the Lord has free course and is glorified." The Bible will not only preserve our Protestantism, but is destined to bring up priest-ridden, down-trodden Catholic countries to the same glorious standard of faith and the same precious liberty. Were this a Roman Catholic country, the eye would be greeted with announcements like the following, and the law made for France, in regard to the quality and extent of instruction, would be the law of the United States:

(OFFICIAL.)

"University of France—Academy at Bordeaux.

"*The Inspector of the Schools of the Dordogne to the Schoolmasters of the Department:*

"MONSIEUR L'INSTITUTOR,—Many of the *curés* and their assistants have reported their schoolmasters as having suffered to be introduced into their respective schools Bibles and Testaments which contain doctrines contrary to *the true religion.* I know that some of the teachers have permitted these books to be used because they were deceived by the *colporteurs*, (!) who told them that they were sent by me. I hasten to request you to remove those *dangerous* books from your school. I will, without delay, in company with the *priest*, visit and inspect your schools, and every copy of these books that we shall find we will cause to be *burned.* I embrace this opportunity of informing you that from this time I will allow only *three books* in the rural schools. viz.,

"1. The *Catechism* of the diocese;

"2. A book of *moral lessons*, easy to be understood by the children;

"3. A book of arithmetic."

Well did one of the poets of that Church say, "*Hail, holy darkness! mother of our Church!*" A better day, however, is dawning upon France. If the Bible is excluded from the children, the masses have access to it, and the two hundred thousand circulated in all parts of that country annually will tend more powerfully to impart and strengthen the spirit of liberty than all other causes combined, for "where the Spirit of God is, there is liberty."

The Bible is honored with a place in the schools of our country, or, rather, it should be said, the schools of our land are honored with the Bible. It is the salt that will save us, the great conservative principle; that which imparts a national conscience and morality, and will forever secure to us and to our children the blessings of a pure Protestant Christianity.

The two great arms of national defense, the army and navy, are regularly and systematically supplied by the society. Thousands upon thousands of copies have been sent to our military stations, and with our armies to foreign lands, to breathe a spirit of peace, and break swords into plow-shares, and spears into pruning-hooks, teaching the nations to cease their warfare. The thousands of seamen and boatmen upon our oceans, lakes, rivers, and canals have been regularly supplied by the parent society through associations specifically designed to operate upon that class of the community. Away from home and kindred, no companion is so valuable to the sailor as the Bible, and numerous instances might be given tending to demonstrate the fact that "the law of the Lord is perfect, converting the soul." Hundreds have been awakened and converted to God solely through its instrumentality. The soldier has borne it in his knapsack on his weary marches and in the deadly strife of battle. Wounded and dying, he has pillowed his aching head upon this sacred treasure. But more of this in another place.

It being the design of the society to supply the whole population of this country, the three millions of the colored race in servitude could not be overlooked. They must be provided for, and the society, at an early period, directed its attention to this work. There were various and conflicting opinions in relation to this subject, and communications from time to time were made to the society, all of which received prompt and respectful attention. The managers determined on acting in accordance with the general principles and settled policy of the society, carefully avoiding any thing and every thing that would in the remotest degree involve a departure from that policy. But, while they lost sight of all societies or parties in promoting the general objects of the institution, they have done all they consistently could do toward supplying the slave population with the Word of God.

During the last two years, a purpose has been

formed by individuals of the northern states to raise a large fund, and place it at the disposal of the American Bible Society for the purpose of furnishing the slaves at the South with the Holy Scriptures. This plan was imbodied in a circular, and sent round to the churches. Funds are being remitted to the treasury for this specific object. Various communications were addressed to the board urging a hearty co-operation, and others desiring to know what views were actually entertained by the conductors of the Bible Society on this subject.

The board appointed a large and well-qualified committee to investigate the subject at large and report. To this committee all the documents bearing upon the subject, or in any way connected with it, were referred. In the month of June, 1847, after several meetings of the committee, in which the subject passed through a patient, protracted, and thorough investigation, a report was presented which was highly satisfactory to the board, and met the hearty concurrence of nearly all the friends of the Bible and the slave.

That all the friends of the society, north and south, may have the action of the board, we present the following, elicited by a proposition made by the American Anti-Slavery Society to the board in relation to the supply of the slave population with the Bible. The committee, after referring to the action of the board in 1844 and 1845, proceed in their report:

"In looking at this subject at the present time, the committee consider that there is little necessity to reaffirm the disposition of the board to furnish the Bible to all classes and conditions of men who are capable of using it. The above resolutions, and the whole history of their operations, show that, so far as this body is concerned, they would gladly reach forth the Inspired Volume to every child of Adam, and bid him read freely.

"Nor is there occasion to restate at length that the American Bible Society is not itself called on or expected to engage in the direct work of distribution in any places where auxiliary societies are or can be formed. It was the original purpose of the general society to act mostly through local auxiliaries; and these auxiliaries, it must be remembered, are some of them large state institutions, organized before the American Bible Society, and became connected with it, as do all auxiliaries, by two simple pledges, namely, that they will circulate the Scriptures 'without note or comment,' and 'will pay over their *surplus* revenue to the general society.' In all other respects they are independent of this Society, more so, by far, than are the several states in our Union in relation to the Federal Government. Those local societies often procure and sustain agents themselves, and when furnished with them by the parent society, they go only where they are welcomed by the local societies, and act but in connection with them. And this is a state of things which the board, on account of its important bearings, would by no means disturb, even if they had the power. They wish the auxiliaries every where to feel their responsibilities, that they are *bound* to see to the supply of their own districts with as little of expense and labor on the part of the parent society as possible. Were this board to undertake the work of distribution throughout the country, they would require several hundreds of paid agents, while the 3000 auxiliaries and branch societies which now act with more or less efficiency would sink into torpor and soon become extinct.

"Motives of economy, then, on the part of the parent society, as well as the *rights* of the auxiliaries, require that local distributions should be made under the direction of the latter. On these organizations at the South devolves the duty, beyond doubt, of supplying the slave population of that region, so far as this work is to be done.

"The only new point of inquiry at this time is, How far those auxiliaries are bound, or can reasonably be expected, to supply the population referred to?

"On this point the committee claim no right to issue positive instructions; they can only state their honest convictions as to what those auxiliaries ought to do, and then leave them to act as they may judge most wise in their circumstances.

"In stating their convictions, the committee would premise that no Bible society in any place is bound to perform all sorts of duty. It is an institution for one great simple object. It is not formed for purposes of education, or missions, or the correction of civil laws; but it is formed for the purpose of circulating the Word of God, without note or comment, *as far as practicable*, among all classes and conditions of men who are capable of using it. So far as there are colored freemen or slaves within the limits of an auxiliary, who can be reached, who are capable of reading the blessed Word of God, and are without, they should unquestionably be furnished with it as well as any other class of our ruined race. This duty is plain and imperious; so plain, that the committee know not a society at the South which calls it in question.

"Many thousands of Bibles and Testaments are sent every year to the societies in that quarter, both on order and gratuitously, and some, it is well known, go to supply the colored man as well as the white. The committee are assured by one of the agents, who has been for two years in the service of the Virginia Bible Society, that in supplying counties there, he found no more obstacles in the way of furnishing the Bible to slaves, when they *could read*, than to any other class of men. One long connected with the North Carolina Bible Society says that he remembers no instance where one of that people wished a Bible, and could use it, of its being refused him. Nearly the same testimony has been given by those connected with smaller auxiliaries, and by agents in other states.

"Still there is no doubt that more or less of colored persons might be found in all those states who could and would make a good use of the Bible, but are yet without it. There is need of new attention to this duty, as all must admit, and it is hoped that it will early receive such attention. No religious object can be more important than this, and to none will the conductors of the parent society more cordially lend their aid, believing, as they seriously do, in the language of their late report, 'that the Word of God is intended for all men, and useful to them in every condition of life.'

"But while the committee speak thus frankly as to the duties of the Southern auxiliaries, they would use the same frankness with those at the North which are proposing to raise funds for the special purpose of supplying slaves with the Bible. While the latter societies seem to act from high and pure motives, they evidently labor under several misapprehensions in relation to the object so eagerly sought.

"They proceed in the first place (judging from several communications received) as if the Managers of the American Bible Society were averse, or at least indifferent, to the duty of furnishing the Bible to the slave, while no class of the community is the subject of more solicitude and careful inquiry. Every opportunity for effecting supplies through the proper channels is promptly embraced, and has been for years.

"In the next place, they seem to labor under the impression that great numbers of the slave population can read the Bible, when few, very few, have that ability. Thorough inquiry on this subject would satisfy any one that before Bible societies, as such, can effect very much, there is a previous work to be done by the schoolmaster or the teacher.

"Another misapprehension is, that if funds can only be raised for supplying slaves with the Bible, the work will be easily accomplished. The fact seems to be overlooked that those who hold slaves are usually men of property, and could and would purchase books and supply their dependent people, if nothing but money were wanting to effect the object. But there is, as stated, an almost universal inability among slaves to read, and an indisposition to instruct them equally extensive. How are funds in the hands of any Bible society, general or local, to remove those obstacles, and how are distributions on any considerable scale to be made until they are removed? Let it be shown that there are numerous slaves at the South who can read the Bible and are yet without it, whose holders consent to their being supplied, and yet will not purchase the books required, then there may, with propriety, be large collections made in all parts of the country to meet so important a demand; but, until the way is thus prepared, the committee see not how collections to any large amount are to be used in the manner proposed. Should the providence of God at any time open the door for an extended distribution of the Bible among the people referred to, and should there be need of general collections to supply the demand, the auxiliaries may rest assured that they will be called upon by the parent board to lend their aid, as they are now called on to supply the destitute of our new settlements, and those in France, Syria, India, and China.

"As the committee have now given their views at length on the communications referred to them, as well as the previous resolutions and doings of the board on the same general subject, they would close by proposing one, and only one, additional resolution:

"'*Resolved*, That while the Managers of the American Bible Society will promptly avail themselves of every opportunity to further the distribution of the Bible among the slave population at the South, they would respectfully suggest to those who contribute to the income of the Society, whether it would be wise to *restrict* their contributions to an object which can only be attained gradually, and the funds for which must remain in part unexpended, while others of the human family, equally destitute and more accessible, are left unsupplied with the Word of God.'"

The American Bible Society has but one great work to perform, and that is, the *universal* circulation of the Scriptures, without note or comment, among all nations, irrespective of country, caste, or color; and it can not travel beyond its appropriate sphere to form a coalescence with the American Tract, Colonization,

Peace, Anti-Slavery, Education, Sunday School, or any other societies, be they ever so benevolent or praiseworthy. Its very existence depends upon its catholicity and unity; and so far from this peculiarity in its organization and operations forming an objection, it should be regarded as the most favorable and valuable type of its character.

CHAPTER IX.

BIBLE IN PRISONS.

THAT unfortunate class of our fellow-men who, for the violation of the laws of the country, are deprived of their personal liberty, shut out from society, and perpetually doomed to their own gloomy thoughts and the compunctious visitings of guilty consciences, which, vulture like, are left to prey upon them in their dark and cheerless cells, though suffering the just penalty of their crimes, are nevertheless the objects of Christian sympathy and labor. The Gospel was preached in prisons in the days of the apostles, and the blessed Savior inculcated the duty of visiting such places with the ministrations of mercy, while the last act of his life was the bestowment of salvation upon a dying thief. Too many appear to think that all punishment for crime should be vindictive to an extent that excludes all mercy, whereas all punishment should partake of the character of that inflicted by the act of God in this life, *reformatory* in its nature.

The place of punishment should be one of penitence and reformation, and all the means productive of these ends of a wise government should be enjoyed by those suffering the penalty of violated laws; hence every states' prison should have its chaplain, every cell a Bible, and every prisoner religious instruction.

With these views, the managers of the American Bible Society early turned their attention to the supply of these institutions of justice.

Many of the penitentiaries, jails, houses of correction and refuge, have been supplied with the Bible by the auxiliaries where they are located, an account of which is embraced in their respective reports. As it would occupy too much space to detail these operations, we shall notice only the grants made by the parent society to the state prisons.

In 1834 a donation of two hundred Bibles and Testaments was made to the Auburn State Prison, on the request of its chaplain, for the use of the convicts.

1836. To the same prison, two hundred and twenty-five for the use of liberated convicts.

To the Connecticut State Prison, on request of its chaplain, fifty Bibles.

To the Virginia Bible Society, for Portuguese pirates in prison, ten Bibles in the Portuguese language.

1837. To the Philadelphia Young Men's Bible Society, for the use of prisoners, one hundred.

1843. To the Auburn State Prison, to be distributed by chaplain among its inmates, ninety.

1845. To the same, one hundred and fifty.

To the prison at Sing Sing, on the request of its chaplain, twenty.

1846. To the New York State Prison, on request of its chaplain, to be distributed among the liberated convicts, fifty.

To the Ohio State Prison, for the use of the convicts, on the request of the moral instructor, Rev. James B. Finley, one hundred Bibles and Testaments.

The writer visited this prison in the year 1847, and

had an opportunity of judging from personal observation, and full and unreserved conversation with its estimable warden, Col. Dewey, and the moral instructor, the great and permanent moral results effected by the reading of the Bible. Many, through its instrumentality and that of the instructor, were truly reformed, and gave satisfactory evidence of having obtained the pardon of their sins. By their confessions, many of their accomplices without the prison walls were made known, much and valuable property was restored to its owners, and the increased industry, and prompt and cheerful obedience to the laws of the institution, gave the pleasing assurance that the Gospel had power to save even the chief of sinners. We were kindly invited to visit the Sabbath school, under the instruction of benevolent Christian gentlemen, in the city of Columbus.

At the ringing of the bell, the different wards marched to the chapel, and we had the pleasure of preaching to four hundred and fifty convicts. The chaplain, in closing the exercises, after taking up a collection in behalf of the Bible Society, addressed himself to the prisoners in the following manner: "My brethren, I know you have nothing to give. Many of you would cheerfully contribute did you possess the ability. God accepts according to what a man hath; but," added he, "I want an expression from you in relation to the Bible, and I wish it perfectly voluntary. All of you that can say the Bible has been a benefit to you, hold up your hands." Instantly every hand in that large assembly was thrust up at arm's length. The effect of this demonstration upon the officers, and ladies and gentlemen from the city, who were present, was thrilling; and the silent tear that coursed its way down the cheek of many an aged and youthful prisoner, told that the response was from the heart. The command of Jesus is to make known the Gospel to *every creature*, and hence there can be no place this side the prison of despair that Christian benevolence should not send the Bible. It strikes us that just in proportion to man's guilt, wretchedness, and danger, should be our efforts to convey to him the means of salvation.

CHAPTER X.

BIBLE AMONG SEAMEN AND BOATMEN.

On the list of the first auxiliaries in 1817 is found the name of the Marine Bible Society in New-York, the specific object of whose organization was the supply of seamen from all quarters frequenting the neighboring ports with the Chart of Life.

The following year the board granted to this society two hundred and fifty Bibles.

In 1819, to the same society there were granted five hundred Bibles; and to the Charleston, S. C., Marine Bible Society, two hundred and fifty.

The following year was granted a donation of five hundred Bibles to the New York Marine Bible Society at one time, and at a subsequent period the same year two hundred and fifty.

To the same society, in 1821, were granted five hundred Bibles and Testaments; also, to the Bath Marine Bible Society, one hundred; to the Saco and Biddeford Marine Bible Society, one hundred; to the Nantucket, New Bedford, and Marblehead Marine Bible Societies, four hundred and fifty.

In 1822, to the Portland Marine Bible Society, two hundred; New Bedford, Fairhaven, and Dartmouth Marine Bible Societies, sixty Bibles.

In 1824, to the Charleston, Saco and Biddeford, Baltimore, and Wiscasset Marine Bible Societies, seven hundred and twenty-five copies.

In 1825, to the New York, Boston, Charleston, Providence, and Saco Marine Bible Societies, seven hundred and fifty, in different languages.

In 1826, to the Baltimore Marine Bible Society, one hundred Spanish Bibles and Testaments.

In 1827, Boston Marine Bible Society, one hundred and fifty.

1829. American Seamen's Friend Society, twenty-four Bibles, in English and French.

1830. American Seamen's Friend Society, two hundred and thirteen.

1832. American Seamen's Friend Society, for Seamen's Retreat on Staten Island, one hundred; and for distribution at foreign ports, in different languages, four hundred and seventy-nine.

1833. American Seamen's Friend Society, five hundred Bibles and Testaments. The report this year contains interesting statistics of the operations of the various benevolent societies for the improvement of the condition of seamen. Bethels and mariners' churches had been erected at our own and foreign ports for their religious accommodation. The Marine Bible Society of New York had employed an agent for the purpose of promoting the object of that institution.

1834. Oneida County Bible Society, for distribution on canal among boatmen, one hundred and fifteen.

American Seamen's Friend Society, for sailors on Lake Erie and boatmen on Ohio Canal, three hundred.

For Sailors' Reading-room at New Bedford, a small supply, in different languages.

American Seamen's Friend Society, for sailors at the island of Java, one hundred.

The board received an interesting communication

from the Rev. Mr. Shaw in relation to the supply of boatmen. He says, "I have ascertained that very many of the boats which pass this place (Utica, N.Y.) are destitute of the Word of God. There are from twelve hundred to fifteen hundred, it is estimated, that float upon this long line of waters, exclusive of rafts and packets. These boats employ from eight to ten hundred hands, and convey from one hundred and fifty to one hundred and seventy-five thousand passengers. Among the emigrants are numerous families from various parts of Europe, as well as from New England, crowding their way to the West. My congregation is a numerous one, and many of them are without the Bread of Life. I want to supply every boat with a Bible, and every boatman with a Testament. I have been engaged in distributing Bibles and Testaments, and the experiment I have made brings to light their destitution, and their willingness to be supplied. A boat's crew were found not long since, on a Sabbath morning, listening to one of their number read the Word of God."

No class of men, perhaps, among us are so necessarily deprived of the preaching of the Gospel as our seamen and boatmen. To them there is no Sabbath nor sanctuary. None are more exposed to sinful temptations; and yet, in their long voyages, none are more favorably situated to read the Bible. The interest in behalf of this portion of our population increases from year to year.

1835. The board granted this year to the Utica Boatmen's Friend Society, for distribution, seven hundred and fifty Bibles and Testaments.

American Seamen's Friend Society, one hundred and fifty.

Young Men's Bible Society, for distribution among seamen, one hundred and fifty.

Merrimac Bible Society, seventy-five.

New York Marine, distribution by chaplains and agent, one hundred and fifty.

New Bedford Marine, one hundred and fifty.

Nantucket Female Marine, one hundred and fifty.

Baltimore, Virginia, Oneida, Erie, Louisiana, Charleston, Warren, Salem, and Philadelphia Bible Societies, each, one hundred and fifty, for distribution among seamen and boatmen in their respective vicinities.

1836. Savannah Young Men's Bible Society, for distribution among seamen, two hundred.

Newark Bethel Union, two hundred.

Sailors' and Boatmen's Friend Society, two hundred.

American Seamen's Friend Society, for distribution in Rio, one hundred and fifty.

Young Men's Western Bible Society, for distribution on steam-boats, seventy-five.

New York Marine Bible Society, one thousand.

The report of this year remarks, that the demand for the Scriptures among this class of our fellow-men is on the increase, and ascribes it to the formation of marine Bible societies, the prevalence of temperance, the diffusion of religious books, the establishment of seamen's chapels, Bethels, reading-rooms, and chaplaincies at our own and foreign ports.

The American Seamen's Friend Society has chaplains at Mobile, Havre, Smyrna, Rio Janeiro, Honolulu, and Canton. These chaplains are kept supplied with the Scriptures in various languages, and thus the Word of God goes out on every sea and touches every shore. The bread is thus cast upon all waters, and the promise is sure that it shall be gathered after many days.

1837. American Seamen's Friend Society, for distribution among seamen and boatmen, at different times during the year, six hundred Bibles and Testaments; for Singapore, three hundred.

Western Seamen's Friend Society, one hundred and forty-seven.

American Bethel Society, for boatmen, one thousand six hundred.

1838. New York Marine Bible Society, for distribution among seamen at Martha's Vineyard, one hundred and twenty-five.

Baltimore Marine Bible Society, one hundred.

American Seamen's Friend Society, at different times, two hundred and twenty-seven.

In regard to distribution on our lakes and inland waters, one who has resided long at the West writes, "The canals of the State of New York, now completed and in operation, extend the distance of five hundred miles through a thickly-populated country. They have on their banks one hundred villages and cities, bear on their bosom one thousand eight hundred boats, and employ in this kind of navigation between ten and twelve thousand men. Pass on to the line of lakes. Ontario, on the north, affords no inconsiderable amount of navigation by steam-boats and sail vessels. Then there is Lake Erie, which forms a most important connection between the West, and East, and North. That beautiful lake is whitened with the sails of one hundred and forty vessels, and will be plied this season by over forty steam-boats, constantly bearing on to the West commerce and the mighty tide of immigration. Glance at the villages, and cities, and beautiful and growing country which lie along the borders of this lake. Then bend your way across Ohio, through the great canal of that state, which is rapidly filling up with boats, and men, and business, and you reach the Ohio River, that beautiful stream so much admired by travelers, and all who have seen it, stretching away a thousand miles through one of the most lovely and picturesque countries in the world, amid a hundred villages which adorn its banks. Then there is the Mississippi, the 'Father of Rivers,' with its twenty-three tributaries, affording navigation for a distance of eight thousand miles, in various directions, into almost every part of the great West.

"The whole distance through which these lakes, rivers, and canals afford navigation is nearly twenty thousand miles, through a fertile and populous country. Their banks are adorned with five hundred villages and cities. On their bosom float two hundred vessels, between three and four hundred steam-boats, two thousand canal-boats, four thousand flat-boats, and innumerable rafts of lumber, employing in this kind of navigation between seventy and eighty thousand men, and transporting annually about two hundred thousand passengers. Besides these, there are probably as many more who are engaged in collateral business, and situated in the vicinity of the waters, who are designed to be benefited by the efforts made in behalf of sailors and boatmen."

During this year, to each of the following societies were granted two hundred Bibles and Testaments, viz., Baltimore, Wheeling, Missouri, Illinois, Louisiana, Galena, Norfolk, and New York.

1839. American Seamen's Friend Society, in English and Spanish, four hundred and seventy-nine Bibles.

New York Marine Society, seventy-five.

1840. Baltimore Marine Society, one hundred and fifty.

1841. Oswego County Bible Society, for distribution among seamen and boatmen, three hundred Bibles.

American Seamen's Friend Society, two hundred and fifty-one.

American Bethel Society, three hundred.

Oswego County Bible Society, for distribution among sailors and boatmen, three hundred.

The report of this year estimates that fifty thousand seamen enter the port of New York annually. The wants of this class are attended to by the agent of the New York City Bible Society.

The Young Men's Bible Society of Cincinnati has been particularly active in supplying boatmen, and in furnishing the cabins of hundreds of steamers with the Bible.

1842. American Bethel Society, seven hundred.

Cincinnati Young Men's Bible Society, for boatmen and emigrants, seven hundred.

Rev. E. T. Taylor, seamen's chaplain at Boston, one hundred.

American Seamen's Friend Society, one hundred and fifty.

1843. Society of Benevolence, Princeton, for boatmen, one hundred and fifty.

Delaware and Hudson Canal, five hundred and fifty.

Bethel Society, Cleveland, four hundred.

American Seamen's Friend Society, four hundred and fifty.

Seamen's Bethel, Baltimore, one hundred and fifty.

Bethel Society, Rochester, N. Y., five hundred.

1844. American Bethel Society, N. Y., for boatmen, one hundred.

Marine Hospital, Kentucky, twenty-four.

Bethel Society, Cleveland, Ohio, one hundred and twenty-five.

1845. American Seamen's Friend Society, four hundred and fifty.

American Bethel Society, five hundred and twenty-five.

1846. American Seamen's Friend Society, four hundred Bibles and Testaments, in English, French, German, and Portuguese.

American Bethel Society, three hundred and eighty.

1848. Protestant Episcopal Missionary Society, on the request of their chaplain, five hundred Bibles and Testaments for the use of seamen at home and abroad.

American Seamen's Friend Society, on request of their chaplain at Mobile, two hundred Bibles and Testaments.

To the same society, for their chaplain at Havana, two hundred and sixty-two Bibles and Testaments.

To the same, for their chaplain at Canton, China, one hundred and eighty Bibles and Testaments.

To the same, for their chaplain at Lahaina, four hundred Bibles and Testaments in different tongues.

CHAPTER XI.

BIBLE IN THE ARMY.

Soon after the organization of the society, an opportunity was afforded of introducing the Bible into the army of the United States.

In 1823, an officer of high rank in the army requested two hundred Bibles to be placed at his disposal, for the supply of the United States troops at remote military posts. Some attention had been paid to this subject by the Michigan Bible Society, and a partial supply had been furnished for the use of soldiers in several of the garrisons of the northwestern frontier.

Arrangements were entered into for a systematic supply of all the subalterns and privates at the distant posts and cantonments.

To complete the supply for military posts, in 1825 the board made a donation of three hundred Bibles.

On the request of Lieutenant Kinsley, the soldiers

at West Point were supplied with Bibles, in various languages, during the year 1831; and the following year one hundred and fifty Bibles and Testaments were sent to the West Point Bible Society for the same object.

During the year 1833, on the request of Captain Loomis, of the army, who marched for the remote military posts of the West, was granted a supply of Bibles, and also to the recruiting station at Utica.

Two hundred Bibles and Testaments were granted to the Bible Society at West Point, for the soldiers stationed at Fort Jessup.

The managers of this society undertook the work of ascertaining the biblical wants of all our military posts, with the view of having every soldier supplied. Permission was granted by the War Department to put Bibles in the bundles of clothing destined for the different posts.

The following extract from the report of the chaplain will show what was done for the supply of the soldiers at the recruiting stations on Governor's and Bedlow's Islands:

"During the past year I have been permitted, by the goodness of God, and through the bounty of your society, to distribute as many as twelve hundred Testaments, in various languages, and one hundred Bibles, to the soldiers stationed on Governor's and Bedlow's Islands, in the harbor of New York. I have been informed by the officers that it is not an uncommon occurrence for half a dozen soldiers to assemble in the open field, or on the parade, and listen to a soldier in the midst, who reads from the Scriptures the words of eternal life. The soldiers who were called by the voice of their country into the dangers of actual service, under the command of General Scott, on the northwestern frontier, were affectionately visited the day preceding their march, and all who were destitute were furnished with Testaments or Bibles. As many of these poor men went out that time to return no more forever, can it do otherwise than cause a happy emotion in your bosoms that they carried with them in their knapsacks, even to their graves, which the pestilence had dug for them in the West, the Book of God, bearing the imprint of your society? In the exercise of my pastoral duty, since the return of the soldiers from the West I have had the pleasure of learning that many of those victims of the cholera died rejoicing in the hopes of the Gospel."

In 1834, a supply of Bibles and Testaments was granted to Major Alexander Thompson, for the use of the soldiers at Cantonment Leavenworth, on the Missouri River; also, to the West Point Bible Society, a supply for soldiers at the various military posts.

For an officer in the army, in 1840, a grant was made of fifty copies of the Bible.

At the military posts in the vicinity of New York, the society for the city circulated one thousand seven hundred Bibles and Testaments. Many of these were furnished to soldiers about to march for Florida and other remote stations.

On the request of a friend of the Bible cause in Philadelphia, one thousand Testaments were granted, to be forwarded in boxes of clothing, through the commissary's department, to soldiers at the remote military posts. A gentleman connected with the department signified his great satisfaction in thus aiding the distribution of these books.

In 1843, to the Rev. N. Sayre Harris, and others, as a committee, were granted eight hundred and sixty New Testaments for the use of soldiers. These books were sent in packages of clothing dispatched from Philadelphia.

This year an association of clergymen, who had once been connected with the army and navy, was formed, for the purpose of promoting the moral welfare of those with whom they were formerly associated. One thousand Testaments were granted this committee, to aid them in their laudable endeavors.

On application of the Rev. Mr. Harris, one of the committee, twelve hundred Testaments, by special desire, were furnished with clasps, which made them particularly acceptable to those for whom designed.

In 1847, to the chaplain at Fort Brooke, Florida, was granted two hundred and twenty-five Bibles and Testaments.

The appropriations made the last few years have been confined mostly to the soldiers who volunteered in the Mexican war, a notice of which will be found in another chapter.

It is hoped that the principles inculcated in the Bible, of love to God and good-will to men, will, through the diffusion thereof, become so prevalent among all nations that they "shall learn war no more."

CHAPTER XII.

BIBLE IN THE NAVY.

The first appropriation made to the navy was a donation of sixty-five Bibles to the United States ship the John Adams, for the use of her crew, in 1818.

During the year 1821, the managers made a proposition to the Hon. Secretary of the Navy for the supply of the navy of the United States with Bibles. The proposition was received by that gentleman in the most pleasing manner. With a view, as suggested by the honorable secretary, of furnishing every officer and seaman with a copy of the Scriptures, the board granted three thousand five hundred Bibles.

In relation to the distribution and preservation of these books, suitable instructions were issued from the Navy Department. The officers readily engaged in circulating the Bibles among their respective crews.

The following naval stations were supplied, namely, Portsmouth, Washington City, Norfolk, Charleston, New Orleans, Charlestown, New York, Philadelphia.

To Captain W. Chauncey, of the United States ship Ontario, for the crew and for distribution on his cruise, sixty-two Bibles, in English, French, and Spanish.

In 1824, to the ship United States, one hundred Bibles.

To Captain Creighton, of the same ship, for distribution in the Mediterranean, fifty Bibles.

In 1826, to the United States naval chaplain, for the sloop of war Boston, five Bibles.

In 1827, to the same, for distribution, four hundred and fifty-five Bibles and Testaments.

United States Navy, Norfolk station, one hundred and five, in English and French.

Norfolk Bible Society, to replace Bibles furnished the United States ship Macedonian, twenty-five.

1828. United States naval chaplain, for sloops of war Natchez, Erie, and Shark, one hundred and ten; and for the West India station, one hundred.

1829. United States Navy, for ships Hornet, Erie, and Hudson, three hundred and twenty.

1830. To the United States naval chaplain, for the sloop of war Peacock, frigate Brandywine, ship Ontario, and frigate United States, one hundred and fifty Bibles.

1831. United States Navy, for officers of ships Boston and Vincennes, forty Bibles.

1832. For the sloop of war Falmouth, ships Franklin and Potomac, and the officers and crew of schooner Enterprise, one hundred Bibles.

1833. United States Navy, three hundred and seventy-two. To Lieutenant Long, United States Navy, one hundred and fifty Bibles, in different languages.

1834. To the United States ship Delaware a grant was made of five hundred Bibles and Testaments.

The following extract of a letter from Captain John C. Long, late commander of the United States schooner Dolphin, in the Pacific, will show the faithful disposition made by him of the Bibles intrusted to his care: "I was absent on the lee coast of Guayaquil, and did not receive the two boxes containing one hundred and fifty Bibles, and one hundred Testaments, in Spanish, until the second of September, since which, however, I have made the following donations, where I doubt very much if a Bible had ever been seen. To the general of marine, for the use of officers and men, eighty-three Bibles and Testaments. To the captain of the sloop of war Libertad, his officers and men, one hundred and fifteen. To the captain of the brig of war Aquipana, sixty-five. To the different ports on the coast, since my last, all of the above in Spanish, thirty-three. To the French brig of war Griffon (in French), fourteen. To the officers of this vessel, since my last report, twenty-seven. As I am to leave the coast for the United States, and shall make one short cruise to windward and to leeward, I think I shall be enabled to dispose of the remainder. I had some doubts about supplying the Peruvian vessels of war, thinking they would dispose of them, as they have the character of doing with every thing belonging to them; but, on reflection, I concluded they would then go into the country, and the object of distribution would be accomplished. I used the precaution to make the following insertion over the index, 'Presented to the Peruvian sloop or brig of war Liberty, by an officer of the United States Navy, in behalf of the North American Bible Society, September 11th, 1833.' Before I sent them, I wrote to the general of marine, as well as to the commanders of the vessels, for their consent, which they granted, and the general of marine said he had not enough to supply the demands of the officers, and to-day I sent him twenty Bibles and three Testaments, being all of the latter I had on hand."

1836. To the Young Men's Bible Society of New York, for the supply of the frigate Constitution and the sloop of war Peacock, one hundred and twenty.

1838. To the New York Young Men's Bible Society, for the navy yard, three hundred.

Spanish seamen on board the ship Manilla, fifty Spanish Bibles.

1839. New York Young Men's Bible Society, for ship Ohio, one hundred and ten English and Spanish.

1840. New York Young Men's Bible Society, for United States ship Constitution, one hundred; United States ship Warren, one hundred; chaplain of the navy, for distribution at navy yard, two hundred; brig United States, of Brazil squadron, one hundred and ninety; and ships Decatur and North Carolina, one hundred.

1842. United States ship Delaware, for officers and crew, three hundred.

The New York Marine Bible Society, for the ship of war Belle Poule, commanded by a son of the French monarch, which conveyed the remains of Napoleon from St. Helena, appropriated seventy-six French Bibles, and one hundred and fifty Testaments, which were gratefully received.

1843. United States ship Columbus, for distribution at Brazil station, two hundred; and ship Ohio, one hundred and twenty-five.

1844. To the army and navy committee was made a large appropriation this year, for distribution in these departments as they should judge best.

1845. To the navy yard, Brooklyn, fifty Bibles.

1846. To the United States frigate Congress, on application of the chaplain, one hundred Bibles, for use on a voyage in the Pacific.

CHAPTER XIII.

BIBLE IN SUNDAY SCHOOLS.

From the interest which had been awakened and seemed to prevail throughout the country in relation to Sabbath schools, and their intimate connection with the reading and study of the Bible as a text-book, the society was induced, at an early day, to publish cheap but substantial editions of the Bible and Testament for Sunday schools. The price of these books has been reduced from time to time, as the means of the society would justify, until now, when a good Nonpareil Bible can be had at the Depository at New York for twenty-five cents, and a Testament at six and a quarter cents.

The society has not only placed the Bible within the reach of all of the most limited means, but it will be seen in this chapter that the most liberal gratuitous appropriations have from year to year been made to this truly benevolent and Christian institution.

The organization of the British and Foreign Bible Society, the great parent of all Bible societies, was suggested by a request for a supply of Bibles for the Sabbath schools in Wales.

In 1802, the Rev. Thomas Charles, of Bala, in the principality of Wales, an ordained minister of the Established Church, but laboring as an itinerant, in connection with the Welsh Calvinistic Methodists, visited London for the purpose of laying before the Religious Tract Society the destitute condition of the Sunday schools and the poorer classes of his field of labor. He proposed a contribution in aid of the plan for printing and distributing the Scriptures in Wales. The proposition gave rise to an interesting and lengthy conversation, in the course of which it was suggested that Wales was not the only part of the kingdom where such a destitution prevailed, and that it would be proper to take such steps as would stir up the Christian community to engage in a *general* distribution of the Scriptures.

This suggestion was made by the Rev. Joseph Hughes, a Baptist minister, who was subsequently one of the secretaries of the British and Foreign Bible Society. The Tract Society requested Mr. Hughes to prepare an address, setting forth more fully his views on the subject.

To this he acceded, and presented an address replete with sound views, and breathing a spirit of the most enlarged Christian philanthropy.

This worthy minister may justly be considered one of the most prominent actors in the formation of that great institution.

The supply of Sabbath schools is thus made an exceedingly appropriate work.

We do not design to notice all the appropriations made to Sabbath schools, or to the local associations which have been formed in various parts of the country, and which from time to time have been supplied, but shall simply direct the reader's attention to those appropriations made to institutions of a general character, organized for the promotion of Sabbath schools.

These schools were first established in England sixty-five years ago. It is said they existed in Italy at a much earlier date. Of this, however, we can not ascertain any thing definite. The seed that was then sown, like the "handful of corn on the top of the mountains, has shaken like Lebanon." The cause at first, like all good causes, met with opposition, and had to struggle against the tide of wordly as well as Christian prejudices. But it has triumphed gloriously, and now there is scarcely to be found a city, village, or neighborhood in all our country unblessed with the Sabbath school. They exist in every Christian country under heaven, and millions of children and youth are thus brought up to the pure fountain of God's truth, and allowed to drink freely of its life-giving waters. At almost every missionary station in heathen lands these schools are established, and working wonders in molding the youthful mind to virtue, and modeling the character after Christian principles. Even men of the world, governed by selfish views and worldly policy, acknowledge the importance of early religious training. A single instance will illustrate this. The King of Prussia, a few years since, ordered the publication of several thousand copies of the Bible, impressed with his own seal, for the use of the schools, remarking that "the youthful mind received impressions with the flexibility of wax, and retained them with the durability of bronze."

The same principle is beautifully illustrated by Tupper: "Scratch the rind of the tender sapling, and the gnarled oak will tell of it for centuries." Every thing depends upon the early bent given to the mind in its forming stage. The same idea is beautifully expressed in the following lines:

"A pebble in the streamlet scant
Has turned the course of many a river;
A dew-drop on the baby plant
Has warped the giant oak forever."

To bless and save this interesting portion of our race the American Bible Society has been actively engaged; and had it accomplished no more than it has accomplished in this extensive and deeply-interesting field of Christian effort, it would well have deserved all the sympathy and support it has received from the Church and the world. But we must not dwell. A theme so interesting has taken captive our pen.

In 1831, the board made a grant of twenty thousand Bibles and Testaments to the American Sunday School Union, for the purpose of supplying destitute schools in the Valley of the Mississippi.

The report of this year states, that "the same motive which has long actuated the managers in urging their auxiliaries to supply every destitute family within their limits with the Bible, has also led them to recommend the supply of all Sunday school pupils with the New Testament." In view of that supply, the following resolutions were passed:

"*Resolved,* That the managers view with great satisfaction the efforts of the present day to encourage the study of the sacred Scriptures in Sunday schools; and that they shall always feel disposed, so far as able, to aid such schools, of every religious denomination, by furnishing on sale at reduced prices, or gratuitously (through their respective unions), such Bibles and Testaments as may be needed.

"*Resolved,* That as the American Sunday School Union has undertaken to establish Sunday schools extensively in the Valley of the Mississippi, a supply of Bibles and Testaments be granted to said union for the purpose of distribution, gratuitously, in such places within their selected field as may need assistance of this kind."

1833. New York Sunday School Union, two thousand four hundred.

1834. To the same union was granted seven hundred and twenty-five.

American Sunday School Union, two thousand Testaments for the supply of destitute schools in the Western States, and five thousand for the use of such schools in the Southern States.

1835. New York Sunday School Union, one thousand.

Massachusetts Sunday School Union, one thousand two hundred.

General Protestant Episcopal Sunday School Union, two thousand five hundred.

Methodist Episcopal Sunday School Union, two thousand five hundred.

1836. New York Sunday School Union, two thousand one hundred.

Protestant Episcopal Sunday School Union, two thousand five hundred.

The following resolutions were adopted for the promotion of the circulation of the Scriptures among youth and children:

"*Resolved*, That the friends of the Bible throughout the country, of every religious denomination, be respectfully invited to co-operate in furnishing, as soon as practicable, a copy of the Bible or New Testament to every child in the United States under fifteen years of age, who is able to read, and is destitute of the sacred volume.

"*Resolved*, That in effecting this contemplated supply, it is desirable that the work be done, so far as possible, through the agency of local auxiliaries, they procuring books, and furnishing them to all the Sunday schools, of every religious name, within their respective limits.

"*Resolved*, That the auxiliaries be requested, so far as they are able, to purchase books requisite for the supply of their respective districts; and when unable to purchase the whole number required, to make known their remaining wants to the American Bible Society, for the purpose of obtaining gratuitous aid.

"*Resolved*, That with such pecuniary assistance from benevolent individuals and the more wealthy auxiliaries as may be reasonably expected, the American Bible Society will endeavor, in the prosecution of this enterprise, to furnish the sacred Scriptures gratuitously whenever this course shall, on examination, seem to be proper and necessary."

These resolutions were highly acceptable, and almost unanimously adopted and carried out by the faithful allies of the parent institution.

1837. American Sunday School Union, eight thousand Bibles and Testaments.

1838. Protestant Episcopal Sunday School Union, one hundred and twenty-four.

American Sunday School Union, one thousand.

1839. New York City Sunday School Union, six hundred.

Methodist Episcopal Sunday School Union, five hundred.

Canada Sunday School Union, three hundred.

Protestant Episcopal Sunday School Union, one hundred and twenty.

1840. New York Sunday School Union, at different times, one thousand.

1841. To the same, one hundred and sixty-eight.

1842. Methodist Episcopal Sunday School Union, one thousand.

Sunday School Union of the Reformed Dutch Church, seven hundred.

1843. To the same union, four hundred and fifty.

1844. American Sunday School Union, two thousand.

In regard to these gratuities to the different Sunday school unions, the board during this year, by a series of resolutions, intended primarily to apply to the American Tract Society, directed them to make no distributions where local auxiliaries existed and could perform the same work.

1845. Sunday School Union of the Methodist Episcopal Church, six hundred.

1846. To the same, three thousand five hundred.

1847. To the same, three thousand five hundred.

American Sunday School Union, three thousand five hundred.

General Synod Sunday School Union of the Reformed Dutch Church, three hundred.

1848. American Sunday School Union, three thousand eight hundred.

CHAPTER XIV.

BIBLE IN BENEVOLENT, LITERARY, AND THEOLOGICAL INSTITUTIONS.

Among the many institutions of the above character which from time to time have received the benefactions of the American Bible Society, we notice the following:

American Colonization Society.

American Tract Society.
African Bible Society.
American Education Society.
Bible Society of the Methodist Episcopal Church.
American Anti-Slavery Society.
American Peace Society.
American Temperance Society.
American Antiquarian Society.
New York City Colonization Society.
Society for Meliorating the Condition of the Jews.
Alms House Schools.
African Free-school Library.
Union Theological Seminary, Virginia.
Theological Seminary of the Dutch Reformed Church.
Theological Seminary of the Synod of South Carolina.
Protestant Episcopal Theological Seminary, Kentucky.
Baptist Literary and Theological Seminary, Kentucky.
Lane Theological Seminary, Cincinnati.
New Haven Theological Seminary.
Classical and Theological Seminary, Quincy, Ill.
Princeton Theological Seminary, New Jersey.
Theological Seminary, Virginia.
Methodist Theological Institute, Newbury.
Episcopal Theological Seminary, Virginia.
Oberlin Theological Institute, Ohio.
Northern Academy of Arts and Sciences, New Haven.
Royal Society North Antiquarians, Copenhagen.
Providence Atheneum.
Asylum for Deaf and Dumb.
Ohio Institution for the Blind.
Nashville Institution for the Blind.

Kentucky Institution for the Blind.
Orphan Asylum, Bloomingdale.
American Philo-Italian Society.
American Protestant Society.
Grand Lodge of Ohio.
Grand Division of Sons of Temperance, Ohio.
Delavan Institution for Reformed Inebriates.

Other institutions have from time to time been furnished with the Holy Scriptures by the various auxiliaries.

CHAPTER XV.

BIBLE DISTRIBUTERS.

In the early history of the society, the distributers were all appointed by the auxiliaries. These distributers were friends of the cause, and from a desire to see the destitute supplied, the county being divided into districts or townships, they offered their services and gratuitously devoted a portion of their time to the work of exploration and supply. This course was universally pursued by the auxiliaries, and by this means a vast expense was saved to the societies, and thousands of families were put in possession of the Lamp of Salvation. The plan, however, had its difficulties. In many places it could not be carried out at all, and where it was adopted the explorations were not sufficiently thorough, and the supply consequently defective.

In 1829, an effort was made to supply every family in the United States with the Bible in the space of two years. This enterprise did not originate with the managers. To a highly respected auxiliary belongs the honor of making the proposition. It was accompanied with a warm Christian commendation, and a pledge of five thousand dollars toward its prosecution. Other auxiliaries approved of and encouraged the undertaking, and the board laid it before the annual meeting. With heartfelt unanimity, resolutions were passed by the great assembly to attempt the work, and vigorous measures were immediately adopted and put in train to secure a successful issue. Never did an object of benevolence meet with more universal approbation. The auxiliaries went to work with new zeal; Bibles were ordered in great numbers; hundreds volunteered their services; professional men, and merchants, and mechanics, and farmers, and laborers came up to the work of distribution, and at the expiration of three years the work was done. More than half a million of Bibles were put into hands, many of whom never possessed the sacred treasure before.

This great paroxysm of excitement, though attended for the time being with good results, in the end proved rather disastrous in reducing the system from its wonted health, and a lethargy supervened, as was anticipated, that was alarming.

It was thought by many that the Bible work was completed, and there would be need of no further effort; and as the work of foreign supply had not then been entered into very extensively, there being but few translations and a limited demand, there was a general apathy. Hundreds of auxiliaries fell into a sleep, from which it would appear, from the ineffectual efforts made to arouse them, there is no awaking. Had the societies, which were most, if not all, actively but noiselessly engaged in the work of home supply, been suffered to move on systematically and regularly, the work would have nevertheless been done, and a constitution, broken down by over-acting, would have been saved for long years of faithful toil. But the excitement was up, and there was no staying the tide. It bore away all opposition. Societies became deeply involved in debt, and the inactivity of many of them is such that they have not sufficient life even to ask to be forgiven. A vast amount was also expended by the employment of special agents for the accomplishment of this work.

In 1839, another proposition was made to the board of great and glorious magnitude. The proposition was, that an attempt be made, in connection with the Bible societies in Europe, to supply the entire world with the Scriptures in the course of twenty years. This proposition also came from one of the society's most important auxiliaries, and was warmly recommended by many of the purest and wisest spirits of the age.

After mature consultation and deliberation, it was resolved at an annual meeting to attempt its accomplishment, not in twenty years, but in the shortest practicable period. As we intend to resume this subject in another chapter, we shall pass it by for the present.

During this year application was made by the American Tract Society to furnish its colporteurs with Bibles and Testaments for distribution among the destitute families found in their respective fields. As the society had furnished the American and other Sunday school unions with grants of a similar character, it was thought by the friends of the tract cause that it would be perfectly right to circulate the Scriptures through their distributers. The society entertained fears in regard to the propriety of this movement, on the ground that it would interfere with the movements of auxiliaries, and constitute an apparent reason for their abandoning the work of distribution. To the writer's own knowledge, these fears were well founded. But, in addition to this, many objected to this plan of distributing the Bible on the ground that it conflicted with the anti-sectarian character of the institution, which required the circulation of the Bible unattended with note or comment, while in almost all the families where Bibles were given away or sold, the society's publications were sold with them.

Whether this objection was valid or not, yet such was the impression wrought upon the minds of thousands. It was objected, again, that by this operation the societies were amalgamated, and the union resulted disastrously to the interests of the Bible Society, inasmuch as the funds which were raised by the agents of the Tract Society, in their appeals to churches and individuals in behalf of those destitute of the Bible and other good books, were devoted exclusively to the aid of the Tract Society.

We have not one word to say of ill intent in regard to the American Tract Society. We believe it to be constructed on the largest and most benevolent principles of Christianity; that its publications are evangelical, and, as far as can be, untinctured with sectarianism. We further believe it is accomplishing a vast amount of good in substituting for the light, trashy, licentious, and infidel literature of the age, the substantial literature of an elevated morality and a pure Christianity; but, while we admit most cheerfully all this, we can not but most heartily subscribe to the views of the board of the American Bible Society, subsequently adopted in regard to Bible distribution, as follows:

"The committee to whom was referred the subject of Bible Distribution by Tract Colporteurs, submit the following Report. It appears, on examination, that in 1844 the managers of the American Bible Society adopted these resolutions:

"'*Resolved*, That the auxiliaries be requested to place in the hands of the colporteurs of the American Tract Society, upon the application of such colporteurs, Bibles and Testaments for distribution, as far as the auxiliaries may think it necessary; and if, to accomplish this, the auxiliaries should need the aid of the parent society, such aid will be cheerfully granted as soon as their wants shall be made known.

"'*Resolved*, That 500 Bibles and 1500 Testaments be granted to said society, to enable its agents and colporteurs to supply the destitute in places where the American Bible Society has no auxiliaries through which distributions can be effected.

"'*Resolved*, That the books thus granted be sold, when practicable, for whole or part cost, and the avails returned to the American Bible Society, or used in purchasing other copies for distribution.

"'*Resolved*, That those who receive and distribute these books be requested to inform the Bible Society, from time to time, as to the manner in which they have been disposed of, and as to the need of further supplies.'

"From the Annual Report of the managers for that year, it is manifest that they had some fears as to the effect of this mode of distribution in the Bible cause, as well as the like mode by the American Sunday School Union, to which donations of the Scriptures had frequently been made. A few extracts from the Report referred to will exhibit the managers' views.

"'The only objections,' say they, 'to these modes of distribution, arose from the apprehension that they might interfere with the favorite and long-tried mode adopted by this society, that is, by means of its own local auxiliaries. The experience of every passing year has tended to confirm the board in the pre-eminent utility of this instrumentality for circulating the Word of God. Nothing is more evident to them than that the various sections of the country are now supplied with the Bible or are destitute of it, just in proportion as they have kept up or neglected these local associations.

"'In relation to no duties connected with this blessed cause are they now more desirous, than that the members and conductors of these associations should keep them in healthful action, and suffer nothing to retard their movements. The wants of the needy within their bounds are then provided for, and moneys raised to carry on, through the parent society, the work of distribution in remoter fields. For these local institutions there is no substitute; and the board desire to see the day when one of them shall be established in every county of the Union, ready to furnish the Bible to every individual. Were such auxiliaries now extant and active in every county, they could supply families and Sunday schools of every condition, and have no occasion for other distributing agencies. Even when they had not the ability to purchase all the books for such a supply, they could derive assistance from the parent institution, which, under such a general system, would be enabled to aid all those that might need.

"'But there are portions of the country where no Bible auxiliaries have as yet been formed, and other portions where they have been inactive and well-nigh extinct. That the needy in such localities may not perish for lack of the Bread of Life, the board are disposed to employ every lawful instrumentality in conveying this blessing to them. They would, in such circumstances, furnish Bibles, so far as in their power, to any benevolent institution which would see them conveyed to the dwellings where they are needed.'

"Under the guidance of these sentiments, when the American Tract Society applied, the past summer, for books, to be circulated by those whom they were sending to the new settlements to distribute other books, the resolutions cited above were adopted.

"A like grant of 500 Bibles and 1500 Testaments was made, the same year, to the American Sunday School Union, and 'it was particularly desired, in both cases, that these books should not be distributed where local auxiliaries of the Bible Society could perform the same work, if requested so to do. It is hoped by the board that these societies, and others of kindred nature, may tend to stimulate the auxiliaries to action, and not, by performing their appropriate duties, to furnish them with an apology for inertness.'

"The committee now find that, in places where there are no Bible auxiliaries, the distributions by tract colporteurs have been timely and useful, and in some instances, where the auxiliaries had become torpid, the call on them for Bibles had led them to a new activity in their work.

"In other instances, where the views of the board, as above given, were not fully understood by the tract agents and colporteurs, there seems to have been a mingling of their duties and labors with those devolving on the Bible Society and its auxiliaries, which evidently needs some correction and future caution.

"The committee, after examining these cases referred to, in connection with the Report and resolutions above given, have been led to propose the following additional statements or articles, as expressing more fully, on some points, the principles and rules designed by the board to be observed in this mode of distribution:

"Article I. In counties where auxiliary Bible societies are ready and willing to supply all the destitute within their limits, and are by their own appointed laborers actually engaged in this work, it is not expected that the colporteurs of the Tract Society will there find it needful to engage in the same work.

"II. When distributions of the Bible are made by the colporteurs of the Tract Society, it is not understood or expected that their distributions will be general, but confined to families which are found to be destitute.

"III. As it is not the design of the Tract Society to go into the work of Bible distribution but to the limited extent specified, and as the Bibles thus distributed are furnished gratuitously by Bible societies, these facts should be clearly stated by tract agents and colporteurs, when soliciting funds, in connection with statements about Bible destitution, lest an impression be made that such funds go wholly or in part (as they never do) for the benefit of the Bible Society.

"As the funds of the Bible Society are furnished for the exclusive purpose of circulating the Scriptures without note or comment, and furnished in part by those who are not connected with the Tract Society, it is not considered proper that any portion of said funds should be used in sustaining tract colporteurs, who circulate other books with the Bible.

"By observing the spirit of these new explanatory articles in connection with the resolutions and statements of the board which precede them, it is believed that the agents and auxiliaries of the American Bible Society, as well as others concerned, will now understand the arrangement for Bible distribution through tract colporteurs, and then, with the exercise of that charity, courtesy, and prudence, which should ever characterize the servants of a common Master, that there will in future be no occurrence but what tends to harmony and increased usefulness."

As our object is to give a faithful history of all the transactions of the society on this particular point, and the policy from time to time adopted, we give the circular of the corresponding secretaries of the American Tract Society, addressed to its colporteurs and agents in 1847, as follows:

"THE BIBLE FOR THE DESTITUTE.

"*To the Colporteurs and Agents of the American Tract Society:*

"DEAR BRETHREN,—The Bible is God's gift to man—the only inspired record of His truth. To it every man has an inalienable right. It commands all men to 'search the Scriptures,' as containing the words of 'eternal life,' and this involves the duty of giving the Bible to those who have it not. Hence the officers of this society rejoice that the colporteurs, while supplying with uninspired works those whom their weary feet have reached, feel that they can not leave them destitute of the Sacred Oracles; and hence we cordially respond to the renewed appeals from colporteurs for so many copies of the Bible as are needed to supply these destitute, and trust we shall spare no effort to provide them.

"As a means of procuring these Bibles, we have naturally looked first to the American Bible Society, from whom partial supplies have already been received. Our Executive Committee, therefore, on the 17th of May, made a request to that society for supplies, by unanimously adopting the following minute, viz.:

"'The society's correspondence of the past year shows that a large number of colporteurs, penetrating the desolations of the country, have not been able to obtain Bibles for the families they have found destitute of the Word of God. By the statistical table in the Annual Report, the number of families *reported* by colporteurs as found destitute of the Bible is 14,665. From 43 colporteurs, however, no report in respect to the Bible has been received; and, on a careful examination, it is estimated that the whole number found destitute is not less than 22,500 families. Of these families, the colporteurs, by their reports, have supplied 7107 with the Bible, leaving about 15,000 families which they were unable to supply with the Bible, although they have reported 6384 Testaments as circulated. Of these 7107 Bibles and 6384 Testaments, 500 Bibles and 1500 Testaments were granted by the American Bible Society. Making every allowance for Bibles which may have been supplied to the destitute and not reported, it appears that *more than ten thousand families visited by colporteurs during the year must have been left unsupplied by them* with the Bible, from the impracticability of their obtaining Bibles.

"'The recent visits of the superintendents of colporteurs at the West to this city were made with a special view to securing supplies of Bibles, the demand for the destitute Protestant and Catholic *Germans*, in their own language, being particularly urgent. This claim for supplies of the Bible they have pressed upon this committee with deep and anxious solicitude. So reluctant have some of the colporteurs been to leave families, whose attention had been awakened, thus destitute of the Word of Life, that, failing in other efforts to obtain supplies, they have purchased Bibles, often at enhanced prices, from their own scanty resources, at much personal sacrifice, and have even given their own pocket Bibles, that they might not leave those whom they might never meet again on earth without the Word of God. It is found that the colporteurs, in more destitute parts of the country, need each an average annual supply, for the destitutions they meet, of at least 100 Bibles and 200 Testaments. In view of these facts, it was unanimously

"'*Resolved,* That this committee respectfully request the board of the American Bible Society, should it be consistent, to furnish such a supply, that in no case, where Bibles can not be procured from other sources, shall the colporteurs of this society be compelled to leave families unsupplied, by sale or gift, with a copy of the Sacred Oracles.

"'*Resolved,* That, grateful for the grants of 1500 Bibles and 4500 Testaments heretofore made, this committee request the board of the American Bible Society to furnish Bibles in English, German, and other languages, in fair type, as shall from time to time be needed during the society's current year, to an amount not exceeding 10,000 Bibles and 15,000 Testaments; and that this committee hereby propose, according as shall be the pleasure of that board, either to return to the Bible Society all the moneys received from the sales, so far as the receipts can be ascertained from the colporteurs' reports; or, if the board prefer, to pay any proportion they may name, not exceeding one third of the value of the books, at the society's prices, the remaining two thirds or more to be a grant from the American Bible Society; this committee wishing to assume no responsibility devolving on the honored sister institution, but simply to invoke her aid in furnishing the Bible to those met in prosecuting the labors of this society who need it, and whom it may guide to the only Redeemer.

"'*Resolved,* That the board be requested to furnish this committee with 2000 Bibles and 3000 Testaments in English, and 1000 Bibles and 1500 Testaments in German, as soon as shall be convenient.'

"In answer to the above request, the Distributing Committee of the Bible Society adopted the following minute, which was sanctioned by their board on the 3d inst., viz.:

"'*Resolved,* That it be recommended to the board to grant the American Tract Society 1000 Bibles and 1500 Testaments in English, and 500 Bibles and 750 Testaments in German, to be disposed of on the principles set forth in the circular adopted in September last, *i. e.*, that the books are to be disposed of where supplies, after proper *effort*, can not be obtained of the local auxiliaries; and that the proceeds of the same, so far as they can be ascertained, be returned to the board, or used in purchasing Sacred Scriptures from the local auxiliaries.

"'The committee would further recommend that these books, in no case, be sold for more than the first cost, together with the cost of transportation to the place where they are distributed.'

"Although the board of the Bible Society did not at once fully meet the request of our committee, we have reason to believe that such grants will be repeated, as far as that board shall become satisfied that destitutions exist which are unsupplied by their own auxiliaries and agencies.

"As their minute implies, they wish to supply the destitute, as far as possible, through their local auxiliaries, making grants for this purpose to such auxiliaries as far as necessary. This principle of action on their part creates no obstacle to the supply of colporteurs, so far as accessible local auxiliaries exist, which have supplies of Bibles, and are ready to furnish them for families found destitute: indeed, Bibles can be more conveniently obtained through such auxiliaries than by applying to the parent society.

"The effort of this society will be simply to procure Bibles for those found destitute, in counties, districts, or neighborhoods, for whom Bibles can not otherwise be promptly procured; and we think it important distinctly to state, that while, on the one hand, this society attempts no general Bible distribution, and can not receive, from any source, even a penny of funds consecrated to the Bible cause, it is, on the other hand, no part of the duty of this society's colporteurs to organize, or make protracted efforts to revive Bible auxiliaries; nor can the colporteur, when entering a destitute field, *wait for a supply of Bibles till after his visits to the destitute are made.* The whole object of the present effort to obtain Bibles for those found destitute by colporteurs will fail, unless the colporteur can have Bibles to take to the people with his other books, and supply the urgent wants *as he meets them.* It is essential, therefore, that colporteurs should, as far as possible, anticipate the want of Bibles for the fields they are to occupy, and in their correspondence clearly state the facts in the case, that, if local supplies can not be obtained, this society may provide them.

"You will perceive the proposal made by this society to pay one third of the cost of all Bibles thus received for distribution by colporteurs; but the Bible Society have liberally made the whole a grant, with the understanding, which we hope every colporteur will scrupulously regard, that Bibles will be *given* by colporteurs only where the destitute can not pay for them in whole or in part; and that all moneys received for the sale of these Bibles will be either accounted in the quarterly reports, to be paid over to the American Bible Society, or used in purchasing Bibles from their local auxiliaries; and that the Bibles will in no case be sold for more than the first cost, together with the cost of transportation.

"Much responsibility will devolve on the colporteurs to conduct the whole matter discreetly, so that, while the destitute shall be supplied, the best interests of both the Bible and the Tract cause shall be advanced, Christian confidence be strengthened, the welfare of dying men be promoted, and the Redeemer honored.

"With respect and Christian love, your brethren and fellow-laborers in the Gospel,

"WM. A. HALLOCK,
"O. EASTMAN,
"R. S. COOK, } *Corresponding Secretaries.*

"New York, June 14, 1847."

With a view of obviating all the difficulties that might exist between these two great benevolent associations, the Committee on Distribution presented a plan, which met the approval of the Board of Managers, providing for the appointment of *Bible Distributers.* After a notice of the fact that the British and Foreign Bible Society employ few distributers in England, where there are vigorous auxiliaries, but adopt a different policy in France, Belgium, and Holland, where there are no such organizations, they remark as follows:

"Now it is believed that there are sections of our widely-extended country where a departure from the auxiliary system is called for in our labors, on grounds similar to those which have led to a departure by the British Society. There are many places where little or nothing is now accomplished, but where active men specially devoted to the work would effect extensive distributions, and among the most needy of all our population.

"The committee are aware that a good number of the local auxiliaries do now, and long have, employed and sustained Bible distributers of their own. This practice they would by all means encourage wherever there is local ability to sustain it, and where distributions can not be effected by voluntary effort. There is, however, a large class of auxiliaries which, though well disposed, are feeble as to numbers, and can not furnish with the Bible the destitute within their limits. They are in localities where immigration is the most extensive; where those without the Scriptures are too many and too widely scattered for the auxiliaries to supply without help both as to books and distributers. It is consequently found that, in many instances where books have been furnished gratuitously by this board, they have gone but slowly into circulation, for want of men to attend to this duty. Could a special Bible distributer have gone with these grants to Wisconsin, Iowa, Missouri, Arkansas, &c., not only would numerous destitute families have been supplied, but many who have a limited supply of Bibles would have purchased all they need when brought at low prices to their doors.

"There seems, then, to the committee to be a *necessity*, not only for employing distributers in places where there are no auxiliaries, but in some where they are too feeble to accomplish all which the situation of those around them requires.

"The following resolutions are therefore submitted:

"1. *Resolved*, That local auxiliaries, where voluntary distributers can not be obtained, be advised and requested to employ, every three or four years, one or more individuals at their own charges to explore their respective fields of operation, selling the Scriptures to all who may wish to purchase, and presenting them as a gratuity when there is inability to purchase.

"2. *Resolved*, That where an auxiliary feels it important that an exploration of its field should be made, but has not the means of accomplishing this work, application (with a full statement of its condition) should be made to the parent society for such assistance as is found *necessary*, either as regards books or the payment of a distributer.

"3. *Resolved*, That where no auxiliaries are yet formed, and there are not materials for sustaining them, the Agency Committee be authorized to procure and send thither well-qualified distributers, provided the compensation shall in no instance exceed one dollar per day, and necessary traveling expenses.

"4. *Resolved*, That the distributer thus employed shall distribute such books *only* as are issued by the American Bible Society; and that these, when sold, shall be sold on the terms proposed by the board in July last, namely, the plainly bound at cost and transportation, the better bound at an advance not exceeding ten per cent.

"5. *Resolved*, That the expense incurred by these men, who are engaged only in the work of distribution, be kept distinct from that of the ordinary collecting agents; that the former shall be defrayed, as far as practicable, by the auxiliaries where they labor, and by special contributions for that purpose.

"6. *Resolved*, That a copy of the above statement and resolutions be forwarded to the society's agents now in employ, and their aid sought in carrying the same into effect.

"7. *Resolved*, That the agents, in seeking distributers, should make thorough inquiry as to their qualifications, and present the result to the agency committee, with name, residence, and amount of compensation required in each case, and the proportion which can probably be paid without calling on the parent society."

The faithful carrying out of this plan will prove more effectual in supplying the destitute with the Scriptures than all the voluntary systems that could be adopted.

It also effectually supersedes the necessity of distributing the Bible through any other agency whatever, especially where auxiliary societies exist.

In almost every part of the home field, distributers, either appointed by auxiliaries or the agency committee, are found engaged in the work, and provision will doubtless ere long be made to cover the entire field with well-qualified distributers. As the auxiliaries become regular and systematic in their operations, by holding regular meetings of the board, keeping on hand a good and well-assorted supply of books, having collections taken up annually in all the churches, holding anniversaries, and making regular reports and remittances to the parent board, we may confidently hope that in a short period, without any fitful excitement, the thousands of our own country will soon be supplied, and the millions of heathen lands visited with the light of salvation.

These distributions, going out, as they do, from the parent society, and circulating through all parts of the country, may not inaptly be compared to the flowing out of the blood from the heart through all the arteries of the system, carrying the pulsations of life to the remotest extremities. We realize in this country emphatically the fulfillment of the promise, "Many shall run to and fro, and knowledge shall be increased."

As the work of exploration progresses, the fact is disclosed that there are thousands of families in our land destitute of the Bible, and in many sections of the country the destitution is as great and greater than when originally supplied. This arises from the rapid increase of population by immigration and otherwise, and will require, in all time to come, increasing efforts on the part of auxiliaries to meet the demand.

CHAPTER XVI.

BIBLE AMONG THE INDIANS.

When our forefathers came to this country, it was the undisputed home and possession of the Indian. On its mountains, and over its vast prairies, and along its mighty rivers, he roamed in native freedom, the lord of the soil. His were these fertile valleys, and rich mines, and beautiful scenery.

It would naturally suggest itself to every Christian and philanthropist, that for the temporal blessings they had received at the hands of the red man, spiritual blessings should be made in return; that for "the bread that perisheth" should be given "the bread that endureth."

How strikingly significant that emblem employed in the early history of our country, and how illustrative of the nature of our holy religion—the device represented an Indian presenting an ear of *corn* to the white man, and in return receiving a *Bible!* Nor is this without its counterpart in history. *The very first Bible printed on the American continent* was *Eliot's Indian Bible.* It was printed at Cambridge, Massachusetts, at the expense of the corporation for the propagation of the Gospel in 1663.

About twenty years afterward a second edition was issued. The translation of the Scriptures into the Indian language was indeed an Herculean labor. The language of the natives had never been reduced to writing, and the work was one of immense toil.

Among the very first objects that claimed the attention of the American Bible Society was the translation of the Scriptures into the Indian languages of our country; and, we believe, the very first appropriation made was a donation of one hundred dollars to the Rev. Mr. Dencke, of the United Brethren Church, to aid him in the work of distributing the Gospels of John and Matthew, and the Epistles of John, in the Indian language, among the Delawares, three hundred copies of which had been sent him by the society.

In 1820, two hundred and fifty of the Epistles of John, in Delaware, and thirty of the Gospel of John, in Mohawk, were sent to the missionaries of the United Brethren, and twenty-four copies of the latter to the Rev. Mr. Crane, a missionary among the Tuscarora Indians.

The succeeding year a supply of the Gospel of John, in the Mohawk language, was sent to a settlement of Mohawk Indians living near Lower Sandusky; also to a village of the same tribe on the St. Lawrence a supply was sent.

In 1826, through the medium of the Montreal Bible Society, many copies of the Gospel of St. John, in Mohawk, had been faithfully circulated among the Indians residing at the Lake of the Two Mountains and at St. Regis, and also at the Caughnawaga village, where they were received with delight. The Indians of the above-named village were members of the Roman Catholic Church, and they convened a council of their chiefs to deliberate upon the propriety of receiving the Scriptures. The result of their deliberations was a unanimous resolve that all their people should be at liberty to accept the Gospel.

A few grants of the Scriptures were made to the mission schools at different places among the Indians during the following year.

In 1829, various grants were made to the aboriginal tribes, and a donation of Bibles and Testaments, in

English, for the use of mission schools among the Senecas, was made; also to the Cherokees and Choctaws.

The following year, one thousand copies of the Gospel of St. Luke, in the Seneca language, was printed by the board, and a supply sent to Rev. Mr. Harris, the missionary to the tribe.

To the American Board of Commissioners for Foreign Missions were granted, at different times through the course of the year 1831, three hundred copies of Bibles and Testaments, for the use of Indian missions under their care.

In 1833, the board made an appropriation of three hundred dollars toward printing an edition of three thousand copies of the Gospel of St. Matthew in the Cherokee language.

An interesting Bible society was formed during the year among the Indians.

An auxiliary having been previously recognized by the board among the Chickasaw Indians, this, on request, was also taken into the great family, and treated as a brother.

A letter, containing the most interesting account of the happy effects of the reading of the Gospel in the conversion of the Indian from the error of his way, was received from the Rev. Mr. Washburn in 1835.

In 1840, for the Methodist Missions in Canada, the board printed a portion of the Scriptures in the Mohawk tongue. The Book of Isaiah has been printed, and the manuscripts were ready for the Books of Genesis and Exodus. It was computed that eight thousand Indians would, by these translations, be put in possession of the Word of Life.

During the following year, a missionary at the Bay of Quinte, in acknowledging the receipt of one hundred copies of the Book of Isaiah in Mohawk, remarks, "At a meeting of the chiefs of the tribes, I was requested by them to assure the society, through you, that they accept this token of the society's interest in their spiritual welfare with sincere thankfulness."

To the Rev. Samuel A. Worcester, of the Cherokee Mission, in 1842, the board made a donation of one hundred and twenty Bibles and Testaments.

On request of Bishop Kemper, one hundred copies of the Book of Isaiah, in Mohawk, for the use of the mission at Green Bay, were granted. The bishop stated that "there were ninety-nine communicants in the station."

Among the disbursements of the year 1844, we find an appropriation of three hundred dollars toward printing portions of the New Testament in the Dacotah tongue, for the use of the Sioux. The translations were made by the Rev. Mr. Riggs and Dr. Williamson, missionaries of the American Board at the Lac qui Parle Mission, and were printed and bound at Cincinnati, Ohio, under the inspection of Mr. Riggs and the Young Men's Bible Society. The work was well executed, and will be used by two or three denominations.

In 1845, to the Missionary Society of the Methodist Episcopal Church, for the Quapaw Indians, a grant was made of two hundred and fifty Bibles and Testaments.

The Ojibwa New Testament, translated by the Rev. Mr. Hall, and other missionaries of the American Board near Lake Superior, had been adopted by the society, and was in a course of publication.

Sixty Bibles were granted in 1845 to the Presbyterian Board of Foreign Missions, for the supply of mission schools among the Creek Indians.

This year there was granted the sum of seven hundred and forty-four dollars to aid in publishing parts of the Bible in the Cherokee language. The Cherokee Bible Society was engaged in systematic distribution. An appropriation was also made for the publication of the Scriptures in the language of the Choctaws.

In 1848, a supply of Bibles was granted to the Presbyterian Board of Missions for the stations among the Indians; and two hundred were also granted to the American Board for the same object.

CHAPTER XVII.

BIBLE IN OREGON AND CALIFORNIA.

A MISSION was established by the Methodist Episcopal Church among the Flat-head Indians near the mouth of the Columbia, on the Willamette River, in the Oregon Territory, in the year 1833, and a small grant of Bibles was made to the missionaries.

In 1844, two hundred Bibles and Testaments were granted to the Missionary Society of the Methodist Episcopal Church for the Oregon Mission.

To the same society, for the same object, in 1845, were granted three hundred Bibles and Testaments.

In 1846, seven hundred Bibles and Testaments, in English and German, for Oregon.

The same year, to an independent missionary, one hundred and twenty-five, for the same territory.

Also, for the same, to the American Board of Commissioners for Foreign Missions, were granted three hundred and thirty-five Bibles and Testaments.

To immigrants for Oregon were granted four hundred Bibles and Testaments.

Seven hundred Bibles and Testaments were granted to the Missionary Society of the Methodist Episcopal Church in 1847, for the Oregon Mission, under the superintendence of the Rev. Mr. Roberts.

To the American Home Missionary Society were granted, in 1848, a large supply of Bibles, in the English, German, French, and Spanish languages, for the same territory.

From the Bibles granted the previous year to the Missionary Society of the Methodist Episcopal Church, for the use of the Oregon mission, the following account was furnished, showing the importance of sending further supplies:

"The box of Bibles and Testaments given to the Methodist Missionary Society, and sent by said society to Oregon, was a blessing to the immigrants of that distant land. They were received by these adventurers on the shores of the Pacific with great thankfulness. Many of these immigrants had lost their Bibles in the rivers, on their way over the mountains, and to find the American Bible Society there with such a timely supply of Bibles was an unexpected and exceedingly pleasurable event."

The superintendent of the mission, Rev. Mr. Roberts, in acknowledging the receipt of two boxes of Bibles in 1848, says, "Nothing more appropriate was ever brought to Oregon. Romanism, Campbellism, Rationalism, Socinianism, and infidelity exist here in a state of crudity, waiting for some molding influence to fashion them, and bring them forth in all their appalling features. A superficial religion, even in our evangelical churches, threatens a destructive prevalence. The country is most trying and captivating to the Church. The high hopes of the colony and Church have recently been somewhat abated by the horrible massacre of Dr. Whitman and wife, and twelve white men, including two lads nearly grown, all Americans. I trust this awful providence will be sanctified to the good of the Church in Oregon, and also to the cause of missions. We are striving to sustain an orphan asylum and a small boarding school at the Tualatin Plains. The number of orphans left by the emigrants, without home or means of instruction, has caused such an institution to be commenced."

To California the board have sent, within a few months past, thousands of Bibles and Testaments. The hundreds of thousands who are flocking to that Ophir of the West and El Dorado of the poet, to wash its dust, and work its mines, and engage in various occupations, must be supplied with the Bible. No country in the world attracts so much attention at the present time as California. Many have gone who are doubtless prompted simply by the love of adventure, but the great majority go to seek its gold. That Word, which, in the language of Zion's king, "is more precious than thousands of gold and silver, and more desirable than much fine gold," assures us, that earthly objects satisfy not. It is a pleasing reflection, that, notwithstanding the precious metal, to which inspiration compares the Bible, has become plentiful, the Word of God is more plentiful and more accessible. Eight hundred acres of valuable land have been given for a single copy of the English Bible; now, it can be had without money and without price by all.

CHAPTER XVIII.

TRANSLATIONS OF THE BIBLE INTO FOREIGN LANGUAGES.

Before proceeding to give a detailed account of the society's operations in regard to translations of the Scriptures into foreign tongues, we hope to be pardoned the digression of giving a short history of the English Bible.

The first translations of any portion of the Scriptures into the English tongue were in Anglo-Saxon verse, in the *seventh century.*

Early in the eighth century the Psalms were translated by Adhelm, the first bishop of Sherborne, and read in the churches. A Saxon version of the four Gospels was made by Egbert, bishop of Lindisfern, who died in 721. At the close of this century the entire Bible was translated into the Saxon by the Venerable Bede.

The death-scene of this venerable man was marked with moral sublimity. His amanuensis is represented to have said, while his pen was tracing upon parchment the last verse of the twentieth chapter of John, "There remains now only one chapter; but it seems difficult for you to speak." "It is easy," replied Bede. "Take your pen, dip it in ink, and write as fast as you can." "Now, master," said the monk, "only one sentence is wanting." Bede repeats it. "It is finished," said the scribe. "It is finished!" replied the dying saint; "lift up my head; let me sit in my cell, in the place where I have been accustomed to pray—and now glory be to the Father, and the Son, and the Holy Ghost." With these words upon his lips, his spirit passed away in peace to its God.

In the ninth century, the Ten Commandments, and other passages from the 21st, 22d, and 23d chapters of Exodus, were translated by Alfred the Great, and prefixed to a code of laws.

Portions of Proverbs, several of the historical books of the Old Testament, and the four Evangelists, were translated into both Anglo-Saxon and Anglo-Norman.

The Waldenses had a translation of the Scriptures made in the year 1160, by Peter Waldo; and the Waldenses were the first colporteurs of the Scriptures, a fact worthy of notice.

Very little more was done in the way of translation into our tongue until the fourteenth century, a period of five hundred years. This did not result so much from the opposition to the use of the Scriptures at that time, as from a general inability to read, which extended to all people, both kings and subjects. The Word of God was now passing through the *dark ages*, and it experienced its greatest obscuration from the tenth to the beginning of the fourteenth century.

In the year 1274, a single copy of the Bible, in manuscript, of small size, was sold for the sum of one thousand dollars in our currency, an amount sufficient to purchase at the present time four thousand copies.

About the middle of the fourteenth century this fearful eclipse began to pass of, and the light of God's Word began to break forth as the morning. The New Testament first, and then the Old, were translated by John Wiclif, and thus the moral Sun was permitted to shine out upon the Anglo-Saxon world in full-orbed splendor. To change the figure, "the treasures of God's Word were unlocked to the English nation." Church and State rose up in opposition to it as though both hated its light, but the Divine hand which sent it sustained and kept it from destruction. Other translations were made by the followers of Wiclif.

In 1526, William Tyndal translated the New Testament, and, eleven years afterward, the *entire* Bible. He had studied the Hebrew and Greek for twenty years, and was well versed in those languages. He wrote to the reigning king, and implored his clemency to grant that the bare text of Scripture might be circulated among his people, offering his body to tortures and death, if necessary, as a sacrifice for so great a boon to man.

He was obliged to flee from England; but his zeal was unconquerable. In his self-banishment he *printed* the New Testament, copies of which found their way back to England. They were read with avidity. They were prohibited, collected together, and burned, and those who possessed them imprisoned; while he himself, the man who first *printed* any part of the Bible in our language, was arrested, strangled to death, and his body burned to ashes.

In 1534, Miles Coverdale commenced a translation soon after Tyndal's imprisonment. The work was completed in one year, and dedicated to Henry VIII. This version was also made and printed on the Continent.

In 1537, through the intercession of Archbishop Cranmer, Tyndal's entire Bible, with a few corrections, was printed in England, under the name of Mathew's Bible, "set forth by the king's most gracious license."

Other translations were made, particularly one by Cranmer, called the "Great Bible." Its printing was commenced in Paris, but the inquisitor general seizing the sheets and burning them, the publishers fled to England and completed it there.

For several years the Scriptures, in different versions, were circulated and read. It was supposed, at the close of Edward's reign in 1553, that one hundred and seventeen thousand copies were in circulation among the English people.

In the reign of Mary the use of the Scriptures was prohibited; but Coverdale, with the English exiles, who had gathered at Geneva, prepared still another version in 1557.

In the time of Elizabeth, in 1560, the Old Testament, of the Geneva version, was published in connection with the New. Cranmer's Bible, corrected by Archbishop Parker, published by authority, was used in the churches for a period of forty years, and called the "Bishop's Bible;" and it was afterward made the basis for the present received version.

In 1609, the Rheimish version was made at Douay. This version was made from the Latin Vulgate, and retains its peculiarities. This is the standard of the Roman Catholics, and, though full of errors, could not be made to teach the dogmas of popery were it not for its copious *notes.*

Our present version was made in the reign and at the instance of King James I. It was first proposed incidentally by Dr. Reynolds, of Oxford, at a convention for other purposes at Hampton Court. The object of the new version was to have a common standard, to which all might appeal in matters of controversy; one that should be free from errors, and untrammeled with notes.

Forty-seven translators were employed, who were selected on the ground of eminent attainments in biblical literature. They were divided into six classes, and held their meetings at Oxford, Cambridge, and Westminster. The names of the persons, the places where they met, together with the portions of Scripture assigned to each company, are as follows:

Ten at Westminster—the Pentateuch; the history from Joshua to the First Book of the Chronicles, exclusively—Dr. Andrews, afterward bishop of Winchester; Dr. Overall, afterward bishop of Norwich; Dr. Saravia, prebendary of Canterbury; Dr. Clark, fellow of Christ's College, Cambridge; Dr. Laifield, fellow of Trinity, Cambridge: being skilled in architecture, his judgment was much relied on for the description of the Tabernacle and Temple; Dr. Leigh, archdeacon of Middlesex; Mr. Burgley, Mr. King, Mr. Thompson, Mr. Bedwell, of Cambridge.

Eight at Cambridge—from the First of Chronicles, with the rest of the history, and the Hagiographa, viz.,

Job, Psalms, Proverbs, Canticles, Ecclesiastes—Mr. Lively, Mr. Richardson, fellows of Emanuel; Mr. Chadderton, Mr. Dillingham, fellow of Christ's College; Mr. Andrews, afterward master of Jesus's College; Mr. Harrison, the reverend vice-master of Trinity College; Mr. Spalding, fellow of St. John's, Cambridge, and Hebrew professor there; Mr. Bing, fellow of Peterhouse, Cambridge, and Hebrew professor there.

Seven at Oxford—the four greater prophets, with the Lamentations, and the twelve lesser prophets—Dr. Harding, president of Magdalen College; Dr. Reynolds, president of Corpus Christi College; Dr. Holland, rector of Exeter College, regius professor; Dr. Kilby, rector of Lincoln College, and regius professor; Mr. Smith, afterward bishop of Gloucester, who composed the learned and religious preface to the translation; Mr. Brett, Mr. Fairclowe.

Cambridge—the Prayer of Manasseh, and the rest of the Apocrypha—Dr. Duport, prebendary of Ely, and master of Jesus College; Dr. Brainthwait, afterward master of Gouvil and Caius College; Dr. Radclyffe, a senior fellow of Trinity College; Mr. Ward, afterward D.D. and Margarett professor; Mr. Downs, fellow of St. John's, and Greek professor; Mr. Boyse, fellow of St. John's; Mr. Ward, of King's College, afterward D.D., prebendary of Chichester.

Oxford—the four Gospels, Acts of the Apostles, and Apocalypse—Dr. Ravis, afterward bishop of London; Dr. Abbot, afterward archbishop of Canterbury; Dr. Eedes (instead of whom Lewis has James Montague, bishop of Bath and Wells); Mr. Thompson, Mr. Savill, Dr. Peryn, Dr. Ravens, Mr. Harmer.

Westminster—the Epistles of St. Paul, and the other canonical epistles—Dr. Barlowe, afterward bishop of Lincoln; Dr. Hutchinson, Dr. Spencer, Mr. Fenton, Mr. Rabbet, Mr. Sanderson, Mr. Dakins.

To each class was assigned a certain portion of the Scriptures. Each and every individual in that department translated by himself the portion assigned to the whole class, and the several translations were read by the class, which together agreed upon the final reading. The portion thus finished was sent to each of the other classes, again to be revised. By this arrangement every part of the Bible passed the scrutiny of all the forty-seven translators successively. These translators were empowered to call to their aid any learned men whose studies enabled them to throw light upon any points of difficulty. The completion of this work occupied three years, and the lives of all the men who commenced the work were spared to witness its successful close.

With this translation all evangelical denominations are satisfied, and, though not regarded by them as the ultimate appeal in matters of religious controversy, yet its authority is regarded as sufficiently valid in all ordinary discussions of a theological character. In the language of one, "The translators seized the very soul and spirit of the original, and transferred it to our language."

Suspicions having been awakened in England some years since in regard to the integrity of the present English Bible, and charges being made of numerous and wide departures from the first edition of the translators, and many letters and pamphlets being published to substantiate those charges, the authorized printers of the Bible at Oxford University published a fac simile of the first edition of King James, in order that it might be compared with modern editions.

The Board of the American Bible Society procured one of these copies, and, feeling it a duty to institute a rigid comparison between it and the standard copy of this Society, appointed a supervising committee, consisting of one member from each religious denomination connected with the society. The editor of the society's publications, having in the library a great number of Bibles issued during the last three centuries, was requested to go through the same, and learn when and where the changes commenced. The committee patiently assisted him in the comparison, and the result of all their labors was that the variations were unimportant, such as capital letters, commas, italic words, &c., such as in no way affected the sense. This investigation has placed that incomparable version of King James on higher ground than ever, and their hope is that all future translations may be equally well guarded.

This Bible is now universally used. Upon this version it may not only be said the sun never sets, for it is found in all parts of the world, but the sun never sets upon its *reading*. It may be said of the English Bible, as of the heavenly Jerusalem which John saw coming down out of heaven, "There shall be no night there." While it is being read where the setting sun flames on Lake Superior, they are reading it where his morning beams have shone for hours in Australia and New Zealand; and while they are reading it where the setting sun gilds the spires of Montreal and Quebec, they are at the same time poring over its pages on the banks of the Ganges, where that same sun lights up the sacred wave.

"God hath not dealt so with any nation;" and if it was the distinguishing privilege of the Jews that "to them were committed the Oracles of God," how much more are we distinguished by the possession ?

But we must not indulge in these pleasing reflections, lest we tire the reader's patience, and shall proceed at once to the subject of the chapter.

By reference to the society's records, we find that

the first translation made under the patronage of the society of the Bible into foreign languages was that for the *Delaware Indians*. In 1818, the Rev. Mr. Dencke, of the United Brethren Church, stationed at New Fairfield, in Upper Canada, translated the Gospel of John. One thousand copies were printed, one hundred of which were given to Mr. Leuchenbach for distribution. The Epistles of John, John's Gospel, and that of Matthew, were printed with the English on one page and the Indian on the other.

The Gospels of John and Mark were translated into Mohawk for the use of the Six Nations, one thousand copies of which were printed.

In 1825, further translations into the extensive language of the Six Nations occupied the attention of the board. This year the New Testament was translated into the Peruvian language.

The translation into the Mohawk of several other parts of the New Testament was made in 1826.

In 1828, the society assisted Dr. Carey in translating the Scriptures into the languages of India.

In 1829, parts of the New Testament were translated into the Hawaiian language, for the use of the Sandwich Islanders, and an edition of fifteen thousand copies was published.

In 1830, an edition of the Gospel of St. Luke, in the Indian language, was translated and printed for the Seneca Indians, and one thousand copies put in circulation.

In 1833, the Gospel of Matthew was translated into the Cherokee language, and also parts of the New Testament in the Mahratta language, for the use of missionaries at Bombay.

In 1835, the Psalms were translated into the Hebrew and Hebrew-Spanish languages, for the use of the Spanish Jews in the Ottoman Empire.

During this year the managers sent the following resolutions to the missionary stations:

"*Resolved*, That the managers view with deep interest and with fervent gratitude to God the growing zeal manifested by auxiliary societies and friends of the Bible in this country toward the circulation of the Holy Scriptures in pagan, Mohammedan, and other foreign countries, and which, in their judgment, is among the signal indications of Divine Providence inviting the nations of Christendom to the great enterprise of converting the world.

"*Resolved*, That from the encouraging prospect of continued and liberal contributions in aid of this work, the managers look with peculiar satisfaction on the efforts of American missionaries, of different religious denominations, in translating the Scriptures into the various tongues and dialects used at their respective stations.

"*Resolved*, That the managers hope to receive intelligence whenever the Old Testament or the New, or any one entire Gospel, or other book of the Bible, is correctly translated and ready (without note or comment) for the press; and that the missionaries be encouraged to expect that, on giving such intelligence, they shall receive the aid requisite for the publication of the same.

"*Resolved*, That any information which the missionaries may communicate from time to time in regard to translations, distributions, mode of receiving the Scriptures in their own vicinity or among surrounding nations, or any suggestions in relation to the great interest of the Bible cause, will be thankfully received and carefully considered by the board.

"*Resolved*, That a copy of the above resolutions be sent to all the American missionary stations abroad, accompanied by a suitable explanatory circular, prepared and signed by the corresponding secretary."

The above resolutions show that the society was constructed upon a scale of benevolence extensive as the wants of man.

The report of 1836 shows an increased interest in regard to the work of translating and circulating the Scriptures in heathen countries.

As all the appropriations for translating and publishing foreign Scriptures had up to this time been made through missionary societies, after mature deliberation, in which the interests of the missionary work in general was carefully consulted, it was determined on by the board to appoint suitable agents, who should be immediately responsible for their operations, and co-operate with the missionaries in translating the Scriptures.

Several important principles were settled in regard to the establishment of these agencies, one of which was, that the Bible agent on each station shall be of the same religious denomination as that to which the missionaries on the ground belong. Another principle was, that they receive the same compensation that the missionaries in similar circumstances receive.

The board were called upon, by circumstances occurring during the year, to fix definitely the principle upon which new translations of the Scriptures into foreign tongues should be made. In regard to the English Scriptures, the character of the version was settled by the Constitution, namely, "the version now in common use," and that "without note or comment."

Although the Constitution is silent in regard to the character of foreign Scriptures, yet the very design of the society, as announced in its first address, in the clearest terms and the most rigid exactness excludes every thing of a *local* or *sectarian* character.

The slightest variation from this principle would mar the harmony of the religious compact, and the confusion of tongues and clash of instruments consequent thereon would arrest the progress of the mighty work.

To preserve the unity and harmony so essential to an institution uniting in its operations all the evangelical churches of the land, the following rules were adopted:

"*Resolved*, That in appropriating money for the translating, printing, or distributing the Sacred Scriptures in foreign languages, the managers feel at liberty to encourage only such versions as conform in the principles of their translation to the common English version, at least so far as that all religious denominations represented in this society can consistently use and circulate said versions in their several schools and communities.

"*Resolved*, That a copy of the above preamble and resolutions be sent to each of the missionary boards accustomed to receive pecuniary grants from this society, with a request that the same may be transmitted to their respective mission stations where the Scriptures are in process of translation, and also that the said several missionary boards be informed that their applications for aid must be accompanied with a declaration that the versions which they propose to circulate are executed in accordance with the above resolutions."

In reply to this wise regulation of the board, the Foreign Committee of the Board of Missions of the Protestant Episcopal Church adopted the following resolution:

"*Resolved*, That this committee entirely approve of the principle adopted by said board, 'in making appropriations for the circulation of the Scriptures in all foreign tongues, viz., that only such versions be encouraged as conform in the principles of their translation to the common English version, at least so far as that all the religious denominations represented in the American Bible Society can consistently use and circulate such versions in their several schools and communities.' "

A copy of the above resolution was sent to the board, and also to their missionaries in Greece, China, India, and Persia.

The Prudential Committee of the American Board of Commissioners for Foreign Missions, after quoting the regulations of the board, passed the following resolution:

"*Resolved*, That the principle contained in the foregoing regulations conforms with the usages of the missionaries of the board in translating the Scriptures, so far as known to the committee; and that the several missions of the board be instructed to make it the basis of every translation made, printed, or distributed at the expense of the board, or of the American or any other Bible society."

The Board of Managers of the Missionary Society of the Methodist Episcopal Church passed the following resolution:

"*Resolved*, That we cordially approve of the regulations of the Board of Managers of the American Bible Society in relation to the translation of the Scriptures into foreign languages, and we will take special care that all future translations made by our society shall conform thereto."

In 1838, the New Testament was translated by the society in Japanese, for the inhabitants of the island of Japan.

The Old Testament, as far as Joshua, was translated this year into the Hawaiian language, for the Sandwich Islanders.

In 1839, one of the Gospels was translated into the Cherokee language.

The Old and New Testaments, in Armenian; the Old, in Armeno-Turkish and Hebrew-Spanish; and some portions of the Arabic and Syriac, were translated, under the direction and at the expense of the society, this year.

The Tamul Scriptures were also translated for the inhabitants of Ceylon.

In 1840, the Gospel of St. Matthew and the Acts of the Apostles were translated into the Grebo tongue, for the inhabitants of Western Africa. The Book of Isaiah was also translated into the Mohawk language.

In 1844, the New Testament, in the Dacotah tongue, for the use of the Sioux, was translated; and also the New Testament in Ojibwa, for a tribe of Indians of that name near Lake Superior.

In 1845, the New Testament was translated into modern Syriac for the Persians at Ooroomiah; and also the Old Testament into modern Armenian.

In 1847, the Hebrew-Spanish Scriptures, for the use of the Spanish Jews, and the Hebrew-German Scriptures, for German and Polish Jews, in Russia, were translated. The Gospel of St. Matthew was also translated in the Urdu tongue, the Punjabee, and Hindee.

Thus it will be seen that the society has been engaged in carrying forward the work of translation, as well as publishing and circulating the Bible in foreign countries.

It has introduced the Bible to the inhabitants of the West Indies, Spanish America and Brazil, France, Russia, Greece, Turkey, Syria, at different points in India, China, Chin-India, the Sandwich Islands, and among five tribes of our aborigines.

Since its organization the society has directly secured the translation of the Bible into upward of twenty different languages, and assisted in rendering it into fifty others, while it has promoted its circulation in all languages.

The subject of Bible translation has constituted one of the most important, and, perhaps, one of the most difficult features of the society's operation since its commencement.

In this connection, we deem it proper to notice an unhappy collision growing out of this subject. The difficulty originated with the Baptist Church, which had, prior to 1835, co-operated with the society in the great work of extending the circulation of the Scriptures.

We will endeavor to state, in a fair and impartial manner, the ground of this difficulty, and the discussions arising therefrom, together with the subsequent action of the Baptist Church in the formation of a separate Bible society.

At a regular meeting of the Board of Managers, Mr. Brigham, corresponding secretary of the parent society, presented a letter from F. A. Packard, dated Philadelphia, July 28, 1835, sending an extract of a letter addressed to him by Mr. Pearce, of Calcutta, Baptist missionary, asking whether aid could be had from the American Bible Society in printing the Bengalee Scriptures, translated on the principle adopted by the American Baptist missionaries in Burmah.

This letter was referred to the Committee on Distribution. As the result of their deliberations, they presented to the board the following resolution:

"*Resolved*, That the committee do not deem it expedient to recommend an appropriation until the board settle a principle in relation to the translation of the Greek word βαπτιζω."

After discussion the resolution was passed, and the subject referred to a committee of seven, one from each denomination represented in the Board of Managers.

The following report was presented by the special committee.

They state that "in the investigation of the subject the following facts have come before them:

"1. The Rev. Messrs. Pearce and Yates, Baptist missionaries in or near Calcutta, have made application to this board for aid in publishing the New Testament in the Bengalee language, in which version the Greek words βαπτιζω and βαπτισμα and their cognates are translated by words signifying *immerse*, *immersion*, &c.

"2. In the Burmese version of the New Testament, and in other versions in the languages and dialects of India, these words are translated in a like manner.

"3. Application has been made to the Calcutta Bible Society and to the British and Foreign Bible Society for aid to print and circulate the Bengalee New Testament translated as aforesaid, which aid has been refused on the ground of its containing said translations; and

"4. Your committee were not aware until now that such translations were made and approved by any denomination of Christians in India or other heathen countries.

"5. Your committee would therefore most respectfully submit, whether it is not highly inexpedient to aid in printing or circulating any version of the Scriptures containing the above or any similar translations differing from the sense of the authorized versions, for the following reasons:

"1. The words βαπτιζω and βαπτισμα and their cognates being left untranslated, as in the English and many other excellent versions, imposes no difficulty on any denomination of Christians, as it leaves every minister or missionary at perfect liberty to explain them according to the peculiar views of his denomination.

"2. The words βαπτιζω and βαπτισμα, &c., being translated *immerse*, *immersion*, &c., will necessarily embarrass, if not wholly exclude, the operations of missionaries of the Methodist, Moravian, Reformed Dutch, Episcopalian, Presbyterian, Congregational, and other Christian denominations, who may endeavor to propagate the Gospel in India, or where the said translations may obtain; and

"3. It is not competent for the American Bible Society to assume any sectarian attitude by favoring the denominational views of any particular church, either at home or abroad."

In view of the above facts and views, the committee submitted the following resolutions:

"1. *Resolved*, That the Board of Managers deem it inexpedient to appropriate any funds belonging to the society in aid of translating or distributing the aforesaid Bengalee Testament, or any other version containing the aforesaid translations, or any similar translations.

"2. *Resolved*, That the Board of Managers, on receiving satisfactory evidence of such corrections having been made in the aforesaid translation of the Bengalee New Testament, or other versions in other languages or dialects, as will comport with the known views of other Christian denominations, or, in other words, with the obvious intention of the authorized English version, will most cheerfully aid in the printing and circulation of said version or versions as heretofore.

"3. *Resolved*, That all persons interested in the foregoing resolutions be informed of their purport forthwith."

To this report Rev. Spencer H. Cone, D.D., a Baptist and one of the committee, protested, on the ground that in 1834 the American Bible Society resolved to distribute the Bible among all the accessible population of the globe, and to this end sent circulars to the missionaries of the different denominations, encouraging them to expect aid, and whenever it should be communicated that they had *correctly* translated the Bible or any portion of it, the society would publish the translation.

The gentleman above named affirmed that the board acted unjustly in refusing the request of Messrs. Pearce and Yates, because their request was but a response to this circular.

It would appear from this that a similar request was never made before by the Baptist missionaries, and hence Mr. Cone bases the application upon the enlarged benevolence of the circular, and justifies Messrs. Pearce and Yates in taking advantage of it. Now all this would do well enough were there not something beneath it of the most doubtful character, to say the least of it. It appears, on investigation, that the Burmese translation made by Dr. Judson, and which had been published by the funds of the American Bible Society, was not in accordance with the principles of the society governing translations, having the disputed words translated as in the Bengalee version, and that the society was kept ignorant of this fact until, upon investigation, *Mr. Spencer H. Cone admitted it for the first time.* The Baptists assume that their translation is "*correct* and *faithful*," the very point in dispute and that which is to be proved. That it was "*correct* and *faithful*" according to the peculiar views of the Baptist denomination, no one, we presume, will be disposed to question; but that it was "correct and faithful" in the estimation of all the other denominations was not true, all of them, without exception, objecting to the exclusive meaning attached to those terms by the Baptists.

That the action of the board in refusing to aid in the publication of a sectarian Bible was "unjust" and "illiberal," we are unwilling to believe there is a candid Baptist acquainted with all the grounds of the controversy will deliberately assume.

It is known that the uniform policy of the society from the commencement down to the present time has been carefully to avoid every thing of the slightest sectarian tendency.

If it were just and proper for the American Bible Society to expend thousands in publishing translations for the Baptists, in which the word *baptize* is rendered *immerse*, then with equal propriety would it be just and proper for it to expend *tens* of thousands in publishing translations where the same word would be rendered to *sprinkle* or *pour*, to suit the numerous Pædo-Baptist denominations represented in the board and co-operating with the society.

Besides, who ever heard of such a demand before? Can it be shown any where that it ever was the practice of any general society, uniting different denominations, to allow one part of that union to appropriate to itself exclusive benefits, though we would be disposed freely to admit its consistency, did such an arrangement enter into the compact?

How is it with the Sunday School, Tract, or Education Societies? Are these unions allowed to make books, and circulate them at home or abroad, that only one denomination can use; or to appropriate their funds for the education of pious and talented young men of only one denomination? No! the very idea is preposterous; and the only thing that astonishes us is that so large, intelligent, and influential a denomination as the Baptists would do itself so much injustice and injury as to make and urge such a claim.

But, lest we should be charged with having given an *ex parte* view of the subject, we shall proceed to present all the arguments offered by the friends of the cause on the Baptist side of the question.

It was urged as a reason why the board should grant the request of the missionaries in publishing the Bengalee Testament, that they had *changed their policy*, inasmuch as they had previously published versions of the same character.

To this it is replied that they *never in a single case* granted aid to a version which they knew at the same time to be of such a character that only a part of their associates could consistently use. They took it for granted that no church would ask for a version favoring exclusively their peculiar views, and hence they aided all who made application. They have since found that they were deceived in two instances. The one was a case where a small edition of an Indian Gospel was printed, in which the word βαπτιζω was translated by a term which signifies to *sprinkle* or *pour*. The other was the aforesaid Burmese translation, where the same word is rendered *immerse*. Had the peculiarity of these translations been known at the time, they never would have been assisted.

Another reason offered on the Baptist side was, that other denominations were allowed to make such foreign versions as suited their peculiar views.

To this it is answered simply that such a charge is wholly without foundation, and that no denomination ever has or ever can be allowed to make translations other than such as can be consistently used by all the denominations in the compact. The society allows of no partiality.

Again, the board are charged with laying down

rules in regard to versions which Baptist translators can not conscientiously follow.

The answer to this is, that the board lay down no rules but such as the general objects of the society require, and such as the compact necessarily enjoins; and, if these rules are unrighteous and oppressive, let those who appoint the board place men there who will reform the Constitution so that Baptists shall have *exclusive* privileges, and be allowed to appropriate its funds for printing Bibles in all the dead and living languages to suit their peculiar views.

It is remarkable that those of our Baptist friends who urge these objections to the American Bible Society from conscientious scruples, do not insist upon "*faithfully*" translating *every* word in the original texts, inasmuch as they object so strongly to transferring. And if the "correct" translation of βαπτιζω is so essential, why does not the "American and *Foreign* Bible Society" translate the word in its English version? It is charged, again, that the board have patronized the use of German and Dutch Bibles, in which the word βαπτιζω is translated *immerse*, or by words which signify the same thing.

The answer to this is simple, and found in the Constitution. The former versions are "*ancient received versions*," such as the founders of the society promised to patronize; and, furthermore, those words referred to have now lost their original meaning, and become of as wide a signification and use as the English word baptize.

Again, it is charged that the board have set up the English Bible as a standard, to which all translations must be conformed.

The resolutions above cited, and to which the society strictly adheres, show this to be unfounded. Missionaries and others, in making new versions, are required by these rules to translate from the original tongues, and their *imitation* of the English is not expected to extend any further than the transference of a few words which either can not be translated, or concerning the meaning of which there are disputes which divide the evangelical churches composing the compact; and even these transfers are not required where the various members of the society can unite in using the versions as they do the English.

The last charge urged is, that the American Bible Society has received forty or fifty thousand dollars from Baptists, and but very partial appropriations have been made to that denomination; that the society is guilty of injustice in not refunding what is still due. This is a very grave and serious charge, and, if true, would certainly present the society in a very unfavorable light.

A subject of such moment demands investigation. As a reference to the science of numbers will be the most satisfactory mode of settlement, perhaps it would be well to publish a statement, and, as figures can not deceive, it will be an easy task to determine the nature of this charge.

It will be necessary, however, before proceeding to this work, to state, that the Baptists, as a church, have seceded from the American Bible Society, and have organized one of their own of a purely denominational character. Notwithstanding this, a highly respectable and valuable portion of the Baptist denomination in the Eastern, Middle, Southern, and Western States are still in union with the national institution, and that portion of the Baptist Church are not to be regarded as claimants on the aforesaid funds.

The following statement is presented:

American Bible Society in account with that portion of the Baptist Church which seceded therefrom in 1835.

Dr.

1830.	To legacy from J. Fleetwood Marsh......	$10,000	
	Do. " " John Withington........	7,000	
1831.	To legacy from Josiah Penfield..........	1,000	
	To five life directors, for which the money was paid by the Baptist Society.......	750	
	To life members, one hundred and fifty....	4,500	
	To donation from Dr. L. Barker, to aid in building the Bible House.............	30	
	To Bible distribution in Burmah	1,000	
	Contributions made through auxiliaries by members of the Baptist Church........	$30,000	$54,280

Cr.

By an equal share of Bibles received for distribution in our country..............	$25,000	
For the Baptist Foreign Missionary Society, for the *exclusive* use of that denomination in preparing and circulating the Scriptures in France, Germany, Bengal, and Burmah	27,00C	
For Messrs. Pasco and Love, Baptist missionaries in Greece, 12,993 portions of the Scriptures.........................	5,000	$57,000
Leaving a balance in favor of the American Bible Society of.....................		$2,720

By the will of the late Mr. Marsh, the American Bible Society is a residuary legatee, of which there are between one and two hundred. Should any thing ever be realized, it will be appropriated in the same way in which the legacy of that benevolent gentleman was appropriated, viz., in furnishing English, German, and French Bibles for the mixed population of our country.

There is one thing connected with this matter that strikes us as remarkable. The Baptists who seceded from the American Bible Society, preferred these grave charges, and set up this claim, in whatever light it may be viewed, did so on the ground of sectarian exclusiveness. They boldly assumed that they were right and all their sister churches were wrong; that *baptism* means *immersion*, whether applied to the case of John or Nebuchadnezzar, and it can not, by any conceivable possibility, have any other meaning.

So rigidly did they adhere to this view of the subject, that when the friends of the American Bible Society—that there might be no collision on account of names—suggested the propriety of naming their society the American and Foreign *Baptist* Bible Society, they utterly refused to comply therewith. But this subject has already occupied more space than its real importance demands. Our Baptist brethren are at liberty to pursue their own course, and we would be the last to throw a single straw in their way. We believe, with them, that *immersion* is baptism and that *baptism* is immersion, but we also believe that Nebuchadnezzar was as thoroughly baptized with the dews of heaven as the Syrian general was baptized with the waters of Jordan. As a society, we are free to acknowledge that they have done more, perhaps, for the conversion of the heathen than any other, and with right good will we bid them God speed.

We will conclude this chapter by giving an exhibit of all the translations made by the different Bible societies in different parts of the world:

Those marked † are New Translations; the rest are reprints of former versions.

The letters *R* and *S* denote the versions of the Russian Bible Society and of the Scrampore Mission, both of which have been aided in former years by large grants from the society.

WESTERN EUROPE.

Versions.	What printed.	Where circulated or for whom designed.
BRITISH ISLES.		
English; authorized version	The entire Bible	British Empire, &c.
Welsh	" " "	Wales.
Gaelic	" " "	Highlands of Scotland.
Irish; in native characters	" " "	Various parts of Ireland, particularly the provinces of Munster and Connaught.
" in Roman "	" " "	
Manks	" " "	Isle of Man.
FRANCE.		
French; the three versions of Martin, Ostervald, and De Sacy	The entire Bible	France, Switzerland, and French colonies.
† Breton or Armorican; Old Testament translated, but not printed	New Testament	Province of Brittany.
French Basque	" "	Departments of the Pyrenees and province of Navarre.
SPAIN AND PORTUGAL.		
Spanish; the two versions of Scio and Enzinas	The entire Bible	Spain generally, and Spanish colonies.
† Catalan; Pentateuch and Psalms not yet printed	New Testament	Provinces of Catalonia and Valencia.
† Spanish Basque or Escuara	Gospel of St. Luke	Provinces of Biscay, Guipuscoa, and Alava.
† Judæo-Spanish	New Testament	Spanish Jews in Turkey, &c.
Portuguese; the two versions of Pereira and Almeida	The entire Bible	Portugal and Portuguese colonies.

NORTHERN EUROPE.

Versions.	What printed.	Where circulated or for whom designed.
Icelandic	The entire Bible	Iceland.
Swedish	" " "	Sweden.
† Lapponese	" " "	Russian and Swedish Lapland.
Finnish	" " "	Finland.
Danish	" " "	Denmark and Norway.
† Faroese or ancient Icelandic (Danish Society)	St. Matthew	Faro Islands, between Shetland and Iceland.

CENTRAL EUROPE.

Versions.	What printed.	Where circulated or for whom designed.
Dutch	The entire Bible	Holland and Dutch colonies.
Flemish	" " "	Belgium.
German; Luther's version	" " "	Protestant Germany, Prussia, &c.
" three versions—Gosner, Van Ess, and Kistemaker	New Testament	For Roman Catholics in Germany.
German and Hebrew (in columns)	Pentateuch, Prophets, and Psalms	For German Jews.
† " in Hebrew characters	New Testament	
Lithuanian	The entire Bible	Province of Lithuania.
† Samogitian	New Testament	In three districts of Wilna.
Polish *R.*	" "	Poland, Posen, Silesia, &c.
† Judæo-Polish	" "	For Polish Jews.
Wendish, Upper	" "	Saxon Lusatia.
" Lower	" "	Prussian Lusatia.
Bohemian	The entire Bible	For Tschehs of Bohemia and Slovaks of Hungary.
Hungarian	" " "	Madgiares of Hungary and Transylvania.

SOUTHERN EUROPE.

Versions.	What printed.	Where circulated or for whom designed.
ITALY AND SWITZERLAND.		
Italian; two versions—Diodati and Martini	The entire Bible	Italy.
Latin	" " "	Chiefly for ecclesiastics.
Romanese	" " "	In the Grisons of Switzerland.
" Lower, or Enghadine	" " "	On the borders of the Tyrol.
† Piedmontese	New Testament	Piedmont.
† " (with Italian)	Psalms	
† " (with French)	Gospels	
† Vaudois (with French)	St. Luke and St. John	For the Vaudois or Waldenses.
GREECE AND TURKEY.		
Greek, ancient	New Testament	For students.
" " *R.*	The entire Bible	For the Greek churches.
" modern	New Testament	For the Greek people in general.
† " "	The Old Testament	
† Albanian (with modern Greek)	New Testament	Province of Albania, on the Adriatic.
Turkish	The entire Bible	Turkey in general.
† " in Greek characters	" " "	For Greek Christians using the Turkish language with Greek characters.
† " in Armenian characters	New Testament	For Armenian Christians using the Turkish language with Armenian characters.
Moldavian or Wallachian	The entire Bible	Moldavia, Wallachia, and part of Transylvania.
† Servian or Serbian *R.*	New Testament	In Servia and some bordering Austrian states.
† Bulgarian	" "	Turkish provinces east and south of Hungary.

RUSSIA.

Versions.	What printed.	Where circulated or for whom designed.
Slavonic, ancient and ecclesiastical language *R.*	The entire Bible	For the purposes of the Russian Church.
† Russ, modern *R.*	Psalms, New Testament, and Octateuch	Russia generally.
Slavonic and † modern Russ (in columns) *R.*	New Testament	" "
Dorpat Esthonian *R.*	New Testament and Psalms	Southern part of Esthonia.
Reval " *R.*	The entire Bible	Northern part of Esthonia, on the Gulf of Finland.
Lettish or Livonian *R.*	" " "	Provinces of Livonia and Courland.
† Karelian *R.*	St. Matthew	For a Finnish tribe in the government of Tver.
† Zirian or Sirenian *R.*	"	For a Finnish tribe in the government of Vologda.
† Mordvinian or Morduin *R.*	New Testament	For a Finnish tribe on the banks of the Oka and Volga, in the governments of Nische-Novogorod and Kasan.
† Tscheremissian *R.*	New Testament	For a Finnish tribe on the banks of the Volga and Kama, in the governments of Kasan and Simbersk.
† Tschuwaschian *R.*	The Gospels	For a Finnish tribe of the mountains in Kasan, Nische-Novogorod, and Orenburgh.
† Orenburgh Tartar *R.*	New Testament	For Tartars in the vicinity of Orenburgh.
† Karass or Turkish Tartar (several other books of the Old Testament translated) *R.*	New Testament and Psalms	For Tartars in the government of Astrachan.
Crimean Tartar *R.*	Genesis	For the Caraite Jews of the Crimea, by way of trial.

CAUCASIAN AND BORDER COUNTRIES.

Versions.	What printed.	Where circulated or for whom designed.
† Ossitinian (in the Russian depôt) *R.*	Gospels, but never circulated	Central regions of the Caucasus.
Georgian (Kedvuli or ecclesiastical characters) *R.*	New Testament	Georgia south of the Caucasus.
Georgian (civil or common characters)	" "	
Armenian, ancient	The entire Bible	Armenia Proper; but also prepared for the Armenians of Constantinople, Calcutta, &c.
† " modern (with ancient in columns)	New Testament	
† Ararat Armenian	" "	Around Mt. Ararat, S. of Georgia.

SEMITIC LANGUAGES.

Hebrew	Old and New Testaments	For the Jews and for students.
Arabic	The entire Bible	For Mohammedans every where.
Syriac	" " "	For the Syrian Church in Travancore and parts of Syria.
Carshun (Arabic in Syriac characters)	New Testament	Mesopotamia, Aleppo, and other parts of Syria.
Syriac and Carshun, in parallel columns	" "	
Syro-Chaldaic (Syriac in Nestorian characters)	Gospels	Mosul, Djezira, Tolamisk, and country west of Kurdistan.

PERSIA.

† Persic (H. Martyn)	New Testament	For the Mohammedans, Parsees, and Persians of India.
† " (Archdeacon Robinson)	Entire Old Testament	
† " (Dr. Glen)	" " "	
† " (Mirza Ibrahim)	Isaiah	Persia Proper.
† " (Mirza Jaffier)	Genesis	
† Pushtoo or Affghan *S.*	New Testament and Historical Books	Affghanistan.
Beloochee or Bulochee *S.*	Three Gospels	Beloochistan, south of Affghanistan, on the Arabian Sea.

INDIA.

† Sanscrit or Sungskrit *S.*	The entire Bible	The sacred and learned language of the Brahmins throughout India.
† Hindustani or Urdu (H. Martyn)	New Testament	For the Mohammedans of India and others, the language being generally understood in all the larger towns.
" by Mr. Thomason	Bible, to 2 Kings	
" Serampore version	The entire Bible	

NORTHERN AND CENTRAL INDIA.

† Bengalee *S.*	The entire Bible.	
† " two versions (Ellerton and Yeates)	New Testament	Province of Bengal.
† " (in Roman characters)		
† " (with English)		
† Maghudha *S.*	" "	Province of South Bahar, now part of the province of Bengal.
† Orissa, or Oreia, or Utcula	The entire Bible	Province of Orissa, the greater part attached to Bengal.
† Hinduwee or Hindooee " (called Hindee by Ser. Trans.), both in the Nagree and Kythee characters *S.*	" " "	For Hindostan or the upper provinces of the Bengal Presidency.
DIALECTS OF THE HINDUWEE.		
† Bughelcundee *S.*	New Testament	A district between the provinces of Bundelcund and the sources of the Nerbudda River.
† Bruj or Brij-bhasa *S.*	" "	Province of Agra.
† Canoj or Canyacubja *S.*	" "	In the Doab of the Ganges and Jumna.
† Kousulu or Koshala *S.*	St. Matthew	Western part of Oude.

NORTHERN AND CENTRAL INDIA—*continued.*

Versions.	What printed.	Where circulated or for whom designed.
DIALECTS FOR CENTRAL INDIA OR RAJPOOT STATES.		
† Harrotee..................... *S.*	New Testament.........	A province west of Bundelcund.
† Oojein or Oujjuyunee......... *S.*	" "	Province of Malwah.
† Oodeypoora.................. *S.*	St. Matthew............	Province of Mewar or Oodeypoor.
† Marwar...................... *S.*	New Testament.......	Province of Joudpoor or Marwar, north of Mewar.
† Juyapoora.................. *S.*	St. Matthew..........	Province of Joypoor, east of Marwar and west of Agra.
† Bikaneera................... *S.*	New Testament.......	Province of Bikaneer, north of Marwar.
† Buttaneer or Virat........... *S.*	" "	Province of Buttaneer, west of Delhi.
† Sindhee...................... *S.*	St. Matthew............	Province of Sindh, east of the Indus.
† Moultan, or Wuch, or Ooch... *S.*	New Testament.......	North of Sindh, between the Indus, Chenaub, and Gharra Rivers.
† Punjabee or Sikh............ *S.*	The entire Bible.........	Province of Lahore.
† Dogura or Jumboo (Mountain Punjabee).................. *S.*	New Testament.....	Mountains or northern districts of Lahore.
† Cashmerian.................. *S.*	New Testament, Pentateuch, and Historical Books........	Cashmere, north of Lahore.
GORKHA DIALECTS.		
† Nepalese, Khaspoora, or Parbutti......................... *S.*	New Testament.....	Kingdom of Nepaul, about Katmanhda.
† Palpa....................... *S.*	" "	Small states north of Oude, below the Himalayas.
† Kumaon..................... *S.*	" "	Province of Kumaon, west of Palpa.
† Gurwhal or Schreenagur...... *S.*	" "	Province of Gurwhal, west of Kumaon.

SOUTHERN INDIA.

Versions.	What printed.	Where circulated or for whom designed.
MADRAS PRESIDENCY.		
† Telinga or Teloogoo.......... *S.*	New Testament and Pentateuch	Northern Circars, Cuddapah, Nellore, and greater part of Hydrabad or Telingana.
† " (Vizagapatam version)..	New Testament and large part of the Old Testament....	
† Karnata or Canarese	New Testament.......	Throughout the Mysore; also in the province of Canara, and as far north as the Kistna River.
† " (Bellary version)	The entire Bible.......	
Tamul or Tamil................	" " "	The Carnatic and northern part of Ceylon.
† Malayalim (Old Test. preparing)	New Testament.........	Travancore and Malabar.
BOMBAY PRESIDENCY.		
† Kunkuna..................... *S.*	New Testament and Pentateuch	The Concan, chiefly the southern part, among the common people.
† Mahratta.................... *S.*	The entire Bible.......	The Concan, and throughout the Mahratta territory.
† " (Bombay version)	" " "	
† Gujerattee .... *S.*	New Testament	Surat and province of Gujerat.
† " (Surat version)......	The entire Bible.......	
† Cutchee or Catchee	New Testament preparing; some of it printed	Province of Cutch; between the Gulf of Cutch and the Indus.

CEYLON.

Versions.	What printed.	Where circulated or for whom designed.
† Pali (in Burmese characters)....	New Testament.......	Sacred and learned language of Ceylon and Indo-Chinese nations.
† Cingalese.....................	The entire Bible.......	Southern part of the island, from Battycola on the east to the River Chilaw on the west, and in the interior.
† Indo-Portuguese (Old Testament preparing).....................	Pentateuch, Psalms, and New Testament	For Portuguese settlers and their descendants in Ceylon and various parts of the Indian seas.

INDO-CHINESE COUNTRIES.

Versions.	What printed.	Where circulated or for whom designed.
† Assamese .... S.	The entire Bible.........	Assam, subject to Bengal Presid.
† Munipoora .... S.	New Testament.........	Munipoor, on the south of Assam.
† Khassee (New Testament translated)	" "	Khassu country, east of Garrow Hills.
† Burmese (by Dr. Judson, for American Bible Society)	The entire Bible.......	Burmese Empire and Arracan.
† Siamese or Thay (New Testament translated)	" " "	Cossya Hills, on the borders of Siam.

CHINESE EMPIRE.

Versions.	What printed.	Where circulated or for whom designed.
† Chinese (Morrison's version)....	The entire Bible.......	China Proper, and numerous Chinese in Indian Archipelago.
" (Marshman's version)...	" " "	
† Mantchou.......................	New Testament.......	Mantchuria: it is also the court language of Pekin.
† Buriat or Eastern Mongolian....	The entire Bible.......	For the Buriats about Lake Baikal in Siberia, and for the Kalka tribes of Mongolia.
† Calmuc or Western Mongolian..	New Testament.......	For Calmucs of the Don and Volga, in Russia; and Eleuths, Calmucs, and Soungars, of Mongolia.

HITHER POLYNESIA.

Versions.	What printed.	Where circulated or for whom designed.
Malay, in Roman characters......	The entire Bible.......	For the Moluccas and eastern part of the Archipelago.
" in Arabic characters	" " "	Malay Peninsula; sea-ports and coasts of Sumatra, Java, and other islands.
† Malay, Low....................	New Testament.........	Batavia and its neighborhood.
† Javanese (Old Testament preparing by the Netherlands Society).	" "	Island of Java.

FURTHER POLYNESIA.

Versions.	What printed.	Where circulated or for whom designed.
† Hawaiian (by American Bible Society).........................	The entire Bible.......	Sandwich Islands.
† Tahitian........................	" " "	Georgian and other islands in the South Seas.
† Rarotonga	New Testament, and portions of the Old Testament........	Hervey Islands, South Seas.
† Marquesan......................	Some portions given, versions preparing	Marquesas Islands, South Seas.
† Tonga	Some portions given, versions preparing	Tonga Islands, South Seas.
† New Zealand	New Testament.........	New Zealand.
† Malagasse......................	The entire Bible.........	Madagascar.
† Samoan	St. Mark, St. Luke, St. John, and the Epistle to the Romans	Navigator's Islands.
† Feejeean.......................	St. Matthew and St. Mark.	Feejee Islands.

AFRICA.

Versions.	What printed.	Where circulated or for whom designed.
Coptic (with the Arabic)	Gospels and Psalms	For the Copts of Egypt.
Ethiopic (ecclesiastical)..........	New Testament and Psalms	For the Church in Abyssinia
† Amharic (vernacular)...........	The entire Bible.........	Abyssinia.
† Berber (four Gospels and Genesis translated)	Part of St. Luke.....	The oases of the African deserts, from Mount Atlas to Egypt.
† Bullom (with English)..........	St. Matthew.............	About Sierra Leone, on west coast.
† Mandingo (four Gospels translated	"	Mandingo country, south of Gambia River.
† Accra	" and St. John .	Gold coast, Western Africa.

AFRICA—*continued.*

Versions.	What printed.	Where circulated or for whom designed.
† Namaqua	Small portions, and others preparing	North of Orange River, Southern Africa.
† Sechuana	New Testament and Psalms	Bechuana, east of Namaqua.
† Caffre	New Testament and portions of the Bible	Caffraria, eastern coast of South Africa.

AMERICA.

NORTH.		
Greenlandish	New Testament and large portion of the Bible	Greenland, for the Moravian Missions.
† Esquimaux	Testament, Genesis, Psalms, and Isaiah	Labrador.
† Mohawk (Pentateuch and Psalms translated)	Isaiah, St. Luke, and St. John	Indian nations west of the Falls of Niagara.
† Chippew or Ojibway	St. John	For the Chippeway or Delaware Indians.
† " (American Society)	New Testament	
† Delaware (" ")	Epistles of St. John	
Creolese (Danish Society)	New Testament	Danish West Indian Islands.
SOUTH.		
† Negro Dialect of Surinam	New Testament and Psalms	Surinam, Dutch Guiana.
† Aimara (with Spanish)	St. Luke	Bolivia.
† Mexican	St. Luke	Mexico.

CHAPTER XIX.

BIBLE IN CANADA.

Through the Vermont Bible Society the managers forwarded a lot of Bibles for distribution in Canada.

In 1822, the want of Bibles was found to be very great, and, at the request of the above-named efficient auxiliary, another supply of French Bibles was sent to that country for sale and gratuitous distribution.

In 1828, on the solicitation of the Rev. Thaddeus Osgood, a distinguished philanthropist, the board presented to the Bible Society of Montreal a supply of Bibles for the use of the poor in that region.

During the year 1834, one thousand Bibles and Testaments were intrusted to Mr. Hoyt for distribution in Canada. The wishes of the Montreal Bible Society were fully met in this matter, and it was by their direction the distribution was effected.

The corresponding secretary of the above society, the year following, remarks as follows in regard to the distribution: "We have reason to believe that the distribution made through Mr. Hoyt has been faithful. The people seem very thankful for the kindness shown them. It is evident, from Mr. Hoyt's report, that the destitution is still very great, and prompt measures should be taken to supply the destitute. In several of the letters which have been received, the demand borders on the clamorous."

In the annual report of the same society, speaking of the section of country where Mr. Hoyt has been laboring, it is stated that, although many books have been distributed, there will be required, according to estimate, an additional supply of more than two thousand.

To Sanstead was sent, in 1836, three hundred Bibles and Testaments. These were presented through the Vermont Bible Society.

During the same year a supply of Bibles was sent, on the request of Archdeacon Wix, of Newfoundland, for the use of fishermen on the coast of Labrador.

A similar request was made by the same person for the use of the destitute of Newfoundland. The population of this island, which was estimated at sixty thousand, were represented as being very poor, and in great spiritual destitution: as an instance, it was stated that some of them had been on the island seventy years, and in all that time had not heard one Gospel sermon. The emissaries of the Church of Rome take advantage of their ignorance of the Word of God, and are active in instilling the superstitions of their Church.

To supply the wants of the settlers between St. John's and the Bay of Islands, near the Straits of Belle Isle, the board sent to the archdeacon four hundred Bibles and Testaments.

In 1837, the board made a grant of one thousand dollars to the Missionary Society of the Methodist Episcopal Church, to aid the work of foreign distribution at their several missionary stations in Canada, South America, and Africa.

In the year following a grant of three hundred Bibles and Testaments was made to the American Baptist Home Missionary Society, for distribution by their missionaries in Canada.

The same year, the Montreal Bible Society having resolved, in the shortest period practicable, to place a copy of the Bible in the hands of all the destitute in the province willing to receive it, the board, for the purpose of assisting them in this benevolent work, made a grant, at two different periods, of six thousand four hundred Bibles and Testaments.

The report of the Montreal Bible Society for 1839 contained encouraging statements of the progress of the work of Bible distribution. Two causes operated unfavorably to the enterprise: the first was the political agitations in the country, and the second the opposition from the Roman Catholic priesthood.

An agent of the British and Foreign Bible Society has been laboring in the provinces, and established a depository at Montreal. A correspondent of the board, in describing the condition of the country, makes the following remarks:

"God only knows what awaits this guilty land, but light kept back for two centuries begins to break in upon papacy, the dark cloud is turning a brighter side on the Egyptian host, there is increasing evidence that the day-star is rising in Catholic Canada, that her long and dreary night is giving the missionary and the traveler tokens of dawn, and the blessings appointed for her make haste. The Scriptures are distributed there with a facility, and received and read with gratitude and tears hitherto unknown. The papal clergy hate and oppose. The Bible burns the priest, and the priest burns the Bible; but this only increases the light, and people inquire, and run together, and read more than if he had not laid his forbidden hand upon the sacred Volume."

The next year five hundred French Testaments were sent to the Montreal Society for distribution and sale.

In 1842, one hundred and fifty Bibles and Testaments were granted to Madame Feller, of the Swiss mission in Canada.

The following year, to the same lady, for the same object, four hundred and fifty French Bibles and Testaments were granted.

During the year 1845, to the French Canadian Missionary Society, on application of the Rev. Caleb Strong, of Montreal, were granted one hundred French Testaments.

During the year 1848, on application of the Rev. Mr. Wolf, there were granted to the French Canadian Missionary Society two hundred and fifty French Bibles and Testaments. For the use of the schools and destitute families at Grand Ligne, on request of Madame Feller, were granted three hundred Bibles and Testaments in the French language.

The previous year, on application of the Rev. H. Wilson, of Canada, for the use of a colony of colored persons, the board granted seven hundred and fifty Bibles and Testaments.

CHAPTER XX.

BIBLE IN MEXICO AND CENTRAL AMERICA.

In presenting to the reader a view of the operations of the society in the countries named at the head of this article, we shall avail ourselves of all the information within our reach which may serve to throw light upon the interesting subject of the introduction of the Bible into these countries, and the extent of its diffusion among the inhabitants.

From an American gentleman residing in Mexico, the managers received information, in 1826, that the Scriptures which had been sent there were gladly received by all classes of people. A correspondence, by the foreign secretary, was immediately opened with an intelligent person in the city of Mexico in relation to the circulation of the Scriptures. A communication from Mr. John C. Brigham, an agent of the American Board, who resided in South America, but who, by his personal knowledge and extensive correspondence, was well acquainted with the condition of Mexico, stated it as his opinion that, in all the states, comprehending a population of seven millions, there had not been distributed more than two thousand Bibles.

Several grants of Bibles, in the Spanish language, were sent during the year to agents in Mexico.

A letter from Mr. Brigham, dated Vera Cruz, states that, on his way from the city of Mexico to that place, he stopped at Puebla, a city of seventy thousand inhabitants, and made an arrangement with the principal bookseller in regard to the purchase of Bibles for resale, and also with the American consul at Vera Cruz, who assured him of his willingness to take charge of them.

During the subsequent year, Spanish and French Bibles and Testaments were sent to Matamoras, Tampico, Puebla, and Mazatlan.

In 1828, five hundred Bibles and Testaments were intrusted to a gentleman who was going to Matamoras, and several boxes of Bibles were sent to the American consul at Mazatlan, to be sent by him to the city of Mexico and other important places in the interior.

A lengthy communication was received during the year from Mr. James Thomson, an agent of the British and Foreign Bible Society, residing in the city of Mexico.

The letter was addressed to the Rev. Dr. Milnor, Secretary for Foreign Correspondence of the American Bible Society, and contained responses to several inquiries addressed to him in regard to the circulation of the Bible in that country.

The principal inquiry related to the reception of the

Protestant Bible, or the *canonical, uncommented* Scriptures. It appears, from his communication, that soon after he had commenced the work of distribution, several articles appeared in the papers impugning, in the strongest terms, the free use of the Scriptures by all classes without note or comment, and they protested stoutly against what they were pleased to call the mutilated Bible in the want of the Apocrypha. These articles were all written by priests. A pleasing fact was developed in this controversy, and that was, that while some priests condemned the Protestant Scriptures, other priests came forward, unsolicited, and, in the same journals, advocated most strongly the unrestricted use of the Bible without note or comment.

The object of the society to translate the Word of God into all languages, and to circulate it among all people, met the favor of many priests in Mexico; and three of them, one of whom was the president of a college, became members of the society by the payment, annually, of a guinea a piece.

We have often wondered why it was that in all papal countries there are some Roman Catholic priests found to favor the reading and circulation of the Bible, while in Protestant countries, bishops, priests, monks, friars, and nuns all join in the general cry of prohibition, and look with horror on Bible societies.

In France there are hundreds of priests engaged in the work of distribution, while in the United States you can not find one. The agent had sent to him, from London, three thousand three hundred Spanish Bibles and Testaments, all of which he disposed of at cost and carriage in less than nine months; fifteen hundred of these were sold in the city of Vera Cruz in a few weeks. The remainder were sold at Queretaro, Zelaya, Guanajuato, San Juan de Los Lagos (where a fair was annually held, a splendid temple erected, and the idol worshiped an image of the Virgin Mary), Aguas Calientes (where the first legal process was instituted by a priest, before the alcalde, against the circulation of the Scriptures in that country, but which signally failed), Zacatecas, San Luis Potosi, and Guadalajara.

Besides these Scriptures, there were sold in these places large quantities of the Gospels, Acts of the Apostles, Psalms, Proverbs, &c., bound in separate volumes.

There was but one diocese in Mexico which prohibited the circulation of the Bible.

In 1829, a gentleman residing at Chihuahua, occupying a public station there, but who was formerly a citizen of the United States, communicated to the board the intelligence that it was his opinion that, among the one hundred and twenty-one thousand inhabitants of that state, there were not eight copies of the Spanish Bible. His official duties led him to every part of the state, and hence he had an opportunity of forming a correct judgment.

A quantity of Bibles and Testaments was sent there, and also a box to the western coast.

The distracted state of the country during the succeeding year prevented the society from accomplishing any thing in the way of the distribution of the Scriptures.

Nothing more was done until 1834, when, on application of Mr. Sumner Bacon, a grant of Spanish and English Bibles was made for the province of Texas. In speaking of the destitution there among natives, and English or Americans, he remarked, that, from an extensive acquaintance, he believed that nine out of every ten in the jurisdiction of Nacogdoches were without the Bible.

This gentleman offered his services as an agent

without compensation. His generous proposals were accepted, and a supply sent to him, as requested.

The following year Mr. Bacon succeeded in organizing several auxiliaries.

In 1838, four hundred Bibles and Testaments were sent to Texas, and five hundred copies of the Gospel of St. Matthew, in Spanish, were sent to the city of Mexico.

It will be recollected that Texas, which originally formed one of the confederacies of Mexico, revolted, became a separate independency, and established a republic; its independence was recognized by other sovereignties, and it was annexed to the United States.

In 1839, when it was a republic, and prior to its admission as a state into the Union of the United States, through the influence of an agent of the American Bible Society, a society was formed at Houston, the capital. Several members of Congress and other distinguished individuals participated in the exercises, and the vice-president of the republic, Hon. David G. Burnett, was chosen president of the society. The agent, having taken with him a large stock of Bibles, sold them to the society, and measures were adopted for organizing auxiliaries and distributing the Scriptures.

Texas being no longer a foreigner or stranger, but a fellow-citizen, we shall not be expected, of course, to say any more in regard to Bible operations in her borders under this chapter, unless it be to remark, that at the anniversary of the Texas Bible Society the following admirable resolutions were passed:

"*Resolved*, That the principles and influence of the Bible tend to the perfection and permanency of all good governments.

"*Resolved*, That we view the Bible as a book proper to be placed in the hands of youth, and recommend its adoption in our schools."

The latter resolution was offered by a member of Congress, and advocated in an able and eloquent manner.

In 1841, a grant of Spanish Bibles was made to an American merchant at Mazatlan, in Mexico, for sale and distribution.

The year immediately succeeding, on the request of the Presbyterian Board of Foreign Missions, were granted five hundred and fifty copies of the Spanish Scriptures.

Dr. Thomson, the agent of the British and Foreign Bible Society, visited Yucatan in 1844, and his representations of the wants of the inhabitants and the great demand for the Scriptures induced the board to send him one thousand Spanish Testaments for distribution in that peninsula.

In 1845, the board sent to William H. Brown, Esq., of Tobasco, Mexico, one hundred copies of Spanish Scriptures for distribution in that region.

During the war which has recently closed by a treaty between the United States and Mexico, by which a part of the Mexican territory was ceded to the United States, our army, rendezvousing at various stations, received a supply of Bibles and Testaments before their departure, and since, large quantities have been sent to New Orleans, Galveston, San Antonia, and Vera Cruz, to supply those who had not previously been provided for.

The board felt called upon to send the Bible to the inhabitants of that ill-fated country in greater numbers than it had previously done. Its unhappy and distracted state was well calculated to awaken Christian sympathy; and if, in defense of the national honor and national rights, it was deemed necessary to send the sword of death, it was equally in accordance with the genius of Christianity to send the Sword of the Spirit, which, like the spear of Telephus, carries a balm upon its point to heal the wound it inflicts.

A prudent and well-qualified agent, in the person of Rev. Mr. Norris, who had returned from a long missionary residence in South America, was commissioned to enter upon the work of distributing the Word of God in that country.

He started for the field of his operations in the summer of 1848, taking with him four thousand Bibles and Testaments in the English, Spanish, French, and German languages.

These Bibles were designed for the supply of our soldiery, as well as Mexicans and foreigners.

Many an interesting incident might be gathered from the distribution of the Bible among the soldiers at the various camps prior to their departure for the scenes of battle.

One of these fell under the notice of the writer. He had requested a grant of two thousand Bibles for the Ohio volunteers, stationed at Camp Washington, on the lawn of Colonel Riddle, near Cincinnati. The grant was made through the Young Men's Bible Society of Cincinnati, one of the most efficient auxiliaries connected with the parent institution. A day was fixed upon by the commandant of the division, Colonel Curtis, and the committee appointed by the society repaired to the camp with the Scriptures. The soldiers were drawn up by companies, and as they marched in solemn order by the station of the committee, each one received a copy, to be deposited in his knapsack, and be the companion of his weary way. The tear trembled in the eye of many a by-stander, and many a soldier's heart felt the influence of the touching scene. Many sons of Ohio received Bibles on that day who now are in eternity. Their bones lie bleaching on the mountains and plains of Mexico.

They met the melancholy fate of "those who take the sword."

As faithfully descriptive of the condition and prospects of Mexico, we shall close this article by copying the letter of Rev. Mr. Norris in relation to his agency in that country.

In his communication to the board, he says, "I need not remind you that Roman Catholicism is the established religion of Mexico—Catholicism unmodified by the Reformation. Protestant worship is not tolerated except in private houses, and by less than twelve persons; if more than that number are present, they are liable to punishment. Except in the city of Mexico, where the English have a cemetery, the privilege of sepulture is denied to Protestants, and their dead must be buried in some obscure place, under cover of darkness, or a grave procured by bribing the priests.

"The great number of churches presents a striking object to travelers. Every village of a dozen huts has one or more of them; every hacienda has its chapel surmounted by a white steeple. In some locations there seems to be a great excess of sacred edifices, as in the vicinity of Puebla. From the Pyramid of Cholula, once occupied as an idol temple, now the site of a beautiful church, upward of fifty churches may be counted, some of them very large, while the population will not exceed a very few thousands. In some parts of this district the sacred edifices outnumber the huts of the inhabitants.

"The religious establishments of the proud and rich city of Puebla are numerous and very wealthy. In the city of Mexico the churches and religious houses, many of them very spacious, and covering nearly an entire square, are said to own in fee one half of all the real estate in the city, in addition to which they hold what is equivalent to perpetual mortgages on one half of the residue, thus controlling three fourths of the real property in the capital.

"The clergy are very numerous in all the cities. With few exceptions, they are reputed to be ignorant, indolent, and exceedingly loose in their morals. Concubinage and its kindred vices are notoriously common among them. Not a few of them are infidels. They still exert considerable political power, while their moral and social influence over the lower class, and the females of all classes, is almost unlimited, and is abused for purposes and to an extent well-nigh incredible. The schools, colleges, and nearly every other institution in the country feel the blighting influence of their interference.

"Like priests, like people as to intelligence and morality. A large proportion of the people in the cities and more populous villages are taught to read and write, but make little use of their acquirements after they leave school. Few of them are able to read fluently. The education of the females is very superficial. Every man professes himself a Catholic, and is very devout and religious in his way; in some respects they are worthy of imitation by enlightened Christians. A fair proportion of men attend the services of the Church.

"In morals the mass of the people are exceedingly depraved. 'The Leperos,' said an intelligent Mexican, 'are all thieves—are liars; they are animals—beasts; they have neither religion nor morality.' 'Three fourths of them,' said a priest, 'live together without marriage.'

"The seventh commandment is universally violated among them, both in spirit and letter, and such violations as must not be named here. The shocking crime of incest is common. The Leperos constitute an overwhelming majority in the cities, particularly the capital, and with the peones, or slaves, and Indians, who are in no respect their superiors, they constitute at least five sevenths of the population of the country. The published accounts of robberies fall far below the truth. On the great roads, nearly every man is a robber. The soldiers rob. The men who are employed to escort the mule-trains, loaded with merchandise, are robbers. Mechanics and shop-keepers in the towns leave their homes and business for a few days to follow the more lucrative business of highwaymen, an employment not generally considered disreputable. Magistrates are known to be accomplices, and protect rather than punish their associates. The drivers of the public stages, keepers of taverns and hotels, are leagued with the robbers, and Santa Anna himself, the Astor of Mexico, was believed to have been engaged in the nefarious business. There is a great deal of intemperance among the common people, and gambling is common among all, from the highest to the lowest, not excepting the clergy and great officers of state. The biblical wants of such a people must be great and pressing. In the light of God's law they are excessively wicked. Their religion helps to make and keep them wicked. The mass of the people are deplorably wicked, even for Roman Catholics, and their spiritual masters (teachers they have none) love to have it so. Hence the Word of God is a prohibited book. To read their own edition of Padre Scio's Bible, with the Apocrypha and notes, edited by a priest, and issued under the approbation of an archbishop, a license must first be obtained. To prevent his people from being injured by reading the Word of God, the Bishop of Mexico bought and burned a box of Bibles sent out by the British and Foreign Bible Society; yet a treatise, too grossly licentious and corrupting in its tendency to be endured any where else than in Mexico, was published for general use as a religious help to conscience. It was hoped that the Mexican war would open the way for Christian enterprise in that country. There was a time when toleration for Protestantism might have been had for asking—could not have been refused; but the favorable moment was allowed to pass, and we have not gained even the privilege of sepulture. By the war, Protestantism has gained nothing but access to the ceded territory. The war has been a great moral evil to Mexico. There are, however, some encouraging features in the present aspect of affairs. A political party now exists, whose avowed object is to limit the power of the priests, confine them to their proper duties, break down the overgrown religious establishments of the country, and devote their great wealth to the cause of popular education. This party has no partiality for Protestantism, yet they are desirous of having the Scriptures circulated, as a means of opening the eyes of the people to the abuses of the Church. Bibles and Testaments have been put by your agents into the hands of hundreds of families in Vera Cruz, Jalapa, Perote, Puebla, and the city of Mexico."

The above communication discloses facts sufficient to make it obvious to the most superficial observer that nothing but the universal circulation and reading of the Bible can elevate this priest-ridden land. There is nothing but the want of Bible instruction to prevent Mexico from being as free, intelligent, virtuous, and happy as our own country. It is the Bible that makes us differ. It is not the native superiority of the Anglo-Saxon over that of the Castilian—it is not that our physical resources are greater, that we have brighter skies, purer air, broader and more fertile plains, mightier rivers, or richer mines—no! it is because we have for our instruction and guide the Oracles of God, and they have nothing but the oracles of a corrupt, designing priesthood, who have usurped the place of God.

CHAPTER XXI.

BIBLE IN SOUTH AMERICA.

The Board of Managers having learned, in 1818, that there was a prospect of introducing the Scriptures into those parts of South America where the Spanish language is spoken, a set of stereotype plates for the New Testament in that language was immediately procured, and, as soon as copies could be printed, they were sent to that country.

A grant of five hundred Testaments was made in 1820, for the use of the primary schools in the municipality of Buenos Ayres. Other grants were made during the same year to different parts of the country, and an extensive correspondence was opened for the purpose of discovering favorable localities for the introduction and circulation of the Scriptures.

Liberal donations of Spanish Scriptures were early made by the British and Foreign Bible Society to the American Bible Society, by which it was enabled to prosecute, with more vigor than it otherwise could have done, the work of distribution.

The changes which had taken place in the Spanish colonies of America favorable to the introduction of the Bible, induced the society to send a further supply to different parts of that country, and a correspondence was opened in relation to the printing of the New Testament in Spanish, in the version of Father Scio.

In 1822, five hundred copies of the Scriptures were sent to different parts of the country.

The year following arrangements were made for the printing of Padre Scio's version of the Bible, and plates were contracted for.

The demand for the Scriptures continued to increase in all parts of the country, persons of rank in Church and State became interested in their perusal, and multitudes were seen with avidity to purchase and read the Word of God.

During the year, two thousand five hundred copies were sent through different channels to all parts of the country.

It will, perhaps, be proper to state here, that the Bibles sent out were a version approved of by the Roman Catholics, and to those who may not have been acquainted with that fact, this statement will relieve their surprise in regard to the favor with which they were received by the inhabitants of a papal country. Notwithstanding the errors found in the Vulgate, from which the versions of the Catholics are made, it contains essential truth enough to "make wise unto salvation." It will be recollected that it was from the Vulgate Luther's mind received its enlightenment in his monastic cell at Erfurt, and through it he was led to renounce the errors of Romanism, and embrace the Gospel doctrine of "salvation by faith."

In 1825, one thousand eight hundred and ninety-five copies of the Bible were sent to Patagonia, in the provinces on both sides of the Parana, to Monte Video, Bahia, the Brazils, Valparaiso, Chili, across the Andes into Mendoza, and other parts of the country. The rays of moral twilight which these Bibles shed abroad in that hitherto Bibleless land, served to show the extent of the darkness which reigned there, and excited a deeper interest in the hearts of the friends of the cause to increase these rays and extend them still further, until the whole land should be illumined by the light of the Gospel.

During the year 1826, intelligence was received of the formation of a national Bible society at Bogota for the Republic of Colombia; and the board, as a pledge of the interest they took in this society, and their good feelings toward it, sent to their depository a donation of eight hundred Spanish Bibles.

They also received intelligence of the establishment of a Bible society in the city of Caraccas, and the agent of the American institution placed at its disposal the Bibles which had been intrusted to his care.

From Mr. John C. Brigham, who is now, and has for many years been, the efficient and popular corresponding secretary of the American Bible Society, but who at that time was the agent of the American Board of Commissioners for Foreign Missions, the board received frequent and interesting communications in regard to the condition and wants of South America, and also in regard to the circulation of the Scriptures in that country. He had visited the republics of Buenos Ayres, Chili, Peru, Colombia, and Mexico, and had in each distributed the Bibles committed to his care. The anxiety to receive the Bible in these republics was so great, that instead of the hundreds which he disposed of, he could with the same ease, he remarks, have sold thousands.

Grants of Spanish Scriptures were made during the year to various agents in that country, and many copies were purchased by merchants and others, who, while they served their own individual interests, at the same time promoted the objects of the society. As an article of traffic, those who engaged in it realized handsome profits. Bibles that were purchased at the Depository for a dollar and a half, were sold by them as high as eight dollars, so great was the demand.

In 1828, Bibles were forwarded to Colombia. A

gentleman who traded up the Magdalena River took with him four boxes of the Scriptures for sale and distribution in the vicinity of Bogota.

Small quantities were also sent to a gentleman from New York residing at Maracaibo. A part of these were sold. Another portion was sent to that place in a vessel which was wrecked on the coast of Colombia, but did not reach the person to whom sent. The board received intelligence, however, of their arrival at Maracaibo. They were taken thither by Indians who visited the wreck, and plundered it of the Bibles, and sold them at a very high price to the citizens. Four hundred and forty-five Bibles were sent to Mr. Parvin and a correspondent at Buenos Ayres. Others were intrusted to a gentleman who intended to visit the west coast of South America and the Philippine Islands.

During the following year, a grant of Dutch Bibles, on the request of one of the missionaries of the United Brethren Church, was made for distribution in Surinam and Paramaribo.

Almost every portion of this country was involved in war during the year, and Peru, Bolivia, Colombia, Guatemala were in a state of continued revolutionary excitement. This, together with the exclusion by the British and Foreign and the American Bible Societies of the apocryphal books from the Spanish Bible, rendered the circulation thereof in that country much more limited than in former years. An ecclesiastical decree was issued, prohibiting the sale or use of any Bible unless accompanied by the Catholic notes. In the preamble of this decree, it was stated that "Bible societies are endeavoring to propagate the lamentable sentiments of Protestant sects, namely, that the only rule of faith is the Bible, interpreted by each one according to his own judgment, a principle directly opposed to that laid down by the holy Council of Trent, by which it was determined that the *living* voice of the *Church* shall settle the meaning of the Scriptures."

A box of Testaments was sent this year to Valparaiso.

The succeeding year but little was accomplished. The objections to the Bible without the uncanonical books still existed. A small quantity of Bibles and Testaments was sent to Carthagena.

In 1831, the unhappy political dissensions which existed prevented the circulation of the Scriptures, and during the year but one hundred Spanish Testaments were forwarded to Buenos Ayres.

In 1833, to an officer in the United States Navy, on the west coast of South America, for distribution at the places where he touched, were granted one hundred and fifty Spanish Bibles.

With a view of effecting an increased interest in the Bible cause, an agent was sent out the following year by the board. He took with him a good supply of Spanish and English Bibles and Testaments, and was instructed to visit the principal towns in Chili, Peru, Equador, New Grenada, and Western Mexico. The agent was at liberty to furnish the New Testament gratuitously to all schools that would agree to use it as a reading book.

A communication was received from the agent which contained the gratifying intelligence that, in the various towns which he visited, the people generally, and some of the priesthood, were favorable to his benevolent mission. One clergyman, a member of the Senate, expressed his full conviction that the Bible should have an unrestricted circulation. The bishop of the diocese, however, thought differently, and, summoning the agent before him, required him to desist from further distributions. The consequence was, that the Bibles which he had deposited for sale had to be taken back to save them from the flames. His distributions in the Republic of Chili amounted to about twelve hundred copies. He next visited Peru, and sold about four hundred copies in Lima and other places.

In 1838, a number of Spanish Gospels were sent to the Hon. Joaquin Mosquera, of New Grenada, for the use of the primary schools at Bogota. A donation of fifty Bibles and one hundred Testaments was sent to the Rev. Mr. Torrey, at St. Catharine's, Brazil, and the same number, in various languages, to the Missionary Society of the Methodist Episcopal Church, for distribution by their missionaries at Rio Janeiro.

The Rev. Mr. Spaulding, in a communication to the board, states that "the sales of Bibles in Portuguese and Latin had increased in various ways. Some circumstances have occurred which have astonished us. Directors and teachers of schools had thronged the house, and upward of sixty notes had been sent requesting Portuguese and French Scriptures."

The following year, to Messrs. Spaulding and Kidder, Methodist Episcopal missionaries in Brazil, were sent one thousand eight hundred and twenty-five Bibles and Testaments, in Portuguese, German, and French. On the part of the people there was a general desire to obtain the Scriptures, notwithstanding the opposition of the priesthood. These missionaries made an eloquent appeal to the board for a supply of an empire embracing a population of five millions. They represented infidelity as having preoccupied the ground in the dissemination of infidel publications. Since the country had gained its independence from Spain, domestic feuds had arisen, in which the Catholic priesthood were particularly conspicuous, manifesting, as from time immemorial, their hatred of and opposition to free institutions. As the most successful way of preventing the prevalence of these institutions, they invariably prohibit the circulation of the Bible.

In 1840, the missionaries report that the supplies sent them had been put into circulation, and the cause was prospering in Brazil.

During the year 1844, to the Rev. Mr. Norris, a Methodist Episcopal clergyman at Buenos Ayres, was sent a supply of Bibles, in Spanish, Danish, and Italian.

To Rio Grande, in Brazil, was sent a small supply of Portuguese and Spanish Bibles, and to a lady at the same place, several Portuguese Testaments for distribution.

To an English friend at Nicaragua, Honduras, were sent two hundred and fifty Spanish Scriptures.

To Rio Grande, Buenos Ayres, and Monte Video, grants of Spanish Bibles were made to a limited extent the following year.

In 1848, a grant of three hundred and twenty-two copies of the Spanish Scriptures was made to the Foreign Evangelical Society for the use of their missionary at Valparaiso, and the same year to the American consul at Santa Martha was sent a supply of Spanish Scriptures for distribution.

This, we believe, embraces all that can be said statistically in relation to the operations of the American Bible Society in South America. Much has been done by other institutions, especially the British and Foreign Bible Society, in scattering abroad over that extensive and interesting field the good seed, much of which has already been productive, and we most ardently hope that the day is not far distant when the sister Republics of that country shall be elevated to the enjoyment of all the blessings of that rational and Christian liberty which we, as a nation, so largely enjoy.

CHAPTER XXII.

BIBLE IN FRANCE.

France is now a republic, and, though nominally a papal country, the Word of God has an unrestricted circulation. The time was when one of her largest cities was searched for a copy of the Bible, that it might be tied to the tail of an ass, and thus dragged in derision through its streets; but that day has passed. That book is now respected, and taken to the council-chamber of many of her most distinguished statesmen.

Among the first donations received by the American Bible Society was a complete set of stereotype plates for the Bible, in the French language, from the British and Foreign Bible Society, in 1818. As a foreign field, the society bestowed its earliest attention in providing for that country the Word of Life.

The managers of the society, having been made acquainted with the labors of the Rev. Frederic Leo, of Paris, by whose extraordinary exertions the printing of two fine stereotype editions of the New Testament, in French, was accomplished, one according to the translation of the Rev. Mr. Osterwald, and the other according to the translation of Le Maistre de Sacy, judged it proper to assist him in a work which he was prosecuting with great personal toil and expense.

A letter from the Secretary of Foreign Correspondence, Rev. Dr. Mason, communicating to the above-named gentleman the intelligence that the board had made him a donation of five hundred dollars to assist him in the printing and distribution of the Scriptures, remarks:

"I hope, my dear sir, that you will see in this act of the American Bible Society a proof that your many and arduous labors in the good work of spreading abroad the Word of Life are not forgotten nor disregarded on this side of the Atlantic, and that you will be encouraged to persevere in your noble undertaking, finding your best recompense in the answer of a good conscience toward God and a benevolent spirit toward man."

The work of Bible distribution was greatly accelerated by the formation of the Protestant Bible Society of Paris about three years afterward.

In 1830, owing to some political events which transpired in France, the field of operations was rendered more inviting, and increased facilities were afforded for the circulation of the Scriptures.

A benevolent gentleman in one of our cities, familiar with the condition and wants of France, offered to furnish one thousand dollars to aid the American Bible Society in circulating the Scriptures in that country, on condition that nine thousand dollars more should be made up from other sources.

During the year 1821, it was estimated that there were put in circulation in that kingdom one hundred and fifty thousand copies of the Bible. This was accomplished principally through the Protestant Bible Society. The circulation was mostly confined to the Protestants, of which there are three millions in that country.

The board, in 1823, made a grant of two thousand dollars to the Protestant Bible Society, to aid it in circulating the Scriptures.

The grounds on which the grant was made may be learned by the following extracts from the Committee of the French and Foreign Bible Society:

"Many motives have induced us to give you official

information of our existence. Besides those bonds of mutual good will which ought to unite both institutions, born of the same faith and for the same end, it has appeared to us that Providence will establish particular ones between your society and ours.

"The name of France awakens in America many generous sentiments. It is associated with the remembrance of the days when God raised you to the rank of an independent nation. It was then that France aided you in gaining that independence, the most precious good (after the possession of the Gospel of salvation) which a nation can enjoy, and which has assigned to your country so honorable a rank among the families of the people—you have never forgotten it.

"Therefore France to you is dear. We are not ignorant how much you interest yourselves in her happiness, and we are assured that it is with particular affection that the Christians of America ask of the Lord that his light may shine upon us, and that his salvation may be known from one end of France to the other.

"It is true that if we compare the immensity of this task with our present resources, we find no proportion between them. But we have learned, even in the book which we labor to distribute, that our God places his glory in using weak things to confound the strong.

"The experience which our elder sisters have had of his blessing encourages us. We believe that there are none of them who have not had, like ourselves, to recollect that the period is still recent when the Bible ceased to be an importation in America and became indigenous there, and that we have lived long enough to see the rapid developments of your society, which can already extend its solicitudes to the remotest nations.

"The necessities around us are immense. The Roman Catholic population, in part detached from the pope, begins to feel its religious wants.

"Brethren of America, we calculate upon your assistance, and we hope to see the day when we can in our turn offer a hand to some new-born society, and, like you, extend our labors beyond the limits of our own country."

In 1824, the board granted to this society six thousand dollars, five hundred dollars of which were for the circulation of the German Scriptures among emigrants passing through France to America.

In 1825, the Protestant Bible Society of Paris numbered seventy-five auxiliaries.

In answer to a letter received from the secretary of the Lyons Bible Society, representing the wants of the two hundred thousand inhabitants of that city and the surrounding country, nearly all of whom were Roman Catholics, the board made a remittance of five hundred dollars, to enable them to purchase Bibles and Testaments from the Depository of the French and Foreign Bible Society in Paris.

During the year 1835, application was made to the board from the French and Foreign Bible Society for aid to enable it to circulate the Spanish Scriptures, and a grant was made to that society of two thousand and seventy dollars.

In 1837, to the above society were granted, on request, one thousand dollars, to enable it to procure a set of stereotype plates for a pica French Testament for aged persons.

In addition to this grant, the sum of one thousand more was forwarded, on the recommendation of the Rev. Robert Baird, to aid in circulating the Scriptures in France and Spain.

A letter from the secretary of this society the following year is of the most encouraging character, and gives a most gratifying account of the circulation of the Scriptures among the sailors and soldiers. It states that the maritime officers and military commanders of many cities, although Roman Catholics, had not opposed them, as was anticipated, but had in many instances granted them assistance.

It was estimated that there were circulated in the different departments of France, during the year 1840, two hundred thousand copies of the Scriptures.

The following year, to the Rev. Mr. Sawtelle, seven hundred Bibles and Testaments were granted for distribution in Havre; and to the Foreign Evangelical Society, to aid in the distribution of Bibles, under the direction of the Rev. Robert Baird, five hundred dollars were granted. In reply to this donation, the above-named gentleman remarks: "I am happy to say that your grant is at this moment furnishing the Scriptures to many people, by means of our colporteurs. An American-Swiss committee employs this winter thirty colporteurs."

Up to this period the societies in France had received, besides grants of money from the British and Foreign Bible Society, upward of a million and a half of Bibles and Testaments. The Depository of this society in Paris, under the direction of the agent, M. Pressense, issued in 1842 one hundred and forty-six thousand Bibles and Testaments, ninety-five thousand of which were distributed by colporteurs.

To the Foreign Evangelical Society, for circulating the Scriptures in France, was remitted the sum of seven hundred dollars.

Soon after this grant, another was made of a thousand dollars to the French and Foreign Bible Society.

A very gratifying letter was received from Count de la Borde, one of the secretaries of the society, acknowledging with gratitude the receipt of the donation.

In this letter the pleasing intelligence is communicated that the circulation of the Bible is attended with the most blessed results. In the Catholic parishes of western France a deep and abiding interest has been awakened among the people, and a general desire to "search the Scriptures" for the foundation of their faith has led many to abandon the soulless system of Romanism, and to ask for pastors who would feed them with the "sincere milk of the Word."

The Archbishop of Toulouse, startled by the encroachments of Bible truth upon the dominions of papacy, revived against the Protestants the false accusation that they were spreading editions of the Bible in which the text was falsified. One of the members of the American-Swiss Committee sent the archbishop a challenge to prove what he had asserted, and soon after published a pamphlet, known by the title of "Reply to the Circular of the Archbishop of Toulouse." This reply induced many inquiries, and the result was, several priests left the Church of Rome, two of whom published pamphlets, entitled, "*Farewell to Rome*," and "*The Pope*," which created a salutary sensation. Thus has the Bible always triumphed when attacked either by papacy or infidelity. Priests, monks, and friars were converted by simply reading the Bible, and became the most zealous colporteurs of the sacred treasure.

To further encourage the labors of the Foreign Evangelical Society, a grant of five hundred dollars was made. In 1847, on the request of Dr. Baird, the board granted five hundred dollars to the Foreign Evangelical Society toward printing and circulating the Scriptures in Switzerland and southern France.

In two different payments to the French and Foreign Bible Society, were granted, during the year, three thousand dollars.

The secretary, Count de la Borde, in his communication, speaks of the determined and persevering opposition of the papal priesthood since the accession of the new pope. It will be recollected that this same Pius IX., by what was in this country termed his *liberal* policy, had obtained for himself the name of a reformer, as though a church infallibly identified with superstition and error could be reformed. While in this country the trumpet of his fame was sounding as a prince of liberal views, his edicts against the rights of conscience were grinding to the dust the sincere inquirers after truth in his own dominions. No thanks to Pope Pius are due, to say the least of it, from Democratic Republicans. That the policy which gave him such favor in the eyes of some, who were ignorant of the motives which actuated him, should be regarded as a matter of *choice*, is not remarkable. Subsequent events in his ill-fated history must certainly have demonstrated to the most obtuse intellect the fact that *necessity*, stern and irrevocable, was the efficient cause of such action. Unacquainted with the laws of progress, or unwilling to yield to their righteous demands, he was obliged to vacate the fabled chair of St. Peter, doff the triple crown, and, disguised as a servant, flee from the seat of his power and take refuge in another state.

The desire to read the Scriptures had been awakened in France, and it was not in the power of the then reigning pontiff or his hireling priesthood to arrest the progress of that spirit of inquiry. The board remitted five hundred dollars to the Evangelical Society, and responded to an appeal from the French and Foreign Bible Society by sending two thousand dollars to aid it in the glorious work.

Since the late revolution, a letter from one of the secretaries contains the following remarks:

"At present our treasury is empty, and in debt twelve thousand francs. Our committee, in addition thereto, has been obliged to make large engagements, amounting to more than thirty thousand francs, in order to renew our stereotype plates, which were worn out; and, as our depository of books is nearly empty, we foresee a large increase of expenses for the purchase of paper and necessary press-work. Certainly such a situation, if made known to the *world*, would draw down upon us its disapprobation, and we should be accused of unpardonable imprudence; but *Christians*, who know the particular circumstances of the religious state of France, far from blaming us, will grant us all their sympathy."

Truly a crisis full of the deepest interest had come —at a time, too, when the political circumstances of the country afforded the widest liberty for the circulation of the Scriptures among a population disturbed and agitated like the waves of the sea in a storm. There was no time to be lost; the liberty gained could only be secured by the infusion into the nation of a Bible morality, and France must have the Bible. The Rev. Mr. Bridel was sent as a delegate to the American Bible Society. His representation of the condition and wants of that country excited an interest in behalf of the Bible cause in France which was vastly greater than any that previously existed. At the anniversary meeting, it was resolved to contribute ten thousand dollars during the year for the support of this cause.

We shall close this chapter by the narration of an interesting incident connected with the circulation of the Bible in France.

The proprietor of the Hotel *Gibbon*, at *Lausanne*,

has charge of a depôt of Bibles in this noted house. In this hotel, bearing the name and built on the very ground so often paced by one who, through life, hated the Gospel, and did all he could to injure its blessed cause, there is a depository of Bibles. The host and hostess have disposed of upward of four thousand copies of the sacred Volume.

It was once said by Voltaire that the time would arrive when the Bible would be regarded only in the light of an old curiosity. The very room in which he penned this sentiment is now piled to the ceiling with that rare old Book.

CHAPTER XXIII.

BIBLE IN SPAIN, ITALY, PORTUGAL, AND AUSTRIA.

From the Annual Reports of the American Bible Society, as well as those of the British and Foreign, together with other sources of information which we have consulted in relation to the introduction and circulation of the Scriptures in this land of "old renown" —the favored country of the "olive and the vine"— the earliest information we can gather is from the annual report of the above-named society for 1826.

Inquiry was made during that year in regard to the dissemination of the Word of Life in that country, but such was its condition that it was deemed proper not to make any special efforts in relation thereto.

During the first year of the American Bible Society's existence, when the board were without funds, and dependent upon the benevolence of friends for a place wherein to hold their meetings, the subject of publishing the Spanish New Testament was brought before them by the donation of certain documents in relation thereto from the New York Missionary Society, which they had collected with a view of undertaking said work.

The subject was favorably entertained by the board, and nothing but sheer inability on their part, arising from want of means to prosecute the work, deterred them from the undertaking at that early day.

In 1828, a few copies of the Spanish Scriptures were introduced through various media.

Nothing more was accomplished until 1832, when small distributions were effected, mostly through natives from Spain residing in England.

In 1835, the secretary of the French and Foreign Bible Society requested a copy of each of the editions of Spanish Scriptures published by the American Bible Society, and also addressed a question to the board in regard to the opinion entertained by well-informed Spaniards of the style and literary merit of the version, with a view of introducing it into Spain, which, from its proximity to France, rendered it more properly the duty of their society to labor for its introduction into that country.

During the same year, the British and Foreign Bible Society sent an agent to Spain, in the person of Mr. Borrow, whose book, entitled "Bible in Spain," has been extensively circulated, and read by thousands with unusual interest. The travels of the above-named gentleman were very extensive, and his description of the condition of the country—its religion, manners, and customs—interesting and truthful.

Spain is Roman Catholic throughout, though, in the language of Mr. Borrow, "she is not blindly wedded to the pope." Though she has done more than any other papal country to enforce the bloody edicts of the Church in the establishment of the Inquisition, which for two centuries was gorged with the blood of thousands—a vast butcher-house—yet this was not so much for the love of Rome as for the title given her of the Vicar of Jesus. When she could no longer wield the sword with success against the Lutherans, and her Inquisition was blown to atoms, so that she was obliged to change her profession as the butcher, she became the banker of Rome. As pride must always have a fall, this being the predominant feature of her character, so was she destined to still further changes.

Wars devastated the country, poverty ensued, the pope clamored for his "*Peter pence*," and complained bitterly of the treatment he received in Spain. In his pastoral letter, he says, "My cathedrals are let down, my priests are insulted, and the revenues of my bishops are curtailed."

The pious lamentations and tears of Gregory XVI. had little effect in moving the hearts of the bull-fighting members of his Church. Mr. Borrow found among the peasantry of Spain a general willingness to read the Bible, and also a disposition to assist him in its circulation.

While in Madrid he translated and printed the Gospel in the Gipsy language, which was extensively circulated, and for which, together with the sale of the Spanish Scriptures, he was arrested by the priesthood of Rome, and thrust into prison. While on his way to prison, in passing the *Carcel de la Corte*, or Prison of the Court, he remarks, "I remembered that this was the place where the Inquisition of Spain was in the habit of holding its solemn *Autos da Fé*, and I cast my eye to the balcony of the City Hall, where the last of the Austrian line in Spain sat, and, after some thirty heretics of both sexes had been burned by fours and fives, wiped his face, perspiring with heat and black with smoke, and calmly inquired, 'No hay mas?' for which exemplary proof of patience he was much applauded by his priests and confessors, who subsequently poisoned him. And here am I, who have done more to wound popery than all the poor Christian martyrs that ever suffered in this accursed square, merely sent to prison, from which I am sure to be liberated in a few days with credit and applause. Pope of Rome! I believe you to be as malicious as ever, but you are sadly deficient in power. You are become paralytic, Batuschca, and your club has degenerated to a crutch!"

All this turned out for the furtherance of the Gospel, the very thing he desired; for, when he wished to get access to its inmates on a former occasion, it was denied him. The word of salvation came to those who otherwise, as in the case of the Philippian jailer, never would have received its joyful intelligence.

In 1838, a civil war raged with unusual violence in Spain, but the indications of Providence seemed to encourage the hope that something could be done for the diffusion of the Scriptures in that country. The board received a communication from a Protestant merchant residing there, requesting a grant of Spanish Scriptures. He says, "There is not the least shade of doubt in my mind that Divine Providence is now opening the way for the dissipation of the horrible abuses and crimes which, under the holy name of religion, have so long stained this most unhappy but finest country of the globe, and of which the intelligent portion of the nation are now beginning to see the effects. Believe me when I tell you, from my own personal observation as well as collected information, that the way is now open, and, if proper and prompt measures are adopted, we may reasonably expect, ay, *even in our time*, to see the Gospel, *founded on the prophets and apostles*, and not on *tradition*, that great corner stone of Romish superstition, established in this country. But let it not be imagined for a moment that this will be the work of a day or of little exertion. No; the prejudices and preoccupations of more than a thousand years are not so easily overcome. Let it not be supposed, that without immense exertion, we can hope to see even a moderate degree of success; people bred from the cradle in the exercise of unhealthy opinions, however they may be convinced of their fallacy, are not so easily, after so long a course of indulgence in them, made to consent to their alteration, and particularly by reasons urged by *foreigners*."

The following year, a box of Bibles and Testaments in Spanish was forwarded to this gentleman at Cadiz.

Nothing more of consequence appears to have been done by either of the Bible societies toward the distribution of the Bible in Spain for several succeeding years.

The irreformable spirit of popery and the distracted state of the country prevented the work from being carried on as it would have been done.

In its labors the Bible Society acts somewhat in accordance with the policy that governed the great Apostle of the Gentiles, who, on being rejected as a missionary to one nation, turned his attention and directed his steps to another.

In 1846, the board granted a box of Bibles and Testaments, in Spanish, to the Foreign Evangelical Society, for distribution on the coast of Spain.

The latest intelligence obtained from official records in regard to Bible distribution in that country is gathered from the last report of the British and Foreign Bible Society. In this there is nothing very encouraging, yet we trust the day is not far distant when Spain and other Catholic countries, like France, will awake to her true interests in the adoption of more liberal principles, and at least consent to the reading and circulation of the Bible.

In Italy, Portugal, Belgium, Austria, and other papal countries, but little had been accomplished in the way of distribution. Through the Philo-Italian Society, the circulation has increased to a great extent for a few years past in Italy.

A correspondent now at Rome says the Bible is freely circulated there at the present time. It is read by all, and frequently appealed to in controversy.

E. Corderoy, Esq., of London, in writing to the editors of the Christian Advocate and Journal, New York, says, a Bible meeting was recently held at the baths of Lucca, a Bible Society formed, and a collection taken up of one hundred dollars in aid of the cause. Thousands of Bibles, on the request of the inhabitants, have been sent to Sicily by the British and Foreign Bible Society.

A correspondent of the London Christian Times, writing from Italy a few weeks since, says:

"Advertisements for the public sale of copies of the Holy Scriptures lie before me, in Italy, where, but a few months ago, even one copy would have been seized by the custom-house officers. We may have depôts for the Bible Society wherever we please, and ought to have one, at least, in every principal town of the Lombardo-Venetian, Tuscan, and Sardinian dominions. We should be able to offer a Bible or a New Testament to every family at a moderate price, and should endeavor to supply the schools. And if some vigorous effort be not made by means of a well-chosen, living agency, the favorable juncture will be missed, future evangelization will be impeded, and infidel reaction will become chronic. Such an agency was established in Spain, although in the face of serious obstacles; and the adventurous Borrow and persevering Graydon, by merely circulating the volumes, effected a benefit which can never be undone.

"In Austria, too, the fetters have dropped from long-imprisoned Christianity as by the touch of an angel. Many thousands of persons are said to have seceded from the Romish communion at Vienna alone, and united themselves, together with many priests, to the German Catholic Church. They see as through a glass darkly—very darkly; but their mind is severed from old attachments, vacillates between truth and error, is inquisitive, and with the profession of candor, at least, is looking for more certain guidance. For Austria, nay, for all Germany, and for Italy and the Italian islands, we need suitable agents and a well-directed system of colportage."

More recent intelligence informs us that a large edition of the Bible is now in course of publication at Rome and another at Florence.

CHAPTER XXIV.

BIBLE PROHIBITION IN ROMAN CATHOLIC COUNTRIES.

Notwithstanding we have, in several instances, alluded to this subject, we present the following additional facts in relation to the systematic and persevering efforts of the Roman Catholic Church to prohibit the reading and circulation of the Holy Scriptures in the vulgar tongue. These facts are drawn from various but well-authenticated sources of information. The first, and that which forms the basis of all subsequent facts in regard to this subject, is found in the Index Prohibitorum of the Council of Trent, ordained in 1564, and beginning "Cum experimento manifestum sit." "Inasmuch as it is manifest by experience that if the Holy Bible, translated into the vulgar tongue, be indiscriminately allowed to every one, the temerity of men will cause more evil than good to arise from it; it is, on this point, referred to the judgment of the bishops or inquisitors, who may, by the advice of the priest or confessor, permit the reading of the Bible, translated into the vulgar tongue by Catholic authors, to those persons whose faith and piety they apprehend will be augmented and not injured by it, and this permission they must have in writing. But if any one shall have the presumption to read or possess it without such written permission, he shall not receive absolution until he have first delivered up such Bible to the ordinary," &c.

It is worthy of remark, that this same papal decree which prohibits the reading of the Word of God, ordains that books "written by the heathens are permitted to be read because of the elegance and propriety of the language." This is what we would call progressing backward.

In Protestant countries, where the ghostly despotism of Rome is held in check, this fourth rule of the Index of Prohibited Books, on which so many popes have dwelt with such fond delight, can only be enforced to the letter where popery is absolutely dominant.

In all the dominions of the Emperor of *Austria*, Bibles, whether in the Hebrew or in the vulgar tongue, are prohibited. In the province of Tyrol, six hundred Protestant Tyrolese were compelled to expatriate themselves in 1837, having been led to renounce the errors and corruptions of popery by the reading of the Bible.

In *France*, popery, as an old dead tree, stretching out its haggard, leafless branches like the ghost of departed greatness and power, is ready to fall. The people, having tasted of the pure waters of life from the fountain of Divine truth, will never again go back to the stagnant pools of Rome.

In *Belgium*, every opposition which can well be conceived has for many years been made to the circulation of the Holy Scriptures.

Bible distributers have not merely been reproached, insulted, and threatened, but mobs have been instigated to maltreat and injure them. Their Bibles have been stolen or forcibly taken away, and torn to pieces or burned before their eyes.

A bishop by the name of Bruges denounced the British and Foreign Bible Society as "a society *hostile to God* and to the holy Church—a society which would rob his dear children of all that is most dear to them." Citing the encyclical letter of Leo XII., he characterized the circulation of the Scriptures as "the infamous project of that anti-Christian society, by which the world was inundated with heretical Bibles, in which the perfidy of heretics had carried sacrilegious temerity to such an extent as shamefully to mutilate the Old Testament by striking out the books of Tobit, Judith, Wisdom, Ecclesiasticus, Baruch, and the Maccabees." These same books, so precious in the eyes of the Roman priests, known as the Apocrypha, were never recognized by the Jews or primitive Christians, or the Greek Church, nor by any general council, as canonical, until the Council of Trent, in the most shameless abandonment of truth, calling itself œcumenical, or general, pronounced them "holy and canonical," with a curse against all who would not receive them as such.

The Roman Church is as superstitious as heathenism. The splendid crown presented on Ascension Day, May 25th, 1843, to a "miraculous image of the Virgin," invoked as the Mother of Mercy, in the presence of the king, queen, and their dear baby, the Duke of Brabant, was as rich in decoration as the scene was ridiculous.

In *Portugal*, the Scriptures are unknown among the peasantry. There the power of the pope is supreme, and his subjects most blindly adhere to the decree infallible of Leo, prohibiting the reading of what he is pleased to term "the Gospel of the Devil and deadly Pastures," on pain of damnation. In this, however, he has not the "unanimous consent of the fathers," for St. Augustine, St. Chrysostom, St. Cyprian, and St. Gregory, all recommended the reading and study of the Holy Scriptures. Now, in regard to this "unanimous consent" for the interpretation of the Scriptures, we have a word to say. If the priests of Holy Mother had intelligence enough to read the fathers, which is far from being the case with many of them, their unanimous consent could never be obtained in support of any one of the dogmas of popery, from the fact that these writings abound in almost endless contradictions. That, as Dr. Brownlee asserts, "the priests are, in general, two hundred years behind the literature of the age," is susceptible of the clearest proof, and the assumption that they are, as a body, learned, is perfectly ridiculous.

In regard to the Scriptures, their ignorance has been proverbial from the days of the Reformation.

When that great event was talked about among the priests, several of them affirmed that the New Testament was a book made by Martin Luther. A monk in Germany, declaiming against the Reformation, said, "A new language has been invented called the Greek," and he exhorted his friends to "guard carefully against it, as the mother of every species of heresy." "The New Testament," said he, "is written in that language, and it is a book full of thorns and serpents."

In *Spain*, the Bible is a prohibited book unless it be accompanied with notes from the fathers and Romish divines, and Felix Torres Amat, bishop of Astorça, could not obtain permission from the Index at Rome for publishing his Spanish version of the Scriptures, with notes, but on the condition "that he would show his readers that *the reading of the Bible is not necessary to salvation.*" This condition he subsequently fulfilled "by duly instructing the readers that they might go to heaven without reading the Word of God."

In 1838, the circulation of the Gospel of Luke, which Mr. Borrow had translated into the dialect of the Gitanos, or Spanish gipsies, was prohibited by an ordinance of the Spanish government, as also the circulation of the same Gospel in the Spanish Basque dialect, which is spoken in the provinces of Guipuscoa and Biscay.

In *Italy*, the Bible is a condemned and prohibited book, and unknown until very recently. The Virgin Mary is the chief object of devout admiration. If a beggar in the streets asks alms, it is for the love of the Virgin.

At Nice, in the dominions of the King of Sardinia, in 1837, twenty-four persons were imprisoned, by order of the Sardinian government, for the heinous crime of having in their possession the Bible. Similar restrictions against the Bible exist in Leghorn.

At Rome, until within a few months past, the Bible was a strange and rare book. The only edition of it authorized to be sold there is in fifteen large volumes, which are filled with popish commentaries. Of course none but the rich can purchase a copy of the Sacred Scriptures; indeed, very few of the common people knew there was such a book in existence as the Bible.

It is stated as a fact in Mendham's "Literary Policy of the Church of Rome," that not one single edition of the New Testament in Greek had ever been issued from the Roman press. Efforts were frequently made, and indulgences granted at different times for the publication, but they were as often revoked, fearing that the publication of the Scriptures in any other than the Latin tongue would prove injurious to the Church.

In *Ireland*, the opposition of the Romish priests to

the circulation of the Scriptures is a matter of notoriety.

The Romish archbishops and bishops, in giving publicity to the encyclical letter of Leo XII., accompanied with "pastoral instructions to all the faithful," declared, "that as the books distributed by the Bible Society, under the name of Bibles and Testaments, treat of religion, and are not sanctioned by us, or by any competent authority in the (Roman) Catholic Church, the use, the perusal, or retaining of them *is entirely and without any exception* PROHIBITED TO YOU; and should any of them be in your possession, they are to be returned to the persons who may have bestowed them on you, or otherwise to be *destroyed*."

The Archbishop of Tuam said to his dear people, "Any person who practices the reading of the Bible will inevitably fall into everlasting destruction. I would therefore, my dear friends and followers, earnestly beseech you, *by the love that you bear to the Virgin Mary* and the dear priests, not to allow these Bible readers near your houses, not to speak to them when you meet them on the roads, but put up your hands and pray to the Virgin Mary to keep you from being contaminated with the poison of the Bible. The worst of all pestilences, the pestilence of the Bible, will entail on yourselves and children the everlasting ruin of your souls. They who send their children to schools where the Scriptures are read give them bound in chains to the devil." Bibles have been burned in Ireland as well as Belgium.

On the departure of the American missionaries from Damascus, in Syria, the Franciscan monks required all the Christian communities to give up their Bibles, and they were burned in the court of the convent.

In *South and Central America*, the same state of things exists in regard to the general ignorance of the

Scriptures and their prohibition. At Ecuador a benevolent individual opened a school and circulated some Bibles. He was denounced by the Bishop of Quito for the "crying enormity" of having "promoted the general reading of the Scriptures in the Spanish tongue, without notes, contrary to the *prohibitions* of the holy Roman Catholic Church."

In the *West Indies*, one of the two Roman bishops resident on the island of Trinidad boasted that he "had taken between two and three hundred Bibles and Testaments from the people of his flock, and placed them under lock and key."

Rome is the same in Protestant as she is in papal countries, and just so far as the influence of the Church extends is the Bible restricted in its circulation. The "faithful" have been deprived of it in England and the United States. In both countries the priests have committed it to the flames.

We need not go back to the times of Henry IV. and Henry VIII., and the sanguinary reign of Mary, to produce evidences of hostility from the papacy to the Bible in England; recent times abound with proofs of the most incontestable character. The hypocritical pretensions and professions of the Rev. Peter Gandolphy, a Romish priest in London, as developed in a letter to Bishop Marsh, in which he says, "If any of the Bible societies feel disposed to try our esteem for the Bible by presenting us with some copies of a Catholic version, *with* or WITHOUT *notes*, we will gratefully accept and faithfully distribute them," shows most conclusively that Rome is driven to the miserable pretext of "keeping up appearances," while, at the same time, she has no intention whatever of making her professions good. Bibles were immediately sent, but they were as promptly put "under lock and key," or committed to the flames.

In 1838, the organization of a "Catholic Bible Society" was announced in Leicestershire. This, to all intents and purposes, was a *secret* society, as none of its operations were ever known to the community, and the name itself has almost passed away from the memory of the inhabitants.

In Ireland, within a very short time past, the Bible has been burned by Roman priests, and poor, defenseless women and children have been beaten and driven from their homes for having it in their possession. Dr. Dill, a delegate from the Presbyterian Church in Ireland to the American Churches, attests these facts.

But the smoke of God's blessed Book has darkened this fair land of religious toleration and liberty. The following well-authenticated statement will speak for itself:

"Chazy, N. Y., June 7, 1843.

"MY DEAR SIR,—Yours of the 28th of April last was duly received, and I should have answered it a long time ago, but, as the occurrence to which you particularly referred in it had taken place during my absence from this place, I thought it best to take all the information I could have on the subject from persons more closely acquainted with the transaction than I was myself. Consequently, I called upon Mr. Woodruff, our Congregationalist minister in this place, and also upon Mr. Hubbell, who had taken considerable pains in ascertaining as near as possible the exact state of that unfortunate and horrible affair of the burning of Bibles at Corbeau. I also received a long letter on the same subject from Mr. Brinkerhoof, the Presbyterian minister of Champlain, and now I hasten to lay before you what I know of this guilty transaction. As far as I can ascertain, from 100 to 150 Bibles were burned last November at Corbeau, through the influence and by the special command of an infuriated Romish Jesuit named Father Telmond, who had been sent there, with several others, by the Bishop of Montreal, to hold a protracted meeting among the votaries of the beast. After much inquiry, I can not find out that there has been any Bible burned out of those which I have personally distributed. I am positive that there is none of your last invoice of last fall which have fallen into the hands of those voracious *birds of prey*. Those burned seem to have been distributed by the Champlain Auxiliary Society; some were from the town of Luvers, others from Beekmantown, and some even from the town of Plattsburgh. As to the effect produced upon the public mind, it has been various. In some quarters it seems to have struck the Protestant population with awe and with deep horror, while it appears, also, to have totally discouraged them as to the probability, and even the possibility, of being ever able to effect some good for the Romish population, and to retrieve them from their errors and present religious degradation. With some other Protestants it struck quite upon another chord; their feelings of indignation against this daring and sacrilegious act, and of deep pity and Christian philanthropy for the poor deluded victims of the crafty Jesuits, appear to have been considerably raised, and they are now more decided than ever to continue their efforts in behalf of the Romans, to open their eyes and enlighten their minds.

"As to the Romish population itself, I believe that this evil designing act of burning publicly the Bibles has done an immense good to them, generally speaking. I can relate instances where it was the visible cause of bringing souls to Christ. There are now in our little church three of the most promising converts, who have been so shocked at this daring outrage upon the sacred Word of God that they forthwith withdrew from the Church of Rome. One is now engaged in the good work of colportage, and proves to be one of the most faithful and most intelligent guardians that has been brought from darkness to light since the beginning of the missionary movements among the Canadians. The other is gifted with the most prayerful soul that has as yet been met with among his converted countrymen. The third one is the wife of the colporteur, and she also walks steadfastly under the eye of her Maker. I have no doubt that the burning of the Bibles has done no harm to the missionary cause, but, on the contrary, I am fully convinced that God has overruled their evil design.

"Before concluding this letter, I must acknowledge that I have received the box of Bibles and of New Testaments which you sent me last fall. I must pay you a very deserved compliment for the nice binding and good print of your Martin's Bibles; and I have thought it more prudent to distribute generally those of other prints, and keep these fine Martin's Bibles for converted families. I have distributed something between thirty and forty out of the hundred which you sent me. The cause of the Almighty is prospering here and in Canada. I am leaving in three days from hence for this latter place, where I am to attend protracted meetings at two or three different places. Pray, my dear sir, for me, that I may grow in knowledge, wisdom, and grace.

"Allow me to subscribe myself, with due regard, your most humble and faithful servant, C. H. O. COTE.

"REV. J. C. BRIGHAM."

More recent than all in regard to Bible burning, we copy the following from a writer in the Montreal Herald of the present year:

> "The Roman Catholic clergy in Canada are, with few exceptions (I know of only two), opposed to the circulation of the Bible; and any one who will take the trouble to go into the houses of the French *habitans*, and make inquiry, will find that they have been quite successful in their opposition. He will scarcely find a Bible or Testament in one house in a thousand, except where Protestant agents have distributed it. In 1839, the Rev. Mr. Rabelle, *curé* of L'Assumption, burned five Bibles and one Testament, which had been circulated in his parish by the agent of the Montreal Bible Society, and for which he afterward paid. In 1842, as stated by the New York Journal of Commerce, between 200 and 300 Bibles were burned at a Roman Catholic protracted meeting in the village of Corbeau, near Lake Champlain. I have before me a letter from Quebec, dated the third of this month, in which the writer informs me that a priest on the island of Orleans, finding a Bible in a house which he visited, told the person who had purchased it that it was 'a bad book,' and persuaded him to tear it to pieces and throw it into the fire. Similar facts might be given, to almost any extent, from the journals of the Montreal Bible Society, and from the French Canadian Missionary Society; but I forbear."

Macaulay, in his inimitable history, says, in regard to Romanism, "During the last three centuries, the chief object of the Church of Rome has been to stunt the growth of the human mind. Throughout Christendom, whatever advance has been made in knowledge, in freedom, in wealth, and in the arts of life, has been made in spite of her, and has every where been in inverse proportion to her power. The loveliest and most fertile provinces of Europe have under her rule been sunk in poverty, in political servitude, and in intellectual torpor, while Protestant countries, once proverbial for sterility and barbarism, have been turned by skill and industry into gardens, and can boast of a long list of heroes and statesmen, philosophers and poets. Whoever, knowing what Italy and Scotland naturally are, and what four hundred years ago they actually were, shall now compare the country round Rome with the country round Edinburgh, will be able to form some judgment as to the tendency of papal domination. The descent of Spain, once the first among monarchies, to the lowest depths of degradation; the elevation of Holland, in spite of many natural disadvantages, to a position such as no commonwealth so small has ever reached, teach the same lesson. Whoever passes in Germany from a Roman Catholic to a Protestant principality; in Switzerland from a Roman Catholic to a Protestant canton; in Ireland from a Roman Catholic to a Protestant county, finds that he has passed from a lower to a higher grade of civilization. On the other side of the Atlantic the same law prevails. The Protestants of the United States have left far behind them the Roman Catholics of Mexico, Peru, and Brazil. The Roman Catholics of Lower Canada remain inert, while the whole continent around them is in a ferment with Protestant activity and enterprise."

CHAPTER XXV.

BIBLE IN THE SANDWICH, WEST INDIA, AND OTHER ISLANDS.

THE "sure word of prophecy" which the society labors to circulate among all nations as "a lamp to their feet and a light to their path," assures us that "*the isles shall wait for his law*," a prediction which has met with a literal fulfillment.

The Sandwich Islands compose one of the groups of the Polynesian Islands far to the north of the great mass of the Polynesian Archipelago.

The attention of the society was called to the condition of these islands in the early part of its history, and the interest then awakened has continued unabated from year to year until the present time, a period of nearly thirty years.

To the first missionaries who started from Boston for the Sandwich Islands, in 1820, under the direction and patronage of the American Board of Commissioners for Foreign Missions, the society made a grant of three hundred Bibles and Testaments. They also sent presents of splendid Bibles to each of the natives of the island of Owhyhee who had been educated at the Mission School in Connecticut, and who accompanied the missionaries. Superior copies were also sent to the late king of Owhyhee, Tam-ah-am-ah-ah, and Tam-o-ree, king of Atooi.

In 1822, the board, at the request of the American Board of Commissioners for Foreign Missions, made a donation of Bibles and Testaments for the use of mariners at the Sandwich Islands.

In 1826, a similar request was made from the same board for a supply of English and Spanish Scriptures for the islands, which was granted.

During the year 1829, the Gospel of Matthew, which had been translated by the missionaries into the Hawaiian language, was published by the society, and fifteen thousand copies were prepared for shipment. In speaking of the demand for the Scriptures, Mr. Loomis, the printer, who had been a resident on the islands, says, "I know not a place in the world where the Scriptures are sought with greater avidity than at the Sandwich Islands. It was the earnest request of the rulers that they might be furnished with the entire volume of inspiration. It is a pleasing consideration that the natives entertain no prejudices against the Word of God. Whatever is known to be there contained is at once admitted to be truth."

The board received, in 1832, from St. Petersburg, Russia, a box of Russian and Slavonian New Testaments, to be forwarded to the Sandwich Islands, for Russian ships which touch there.

The Rev. Mr. Knill sent, in company with the books, a very interesting letter, from which we make the following extract. Speaking of St. Petersburg, he says, "We live at the gate of a mighty empire, among sixty millions of people, and we are enabled to distribute the sacred Word in all directions. In three years we have distributed twenty thousand volumes of the New Testament in various languages."

During this year a letter was received from the Rev. Mr. Green, from the islands, in which he says, "The smiles of Jesus on the efforts made to convert the inhabitants of Hawaii have been signal. It is literally and emphatically true that these 'isles wait for his law.' With the continued smiles of the Savior, we hope to print the entire New Testament in the course of the next year. We shall greatly need paper, type, and ink, and we assure you that any donation your society may be pleased to make us shall be faithfully appropriated to this object."

Accordingly, a grant of five thousand dollars was made for the object above specified.

On the reception of the above grant, the missionaries, which were at that time twenty in number, at their annual meeting passed several resolutions expressive of their gratitude, in behalf of the islanders, for the liberal donation.

The number of natives reported at this meeting as able to read was twenty-three thousand one hundred and twenty-seven.

In 1837, the board granted to the American Board

of Missions three thousand dollars to promote the publication and diffusion of the Scriptures in the Hawaiian language. The missionaries, in a communication to the board, use the following language:

"We have completed the printing of an edition of ten thousand copies of our revised translation of the New Testament, at your expense. It is now binding and distributing, and is called for by the people as fast as a dozen native binders can put them up. We are prosecuting the translation of the Old Testament, and printing it in separate books, some of very small editions. We cherish the hope of having the translation completed in eighteen months, perhaps a year from this date."

A letter from one of the missionaries, in 1839, communicates the cheering intelligence that a gracious revival of religion was in progress. The Spirit of God had been poured out copiously upon the seventeen churches, embracing twenty thousand regular hearers. The writer remarks, that "the glorious Gospel, through the agency of the American Missionary, Bible, and Tract Societies, had been made a savor of life unto life to the multitudes, who were dead as the dry bones in Ezekiel's vision."

Thirty thousand copies of the New Testament had been printed, and also a large portion of the Old Testament.

Two thousand five hundred dollars were appropriated for the promotion of the circulation of the Bible during the year.

In 1841, for the publication of the Hawaiian Scriptures, the board granted five thousand five hundred dollars.

The translation of the entire Bible in the Hawaiian tongue was completed in 1839, and the board having examined it, no doubt was left on their minds in regard both to its fidelity, and in reference to its catholic character. In the eighteen churches on the Sandwich Islands there were, in 1841, fifteen thousand nine hundred and fifteen communicants, and not far from nineteen thousand pupils connected with the common schools. The number of those who could read was estimated at between thirty and forty thousand.

Two editions of the New Testament had been published of ten thousand copies each, and one edition of ten thousand copies of the entire Bible.

The forcible establishment of French papal missionaries rendered it increasingly important to have the Word of God placed in every household.

To the chaplain of the American Seamen's Friend Society stationed at the islands was granted a supply of Bibles and Testaments in different languages.

To the Sandwich Island mission, in 1842, was paid the sum of five thousand dollars, toward the appropriation of ten thousand dollars made by the board.

A society was organized at the Sandwich Islands, denominated the "Hawaiian Bible Society," auxiliary to the American Bible Society. To this society was granted by the board, in 1844, the sum of three thousand dollars. The following statement, from its second Report, will convey some idea of the nature and extent of its operations:

"During the past, as in former years, the distribution of the Scriptures has, to a great extent, been gratuitous. The people are poor, and it is with much difficulty that the mass can obtain the money requisite for the payment of their taxes. The distribution has been in proportion to the readers in all parts of the field. Our plan of division is to give to each missionary station a just proportion of all the books printed, so that the divisions of islands, where the people are the poorest and least able to pay, are furnished as am-ply as the portions enjoying greater means and facilities."

The influence of the Bible, forming, as it does, the basis of all their laws, exerts a happy and controlling power over all classes of the people.

In 1845, a grant of fifteen hundred dollars was made to aid in the publication of the Hawaiian Scriptures. From the Report of the Hawaiian Bible Society we learn that an increased interest was manifested in the circulation of the Scriptures in the islands.

For the same object there were forwarded to the Sandwich Islands fifteen hundred dollars in 1847.

The society there is represented to be one of efficiency and system, and it is anticipated that incalculable good will result from its labors.

As letters were expected by which grants were to be regulated, but had not arrived before the close of the financial year, no appropriations were made for the work of Bible distribution in the islands for 1848.

As early as 1820, the Board of Managers sent a small quantity of Spanish Bibles and Testaments to Trinidad and St. Croix, the former of which is known as the most southerly of the Caribbee Islands, and is represented as being exceedingly fertile and beautiful.

During the year 1825, a quantity of Bibles and Testaments was sent to St. Martin's and St. Croix. This year the society, as the almoners of the British and Foreign Bible Society, sent to Porto Praya three hundred Bibles and Testaments in the Portuguese language.

Through the liberality of the New York Bible Society, the immigrants to the island of Hayti were furnished with a suitable supply. A small number was also granted for the use of the schools.

To Antigua was also sent a supply of Bibles and Testaments.

In 1826, several boxes of Spanish Scriptures were sent to Cuba for sale and distribution at different places by Roman Catholic clergymen.

Another box of Spanish and French Bibles and Testaments was sent to Hayti.

In 1828, Bibles and Testaments were sent to Matanzas and Port au Platte, and intrusted to Catholic clergymen.

A small supply of French Testaments was sent to a religious captain of a vessel for Aux Cayes.

On request of Mr. Wainwright, of Port au Prince, Hayti, a small quantity of French Bibles and Testaments was sent for distribution.

In 1833, to a colony near Baracao, was sent a small supply of Spanish Bibles and Testaments.

On application of a missionary at one of the Bahama Islands, in 1835, a grant of one hundred and fifty Bibles and Testaments was made.

These books were portioned out to the inhabitants of New Providence, Turk's Island, Rum Key, Wolling's Sound, Exuma, Grand Bahama, and Andros Island.

In 1843, to the Rev. Dr. M'Elroy, who had been in Santa Cruz, was granted fifteen hundred Bibles and Testaments for the Danish Islands. The propriety of the grant can be learned from the doctor's letter. He says, "The government has recently established schools at different points on the island of Santa Cruz, to sustain which would cost the treasury ten thousand dollars per annum. By law, planters are required to send all their young slaves to these schools for a period of four years, commencing with their fifth year. To keep pace with the intellectual improvement, and make provision for the religious training of the youth, the wise and good have fallen upon the expedient of Sabbath schools, and gentlemen and ladies of the first respectability are seen from Sabbath to Sabbath instructing the slaves, together with their own children. Multitudes of these children are without the Scriptures, and those who have the heart have not the means to procure them for gratuitous distribution."

Other grants to a small amount were made to Hayti and Cuba the same year.

In 1844, to Mr. Stevenson and a lady at St. Croix, for distribution, were granted seventy-three Bibles and Testaments in Danish and French; and to the Rev. Mr. Hanson, a Protestant Episcopal missionary at Key West, were sent one hundred and eighteen Bibles and Testaments for the destitute.

To the Rev. Mr. Brett were sent five hundred and fifty Bibles and Testaments, to the island of St. Thomas; and to the Rev. Mr. Towler, Wesleyan missionary at Hayti, were granted one hundred and seven Bibles and Spanish Gospels.

During the year 1845, to a Wesleyan missionary at Hayti, were sent French Bibles and Testaments; and to a gentleman at St. Croix were sent one hundred and fifty Bibles for distribution.

To the Rev. Mr. Brett, of the Reformed Dutch Church at St. Thomas, were sent four hundred and seventy-five Bibles and Testaments in English, German, and Spanish.

One hundred Portuguese Testaments were sent to Mr. Dabney at the Azore Islands for distribution.

During the following year, grants of Bibles were made to Key West, St. Croix, St. Thomas, and Cuba.

In 1847, for the use of the slave population of St. Croix, on the recommendation of the Rev. Mr. Mines, there were granted by the board five hundred Bibles and Testaments.

To a resident of Cuba, a small quantity of Spanish Bibles and Testaments was granted for distribution.

To a missionary of the Reformed Presbyterian

Church were granted, in 1848, one hundred and fifty Bibles and Testaments, in French, for Hayti. These books were for the use of the mission.

At the same time there were granted to the Bahama Bible Society, on the request of its secretary, two hundred Spanish Bibles and the same number of Testaments, and two hundred Spanish Gospels, the latter being designed for distribution by a friend at Matanzas, Cuba.

All hither as well as farther Polynesia presents a most inviting field; and every island of the numerous groups invites occupancy, and promises a rich and plentiful harvest.

CHAPTER XXVI.

BIBLE IN THE CHINESE EMPIRE.

THIS country embraces the southeastern part of the continent of Asia. It derives its name from the dynasty of *Tsin.* It was anciently called *Tien-sha,* which signifies *under heaven*, and implies that it is only inferior to heaven; hence the Chinese call it the "Celestial Empire." Like the ancient Egyptians, the Chinese lay claim to the most extravagant antiquity, while their authentic history does not commence until the age of Confucius, who flourished about five centuries before the Christian era.

The extent of the country from north to south is about one thousand four hundred and fifty miles, and from east to west about one thousand two hundred and sixty miles, an area larger than the United States.

Its population is variously estimated. The most accurate statement, perhaps, is that contained in Goodrich's Modern History, which puts it down at three hundred and fifty millions, a number seventeen times greater than that of the United States. The government of the country is despotic, the emperor claiming to rule by the appointment of heaven.

As a missionary field, there is, perhaps, no one in the world more interesting or inviting. If the population of the heathen world be estimated at seven hundred millions, then China alone embraces one half of the entire heathen world.

Whatever relates to the introduction of the Bible into the "Celestial Empire" must prove of interesting importance to all who desire to see heathen rites and barbarous customs superseded by Christian civilization and refinement.

Though we are disposed to place little reliance upon traditional accounts, yet the following from Townley's Biblical Literature is worthy of notice, and, if true, will show that this vast population was early visited by the missionary:

"In 637, a Christian mission from Syria arrived in China, under the superintendence of a minister whom the Chinese call Olopen, and had the good fortune to obtain the emperor's protection, who ordered his prime minister to translate the Scriptures brought by Olopen into the Chinese language. During some following centuries Christianity prevailed, with a few variations, in the Chinese Empire, where the names of several bishops and other ministers are left on record."

Professor Lassar, of the Anglo-Hindoo College at Calcutta, an Armenian Christian, in 1807 translated the Gospel of Matthew into the Chinese language; and in 1808, the same gentleman, in connection with his pupils, among whom was Mr. Marshman, completed the translation of all the Gospels into that tongue.

The Bible was translated into the Chinese language, at great toil and expense, by Dr. Marshman, the elder pupil of Professor Lassar, in 1819, since which time the British and Foreign and American Bible Societies have labored assiduously to promote the circulation of the Scriptures in that country.

A communication to the Board of the American Bible Society from Dr. Morrison, at Canton, in 1822, states that the free dissemination of the Bible in China proper was impracticable, and the same was the case with all books that exhibited the claims of Jesus and treated of his salvation.

In 1823, the whole Bible was printed in Chinese, from a translation by Drs. Morrison and Milne, thousands of copies of which were put in circulation.

Nothing more occurs in the reports until the year 1832, when the board received a communication from the Rev. Mr. Bridgman, at Canton, containing a strong appeal for means to prepare and circulate the Chinese Scriptures. He states that, since the translation of the Bible in that language, changes that caused joy in heaven had taken place. Two editions of Bibles, three of the New Testament, and four of the Psalms had been printed and put in circulation, to the number of between twelve and fifteen thousand.

Another fact, he says, which gives them a strong claim to the attention of the society is, "that they are a reading people. In this respect they are probably superior to any pagan nation of ancient or modern times. Buddhism, with all its absurdities, has worked its way into every nook and corner of the empire, through all the grades of society, by means of books, without the aid of teachers. Give the Chinese the Bible, and at once a very large proportion of the population can read it. Thousands are now accessible, and would willingly receive the bread of life. There is no one language on earth in which the Bible, were it universally distributed, could be read by so many millions as in the Chinese language. Take a survey of the field. From Canton pass up through Formosa, Loo Choo on to Corea, thence pass westward along the Russian frontiers for more than two thousand miles to the center of Asia, from thence, in a south-eastern direction, travel down through Thibet, Siam, Penang, Malacca, across the equator on to Java, and by a circuitous route, including the numerous islands in the Indian Archipelago, return to the place of your departure, and you will have included in the vast area *one third part of the human family*. Though there are different languages and dialects within these limits, yet throughout the whole extent, the Bible, if possessed in the Chinese language, can be read. With such a territory, and such a waiting and reading population, we feel impelled and encouraged to ask for the prayers and charities of the American Bible Society."

Although the walls of the "Celestial Empire" remained impervious to the distributer of the Bible, yet the intelligence received through the labors of that indefatigable philanthropist, Gutzlaff, whose tours extended along the eastern and northern parts of China, encouraged the hope that at no distant day the Bible would enter and have free course within the walls of that vast empire.

In Siam and along the southern borders of China the people are accessible. Four hundred and forty thousand Siamese were represented as being ready for the Bible in 1833.

The board made an appropriation of three thousand dollars for the circulation of the Bible in China.

In 1843, a letter from the mission established in Canton, after expressing thankfulness to the board for its grant, and also a hope that it will be succeeded by others, states that Leang Afa, a distinguished Christian convert, was in that city distributing portions of the Scripture to the inhabitants, but more particularly among the students and literati.

Mr. Gutzlaff, while in Corea, presented the king with twenty-one volumes of the Scriptures, which were accepted. In visiting the province of Cheteang and the Chusa Islands, he writes, "All that I had formerly seen was nothing compared with the ardent desire evinced by the natives to obtain books. Had I fifty thousand copies of the Scriptures, they would all have been scattered among eager readers."

From Fokin province, four hundred miles interior from Canton, he writes, "Here is a wide door opened. I have traversed large tracts of country with boxes of books, and had only to regret that I had not the pleasure of distributing them, for the people robbed me of every volume, such was the eagerness with which they seized upon them. There is a great error abroad concerning China, in a spiritual point of view. No country of Asia, ruled by native princes, is so easy of access. I am now writing a work against the three prevailing superstitions of China, and hope to follow this by an essay on the Trinity." He states it as his confident opinion that China would be visited with the glorious Gospel. He says, in conclusion, "My whole heart is set upon the work. If the Savior grants me grace, I shall labor to the last, and my last breath be a prayer in behalf of China's salvation."

In 1835, another communication was received from the Rev. Mr. Bridgman, missionary at Canton. Among other things, he says, "It is impossible for those who have not given particular attention to the condition and situation of these Eastern nations to believe that the Chinese Empire contains three hundred and sixty millions of human beings, or that those who can *read* the Scriptures in the Chinese language constitute more than one third of our race.

"The principal part of your grant will be employed in printing the Chinese Bible at Malacca. Many copies will be needed for immediate circulation, and should a missionary ship be sent out to visit the coast and the Chinese settlements, many thousand copies will at once be required, and perhaps, very soon, many millions."

A letter from the evangelist Leang Afa, giving an account of his conversion, his punishment by government for printing portions of the Scriptures from blocks prepared by himself, the instructions he received from Dr. Milne at the Anglo-Chinese College at Malacca, and closing by an appeal to the society for aid in printing the Chinese Bible, that he might circulate it among his countrymen, was received by the board.

A letter from the Rev. Charles Gutzlaff, in regard to Bible distribution, says, "If only the one hundredth Chinaman was to get a Bible from you, a ten-year's income would not be sufficient to defray the expenses. Pray to the Lord that he will not only open an effectual door to all the maritime provinces, but also to the whole empire. I inform you that all the parts of Scripture which were sent to my care were distributed to eager readers at Formosa and in Fokin. A total revision of the whole Chinese Scripture is a matter of urgent necessity; and we have therefore set to work to furnish a new edition in order to answer the wants of the people. Every care and attention will be bestowed upon this important undertaking."

The following truthful and beautiful allegory, from the pen of the Rev. Mr. Abeel, represents the utility of the Bible in China:

"He knew but one missionary in whom he could place complete confidence. That missionary he had met in China. He was instructed in the languages, and diligent in exertion; he had made voyages from island to island; he had gone forth unaided and alone; he had entered villages and hamlets; he dared to enter the place of him who was called 'The Son of Heaven,' and had ventured to tell him the true way to heaven. That missionary had done him the honor to be his companion, and such another companion he never expected to find. Where he could not go, that missionary went. He had never left him. In entering regions which had no teacher, he was still his companion. He went among all classes; he abode with him for weeks at a time; he animated all his exertions, and, what was most remarkable, with all his powers, with all his elevation of soul, he became his servant; he entered even the junks, and taught the mariners; he went on, and entered China itself. Surely all will desire to know who he was. He would tell them who he was not. He was not a Churchman nor a Dissenter; he was not a Calvinist nor an Arminian; he was not an American, nor an Englishman, nor a Scotchman, nor a Hollander. He appeared to hate all sects, and many of those who were the most prominent he had never even mentioned. That missionary was THE BIBLE!"

The report of 1836 states that Messrs. Gutzlaff, Bridgman, Medhurst, and Morrison were engaged conjointly in revising the Chinese Scriptures.

The board this year granted one thousand dollars to the Baptist Board of Foreign Missions for the purpose of circulating the Scriptures in China.

To the American Board of Missions, for preparing the Chinese Scriptures, five hundred dollars.

To Messrs. Oliphant and associates at Canton, toward transporting and distributing the same in China, one thousand dollars.

To the Protestant Episcopal Board of Missions, for Chinese Scriptures, five hundred dollars.

To the American Board of Foreign Missions, for Chinese Scriptures, four thousand dollars.

To the same, for the Chinese, Malay, Siamese, and Bugis Scriptures, seven thousand five hundred dollars.

In 1838, the Rev. Mr. Gutzlaff communicated to the board information of the preparation, under his supervision, of the New Testament in Japanese. He had in his family two natives of Japan, one of whom was wholly devoted to the prosecution of the work. The board, on request, paid for the services of this translator seventy-two dollars per year.

The new Chinese version, alluded to in a former report, created a difference of sentiment among the missionaries in regard to its merits. The principal objection was in regard to the retention of the Chinese idiom. This peculiarity rendered it more acceptable to the Chinese than a more literal one. The British and Foreign Bible Society withdrew their patronage from it, and the American Society postponed their decision until further advised.

An interesting letter was received from the Rev. Mr. Rottger, a Dutch missionary at Rio, in relation to his labors in distributing the Bible among the Chinese. He had visited and distributed the Scriptures at Rio, at Banca, and at Palembang in Sumatra. At Muntok, in Banca, he says, "They built a new Chinese temple. I went in with the eternal Gospel in my hand, and gave the workmen some copies. I spoke to them about that one thing which is needful for the salvation of their immortal souls. Immediately the temple was crowded with Chinamen, seeming to be glad of what they heard and read. In this way the Gospel has been preached in this temple before it was ready to act their idolatrous superstition in it."

The prospects for the Bible cause in China, in 1839, were more gloomy than they had been previously. This was attributable to several causes. The doubts entertained in regard to the propriety of circulating the new version—the cutting off the communication with the remote provinces, where most of the distributions had previously been made, except by vessels engaged in the illicit and ruinous opium trade, embarkation in which, by religious men, would have been as questionable as the taking a passage in a slaver—these combined, served to produce despondency in the minds of the friends of the cause at home and abroad. Incipient measures were taken, however, to remedy the last-named difficulty, by procuring and sending to Canton a small vessel for the purpose of transporting the Bible and its distributer.

A communication from Mr. Gutzlaff in relation to distributions at Macao was more encouraging.

In the environs of that place he visited thirty villages, several hundred national vessels, and distributed about two hundred volumes of Testaments.

1840. The disturbed relation between the Chinese and foreigners was of such a nature as to preclude almost entirely the circulation of the Scriptures.

In consequence of the difficulty connected with the circulation of the versions of the Chinese Scriptures, to which allusion has already been made, the first translation, by Dr. Morrison, being too literal and simple in style to suit the Chinese, especially the educated portion, and the latter, though popular with that class, yet exceptionable to the missionaries and the British and Foreign Bible Society on account of its figurative and paraphrastic character—in 1843, the missionaries of Europe and America, of all denominations except the papal, undertook to prepare a version retaining all the good features, without the defects of the two previous translations.

The meeting of the above-named missionaries was held at Hong Kong.

Present, Messrs. Dyer, Hobson, Legge, Medhurst, Milne, and A. and J. Stronach, of the London Missionary Society; Messrs. Bridgman and Ball, of the American Board of Commissioners for Foreign Missions; Messrs. Dean and Roberts, of the American Baptist Board; and Mr. Brown, of the Morrison Education Society.

The present state of the Chinese version was fully discussed, and the following resolution was passed unanimously:

"*Resolved*, That it is desirable to have a version of the Sacred Scriptures translated into the Chinese language, better adapted for general circulation than any hitherto published. In regard to the New Testament, while the meeting readily acknowledge the superiority of the latest over every former version, they would recommend that all that has been done be submitted to a committee for the purpose of being thoroughly revised, and that the same committee be instructed to prepare a version of the Old Testament in conformity with the above revised version of the New Testament."

At an adjourned meeting, held subsequently, present as before, with the exception of Messrs. Dean and Roberts, of the Baptist Board, whose places were supplied by Messrs. Shuck and Macgowan, it was

Resolved, That any translation of the Scriptures into Chinese, issued with the approbation of the body of Protestant missionaries, be in exact conformity to the Hebrew and Greek originals in sense, and, so far as the idiom of the Chinese language will allow, in style and manner also.

Resolved, That the Textus Receptus shall form the basis of the proposed revised version.

Resolved, That the amounts of weights, measures, and pieces of money being ascertained, the same be translated by corresponding terms in Chinese.

At the third meeting, present as before, it was resolved,

"That the passages occurring in different places, but expressed in the same way in the original, be translated in a uniform manner, and that the spirit of this resolution be applied as far as possible in the case of individual terms. That no periphrasis be substituted for the possessive pronoun when used in connection with the name of God.

"That the interchange of the noun and pronoun be allowed when deemed necessary by the translators.

"That euphemisms in the originals be rendered by corresponding euphemisms in Chinese."

At the fourth meeting, the same members present, it was

"*Resolved*, That the subject of rendering the word βαπτιζω and its derivatives into Chinese be referred to a committee consisting of Messrs. Bridgman and Dean.

"That the rendering of the names of the Deity into Chinese be referred to a committee consisting of Messrs. Medhurst and Legge.

"That the rendering of Scripture names generally be referred to a committee consisting of Messrs. Medhurst and Milne, with the assistance of Mr. J. R. Morrison, and that in the arrangement of sounds uniformity and brevity be studied.

"That the whole body of Protestant missionaries to the Chinese form a general committee for the purpose of revising the translation of the Scriptures in the Chinese language, and that this committee be subdivided into local committees of stations, each to consist of all the missionaries at that station—that the work of revision be subdivided and apportioned to the several stations. That when each local committee has completed its task, a transcript thereof shall be sent to each station for further revision, and then these transcripts, with the corrections upon them, shall be submitted to the original revisers. When the whole of the New Testament shall have been thus revised, each station shall select one or more of its most experienced men to act as delegates in a meeting of the general committee, it being understood that each station will be entitled to one vote only, and these shall be the final judges as to the propriety of each revision, after which the whole shall be submitted to the Bible societies in Great Britain and America for their acceptance."

At the fifth meeting of the committee, same as before present, with the addition of W. C. Lowrie, of the American Board of Foreign Missions, it was

"*Resolved*, That Mr. Medhurst be requested to act as secretary to the general committee.

"That the Bible societies in England and America be requested to reimburse any reasonable expenditure which may be incurred by the brethren in making the revision.

"That no portion of this revision shall be printed until finally revised by the committee of delegates, and not then, at the expense of the British and Foreign and American Bible Societies, until approved by them.

"That the work of revision be divided into five portions, as follows:

"1st. Acts and Hebrews to 2d Peter.

"2d. Mark and 1st and 2d Corinthians.

"3d. Matthew and Philippians to Philemon.

"4th. Luke, Romans, Galatians, and Ephesians.

"5th. John, Epistles of John, Jude, and Revelation."

At the sixth meeting, the committee appointed to report upon the proper mode of rendering the word βαπτιζω stated that "they were not prepared to recommend any one term to express it so as to harmonize the views of the Baptists and Pædo-Baptists," and hence the meeting resolved

"That we proceed harmoniously in the work of revision, employing the talents of missionaries of both these sections of the Church to conduct it and to bring it to as perfect a state as possible; that, when this is done, should difficulties still exist on this subject, each section shall be at liberty to recommend for publication separate editions of the same version, agreeing in all other respects, and only differing as to the rendering of this term; and that the revision go forth to the world, not as the work of one party or of the other, but as the result of the combined efforts of the whole."

At the seventh and last meeting it was

"*Resolved*, That as it is difficult to decide upon the most appropriate word for expressing the name of God in Chinese, each station may for the present use such word as it shall prefer, leaving the ultimate decision to the general committee.

"*Resolved*, That the above resolutions be printed, and that authenticated copies, signed by the chairman and secretary, be sent to the Bible and missionary societies of England and America."

In the report of 1846, the intelligence was communicated that Chinese youth at Hong Kong were learning the English language, and the board made a grant during the year of English Bibles for the use of schools in that place.

Of the thousands of youth receiving Christian instruction, many are just emerging into manhood, and are themselves becoming teachers to their benighted countrymen. This state of things encourages the fond hope that the day is not far distant when the millions of that long-lost empire will be saved by the power of the Gospel of Christ, in the onward march of which pagan temples, and altars, and idol gods shall fade away as mist from the mountains when the sun breaks across the threshold of the Eastern world.

In 1847, the board made an appropriation of ten thousand dollars toward procuring and circulating, by the American missionaries, the new version of the Scriptures about to be issued in China. This appropriation will be paid in instalments, from time to time, as it is needed by the missionaries.

The British and Foreign Bible Society granted to the London Missionary Society one thousand pounds, for the purchase of a cylinder press for printing the new version.

The time for realizing those things spoken of by Dr. Milne just before his death has already come to China. When asked by a friend, "What are you doing in China?" he replied, "I have to tell you we are here standing and knocking at the gates of China, calling upon the emperor, in the name of the Lord Jesus Christ, to open the gates of his empire for the admission of the Gospel. To the above summons, the emperor's reply is, 'No! my gates are forever closed against you and your message!' While the emperor is setting at defiance the mandates of our divine Master, the Prince of the kings of the earth, who shutteth and no man openeth, and who openeth and no man shutteth, and who has the keys of the gates of the nations of the earth at his girdle, is calling upon us to go on with our work—to continue knocking; and if the Emperor of China will not open his gates, he says, 'I have a Key that will open them!'"

Those gates are now open; the Bible and missionary have free access to the population within these hitherto impassable walls. The attention of almost every denomination in the Christian world is now turned to China; and the sixty missionaries on the ground, mastering its language and laboring for its salvation, will receive re-enforcements from year to year, until that whole vast empire shall see the salvation of God.

CHAPTER XXVII.

BIBLE IN INDIA AND INDO-CHINESE COUNTRIES.

THE ancient history of Hindostan, or India, according to the native annals, goes back to a very remote antiquity, like that of China, and is equally absurd. The country was not known to Europe until the time of Alexander the Great.

It contains one million one hundred thousand square miles of territory, and a population of one hundred and thirty millions. Of these about fifty thousand are of European descent.

The Portuguese, Dutch, Spanish, French, and British all have possessions in this country of greater or less extent.

As a missionary field, it was among the number of the "nations from afar" that was visited when the apostles were "scattered abroad, and went every where preaching the Word."

When the Portuguese visited this country in the sixteenth century, they discovered certain traditions, and the existence of some monuments, that the Apostle "Thomas, one of the Twelve," had preached there; and it was asserted that he was murdered by some

Brahmins, who feared that his labors might eventually prove subversive of their idolatrous superstitions. This martyrdom took place at Malabar, on the coast of Coromandel. He was carried to Edessa, and there buried. This, if true, presents in a striking light the estimation in which that apostle held the commission of his Lord, to "go into *all* the world, and preach the Gospel to *every* creature." It is also a living comment and testimony both of the nature and extent of that commission.

But India is interesting to the philosopher as well as the Christian. Dr. Henry, in his "History of Philosophy," speaking of the origin of science, conveys the idea that, of all the nations of pagan antiquity, the philosophical conceptions of none appear to ascend an epoch so near the deluge as that of India, or to have risen to speculations so lofty, and infers therefrom that they were enlightened with the primitive theology handed down to them by oral tradition from the primeval world.

Of China, Persia, and Egypt, he says, "They form, as it were, the three angles of a luminous triangle, within which the Oriental genius exerts its activity, and of which Chaldea and India occupy nearly the middle. Neither of these angles, in the actual state of our historical knowledge of the Oriental mind, presents any traces of a philosophical development on a large scale.

"To find this, we must go to *India*. This magnificent country, which extends through every degree of temperature, from the icy summits of the Himalaya to the burning seas of the Polynesia, has been the scene of a vast and long-continued philosophical conflict, of which some monuments have already passed into the domain of European science."

But we must not dwell upon speculations of this

character, however interesting they may be. Our business relates to *facts* in regard to the religious condition of India; and in the narration of these facts, it will be seen that, whatever may be said of its primitive theology or philosophy, they neither "know the true God nor Jesus Christ whom he has sent," and that if they ever did, "they glorified him not as God, but their foolish hearts became darkened, and they changed the glory of the incorruptible God into images, made like to corruptible man, and to birds, and four-footed beasts, and creeping things, and changed the truth of God into a lie, and abandoned themselves to lust, rage, revenge, polygamy, incest, and bestiality." Thus it is, and thus it ever has been, and will be, with all the philosophy of the world that has no God in it to purify its principles and direct its tendencies.

Chin-India, or Indo China, as it is called, instead of Farther India, or India beyond the Ganges, lies between China on the north and east, and Hindostan or India proper on the west. Its southern coast is washed by the China Sea and the waters of the Straits of Malacca. It comprises Birmah, Cochin China, Tonquin, Pegu, Cambodia, Laos, Siam, and the peninsula of Malacca. This interesting country once belonged to the Chinese, and the inhabitants in many important features resemble the Chinese.

We had thought of assigning to this a separate article; but as there is such an identity of language and manners among the people, and the operations of the Bible and missionary societies, with those of China and India proper, we concluded to embrace these operations under one head. In this portion of the Bible field there are some interesting points. Here is Birmah, where our Baptist brethren have been so long and faithfully laboring, the very name of which awakens a thousand hallowed associations in the minds of all who love the cause of Christ. Here, too, is Malacca, the Ophir of the Old Testament, whose wedges of gold enriched and beautified the Temple of God at Jerusalem, and whose principal sea-port contains the ashes of the lamented *Milne*, who, with the lamented *Morrison*, of China, labored with such untiring industry to open up the treasures of God's Word to four hundred millions of our race. Here, in the city of Malacca, with its forty thousand inhabitants, was established the Anglo-Chinese college for the education of youth in the English language, and also of missionaries in the language and literature of China.

Having made these preliminary remarks, we shall proceed to direct the reader's attention to the introduction of the Bible among these sin-ruined millions.

The College of Fort William, at Bengal, called the Anglo-Hindoo College, was founded in 1800. During the first seven years of its existence it translated the Scriptures into five languages, and produced one hundred volumes in Oriental literature.

The first Protestant mission in India was founded by Ziegenbalg, at Tranquebar, a man of erudition and piety from the University of Halle. In 1719 he finished the translation of the Bible in the Tamul tongue, having devoted fourteen years to that work.

At Calcutta and Serampore, Bible societies were instituted in 1811, at Bombay in 1813, and at Madras in 1820. These institutions have been engaged zealously, efficiently, and perseveringly in translating, printing, and circulating the Scriptures in the various languages of India.

In a report of the former of these societies in 1821, the secretary uses the following language: "Fearing lest even the sacred Scriptures might, by a profuse and inconsiderate distribution, be unprofitably consumed, I thought it expedient to warn our fellow-laborer, Mr.

Bowley, of the danger there was of throwing away our precious stores, and coming to an end of our editions before the time. His answer was, 'Permit me to beg you to picture yourself in the midst of an annual Hindoo fair, as I was the other day at Mirzapore, surrounded by forty thousand people, pent up literally so closely as to be unable to move by reason of the pressure of those heathens, soliciting for the words of eternal life, which were translated, printed, and sent you purposely for distribution among them—could you have refused those who could read and were importunate with you for them?'"

In 1822, the following communication to the Managers of the American Bible Society from Drs. Carey and Marshman, was received:

"*Dear Brethren in Christ:* Aware of the liberal principles on which your society is founded, and that it is by no means your wish to confine your endeavors to disseminate the sacred Scriptures to America alone, but, as much as in you lieth, to assist in giving them to the whole family of man, we make the following appeal: The circumstances under which the work was begun by our elder brother, Dr. Carey, twenty-six years ago, are not altogether unknown to you, nor the endeavors made by us as a united body, for nearly twenty years past, to give the Scriptures, in the various languages of India, as far as the Lord might enable us. In the accompanying memoir, you will perceive that the whole of the sacred Scriptures have been published in *five* of the languages of India; the New Testament and certain parts of the Old in *ten* more; and in *six* more the New Testament is brought more than half through the press; in the remaining *ten* some one of the Gospels is printed, and in several all four of the Gospels.

"The expense which has attended this work has

been defrayed by the liberality of the public in Britain and America, among whom we feel eminently indebted to the generosity of the British and Foreign Bible Society. For the expense of printing the Old Testament in the few languages wherein it is now going forward, and that of printing further editions of the New Testament now in the press, we are constrained to appeal to the Christian public at large both in Britain and America."

To assist in preparing new editions of the Scriptures in Sanscrit, Bengalee, Hindee, Mahratta, and Orissa, the board granted to the above-named gentlemen the sum of one thousand dollars.

In the Report of the British and Foreign Bible Society for 1828, it is stated that the societies at Madras and Bombay had distributed, since their organization, thirty thousand copies of Bibles and Testaments in thirty of the tongues of India, among which were the Anglo-Chinese, the Tamul, Goojurattu, Cingalese, and Pali languages, the latter of which is the language of the literati of the Burman Empire. At Singapore, Malacca, the Bible was distributed among the Chinese junks in the harbor.

In 1829, the board granted one thousand two hundred dollars toward printing Judson's translation of the New Testament in the Burman language.

The publication of the Scriptures in this language opened up the word of life and salvation to a population of seventeen millions in that empire.

In 1832, a communication was received from the American Board of Commissioners for Foreign Missions, presenting the claims of India to the society, and an appropriation was made of five thousand dollars to aid in printing the Mahratta Scriptures at Bombay, and also five thousand dollars toward printing the Scriptures in the Burman tongue.

In relation to the operations of the Bible cause in India in 1833, the managers state that the whole of the New Testament, with the Pentateuch and Psalms of the Old, have been translated into the Mahratta language by the American missionaries. The versions were made from the originals. Most of the copies of the Book of Genesis and of the New Testament which had been printed were put in circulation. Other versions of parts of the Bible, under the patronage of the Church Missionary Society, were printed at Bombay.

The versions of our missionaries were made to conform to our English version, in being literal and not free translations of the Word of God.

Mr. Graves, one of the missionaries of the American Board, stated, while on a visit to this country, that about one in forty of the Mahratta people were able to read; hence the number of those who could read was not far from four hundred thousand.

In 1834, the board granted to the American missionaries at Bombay, to aid in printing the Mahratta Scriptures, three thousand dollars.

To the mission station in the Burman Empire, for printing the Burman Scriptures, five thousand dollars.

The following extracts from a communication to the board will show the progress made in the work of distribution.

The letter contains the following interesting items: The demand for the Scriptures at Bombay was on the increase. Copies were distributed in Hindoostanee and Persian among the Mussulmans. The Book of Exodus, prepared by Mr. Graves, had been lithographed, mostly at the expense of the board. The demand for these by the Jews was great.

An edition of Leviticus was also in preparation. Mohammedans, Jews, and Mahrattas were all receiving the Word of Life.

The Mahrattas numbered about twelve millions, and to supply them with the Word of God there were only eleven missionaries in the field.

Schools were multiplying in the country, and thousands of youth were yearly sent out into active life who had been taught to read the Bible.

From Birmah cheering intelligence was received of the progress of the work of printing and circulating the Scriptures. The Baptist Board at Maulmein had printed the first edition of three thousand copies of the New Testament in the Burman language, and, so urgent were the demands for them, another edition was contemplated.

A very interesting account of the Rev. Mr. Kincaid's voyage up the Irrawaddy River, from Rangoon to Ava, describes the people as willing every where to read the "Sacred Book."

To the Western Foreign Missionary Society at Pittsburgh, Pennsylvania, there was made a grant, in 1835, of five hundred dollars, to be expended by their missionaries in circulating the Scriptures in Northern India, in the province of Lahore.

For the circulation of the Scriptures among the Baptist missions in the Burman Empire, a grant of seven thousand dollars was made during the year.

The Secretary of the Baptist Board stated that, in addition to the printing of the New Testament, the Old Testament would soon be in a course of publication.

They had it in contemplation to send out a fifth press, that copies of the Bible might more rapidly be multiplied.

In the year 1836, a box of Bibles and Testaments was sent, through Mr. Medhurst, to Singapore, for distribution among the seamen, vast numbers of whom, from almost all countries, visit this port.

During the year the following appropriations were made:

To the Baptist Board of Foreign Missions, for circulating the Orissa Scriptures in India, by the Rev. Mr. Sutton and associates, one thousand dollars.

To the same for Burmese Scriptures, five thousand dollars.

To the Western Foreign Missionary Society, toward circulating the Scriptures in Northern India, one thousand dollars.

To the American Board of Commissioners for Foreign Missions, for Siamese and other Scriptures in Siam, two thousand dollars.

To the same for Malay, Siamese, and other Scriptures at Singapore, seven thousand five hundred dollars.

To the same for Mongolian Scriptures, one thousand two hundred dollars.

From the Rev. Amos Sutton and his associates, Baptist missionaries at Orissa, to whom a grant had been made, the board received the following communication in 1837:

"I need not tell you how much the life-giving Word is needed in this land of darkness and the shadow of death. I have just returned from the annual festival of Juggernaut, distant from Cuttuck about fifty miles, and, though it was the thinnest attendance of any festival I have seen of a similar kind, yet there was probably not less than one hundred thousand immortal beings prostrated before that bloody Moloch. But we had not a single Gospel to bestow upon them—nothing of the Scriptures but a few bound Testaments, and a collection of certain passages from the whole Bible printed as extracts. I labored hard to get an edition of Matthew printed off in time, but was prevented by sickness and loss of types from accomplishing it. I leave it with your committee to determine, when looking over the waste places of the earth, if Orissa does not demand their sympathy and aid."

In 1838, the board received from the Rev. Messrs. Scudder and Winslow, missionaries at Madras, in relation to the preparation and circulation of the Scriptures in the Tamul language, the following: "Do you ask as to the probable number of families in the district, whose language we speak, in which the Word of God can be read? We answer, five hundred thousand. Will the American Bible Society not come to the resolution that they will supply these thousands of families in the Tamul district who can read with at least a New Testament or single Gospel? We say nothing of those who speak the Zeloogoo language, whose wants are even greater than those of the Tamul people. We are now pursuing the study of their language, and hope soon to be able to communicate with them through it. The Madras mission was commenced with the expectation of having a large printing establishment connected with it, and something like an agency for the American Bible Society, to afford them the means of furnishing, to some extent, the Tamul and Zeloogoo population of this peninsula with the Word of Life. Can not you give us twenty, ten, or five thousand dollars a year for Southern India?"

In 1839, a correspondent of the board communicates the intelligence that during the year the Mahratta Scriptures entire would be brought into that language.

At Madras, a communication from one of the missionaries there states that, "as to the inhabitants being converted through the instrumentality of the oral Word, it is quite out of the question. They can not be reached in any great numbers in this way, for there are not men to do it. In all the tours I have taken since I came to Madras, I have not found a single missionary. It appears to me that the American Bible

Society, in conjunction with the British and Foreign Bible Society, can supply all the calls made by those who can and will distribute. I shall soon leave Madras with fourteen thousand portions of the Scriptures, and shall be absent about two months in distributing them."

To meet the above call, in part, the board appropriated four thousand dollars.

The prospects for Bible distribution in Madras, in 1840, were quite encouraging. A communication made to the board during the year states that "the land, in its length and breadth, is open for the distribution of the Bible. Viewed in all its bearings, there is no place in any part of the world, embracing a population of seventy-five millions, which affords greater facilities for the distribution of the Word than India. The government is favorable, and there is no place to which we go with this precious volume where the people do not come in crowds to obtain it.

"Exclusive of our distributions in the city, we have given away on our tours, in little more than a year, twenty-five thousand portions of the Bible. The Madras Bible Society have asked of the British and Foreign Bible Society five thousand pounds a year. We have asked, and still ask of your board, twenty thousand dollars a year to begin with."

A further request was made in the course of the year from the Madura mission, which received supplies through the mission at Madras.

At Madura it is customary for the people to hold bazars or fairs regularly, in different places, within a circumference of twenty miles, on every day of the week. This is common throughout the district. These bazars are visited by distributers, and the number of copies of the Scriptures circulated by them is very large.

In 1841, for purchasing Scriptures printed at Madras, for distribution at Madura, and employing native converts to distribute them, the board sent two thousand dollars.

For the station at Madras was granted, during the year, six thousand dollars.

A communication from a gentleman at Bombay states that the population of that city is over three hundred thousand, among which are many Jews, Persians, and other nations, and as each retains its original language, the prejudice of caste tends to perpetuate them, by preventing social intercourse.

The Mahratta language is more generally used than any other, and, though the Bombay Bible Society, which is auxiliary to the British and Foreign, possesses the Scriptures in the Hebrew and Parsee, yet the obstacles in the way of their circulation are great, and somewhat difficult to be overcome. The Jews, however, will take the Old Testament, and sometimes the New, and read them. The Goojurattee is used by a large body of the inhabitants, and to this class the Parsees belong, who follow the religion of Zoroaster. The priests of this faith made preparation for printing a translation of Paine's Age of Reason, for the purpose of overthrowing the Christian religion, some of their followers having embraced it, but it was abandoned. Soon after, a work was published, having the same ostensible purpose, entitled "The Doctrine of Zoroaster." It was prepared by a Parsee priest, consisting chiefly of extracts from the Scriptures, with sneers and caviling remarks thereon, and selections from Voltaire.

The great extension of British power acquired by the government in countries lying between India and Persia opened up new and large provinces for the circulation of the Scriptures.

In 1842, the board granted a supply of Bibles and

Testaments in the English tongue, for the use of those learning that language at Madras. The demand for these Scriptures in the schools of Madura and Madras, and for East Indians, was represented as very great.

To the mission of the Presbyterian Board for Foreign Missions was granted the sum of two thousand dollars for publishing the Scriptures in Northern India. A letter from the secretary of the board, Walter Lowrie, Esq., shows the importance of this grant:

"Our printing presses in India are now double what they were last year, and the demand for the Scriptures is beyond any thing those presses can supply, even if constantly employed. Whatever sum you can spare for this field, we would at once invest in paper, and try to furnish the means for the printing and binding from our own funds. The paper we wish to send by the first ship to Calcutta. Thus I have given you the facts in relation to printing and distributing the Bible in Northern India."

To the Rev. Mr. Sutton, of the Baptist mission at Orissa, was sent one hundred dollars, in part to be used in circulating portions of the Old Testament.

In 1843, to the Board of Missions of the Presbyterian Church, on the request of Walter Lowrie, Esq., were granted four hundred Bibles and Testaments for the use of the government schools in Northern India, and also for those who are learning the English language.

The board authorized the Rev. Mr. Winslow, of Madras, to furnish two hundred dollars worth of Tamul Scriptures to the Rev. Mr. Heyer, a missionary of the Lutheran Church of the United States, resident in India.

To the Presbyterian Board, to aid in the publication of the Scriptures at Lodiana, Northern India, was granted the sum of three thousand dollars.

The board was favored with samples of the Scriptures published at their expense, and were highly satisfied with the manner of their execution.

To the mission station at Madras a grant was made of three thousand dollars, for the preparation and distribution of the Scriptures in the southern part of India.

To the station at Madura, for the same purpose, the board sent five hundred dollars.

In 1844, to Bombay, to aid in the circulation of the Scriptures, were granted one thousand dollars.

A communication from Mr. Hume to the secretary of the Bombay Bible Society, in regard to the work of distribution, contains many interesting facts.

To Hindoos, Mussulmans, and Jews in Bombay the Word of Life is distributed with interesting results, particularly to the Jews, who, though they read with the veil upon their hearts, are yet disposed to inquire after truth.

He had made a tour to Goa, and passed through the whole southern Concan, and, though he expected opposition from the priests, yet the New Testament was eagerly sought by the ecclesiastics, by persons connected with the government, and others. The whole Bible was often asked for, but, as he had none in Portuguese, he could not supply the demand.

In few portions of the heathen world was there so large a proportion of intelligent readers as in the Southern Concan. The Brahminical class was very numerous, and were generally educated.

In Goa the majority speak the Portuguese, and a considerable number a corrupted Mahratta. Goa is the residence of the Roman Catholic archbishop, who has jurisdiction of the Roman Catholics in that part of the world.

Buchanan, in 1808, speaking of Goa, says, "The

magnificence of the churches of Goa far exceeds any idea I had formed from the previous description. Goa is properly a city of churches, and the wealth of provinces seems to have been expended in their erection. The ancient specimens of architecture in this place far excel any thing that has been attempted in modern times in any other part of the East, both in grandeur and taste. The Cathedral of Goa is worthy of one of the principal cities of Europe. In this, mass is celebrated by some twenty or thirty priests, but there are none others present to witness the performance—the priests themselves are the congregation. Soon all the magnificence of Goa will have passed away. The convents, once filled with ecclesiastics, will soon be heaps of ruins; the external pomp and magnificence, the remains of which are still visible, were, doubtless, well fitted to make an impression upon an ignorant people, but the spirit of true Christianity was a stranger here."

Mr. Hume remarks: "While standing on the ruins of the dreadful Inquisition, and surrounded by the fast-decaying monuments of popish power and superstition, I rejoiced that the decay of these things seemed apparently to be preparing the way for the free progress of the Gospel. The fear of the holy Inquisition can not now, as formerly, restrain the people from receiving and perusing the Word of God."

There is much intercourse between Bombay and Goa, which facilitates the distribution of the Bible there.

To the missionaries at Siam, to aid the publication of the Scriptures in that region, the board remitted one thousand dollars. In the Siamese language, the Rev. Mr. Robinson says, that, "in addition to the publication of one edition of Genesis, the Gospel and three epistles of John, the Acts of the Apostles, and the

Epistle to the Colossians, and two editions of the Gospel of St. Mark, the Books of Daniel and Exodus, and all the Gospels, are ready for the press. They had introduced in printing the *division of the words* and the *marks of punctuation*, with which the Siamese are well pleased."

Parts of the Bible were also translated into other Indo-Chinese languages.

To the station at Madras, to be expended, under the direction of the Rev. Mr. Winslow, in circulating the Tamul and Zeloogoo Scriptures, and also to the station at Madura, were granted, to the former one thousand, and to the latter five hundred dollars.

In 1847, for printing and circulating the Mahratta Scriptures, one thousand dollars were granted to the American Board of Foreign Missions.

For publishing the same in Northern India, under the care of the Presbyterian Board of Foreign Missions, a grant of five thousand dollars was made.

For the further publication of the Scriptures at Madras, the same board was granted two thousand dollars.

A still further grant of one thousand dollars was solicited, so urgent were the appeals for the Scriptures among the millions of India.

We shall close our article by an extract from a communication to the board in relation to the condition of the inhabitants of the cities of India: "In Bombay, as in most of the cities of India, where many persons are acquiring a knowledge of the English language and of European literature, there is much skepticism in respect to religion of every kind. This class of persons practice their own religious rites and ceremonies just enough to keep themselves within the rules of caste. Their feelings are those of indifference toward those systems of religion which allow every man to live much as he pleases, or which teach that every man should continue in the religion in which he was born, and then all will be well with him in the future world. They *hate* Christianity because of its exclusive and aggressive character, which requires all, whoever they may be, and whatever may have been their faith and practice, to receive its doctrines and obey its precepts. The native papers and magazines, of which there are several in Bombay, contain much that is aimed directly or indirectly, according as they think it will produce the greatest effect, against the Scriptures. The editors of such papers are generally well acquainted with the works of infidel authors which have been published in Christian countries. They have sometimes been at much expense to procure such books from Europe. Probably no English works are read more among the native population than those of this character."

Thus it will be seen that the enemy is also in possession of that mighty engine for good or ill, the press, and is perverting it in diffusing an infidel theology and a corrupt literature.

The board received very recently a complete copy of the Koran in the Arabic tongue, the first ever printed in India. Several zealous Mohammedans, provoked by the efforts of the Bible Society in furnishing the Holy Scriptures for those followers of the false prophet who were willing to receive and read them, and fearing that the Koran would become a dead letter, and Islamism lose its power over them, organized a Koran Society, for the purpose of printing, for gratuitous circulation, the Bible of Mohammed among the sixty thousand Mohammedans of Bombay, and for those of Arabia and Persia. So mightily does the Word of God grow and prevail, that old exploded systems of error, like galvanized dead bodies, begin to writhe and show signs of life. It is only, however, that they may relapse again into that sleep from whence there will be no awaking, for the "Word has gone forth, and it shall not return void," but prove "the power of God unto salvation to every one that believeth."

CHAPTER XXVIII.

BIBLE IN CEYLON.

The island of Ceylon lies near the equator in the Indian Ocean. It contains near twenty thousand square miles, and has a population of two millions. It was taken possession of by the Portuguese in the sixteenth century, who were subsequently displaced by the Dutch, and they, in turn, by the British, to whom it was formally ceded in 1795. The native inhabitants are divided into Weddas, a rude people living in the interior of the forests, and the Cingalese, who had attained a certain degree of civilization. The Cingalese are divided, like the Hindoos, into castes, and are of the religion of Buddha.

Efforts to convert it to Christianity were early made by the different religious denominations, and if St. Jerome is to be believed, Ceylon, like Hither India, has been made sacred by the visit of one of the twelve apostles of our Lord.

It is not our work to treat of it as a missionary field only so far as the missionary cause is identified with that of the Bible, and we confess, in the language of one, "All other means for saving sinners, compared with the circulation of the Bible, are like stars and moons deriving all their light from this."

In this connection, we ask the indulgence of the reader while we give a few items of historical information in regard to the introduction of Christianity in the island.

It is said that Francis Xavier, a Roman Catholic priest, visited the island and preached with some success. Whether Romanism were established by him or not in the sixteenth century is a matter of speculation, but that Romanism was there when the first Protestant missionaries visited it is beyond question, unless, perhaps, we except the Dutch, who, at the commencement of the seventeenth century, wrested the island from the crown of Portugal, and attempted to convert the natives to the Protestant faith. Unfortunately, however, they induced the Cingalese to become hypocrites rather than Christians, by absurdly ordaining that no native should be admitted to any employment under the government unless he subscribed the Helvetic Confession and became a member of the Reformed Church. All who aspired after dignity or office professed their readiness to change their religion; and as nothing more was required of the candidates for baptism than a repetition of the Lord's Prayer, the Ten Commandments, a short morning and evening prayer, and a grace before and after meat, they flocked in such numbers to the font, that in the year 1663, in the district of Jaffnapatam alone, there were, according to the Church registers, sixty-two thousand five hundred and fifty-eight men and women who professed Christianity, besides two thousand five hundred and eighty-seven slaves; and the children who had been baptized within a few years amounted to twelve thousand three hundred and eighty-seven.

In the year 1740, the Moravians sent two missionaries to Ceylon. On their arrival at Colombo they were received by the governor with great kindness, and every facility afforded them for prosecuting the objects of their mission. Shortly after, however, another governor succeeded "who knew not Joseph," and, on account of slanders propagated against them, they were ordered from the island. Their labors, though short, were not without fruit; a distinguished surgeon was converted to God through their instrumentality, who was left as a living epistle of the truth of Christianity.

In 1813, the Rev. Dr. Coke, of the Wesleyan Methodist Church in England, whose mind had been long and deeply impressed with the importance of a mission to Ceylon, and who proposed to the Conference to defray all the expenses of the first missionaries, under the sanction and direction of the Conference, set out, with Messrs. Harvard, Clough, Ault, Erskine, Squance, and Lynch, for the island, for the purpose of establishing a mission. It will be recollected that, by an inscrutable Providence, the rationale of which we can not now know, the doctor died on the passage, and was buried in the Indian Ocean. The remainder reached the island in safety, were kindly received by the missionaries and dignitaries of government, and at once entered upon their work, which from time to time has been crowned with success. To them must be awarded the honor of having established the first Sunday school in Ceylon.

In 1815, the Prudential Committee of the American Board of Commissioners for Foreign Missions sent out the following missionaries: the Rev. Messrs. Richards, Warren, Poor, Meigs, and Bardwell. Their voyage was prosperous in every respect. On their arrival at Colombo they were received by the governor and missionaries from England with every expression of respect, and every facility afforded them for the furtherance of the objects of their mission. In the educational department, this mission has perhaps accomplished more than any other denomination. They established a college at Batticotta for the education of pious young natives for the ministry, and to act as teachers in the schools of the island.

The English Baptists have also a mission with two stations, one at Colombo, the capital, and another at Hanwell.

As a *Bible* field, Ceylon presents a rich variety of facts, fruitful and fragrant as her savannas and mountains, and grateful to every lover of the cause of Christ.

A Bible Society was instituted at Colombo, auxiliary to the British and Foreign Bible Society, in 1812.

At Jaffna, also, a Bible Society was organized during the same year.

The first notice we have of this field, in connection with the operations of the American Bible Society, is found in the Report of 1823, when the board made a donation of five hundred dollars to the Board of Commissioners for Foreign Missions in the island of Ceylon, to be employed by them in purchasing Scriptures in the Tamul language for distribution.

About this time the Old Testament, under the direction of the Colombo Bible Society, was translated into the Cingalese language, assisted by missionaries of the Episcopal, Baptist, and Methodist Churches.

The memorial of the missionaries represented the Tamul language as spoken by the inhabitants of the northern part of the island, from Batticaloe to Jaffnapatan. It was supposed that three hundred thousand spoke that language in the island. The Scriptures having already been translated into that language by Danish missionaries in 1715, and since then eight or ten editions having been published, they could readily be procured by the missionaries at Tranquebar and Colombo.

In 1829, a communication was received from American missionaries at Ceylon, representing the great demand for the Scriptures, and the great facilities possessed by them for their distribution, and asking for more aid, which was responded to by sending a donation of five hundred dollars more.

In 1831, to the same missionaries were sent the sum of six hundred dollars, to aid in the work of printing and distributing the Tamul Scriptures.

In 1833, to the same mission was sent one hundred English Bibles for the use of pupils in the schools at Jaffna.

From the "Prudential Committee" of the American Board for Foreign Missions the managers received a communication in relation to the facilities and prospects for circulating the Scriptures. In regard to Jaffna station, they say the mission is established in the center of a population of two hundred thousand who speak the Tamul language, and near the Coromandel coast, where the same tongue is spoken by eight or nine millions. They propose sending out a printing establishment for the purpose of printing the Scriptures on the island. The demands for the Scriptures were such that they ought to have at least ten thousand copies of the New Testament for immediate circulation.

A grant of two thousand dollars was made by the board to the missionaries above named to assist them in the work of supplying the destitute with the Scriptures.

Letters were received from the missionaries in 1835, asking for printing paper, or means to procure it, for the purpose of publishing the Tamul Scriptures.

From one of these communications the following extract is taken:

"There are probably between four and five thousand children under Christian instruction in the schools of the different missionary establishments in the district, a good proportion of whom are able to read. It is important that these schools should be furnished with a supply of the Gospels, not only for the purpose of training the children to read the printed character, but more especially to imbue their tender minds with scriptural truth, with the hope that, by the Divine blessing, they may be preserved from the pernicious and contaminating influence of heathenism under which most of the adult population is so powerfully held. To supply each school with ten books, which can not be considered a great number, would probably require more than a thousand copies. They were also anxious to furnish youth on leaving the schools a portion of Holy Writ." In view of these demands, the board made a grant of six thousand dollars, to enable them to print and circulate the Scriptures in Ceylon.

In 1837, to the American Board was granted two thousand dollars, to aid in distribution.

The following year a supply of Bibles and Testaments were sent for the use of the schools.

Communications were received in 1839 and 1840 for additional aid, by way of Bibles and Testaments, for the use of those learning the English language, and also for money to enable the missionaries to print and circulate the Tamul and Cingalese Scriptures.

The Report of the Jaffna Bible Society for the latter year shows that there had been printed for the society at Manepy five thousand copies of the Book of Genesis and the first twenty chapters of Exodus, fifteen thousand copies of the Psalms, five thousand copies of which had been sold to the American mission on behalf of the American Bible Society. The following portions had been carried through the press: Acts of the Apostles, Proverbs, Epistles of Timothy, James, and John, Genesis, Exodus, and Psalms, making in all seventy thousand copies.

In the year 1841, for preparing the Tamul Scriptures, the board made a grant of four thousand dollars to the American Board of Missions.

Also to the same, the following year, two thousand dollars.

To the Rev. Mr. Johnston, an English Episcopal missionary, was granted five hundred Bibles and Testaments.

In alluding to the Tamul Scriptures, he says, "The copy of Genesis, as revised, has been disseminated through the island, and also through the southern part of India, for the opinions and suggestions of the Tamul writers. We trust in this way to secure as near an approximation to a good translation as may, in this early state of things, be reasonably hoped for; and, above all, we especially hope, by the favor of our Master upon us, to avoid the use of diverse editions of the Holy Scriptures, which in infant churches can not but be hurtful. We desire to give the Tamul people the Word of God pure—*genuine*. The number of persons who can now read English is vastly increased, and the extreme desire felt by *all* persons, whatever the other castes may be, to learn English, is greatly in favor of our missionary operations. But it will be obvious to all, that in the study of the English, as well as any thing else, the Bible should be the text-book. Now we are not able to do this. We have not a copy of the *whole* Bible in our Depository, and cries from Madura and other parts of the island are sounding in our ears for want of them. The grant for which we ask is designed for the mission at Madura as well as that of Jaffna."

The board granted, in 1844, to Ceylon, the sum of three thousand dollars, to aid the missionaries in their work, the American and English cordially co-operating in the Jaffna Bible Society.

In 1846, a supply of English Bibles and Testaments was sent to Ceylon, for the use of the schools in that island connected with the missions. It is an interesting fact, and one full of cheering promise, that thousands upon thousands of heathen youth, in all parts of the pagan world, through the agency of the society, are annually becoming acquainted with the English language through the reading and study of the English Bible.

The following year, so increasing were the demands for the English Scriptures, the board sent five hundred Bibles to the Jaffna Bible Society for the use of native youth; a still larger grant was also received from the British and Foreign Bible Society.

During the year 1848, for publishing a new edition of the Scriptures in the Tamul language, the board sent one thousand dollars.

Through the influence of the Bible and the missionary, this beautiful island has been made to bud and blossom with the fruits of righteousness. Its desert mountains, cinnamon groves, and flowery plains "have been made glad for them." *The word of God has not returned void, but it has accomplished that for which it was sent by its Divine Author.*

CHAPTER XXIX.

BIBLE IN AFRICA.

This immense country, stretching through eighty degrees of longitude, and embracing seventy degrees of latitude, forming a vast triangular peninsula, and containing a population of fifty-seven millions, is in a more wretched and helpless condition than any other country in the world. It was once the seat of the most powerful empire, the center of learning and the arts, and from its shores Egyptian colonies, in the most remote times, carried to savage Europe the germs of civilization. Until recently, Christianity never succeeded in shedding its light upon the west, the center, and the south of Africa. The fanatic Arab, mounted on his fleet dromedary, flew to plant the standard of the false prophet on the banks of the Senegal and the shores of Sofala, and now, from Zanguebar to the Mediterranean, and from the Red Sea to the Desert coast, Mohammedanism holds its sway.

The Bible, and with it Christianity, were introduced into Africa at a very early period in the history of the Christian Church. When the nations of the world were assembled at Jerusalem on the day of Pentecost, Egypt and Abyssinia were represented. The Ethiopian eunuch, an officer of the court of Queen Candace, was there, and, returning in his chariot, reading the prophecy of Isaiah in relation to the sufferings of Christ, was instructed by Philip, who "preached to him Jesus," and, believing on Christ with all his heart, he was converted and baptized, and went to his distant home rejoicing in the salvation of the Gospel. On his return the Abyssinian Church was established, which exists to the present day.

The first translation of the Bible was made into Hebrew-Greek in Egypt in the reign of Ptolemy Philadelphus, from whence it was copied from time to time, and circulated throughout Southern Europe and Western Asia among the synagogues of the Jews, and thus it was the only book that survived the torch of the ruthless Saracen when the Alexandrian library was destroyed. Perhaps it was the only one worthy of preservation. Of one thing we are quite certain, and that is, that the Holy Scriptures are worth all the Alexandrian libraries in the world.

From the Reports of the British and Foreign Bible Society, we have information of the formation of Bible societies in Africa, at Sierra Leone, the Cape of Good Hope, and Abyssinia, as early as 1820. These were all auxiliary to the above-named institution. The Scriptures were translated into the Amharic language for the use of the Abyssinians.

In 1821, the Sierra Leone Bible Society distributed nearly two thousand Gospels in the Bullom and English languages.

In one town among the Hottentots, in South Africa, more than one hundred of this people had been taught to read the Bible. Instances were known of their coming from fifty to one hundred miles to get a copy of the Scriptures.

In 1825, Dr. Philip communicated to the British and Foreign Bible Society some interesting facts in relation to the languages of Africa. The discoveries which had been made led to the belief that all the languages spoken, from Kieskamma to the Arabian Gulf, and from the mouth of the Zembeze to that of Congo, were derived from the parent stock, and so nearly allied to each other that there would be no difficulty in translating the Scriptures for the use of this vast field.

The foundation of a temple, in which all the numerous dialects of the Bootchuana language would be consecrated to the service of the living God, was laid, and the numerous tribes might repair to this temple and receive the light of salvation.

The Bible in Ethiopic, Coptic, and Arabic had been translated by the British and Foreign Bible Society, and thousands of copies were annually distributed at various points.

In 1829, the American Bible Society granted to the colony of Liberia four hundred and fifty Bibles and

Testaments. It had previously sent Bibles to this colony, and several fine copies as presents to neighboring African kings.

Bibles were sent during this year to the island of Madagascar; and in 1833, the Old Testament was translated into the Madagasse, the language of that island, the New having already been issued from the press.

A supply of Bibles and Testaments were sent the following year, through Messrs. Landers, to Central Africa, by the British and Foreign Bible Society.

In 1837, a letter from a Wesleyan missionary at Cape Town communicates the following in relation to the circulation of the Scriptures in the schools of the country: "Our schools at Cape Town, Simon's Town, Wynberg, Hottentot's Holland, Little Namaqua-land, and the Great Namaqua mission beyond the Orange River, have all been supplied. In these various schools there are scholars from six to sixty years of age, persons of almost every color, and of every expression of countenance. What a blessing for them to possess that holy Book, from which they learn that its Author is the Father of the spirits of all flesh! Part of the supply had been sent to the prisons and among the convicts on the public roads; poor widows have also shared the bounty, and other sons and daughters of affliction. Many of the slaves (now apprentices) have received the Testaments with gladness, and several of the colored boys and girls are now reading the words of eternal life."

In 1838, the Rev. Dr. Philip and the Rev. Mr. Read, who had been a missionary in Africa seventeen years, visited London, accompanied by a Christian Caffre chief and a Christian Hottentot.

The following extracts from the addresses of the Caffre and Hottentot will show the importance of Bible distribution among the heathen:

"When the Word of God," said the Caffre, "came among us, we were like the wild beasts; we knew nothing; we were so wild that there was nothing but war and bloodshed. Every one was against his neighbor; there was no confidence between man and man, and each man tried to destroy his brother. The Word of God has turned us; the Bible has brought peace, has reconciled one man to another, and in us is fulfilled the text of Scripture, 'The wolf shall dwell with the lamb.' I thank the English nation for what we have received."

The Hottentot said, "I will not dwell upon what we were before, but I will tell you what the Bible has done for us. There are three gentlemen in this country who are witnesses to what Africans were, Dr. Philip, Mr. Read, and Mr. Campbell. I wish to tell you what the Bible has done for Africa. What would have become of the Hottentot nation, and every black man in South Africa, had you kept the Word of God to yourselves? When you received the Word of God, you thought of other nations who had not that word. When the Bible came among us we were naked, we lived in caves and on the tops of mountains. The Bible made us throw away all our old customs and practices, and we lived among civilized men. We are tame men now. Now we know there is a God; now we know we are accountable creatures before God. Before the Bible came we knew none of these things. We knew nothing about heaven—we knew not who made heaven and earth. The Bible is the only light for every man that dwells on the face of the earth. I thank God in the name of every Hottentot for the Bible. I have gone with the missionaries in taking the Bible to the Bushmen and other nations. When the Word of God was preached, the Bushman threw away his bow and arrows. I have gone with the Bible to the Caffre nation; and when the Bible spoke to the Caffre, he threw away his shield and all his vain customs. I went to Lattakoo, and they threw away all their evil works; they threw away their assagais, and became the children of God. Where the Bible is not, there is nothing but darkness: it is dangerous to travel through such a nation. Where the Bible is not, man does not hesitate to kill his neighbor; he never even repents afterward of having committed murder. I thank you to-day—I do nothing but thank you to-day."

This simple, truthful language is descriptive of heathenism every where, unenlightened by the Bible, and also of the happy results produced by its distribution in all "the dark places of the earth filled with the habitations of cruelty."

In 1840, the board received a communication from the Rev. J. L. Wilson, missionary at Cape Palmas, acquainting them with the fact that the Gospel of Matthew had been translated into the Grebo tongue, and that one thousand copies had been printed. The Acts of the Apostles had also been translated, and would soon be ready for publication. One thousand dollars had already been furnished by the board toward that work.

The next year the board made an additional grant of three hundred and fifty dollars to aid in printing the Gospels under the superintendence of Mr. Wilson.

The auxiliaries of the British and Foreign Bible Society at Sierra Leone, Cape Town, and other places, were engaged in the work of translating, printing, and circulating the Scriptures in the languages of Africa. At Sierra Leone the interest was increasing, and distributions had been made to some good extent among the Jews at Tunis.

In 1846, a Wesleyan missionary from South Africa

writes, "I think, in Caffreland, on the various stations occupied by the London and Glasgow Societies and German missionaries, there are at least five or six thousand who can read the Word of God. Within the last few years, education has progressed with astonishing rapidity. We publish a monthly magazine in Caffre, the articles mainly furnished by natives, and in our stations we have several hundred subscribers (natives). The first edition of the New Testament (or rather part of it, including the four Gospels, Acts, James, John, Peter, and Jude), of one thousand copies, was out of print in a very short time. When I left, in February, 1843, we were printing an edition of five thousand, and there were readers and a demand for every copy as fast as the book could be finished."

In 1848, the board made a grant of two hundred Bibles and Testaments to the American Board of Commissioners for Foreign Missions for missions in Africa.

The society is at present engaged in printing the Gospel of Luke and the Book of Acts in the Grebo language, translated by the Rev. Mr. Payne, an Episcopal missionary in Western Africa. Other portions of the New Testament have been translated by the same gentleman, and the board have entered into engagements to publish them when forwarded to the Bible House.

The Rev. Mr. Moffat, a missionary among the Bechuanas, writes: "We have seen the usefulness of the written Word verified again and again. This was well expressed by one of the native converts, now a leader and witness to the people. He had been placed in trying circumstances, which were well calculated to shake a stronger faith than his. 'But for the New Testament,' said he, 'you would not have found me among the faithful, nor even an inhabitant of a missionary station; and but for the written Word of God,

I should have parted with my faith, and become as a dead man.' This was impressive, especially from one who could say as he did, in his last address or sermon here, before going to occupy a station as native teacher in the far interior. Lifting the Testament from the desk, he asked his countrymen, 'What did we think of this book before we were taught to read? Just the same as those think of it who are yet in that state of darkness and death in which we ourselves once were. We imagined it to be a charm of the white people to keep off sickness, a *thing* only like other things, or that it was a trap to catch us. We never heard of such a thing. Our fathers, who have all died in darkness, could not tell us about it. It was a new thing in our nation, and it was a *seo hèla*, a trifle nobody cared for; but now we not only hear with our ears, and see with our eyes, but we read it to our children, and we teach them to read it too. We can find nothing bad in it. It is all good. *It is a charm*, for it preserves us from the second death in hell. It is a thing, it is true, but it is a thing compared to which all other things are nothing. We thought it was a thing to be spoken *to*, but now we know it has a tongue. It speaks, and will speak to the whole world.'"

What comment more striking than this do we wish of the declarations of the Psalmist, "The law of the Lord is perfect, converting the soul. The testimony of the Lord is sure, making wise the simple."

We remarked, in the beginning of this article, that Africa was the most wretched and helpless of all portions of the heathen world; and yet it would seem that less has been done for her salvation by the friends of missions and the Bible than for any other quarter of the globe. A hundred fold more has been done even for one single island. Why is this? Is it because the field is not white unto harvest? or that the fruits will not repay the laborer's toil? It can not be. Souls are as precious in Africa as in Asia, or Europe, or America. Of all countries under heaven, we owe her the most, for we have wronged her the most. While she imploringly stretches out her hand in the name of her God, let us labor to deliver "*her land from error's chain.*" We feel grateful that the Bible is there—that a Mills and a Cox sleep upon her shores. If the sight of the wild boy in the wood learning his letters be, according to Dr. Chalmers, the most sublime spectacle on earth, what heart can be insensible to the grandeur of those results produced by the introduction of the Bible, the missionary, the teacher, the school, the printing press, and all the blessings of civil and religious liberty.

CHAPTER XXX.

BIBLE IN THE LEVANT.

UNDER this designation we shall embrace all those countries in the East where the society has extended its operations, but more particularly those to which the term specifically applies, such as Greece, Syria, Egypt, Turkey, Persia, Asia Minor, and Arabia.

As we advance in our Biblical researches, the ground over which we tread becomes more and more sacred, and our interest in tracing the flight of the Apocalyptic angel speeding his way to the nations with "the everlasting Gospel" increases as we contemplate his wondrous journey.

When we consider that seven tenths of the world's population have already been startled by the rush of his wings, and enraptured by the melody of his song, we anticipate the day as not far distant when the "glad tidings" of his message shall break the silence of every shore.

Whatever relates to the reintroduction of the Bible into those countries where it was first written and published—where the Divine Author of the Gospel himself lived and labored, suffered and died, must be of thrilling interest to all who love the cause of true religion.

We propose, in our researches, to conduct our readers to the deserts of Arabia, to the ancient sites of the schools of the prophets on the banks of the Jordan, to the sumptuous palaces of Babylon, to the Temple at Jerusalem, to the proud cities of Greece and Rome; and while, with melancholy interest, we gaze upon their ruins in the absence of that divine revelation which once rayed out from these points, we shall direct the attention to the faint light of a returning morn breaking upon their mountains and heralding a coming day.

After the captivity in Babylon, in the days of Ezra, the compiler and publisher of the Scriptures, the Word was read by him and the Levites from an elevated platform to an audience of fifty thousand; and so sacredly did the Jews regard the words of the Law, that as soon as the reader ascended the platform and opened the Book, the whole audience simultaneously rose to their feet.

In the days of the Savior, manuscript copies of the Bible, in the translation of the LXX., at Alexandria, were found in all the synagogues of the Jews, but, like the many monuments of ancient grandeur scattered all over those countries, few traces of the divine Record are to be found.

Since the era of Bible societies, the living Oracles,

like the exiled Jews to whom they were first committed, are returning to their native land. After having dispensed blessings to almost every portion of the Gentile world, the Waters of Life are returning to refill the founts from whence they sprang.

The first notice we have of any regular and systematic efforts to circulate the Bible in those countries which form the subject of this article, were those made by the London Missionary Society in 1811.

That society sent the Rev. Mr. Bloomfield to Malta, in the Mediterranean, as a point from whence he could circulate the Scriptures in those countries bordering upon that sea.

In 1815, the Church Missionary Society, for the promotion of the same object, and as a literary representative, sent the Rev. Mr. Jowett to that island.

In 1820, the American Board of Commissioners for Foreign Missions commenced a mission there, with the design of benefiting the mingled inhabitants of Palestine.

They also sent a printing establishment, with three presses and fonts of type, for printing the English, Italian, Greek, Greco-Turkish, Armenian, Armeno-Turkish, and Arabic.

The selection of Malta as the emporium of Bible and missionary operations for countries bordering on the Mediterranean was the most desirable thing that could have been wished for in the promotion of these benevolent objects.

This island may be regarded as the key by which all the doors in the East could be unlocked. No position could be more commanding. Contiguous to it are the Black Sea and Arabian Gulf, which, in connection with the Mediterranean, in which it is situated, present a line of coast which, if drawn out in length, would encircle one half of the globe.

All the territory adjacent to this boundary line is solid continent, extending thousands of miles. From the greater part of these countries Malta is not more than fifteen days' sail distant. All the surrounding country, and the numerous islands that adorn this vast expanse of waters, are well peopled.

In addition to the societies above named which have selected this favorable spot, we mention the London Jew's Society and the Wesleyan Methodist Missionary Society.

In 1821, measures were adopted by the Malta Bible Society to translate the entire Bible into the modern Greek.

In 1823, the society reports the distribution of the Scriptures in Italian, Greek, Armenian, Syriac, Ethiopic, and the common European versions.

At Aleppo, four hundred and ninety-nine Arabic Testaments, and six hundred and forty Arabic Psalters, were distributed in three days.

The translation of the modern Greek Testament had been accomplished, and measures adopted for its publication. The Testament had been translated into the Albanian language, and was under revision for publication.

An interesting communication was received from the Rev. Pliny Fisk, describing his visits to Smyrna, Teos, Vourla, Scio, Ephesus, and Tenedos, in all which places he left some copies of the Scriptures, which were thankfully received.

In 1824, the society at Malta issued nearly eight thousand copies of the Scriptures, or parts of them, in different languages. They were sent to Alexandria, Cairo, Smyrna, Aleppo, Candia, Cyprus, Algiers, Tunis, Joannina, and other places. The Turkish Bible was completed and in the press.

The Gospels were translated into modern Armenian.

Thirteen hundred Bibles and Testaments had been sent to Constantinople, Syria, and Armenia.

In 1825, the report of that society states that the light of divine Truth was shining upon the darkness of Egypt. The Coptic Church had lifted up its voice in favor of the Bible Society, and its priests were urging the people to purchase the Word of God. The patriarch and bishops also called upon the Bible Society for help.

To Palestine were sent Scriptures in the Arabic, Armenian, French, Hebrew, English, Italian, Greek, Ethiopic, Syrian, and Slavonian languages.

The British and Foreign Bible Society had sent the Gospels in the Amharic language to Abyssinia. Distributions were also effected through the Ionian Bible Society.

In 1826, the Malta Bible Society issued upward of ten thousand copies of the Scriptures in fifteen different languages.

The Ionian Bible Society had sent thousands of copies to the suffering Greeks, many of whom were seen reading the sacred page while encamped and in expectation of the enemy.

In Turkey, the firman of the grand seignior, prohibiting the circulation of the Bible, proved an extensive publication of the fact of their existence, and excited many to procure the prohibited books.

From the depositories at Smyrna, Aleppo, and Constantinople, four thousand copies, in the Arabic, Syriac, Turkish, and Armenian languages, had been issued. Also at Jerusalem, Tyre, Sidon, Tripoli, and Damascus, the Scriptures have been circulated.

In the Persian language the Pentateuch had been translated, and a version of the historical books in progress.

The following year witnessed a like zeal on the behalf of the above-named institutions to circulate the Bible in the Levant.

Having thus briefly alluded to the operations of other societies in this interesting field, by way of introduction to the history of the operations of the American Bible Society, we shall dismiss that subject, and confine our observations to the society, the history of whose operations we are endeavoring to give.

In 1828, it being determined that the Rev. Jonas King, who had been a missionary to Palestine, should visit Greece for moral and religious purposes, the society appropriated one thousand five hundred dollars to supply that gentleman with Greek Scriptures for that oppressed country. Great sympathy was manifested at that time in behalf of the Greeks all over the country, and large quantities of provisions, clothing, and money were sent to their relief. It was but right and proper that with these benefactions should be sent the word of eternal life.

In 1829, to the Missionary Society of the Protestant Episcopal Church, for the purpose of circulating the Scriptures in Greece, the board made a grant of five hundred dollars.

A letter from Mr. King, addressed to the Corresponding Secretary, Rev. J. C. Brigham, communicated the facts that the desire for the Scriptures in Greece was very great, and that they were in a very poor and wretched condition generally, many of them destitute of the necessaries of life. The demand for the Scriptures was such that he ought immediately to be put in possession of thirty thousand copies for gratuitous distribution.

In 1830, interesting accounts of Bible circulation in Greece were received from the Rev. Messrs. King and Robertson. These gentlemen were authorized by the board to purchase Greek Scriptures from the British and Foreign Bible Society.

In 1831, a communication was received from Mr. Brewer, in which he says, "The circulation of the Scriptures in different parts of the Turkish empire is going on more and more extensively. The depôts at Smyrna and Constantinople were issuing their thousands annually in different parts of the country."

In 1832, a letter from the Rev. Mr. Brewer, dated at the Isle of Patmos, to the board, says, in speaking of the Seven Churches of Asia, "Why should you not undertake to furnish every family dwelling where the churches mentioned in the New Testament are located, and especially those to which its holy epistles were addressed? Beginning at Jerusalem, whither we trust shortly to send a pious Greek, more especially for carrying forward school operations, the hundreds of Greek and Armenian families could be supplied through his agency and that of the missionaries who visit there during the Passover season."

In 1833, the board resolved on an appropriation of two thousand dollars for the use of the missions of the various denominations in the Mediterranean, which was subsequently remitted.

This year the British and Foreign Bible Society were called to mourn the loss of that distinguished Oriental scholar, Mr. William Greenfield, professor of the Turkish language in the College of France. For ten years he was engaged in the translation of the Turkish Bible, which he published for that society. He also superintended various editions of the Scriptures in other tongues for the society, and was untiring in his efforts to put them in circulation. In the course of one year previous to his death, he effected the distribution of two hundred thousand Bibles and Testaments, mostly in France.

A letter from one of the missionaries at Malta to Dr. Brigham congratulates the society for having completed the plates for printing the New Testament in modern Greek, and also communicating the intelligence that the Armenian Bishop Carabet had finished the translation of the Old Testament into the Armeno-Turkish language, and expressing a desire that the society should undertake its publication.

It also suggested the propriety of sending an agent of the society to the Levant.

In 1834, the board made the following grants: To the Rev. J. Brewer, at Smyrna, five hundred copies of the modern Greek Testament. To the Rev. Dr. King, of Athens, Greece, two hundred copies of the same. To the Rev. J. Robinson, of Syra, two hundred; and a like number to the Rev. Mr. Goodell, at Constantinople.

In 1835, a communication was received from the Rev. Mr. Schauffler, missionary of the American Board of Foreign Missions among the Jews at Constantinople and countries around it. The object of this communication was to make the board acquainted with the condition of the Jewish population in the Ottoman empire, and to propose the publication of the Scriptures of the Old Testament in the Hebrew and Hebrew-Spanish languages, that the three hundred thousand souls who are still heirs of many divine promises may not perish at our very doors without an effort to save them from the judicial blindness in which they grope at noonday.

He had commenced revising the Psalms, with the intention of printing an edition of three thousand. This, with the Jews, is the most desirable book in the Old Testament canon. After learning that the proposed translation of Mr. Schauffler was in accordance with the regulations of the board, and that the printing could be done at Smyrna or Constantinople, the board granted one thousand dollars to aid in the publication of the Psalms in Hebrew-Spanish.

To the same society was granted eight hundred dollars, for the purpose of procuring Arabic Scriptures to be distributed by their missionaries in Syria.

Another grant to the same society of five hundred dollars was made for the purpose of supplying the Rev. Mr. Perkins with Syriac Scriptures for distribution among the Nestorians in Persia.

In 1836, the board granted to the Rev. Dr. King, missionary at Greece, a good supply of modern Greek Testaments. A letter from that gentleman represents the demand for the Scriptures as increasingly great.

The board having authorized him to employ a native agent for distributing the Scriptures in that country, he accordingly employed a priest who had been a teacher in his gymnasium for three years, a native of Sparta, by the name of Damianos.

Damianos was recommended by the Bishop of Sparta, and, belonging to the priesthood, he had access to all the churches, where he could preach to the people on the subject of reading and circulating the Word of God.

Five hundred copies of Testaments were also sent to the Rev. Mr. Hill, missionary of the Protestant Episcopal Church in Athens.

During the year the board granted to the Missionary Society of the Protestant Episcopal Church, for Greco-Turkish and other Scriptures for Greece and the Grecian Archipelago, three thousand dollars.

To the same society, for Persian and other Scriptures, by their missionary in Persia, five hundred dollars.

To the American Board, for Persian and other Scriptures, five hundred dollars.

To the same board, for Armeno-Turkish Scriptures, five thousand dollars.

During the year 1837, the managers, in accordance with their previous determination of sending agents abroad to assist in preparing and circulating the Scriptures at the more important missionary stations, appointed the Rev. Simeon H. Calhoun to superintend the operations of the society in the Levant.

He was cordially received by the American and English missionaries, and the agent of the British and Foreign Bible Society at Smyrna.

An arrangement was made through Mr. Calhoun to have the Hebrew-Spanish Old Testament translated at the joint expense of the British and Foreign and the American Bible Societies. This arrangement was highly satisfactory to all the missionaries. Objections being made to the version of the Greek Testament on account of its idiom, Professor Bambas, an eminent Greek scholar of high moral qualifications, made a new translation.

To the American missionaries at Constantinople the board sent a supply of Bibles and Testaments in the German, French, Italian, and modern Greek, for the benefit of those speaking the above tongue in Turkey and the surrounding regions.

To the Rev. Mr. Smith, for the purpose of circulating the Arabic Scriptures in schools among the destitute in Syria, the board appropriated five hundred dollars.

In regard to the circulation of the Bible in Syria, the Rev. Mr. Thompson, in a letter to the board, says, "I am in favor of putting a Bible into the hands of every one of the thousands of pilgrims who annually flock to Jerusalem, the city of sacred associations. In this way Bibles will find their way to every country from Ethiopia to Siberia, and from India to Spain.

The only possible way by which we can reach the millions of this country is by sending them the Bible. The few and feeble missionaries in the field can not supply them. *From that quarter there is absolutely no hope.* There are several hundred thousand Christians of the Syriac and other churches in and around Mosul. They are destitute of both Bibles and priests, but keep up a most inveterate hostility to the pope, and are anxious to receive the Word of God. Various Oriental sects in Aleppo, Torsoos, and Cesara, with the countries around them, are equally destitute."

From the Rev. Justin Perkins, missionary in Persia, the board received the following:

"The field for the distribution of the Scriptures among the Nestorian Christians is *wide*, and *wide open.* They have reverence for the sacred Volume, and, unlike all other Oriental Christian sects, they make it their *only rule of faith* and professedly of practice. Until I came to Persia, they could procure no copies of the Bible save those furnished at long intervals by the slow motion of the pen. The entire Scriptures were printed long ago in ancient Syriac by the British and Foreign Bible Society, but scarcely a printed copy had reached them before my arrival. The deep reverence with which they kiss and fold it to their bosoms when I present it to them, at the same time imploring innumerable blessings to rest on those who send them such a treasure, is truly affecting. This best of missionaries will, I feel assured, become 'the power of God unto salvation' to multitudes of this poor people who were 'ready to perish,' and soon prepare them, in turn, to become the heralds of the pure Gospel to the benighted millions of Persia and all Asia."

From the Rev. Mr. Calhoun, the society's agent in the Levant, an interesting letter was received in 1838, in relation to the translations, printing, and circulation of the Scriptures in various languages in that country.

To the Rev. Mr. Whiting, missionary at Jerusalem, he had sent a supply of Bibles and Testaments in the Arabic, Greek, modern Greek, modern Armenian, and Greco-Turkish languages, designed for circulation among the thousands of pilgrims who visit the Holy City from all parts of the world at the season of the Passover.

To the Rev. Mr. Love, of the Baptist mission at Patras, he sent eight hundred and thirty copies of the Scriptures in modern Greek and Italian.

From Dr. Grant, of the Ooroomiah mission in Persia, a letter was received urging the publication of the Scriptures in the ancient Syriac, the written language of the Nestorian Christians.

The doctor stated that there was not a complete copy of the Bible in the Nestorian character in the whole province of Ooroomiah. The same was true in regard to the numerous Nestorian population bordering upon the Tigris. Detached portions were found, but so scarce that it was thought necessary to teach the children to read upward, or downward, or sidewise, so that five or six persons might, by forming a circle round it, read from a single book. Besides the Psalms of David, which formed an important part of their devotional exercises, there was but *one* copy of the Old Testament in all the province, containing a population of twenty thousand souls, and that was in three or four separate volumes, the property of several individuals. The supply of the Gospels in the Nestorian character, printed by the British and Foreign Bible Society, was tolerably good, but none of the Epistles or Acts of the Apostles could be found, while the Book of Revelations in the Nestorian character had never reached them.

The communications of the society's agent in relation to the circulation of the Scriptures among the Greeks, Persians, Arabians, Turks, Russians, and Jews, as found in the Reports of the society, are of an exceedingly interesting character.

In 1840, at the urgent request of missionaries, fifteen hundred German Bibles and five hundred Testaments had been forwarded to the poor colonists in Southern Russia bordering on the Black Sea. Four hundred and seventy five Bibles and Testaments, in different tongues, were sent to the agent, to meet the frequent demands from seamen, missionary stations, pilgrims, and others. The agent also made extensive purchases of Bibles from other societies and delivered them to missionaries.

In relation to Greece, it was stated that a warm discussion was going on in Athens in regard to the subject of translations. The controversy was confined to the Greeks themselves, while the missionaries are actively engaged in the work of distribution, and thus, in the most effectual manner, defeating the schemes of those who would lock up the Word of God in a dead language. The more light the people get, the more unwilling are they to go back to the days of darkness.

Copies were furnished to the Baptist missionaries at Patras. The missionaries state that officers, civil and military, and priests, had made application for the Bible, and that, through Albanian Greeks, it had been communicated throughout the extreme districts of Albania in Turkey.

At Athens there were upward of eight thousand furnished by the agent.

At Constantinople, Salonica, Broosa, and Jerusalem, one thousand two hundred in Hebrew-Spanish.

The agent also procured Greco-Turkish Scriptures for American missionaries. Also copies of Arabic,

Turkish, Italian, and Armenian, to be distributed in Turkey and Syria.

The agent received and disbursed funds for the translation and printing of the Scriptures in different languages.

During the year he made a visit to Egypt, and from thence into Syria, visiting the missionaries at Beyrout and Jerusalem. He found at Alexandria a box of Bibles in the hands of the American consul, which had been sent to Mr. Wolf, the Jewish missionary. At Beyrout the missionaries had printed, at the expense of the society, the Book of Psalms in Arabic.

In the island of Cyprus, where an American mission is established, the Greek Scriptures were extensively circulated without opposition.

In 1841, to aid in the publication of the Hebrew-Spanish Old Testament at Vienna, under the superintendence of the Rev. Mr. Schauffler, the board made an appropriation of six thousand dollars.

This being the year in which the agent visited the United States, there were no communications from the Levant in regard to the special operations of the society in that region.

In 1842, a supply of Bibles was sent to Dr. Grant for the use of the Nestorian clergy.

For preparing and circulating the Scriptures in Greece, Turkey, Persia, and Syria, under the direction of the society's agent, two thousand four hundred and ninety-nine dollars were appropriated.

The rabbis at Constantinople had manifested much hostility to the Christian missionaries, and forbade their brethren from entering the house of Mr. Schauffler, who was engaged in translating the Old Testament into the Hebrew-Spanish language, and it was thought that their opposition would prevent the circulation of the Bible among those for whom it was designed, but the wonderful providence of God ordered it otherwise. To the astonishment of every one, the chief rabbi of Constantinople issued a certificate in favor of that very translation in the following words, translated from the Hebrew:

"*Consider, my people, and act.*

"Approbation of the exalted rabbi in the city of Constantinople to the twenty-four sacred books translated into Spanish, and printed in the city of Vienna, by the celebrated William Schauffler, an upright and pious man, well acquainted with the grammatical science of the language, and worthy the support and confidence of every individual.

"Ye men, come and see how good and beautiful is the work the mighty One has composed. His work is his ornament, the token of his power, the proclamation of his goodness; a flowing well, a fountain of wisdom. He has displayed the banner of his law, putting it into a pure, intelligible language, informing each one of what he reads by what method the youth can direct his way in obscure paths. He offers pleasing tidings, serving to us not only as light, but as honey and cream to our tongue; explaining the words of the King and of his law, emanating from justice; making understood the words of Wisdom, that all his works are faithful; showing us how to learn and to teach proper actions. Its contents are like fresh water to one who is thirsty; it does not weary, but gives strength to those who have none. With knowledge he speaks pure words that are clear to be understood, and so taught that the young and old may walk uprightly. Read and study according to the will of Him who dwelt in the bush. He has brought to light here every thing that is obscure, that each might come and open, and examine the truth in its length, and breadth, and height. Such a work has not before been among us. It is a benefit which our forefathers could not avail themselves of; it is now plain, and strong like an oak. Every one will say our eyes have beheld something new. The Lord gave him wisdom, and placed in his mouth to say, 'Thus speak to the house of Jacob from a foreign nation;' the Lord shall recompense him, and his reward shall be perfect. May the Lord consider it favorably. And now, my brethren, come and take hold of the good which is provided; search from the Book of the Lord, and read it daily, that you may know how to walk in the desert and in the plain. There is none before this man versed in the grammatical structure of the language of the law which Moses hath given; he well knows each portion of it. Whoever desires life should weigh his silver to purchase this Book. Hear and obey this Word, and the earth shall be filled with knowledge out of the fountain of salvation which rises for us in heaven. May the Lord grant you mercy manifold, to children and children's children, to study the law, and reward you bountifully. Whoever will obey shall be blessed by the Most High, and upon him happiness shall descend, and peace shall be in his possession until Shiloh appears, and the Redeemer comes to Zion. Amen! Given on the first day of Thamuz, in the year 5590 from the creation of the world.

"He who thus sends forth this message and salutation is SAMUEL HEIMANN."

The Armeno-Turkish Old Testament, by the Rev. Mr. Goodell, was finished this year, and its publication was going on.

The preparation of the above work was a long and difficult one, consuming the time and strength of many years. The translator made an effort to carry it forward in connection with his other labors as a missionary, but he found it necessary, after a short trial, to devote himself exclusively to the one work. The work of Mr. Goodell is not a version or revision of another translation, for there were none in existence. The whole was taken from the Hebrew. When he had finished it, he wrote at the bottom of the page, "Bless the Lord, O my soul! and forget not all his benefits." He then rose up, shut all the books that had been open before him for years, fell on his knees, and gave thanks unto the name of the Lord, "who had not dealt with us according to our sins," but who had given us his blessed Word to be "a light unto our feet," and whose wondrous love permits us to hold it up to "lighten every man that cometh into the world."

The society's agent, in relation to the field of operation assigned him, says, "It is most gratifying to be able to state that the field for the distribution of the Scriptures in these regions has never been more open, or the obstacles less than at the present moment. In Syria and Greece, at Constantinople and Broosa, and South Russia, we are permitted to go forward without material hinderance. It is a fact worthy of record, that the field has become more open to us just at a time when we are becoming better supplied with the Scriptures. Hitherto the missionaries have been employed much in translations. As their labors are approaching a termination, and we are getting their works through the press, we find that the Lord is opening the way before us for their circulation. Thus are we taught to wait patiently for the Lord."

An urgent request was made by the board this year to print the Arabic Testament, and the agent entered upon the work.

On the request of Dr. King, of Athens, the board

resolved to publish an edition of the modern Greek Testament, from the plates in the possession of the society.

In 1843, the board sent to the agent in the Levant five thousand dollars, to be appropriated by him in translating, printing, and circulating the Scriptures in that country.

The Rev. Mr. Schauffler, while at Vienna, with the advice of the agent, published an edition of the New Testament in German, with the Book of Psalms annexed. This was designed for the multitudes in that papal country, and in Hungary, where it was gladly received, the Queen of Hungary herself engaging in the work of distribution.

The society, at its own expense, has published the following Scriptures in the Levant:

Armeno-Turkish Old Testament, three thousand copies, printed at Smyrna.

Armeno-Turkish Pentateuch, two thousand copies, printed at Smyrna.

Hebrew-Spanish Old Testament, three thousand copies, printed at Vienna.

Hebrew-Spanish Psalms, three thousand, printed at Constantinople.

Hebrew-Spanish Pentateuch, five hundred, printed at Vienna.

Ancient Armenian New Testament, two thousand, printed at Smyrna.

Ancient Armenian four Gospels, one thousand, printed at Smyrna.

Gospel of John, in modern Greek, two thousand, printed at Smyrna.

Modern Armenian Psalms, one thousand, printed at Smyrna.

Psalms in Arabic, two thousand, printed at Beyrout.

Acts of the Apostles, in Arabic, two thousand, printed at Beyrout.

Psalms, in ancient Syriac, one thousand, printed at Ooroomiah.

Galatians, in ancient Syriac, one thousand, printed at Ooroomiah.

Acts of the Apostles, in ancient Syriac, one thousand, printed at Ooroomiah.

German New Testament and Psalms, two thousand, printed in Austria.

The Old Testament in modern Armenian, the Old Testament in Syriac, the New Testament in Arabic, Proverbs in Arabic, and another edition of Psalms in Arabic, were in process of publication.

A letter from Dr. Goodell to the board, reviewing his labors, and communicating his intentions in regard to future action in the open field of missionary toil, contains some just and admirable sentiments in regard to the absolute importance of the Bible to the missionary in the same language in which he preaches the word of salvation. He says, "Without the Bible we could say one thing, and the priest of a false religion could say another, but where would be the umpire? It would be *nowhere*, and all our efforts would be, of course, like 'beating the air.' And we may ask, What could even the apostles have done without the Bible? Among the Jews he could have done absolutely nothing: they based their whole new revelation upon it. They appealed to it always, and they asserted it to be more sure and certain than any voice they had themselves heard in the holy mount. And so our Savior himself appealed to it. Instead of requiring the Jews to take his mere word for the truth, he either confirmed it to them by a miracle, or referred them to their own Scriptures for the truth of it. With the Bible in our hands and in the hands of the people, we stand on the Rock of Ages and build for eternity, but without it we build on the sand, and our house is exposed to be blown down by every storm."

In 1844, for printing and distributing the Scriptures in various languages in the countries of the Levant, the board appropriated eight thousand one hundred and forty-five dollars.

Interesting accounts were forwarded to the board by the agent from Bible distributers in Turkey. At Koolah, Ushak, Cara, Hissar, Broosa, Kansack, Solus, Kermasti, and Trebizonde, hundreds of books were sold, and their reports furnished gratifying evidence of the benefits resulting from their circulation.

In 1845, on the request of the agent, the board granted to the Baptist Foreign Missionary Society, for distribution by their missionaries in Greece, fifteen hundred modern Greek Testaments.

The board granted one thousand dollars to aid the Rev. Dr. Perkins, missionary of the American Board of Foreign Missions in Ooroomiah, Persia, in publishing the New Testament in modern Syriac, which he and others had translated. In addition to the recommendation of the society's agent, the secretary of the missionary board gave ample assurance of the fidelity of the translation.

To the same board was also granted one thousand dollars to aid in translating and printing the Old Testament in modern Armenian, the New Testament having been published by the British and Foreign Bible Society some years before.

To the agent, for printing portions of the Bible in different languages, the board appropriated five thousand dollars.

Mr. Calhoun feeling it his duty to go to Mount Lebanon and engage in the duties of a missionary, his Bible agency was brought to a close.

His last letter to the board contains the following statements: "During eight years the society has printed, chiefly at Smyrna and Beyrout, three thousand five hundred copies of the Scriptures, in whole or in part. It had distributed in the Levant about sixty thousand, obtained from different places. These Scriptures were in the following languages: Hebrew, Hebrew-Spanish, Arabic, Syriac, Persian, Turkish, Armeno-Turkish, Greco-Turkish, ancient and modern Armenian, ancient and modern Greek, Albanian, German, Italian, French, and English." With this truly pious and devoted servant of Christ we have the honor of a personal acquaintance, and most ardently do we hope he may long be permitted to live and to labor in the ancient Gospel land.

In 1846, the board entered into engagements to furnish ten thousand dollars for the purpose of printing a new edition of the Hebrew-Spanish Scriptures for the use of the Spanish Jews; also to furnish means for translating and publishing the Hebrew-German Scriptures for the use of the German and Polish Jews in Russia and Turkey.

A further engagement was made to prepare and publish the Old Testament in modern Armenian, and the New Testament in modern Syriac, at Ooroomiah, in Persia, under the direction of the Rev. Dr. Perkins, one thousand dollars toward which were remitted last year.

In 1847, the board granted two thousand five hundred dollars to the American Board of Foreign Missions to aid in the publication of the entire Bible in modern Syriac, for the use of the Nestorians in Persia, the increasing interest manifested by this people in religion making it particularly desirable that they should be furnished with the Word of God.

To aid in the publication of the Hebrew-German

Scriptures, for the use of the German Jews, prepared by Mr. Schauffler, five hundred dollars were granted.

In 1848, for the purpose of publishing the Scriptures in Turkey, under the direction of the American missionaries, five thousand dollars were remitted during the year.

From a committee of missionaries in Turkey the board received the cheering intelligence that, throughout all the countries of the Levant, the Word of God, in the various languages in which it had been published by the society, had free course, and was glorified in the salvation of those to whom it was sent. "The diffusion of the sacred Volume," say they, "must always form an important part of our work. The Bible is the first book we wish to put into the hands of this people, and nothing can be better adapted to show them their errors, and their helpless and hapless condition without saving faith in Christ. We are, therefore, fully prepared to urge the society not to slacken, but rather to prosecute with renewed zeal their operations in this field. It surely holds out to them many encouragements. It promises a plentiful harvest at no distant day; of this we feel more and more assured. The Christian sects of this empire are to be brought under the purifying and saving influences of the Bible. The developments of every year are tending more and more to this result."

CHAPTER XXXI.

BIBLE IN RUSSIA.

A Bible society was established in Russia at an early day. At the organization of the American Bible Society a fraternal correspondence was commenced, which has been kept up without interruption to the present time.

In 1818 the board received a copy of its Reports, and several copies of Bibles and portions of Scripture published by that society in the various languages of the Russian empire, such as the Calmuc-Armenian, Finnish, German, Polish, French, Sclavonian, Dorpatian-Esthonian, Reval-Esthonian, Lettonian, Persian, Georgian, Samogatian, ancient Greek, modern Greek, Moldavian, and Tartar. The society has been patronized by the emperor with distinguished liberality, and by his nobles and the dignitaries of the Church with uncommon union.

Though five years younger than the great parent of all Bible societies, the British and Foreign, it has been more extensively useful, perhaps, to the Eastern Continent than its illustrious prototype.

In 1820 it had promoted the translation and circulation of the Scriptures in forty-six different languages.

The society started out upon its boundless field with the determination to furnish the Bible to every family, from the Swedish frontier to the Straits of Behring, and from the shores of the Frozen Ocean to the boundaries of Turkey and China.

In 1826, an imperial ukase, dictated by ignorance and prejudice, silenced the Bible press. The Russian

Bible Society, at this melancholy period of its history, had two hundred and eighty-nine auxiliaries, and had issued the Scriptures in various languages to the amount of one million of copies.

The prohibition, however, did not extend to the sale and distribution of the Scriptures, nor to the existence of Bible societies.

The same year the Russian Protestant Bible Society was organized at St. Petersburg.

Through the labors of the Rev. Mr. Knill, who was furnished with Bibles and Testaments by the British and Foreign Bible Society, the St. Petersburg Society circulated in two years twenty-two thousand copies.

In 1835, the board made a grant of three hundred dollars to the St. Petersburg Bible Society, on the request of William Ropes, Esq., an American merchant at that place. He sent an extract from a letter to him from Pastor Malenberg, of Finland, showing the need of assistance: "You inquire," said he, "if I have any Finnish Bibles or New Testaments? I have hitherto had them, but have only six remaining. I would propose that you send me such books as I need, but I am afraid to do so. Who will pay for them? and can I ascertain the price? and how shall I be able to send you the money for them, having no more money than I need, and not always that? I wish, from my inmost soul, that I could obtain New Testaments, but I know not how. Ponder these things, and tell me what is best, and what can be done."

This society obtained the protection of the government, and quietly moved forward dispensing blessings.

In 1836, the board granted to William Ropes, Esq., and associates, at St. Petersburg, for the purpose of extending the circulation of the Scriptures, one thousand dollars.

This year one thousand four hundred Testaments

and Psalters were purchased by two ladies in Sheffield for distribution in Siberia.

An interesting communication was received from the Rev. Mr. Brown and Mr. Ropes in relation to Bible distribution in Russia in 1838. With a view of supplying the destitute, through the liberality of the American Bible Society, these gentlemen requested the pastors to make inquiry in regard to the condition of the people. Several of them addressed circulars to their charges. One Lutheran pastor in Esthonia asked for five hundred New Testaments to supply his destitute parishioners. The general superintendent of the churches, subject to the Southern Consistorium of Moscow, wrote to all the pastors under his care, requesting information in regard to the number of families destitute of the Bible. He furnished the Rev. Mr. Brown with the names of twenty pastors whose people were destitute. The Archbishop of Finland expressed his belief that there were forty thousand families without the Scriptures. He stated that, though poor, they were mostly able to read, and would be thankful for the Word of God through the benevolence of American Christians.

To supply these destitute, the board made a grant of one thousand five hundred dollars.

In 1839, a letter from the Rev. Mr. Brown communicated interesting intelligence in regard to the society's benefactions in Russia. One pastor says: "The supply of the destitute by the American Bible Society caused great astonishment and admiration. The people expressed themselves deeply gratified at the love which stretched out its arms over the sea to brethren it never saw. Two parishes, including fifteen thousand souls, were represented as containing one thousand nine hundred and fifty destitute families."

Another pastor stated that his parish contained eleven thousand two hundred souls, and that one thousand and ninety families were entirely destitute.

Another parish, containing eight thousand souls, had six hundred destitute families.

To meet these and similar wants, the board sent five hundred dollars, and one thousand five hundred German Bibles, for those speaking that language in the southern part of the empire.

In 1841, on the request of Messrs. Ropes and Gilibrand, for the circulation of the Bible in Russia and Finland, the board granted one thousand dollars.

In 1842, for the circulation of the Scriptures as above, one thousand dollars more were granted to the committee at St. Petersburg.

To procure and distribute the Scriptures in Sweden, under the direction of the Rev. George Scott, the sum of one thousand five hundred dollars was paid.

The following year, to the St. Petersburg committee were sent one thousand dollars. The appropriation was designed to be employed in purchasing the Scriptures in Reval-Esthonian and other tongues, for the destitute congregations in Livonia and Esthonia.

The succeeding year, from the Report of the British and Foreign Bible Society, we learn that forty thousand destitute families had been supplied with the Scriptures.

In 1847, the board sent to Russia the sum of two thousand dollars, to be expended as above stated. The books distributed by the funds of the society were mostly in the provinces of Esthonia and Livonia. The committee under whose direction they were circulated, after speaking of the success of the cause in Finland, adds:

"Scarcely less interesting is the religious aspect of Esthonia, whose population has manifested for years past tne utmost eagerness for the possession of the precious volume of God's Word. At the sole charge of the American Bible Society, thirteen thousand copies have been distributed since 1841, and a very large, if not an equal number, by the British and Foreign Bible Society. Our brethren of the American society having expressed a desire that the Baltic provinces should be their peculiar sphere of labor, we have for some time past supplied both Esthonia and Livonia with the Holy Scriptures, from funds placed by them at our disposal. The latter province presents a scene of painful interest. Statistics have been furnished us, from which we gather that not less than fourteen thousand families are altogether destitute of a single copy of the Old or New Testament."

In 1848, at the expense of the American Bible Society, there were circulated three thousand eight hundred and twenty copies of the Scriptures in Russia.

Through the British and Foreign Bible Society, which has an agent at St. Petersburg, several translations have been made for the various languages in that vast empire; and the time is no doubt near at hand when it may be said of Russia, as of every other country in the world, the people all are permitted to read "the wonderful works of God in their own tongue in which they were born."

May God, in the dispensations of his providence and grace, usher on that day.

CHAPTER XXXII.

AN APPEAL TO THE FRIENDS OF THE BIBLE.

With our present knowledge of the contents of the sacred Oracles, and the conviction of their importance as a source of instruction in all the essential departments of faith and duty as connected with our present happiness and everlasting welfare, were we to suppose for a moment, by way of illustration, that there was but one single copy of this sacred Book in existence, with what eagerness would we desire to gaze upon its wondrous pages!

What pilgrimages from every land would be made to that holy shrine, and what multitudes would flock to see the Book of God and hear its divine revelations!

The oracle of Apollo at Delphos, the tomb of Mohammed at Mecca, and the car of Juggernaut at Orissa, visited in other times by almost countless thousands of devotees, would be outnumbered by the hosts that would cover the plains and darken the mountains of that land which held the "living Oracles" of the "living God."

The oracle of Apollo has ceased its responses, the temple is in ruins, and the pythoness has departed. The ashes of the prophet have lost their power to charm, and the Mussulman seeks not, as of old, to bow at the shrine of him who conquered by the sword.

The Hindoo, who vainly thought that death within ten miles of Orissa, which contained the car of his bloody god, was a certain passport to heaven, no longer risks his life to traverse burning deserts nor joins the shout of wild and hideous revelry as the car of death rolls on.

The Scriptures of Confucius, the Zendavesta of Zoroaster, the Hieroglyphics of the Thaumaturgists, the Shasters of the priests of India, the Koran of Mohammed, the funeral pile, the sacred waters, whether of Ganges or Ilissus, have all become powerless, and, as the old, time-decayed monuments of ancient superstition, they are passing away.

Now, when the lurid twilight of pagan mythology has ceased to satisfy, and has left its votaries to wander in bewilderment, the Sun of righteousness, as it shines in peerless majesty through the Gospel of salvation, is ascending the meridian, and shedding abroad its light and heat to illumine the remotest corners of the realm of night, to reanimate and gladden the nations still prostrate in the region and shadow of death; and even blank and cheerless infidelity, to its own dismay and confusion, has evoked the light of science from the deepest recesses of earth and the gem-set canopy of heaven only to confirm the truth of Bible theology and stamp its origin Divine.

We are not called upon to contemplate the Bible as an oracle, magnificently resting in the temple of some far-distant land only accessible to the pilgrim; it has "grown, and prevailed," and multiplied, until its millions of fac similes have found a place and yield a clear response to every inquirer in every land. Nor is it the less precious because it has become thus plentiful. The light is not the less pleasant and beautiful to behold because it pours its wide, diffusing ray on every mountain and plain, and ocean and river. Nor is the glorious moral sun "which Mercy took from off the throne" less precious because its beams enlighten every nation, and its glad tidings break in melody upon every ear.

As it is in nature, so it is in grace and providence, our most valuable blessings are the most common and universal; but is this a reason why the Giver and the gift should be less esteemed? Rather let the value of the one increase our respect and love for the other, until, in the blessings of our God, we shall constantly behold the evidences of a love enough to make "the rocks and hills break their everlasting silence."

The time was when the Jews, to whom were committed the living Oracles, lost them as they lost their temple and its sacred vessels. The very language in which they were written was also passing away. Darkness was in all their dwellings and synagogues, like that which hung over Egypt on the fearful day of its curse. It was a gloomy, starless night to the descendants of Israel. "The law and the testimony" were buried amid the ruins of their most holy place. The Oracle was gone, the Ark was taken, and the Urim and Thummim had lost their power. But the same hand that wrote its everlasting law upon tables of stone, preserved it from the touch of the destroyer until piety could again take it from the hiding-place, and cause it to be read in the presence of all the people.

When, at the conflagration of the Alexandrian library, which contained in its alcoves the literature of the world, it fell a victim to the torch of the incendiary, unlike the works of renowned authors of antiquity, it was not destroyed. The synagogues of Judea contained the sacred Treasure.

Its divine Author preserved it during the centuries of pagan and Christian darkness through which it passed, and through all the fires of the persecution to which it has been subjected, until it has become the most plentiful and accessible of all books in the world.

Prophecy and fact are remarkably coincident in regard to the Bible: "The Word of our God shall stand forever;" it "shall cover the earth as the waters cover the sea;" "shall have free course and be glorified;" "shall not return void," but shall fill the earth with fruitfulness, while songs and everlasting joy shall follow its glorious way!

To those who are the friends of the Bible, believing in its pre-eminent importance, and tracing the movements of the divine Hand in its production, preservation, and diffusion abroad, what becomes obviously their duty in regard to it? To possess it ourselves; to read, mark, learn, believe, and practice what it teaches, is evidently our duty. But duty stops not there. It inculcates a regard for others equivalent to the love we bear for ourselves, and assures us that "to do good and to communicate" thrill the mind of God himself with pleasurable emotions.

The term neighbor has a world-wide signification. Cast in the scanty mold of some minds, it extends but a step from the threshold of our own habitation; but in the light of true Christian charity, it is boundless as the wants and woes of humanity. Diffusive as the light of heaven, Christian charity shines on all, and blesses all on whom it shines.

If it subjects him to the charge of a "denial of the faith and a gross infidelity" who provides not for the spiritual wants of his own household, he who withholds what his Lord rightfully demands is not only an infidel in heart, but a "*robber of God*," and the very blessings of Heaven will turn to curses in his hand. Those who seek to save that which should have been given to the Lord for the promotion of his cause and kingdom on earth, must suffer its loss; and if not with it the loss of his own soul, it will be because of his hearty repentance and true faith in turning to God.

What is given to the Lord is "a treasure laid up in heaven that moth can not rust, nor thieves break through and steal;" and it will be all we shall possess when we come to die. The ownership in every thing else must be relinquished then; that is invested in the treasury of Heaven, the profits of which will accumulate forever.

It is this that the Savior denominates a riches toward God.

Possessing the distinguished blessing of the Gospel in such rich abundance, the claims of God are on us to send it to the destitute.

There is a fearful amount of incredulity in the world, and not a little in the Church, in regard to the destitution of the Word of God in our own country; and many are disposed to think that, in a land of Bibles, emphatically so speaking, there certainly can not be many that are destitute; and even if such could be found, so cheap are the Scriptures, and so easy of access in all parts of the country, that Christian charity does not require any specific action in relation thereto.

A reference to a few facts will show that notwithstanding the American Bible Society has been in operation for thirty-three years, during which time it has circulated nearly five millions of copies of the Scriptures in the different states and territories of the Union, yet, startling as it may appear, there is at this moment a greater destitution in this country than there was when the first Bible was issued from the society's press.

Twenty years ago a resolution to supply the United States in two years was unanimously adopted by the parent society, and concurred in by the auxiliaries. Bible associations went vigorously to work, copies were scattered by the million all through the length and breadth of the land, and the work was done—every family was reported as supplied.

Explorations were recommenced a few years afterward, and it was ascertained that the destitution was as great as ever.

An array of facts could easily be presented, showing that, in consequence of the increase of population, the creation of new families, and the influx of foreigners, the destitution absolutely increases instead of being lessened every year. A few will suffice.

Take the State of Massachusetts, the landing-place and home of the Puritan, where—as beautifully illustrated in one of the paintings in the Rotunda of the Capitol at Washington—the light of heaven first fell upon an open Bible in our beloved country, and where it was first baptized with the prayers, and tears, and blood of the purest and bravest hearts that ever beat. In Massachusetts, fast and firm as her granite mountains, free and boundless as her ocean waves, there are hundreds of families unblessed by the light of the written Word.

Plymouth county, forever consecrated as the spot where pilgrim feet were permitted, for the first time, to stand upon a free soil, was explored about three years since, and hundreds of families were found without the Bible. One would think this a fancy sketch were it not sustained by cold New England facts.

Next we come to the proud Empire State of New York, and we find a still greater destitution. Right under the glorious shadow of the parent tree, which has struck deep its roots and spread out its branches, the leaves of which are for the healing of the nation, the destitute are to be found.

Jefferson county was reported as supplied in 1830, when the general supply was effected.

Five years afterward it was re-explored, and one thousand families were found destitute.

After the lapse of five more years it was again canvassed, and eleven hundred families were found without the Bible.

At the close of the next five years it was ascertained that *fifteen* hundred families were in a state of Bible destitution.

We discover in this the clearest indication of duty to engage in a perpetual distribution, as the only way of keeping up a regular supply.

We next pass to Virginia, denominated the "Old Dominion." There the destitution is as great, if not greater, than in any of the Northern, Eastern, or Western States.

On the authority of the Rev. Mr. Poisal, the agent of the State Bible Society, there were fifteen thousand families destitute of the Scriptures in that state. In Western Virginia nearly one half of the white families were without the Bible, and this is put down as a low estimate by those who have made the exploration.

Ohio, the third state in the Union, filled with an active and enterprising population, second to none for her zeal in the promotion of schools and churches, and among the earliest in the Bible field, there is a destitution amounting to about one fifth of the families in the state.

About two thirds of the county of Clermont was visited, and upward of three hundred families were found destitute.

We have selected the above states as representing the four great divisions of the Union; and if they furnish a criterion by which the others are to be judged, then, at the lowest calculation, there are at this time three hundred and fifty thousand Protestant families without the blessings of God's Word.

A period never will perhaps arrive when it can be said the society has fulfilled its mission, and its presses may stop. To keep up the supply in our own country alone will require its ceaseless operations, and on a vastly increased scale from the present. If the estimate be a correct one, that the population of the country increases at the rate of thirty-three per cent. every ten years, then in less than fifty years we shall have a population of one hundred millions, and they must have the ever-luminous revelations of the Word of God to guide and control them in the mighty whirl of human progress.

Vast as the *home field* is, yet the entire world has claims upon us, and we must meet the demand. God is preparing his way among all nations. The vast valley of the dead is shaken with the word of his mouth, and betokens a resurrection from the sleep of centuries. Heathen temples and idols, old systems of religion and superannuated forms of worship, are fading away, and soon will be numbered with the things that were.

The signs of the times, which are but the indications of Providence for the Church's direction, are clear as noonday that the world-wide field is white unto harvest. A few years ago, and many of the most interesting portions of the heathen world were inaccessible to the light of Divine Revelation; now, there is not a heathen country under heaven where it has not an unrestricted circulation.

To the three hundred thousand dollars which have been expended by the society to translate, print, and circulate the Scriptures in foreign lands, must be added millions before the world is supplied. A general desire is awakened in all lands for the Word of Life. The cry for help comes up from every valley, echoes from every mountain, resounds from every shore, is borne on every breeze, and he must be either a stupid or heartless Christian who has no ear for that cry, and no hand to extend to them the means of salvation.

We admit the importance of the missionary enterprise in all its length and breadth, but the details of this book will show most conclusively that the Bible is the great and leading star in the world's conversion. A missionary may enter a heathen land, mingle with its inhabitants, and learn their language, but, unless he have for them a vernacular Bible, he can accomplish nothing. Without this, he would be as a minister at a foreign court without his commission. All his assertions and exhortations, unbacked by the divine authority of the written Word, could be set aside by the mere dictum of a heathen priest.

We only ask that the cause we advocate receive aid in proportion to its importance, when compared with all the other benevolent institutions of the Church, and we shall be satisfied with the result. We desire that the Bible may become to every nation as free and exhaustless as the air of the mountain or the water of the river.

A traveler once, wearied and faint with the toils of his journey, approached a fountain on the borders of the desert, and he hasted with eagerness to quench his burning thirst with its refreshing waters. Engraved on a marble slab surmounting the fountain were the following beautiful lines:

> "Come, traveler, slake thy burning thirst,
> And drive away dull care;
> Thou need'st not broach thy little purse,
> For I am free as air.
> My home is on the mountain side,
> My course is to the sea;
> Then drink till thou art satisfied,
> Yea, drink, for I am free."

Thus would we say to all earth's toil-worn travelers, fainting and dying amid the deserts of heathenism, come: "Ho! every one that thirsteth, come to the waters, and he that hath no money, come; yea, come, buy wine and milk without money and without price." The Bible has opened up a broad and mighty river all through the desert earth, on the banks of which three thousand missionaries stand and exclaim,

"Ho! ye that pant for living streams,
And pine away and die,
Here you may quench your raging thirst
With streams that never dry."

CHAPTER XXXIII.

BIBLE SOCIETIES IN DIFFERENT PARTS OF THE WORLD.

The following list will show the names and localities of these institutions, together with the date of their organization, and issues of Bibles and Testaments. They are all parent societies, and have their thousands of auxiliaries and branches in the different countries embraced within the sphere of their operations.

These societies are multiplying from year to year, and are to be found in almost all parts of the world. They are also being organized in heathen and papal countries. The present year adds to the number a society for the circulation of the Scriptures, a large edition of which is now being published, in the very center and citadel of the Roman hierarchy.

	Copies of Scriptures issued.
British and Foreign Bible Society, instituted 1804	20,000,000
American Bible Society, instituted 1816	6,000,000
Protestant Bible Society at Paris, instituted 1818, with 132 auxiliaries	300,000
French and Foreign Bible Society at Paris, instituted 1833, with auxiliaries	100,000
Strasburg Bible Society, instituted 1815 (chiefly German Bibles and Testaments)	66,087

	Copies of Scriptures issued.
Issued from the British and Foreign Bible Society's Depôt in Paris, from April, 1820	2,089,211
Icelandic Bible Society, instituted 1815	10,445
Swedish Bible Society, instituted 1808, with auxiliaries	564,378
The Agency at Stockholm, formed 1832	231,900
Norwegian Bible Society, instituted 1816	30,995
The Agency at Christiana, formed 1832	26,240
Stavanger Bible Society, instituted 1828	6,693
Finnish Bible Society, instituted 1812, at Abo, with many branches	110,561
Danish Bible Society, instituted 1814, with auxiliaries	172,554
Netherlands Bible Society, with auxiliaries	274,738
The Agency at Amsterdam, appointed 1843	47,659
Belgian and For. Bible Society at Brussels, instituted 1834	7,623
Belgian Bible Associations, instituted 1839	3,903
The Agency at Brussels, appointed 1835	119,585
Antwerp Bible Society, instituted 1834	439
Ghent Bible Society, instituted 1834	8,980
Sleswick-Holstein Bible Society, instituted 1815, with auxiliaries	107,213
Eutin Bible Society, instituted 1817, for the Principality of Lübec	5,296
Lübec Bible Society, instituted 1814	11,472
Hamburg Bible Society, instituted 1814, with branches	83,752
Bremen Bible Society, instituted 1815, with an auxiliary	20,163
Lauenburg-Ratzeburg Bible Society, instituted 1816	10,675
Rostock Bible Society, instituted 1816	19,154
Hanover Bible Society, instituted 1814, with auxiliaries	99,229
Lippe-Detmold Bible Society, instituted 1816	3,569
Waldeck and Pyrmont Bible Society, instituted 1817	2,800
Hesse-Cassel Bible Society, instituted 1818	30,000
Hanau Bible Society, instituted 1818	3,316
Marburg Bible Society, instituted 1825	7,065
Frankfort Bible Society, instituted 1816	73,565
The Agency at Frankfort, appointed 1830	701,027
Hesse-Darmstadt Bible Society, instituted 1817, with auxiliaries	31,484
Duchy of Baden Bible Society, instituted 1820, with auxiliaries	18,585
Würtemberg Bible Society, instituted 1812, with auxiliaries	464,576
Bavarian Protestant Bible Institution at Nuremberg, instituted 1821, with auxiliaries	108,990

	Copies of Scriptures issued.
Saxon Bible Society, instituted 1814, with auxiliaries....	159,536
Anhalt-Bernburg Bible Society, instituted 1821.........	4,786
Anhalt-Dessau Bible Society	3,310
Weimar Bible Society, instituted 1821................	3,773
Eisenach Bible Society, instituted 1818	4,938
Brunswick Bible Society, instituted 1815	700
Prussian Bible Society at Berlin, instituted 1805, with auxiliaries	1,271,194
Issued to the Prussian Troops since 1830..............	235,916
Bâsle Bible Society, instituted 1804	336,184
Schaffhausen Bible Society, instituted 1813............	8,382
Zürich Bible Society, instituted 1812, with auxiliary at Winterthur	14,656
St. Gall Bible Society, instituted 1813................	34,429
Aargovian Bible Society, instituted 1815	13,802
Berne Bible Society............................	40,841
Neufchatel Bible Society, instituted 1816..............	6,430
Lausanne Bible Society, instituted 1814...............	32,000
Geneva Bible Society, instituted 1814.................	36,651
Glarus Bible Society, instituted 1819.................	5,000
Coire or Chur Bible Society, instituted 1813	12,267
Waldenses Bible Society at Tour, instituted 1816.......	4,238
Ionian Bible Society, instituted 1819 at Corfu, with three auxiliaries	7,377
Russian Bible Society, Petersburg, previous to its suspension by an imperial ukase in 1826, had 289 auxiliaries, and had printed the Scriptures in various languages, the circulation of which is still allowed.................	861,105
Russian Protestant Bible Society at St. Petersburg, instituted 1826, with numerous auxiliaries...............	132,464
Calcutta Bible Society, instituted 1811, with various branches	491,567
Serampore Missionaries	200,000
Madras Bible Society, instituted 1820.................	462,505
Bombay Bible Society, instituted 1813................	139,928
Colombo Bible Society, instituted 1812, with various branches in Ceylon.............................	36,114
Jaffna Bible Society.............................	62,625

We have not the means of ascertaining definitely the precise number of Bibles issued from the various depositories. An international correspondence is kept up with the different societies, but complete reports are not always received, and consequently the exact number can not be given. As far as the table goes it is strictly correct, but the number of issues is greater by thousands than is here exhibited. We may safely put down the number at 40,000,000. Many of the above societies increase their operations from year to year, and thus, from many different and distant points, the rays of divine truth go out for the healing of the nations.

CHAPTER XXXIV.

AGENCIES.

The appointment of agents early engrossed the attention of the Board of Managers.

No society, perhaps, ever labored more assiduously to forward its interests, without fee or reward, than did the American Bible Society. For several years all its business was conducted without the employment of an agent, nor did the managers adopt this policy until every other measure was exhausted.

The importance of having some one to organize auxiliary societies, and keep them in existence and action when organized, was early felt, and the repeated neglect of many auxiliaries to hold meetings, take up collections, explore and supply their respective fields, was equally deplored.

To obviate this difficulty, an Auxiliary Committee was appointed, whose duty it was, as far as practicable, to attend the anniversaries, or depute some one to attend. They were authorized to pay the expenses of such representatives, and urged to use their utmost endeavors to stimulate the societies to increased exertion.

This committee addressed various circulars to different parts of the country, many of which remained dead in the offices, and but few produced the desired effect. The following is one of those circulars:

"GENTLEMEN,

"The undersigned are a committee appointed by the managers of the American Bible Society in order to increase the number and animate the efforts of its auxiliaries.

"We trust that it is not necessary to dwell on the benefits resulting from this national institution. The simplicity of its object, and the comprehensiveness of its plan, must commend it to the approbation of every observer. Its 'sole object is to encourage a wider circulation of the Holy Scriptures without note or comment;' and it admits to equal privileges Christians of every religious denomination. Its effect has already been felt in the growth of that catholic charity which is an ornament to the Christian name, in the production of that mutual good-will between the most distant parts of our land, which promises to be a blessing both to the country as such, and to the Church which God has planted in it, and in the spread of the Bible to thousands who were formerly destitute of this sacred Volume.

"It is very evident, however, that the abilities of this institution to render its blessing permanently and extensively felt must depend on the number and activity of its tributary institutions. Although the British and Foreign Bible Society is patronized by many who are distinguished for the elevation of their rank and the abundance of their wealth, yet is the proportion of five sixths of their vast income annually derived from auxiliary societies and Bible associations; and if ever the American Bible Society is to become equally distinguished for zeal and success, it too must depend on the aid furnished from similar sources as its great means of replenishing its treasury. At the same time, it should be observed, that auxiliaries are equally necessary for the wise and economical distribution of the Scriptures themselves. Experience has convinced the Board of Managers that in ordinary cases, occurring within the United States, it is inconsistent with the best interest of the society to distribute the Bible gratuitously, except through the medium of auxiliary societies; and of course it is hoped that, in the most impoverished and destitute parts of our country, auxiliaries may be formed as means of sharing in the bounty of the national institution; and in those regions where auxiliaries may have funds sufficient to pay for the Bibles they may need to supply the destitute within their reach, their usefulness, as organs of distribution, must be obvious; for they alone can form a just opinion as to the extent of the existing wants, and the best means of furnishing a supply.

"To these general observations we beg leave to subjoin the following summary of regulations adopted by the Board of Managers of the American Bible Society in relation to auxiliaries.

"'All such Bible societies as shall agree to place their surplus revenue, after supplying their own districts with Bibles, at the disposal of this society, shall be considered auxiliary; and the members of such societies shall be entitled to vote in all meetings of this, and the officers of such societies shall be, *ex officio*, directors of this.

"'Every auxiliary will determine for itself what is their surplus revenue after supplying their own wants; but that revenue, when given, remains at the sole disposal of the managers; who will, however, thankfully receive any recommendation as to the best way of disposing of it, reserving to themselves the right of adopting or rejecting the recommendation.

"'Any society becoming auxiliary has a right of withdrawing from the connection when it sees fit so to do.

"'Bibles are sold at cost prices to any Bible society not auxiliary, and at a deduction of five per cent. from said cost prices to societies that are auxiliary.

"'No society is considered as an auxiliary to this which shall unite any other object with that of circulating the Scriptures without note or comment.

"'The auxiliaries now in existence, and those hereafter to be formed, are desired to transmit their annual reports to the parent institution before the first of March in each year, in order to afford the opportunity of embodying the information so communicated in the annual reports of this board.'

"For any further information which you may desire on the subject, we would refer you to the annual reports, and the quarterly extracts from the correspondence of the board; from all which you will see that the sole object of the American Bible Society is to spread the sacred Volume on such terms and to such extent that neither rich nor poor shall be found without the Oracles of Life.

"Hoping that you will see fit to unite with us in this good cause, in such way as to you shall seem most expedient, we are, gentlemen, your obedient servants,

"J. M. MATTHEWS,
"JOSHUA SOULE,
"PETER A. JAY,
"THEODORE DWIGHT,
"JOHN CAULDWELL,
} Committee."

In 1820 the committee were instructed, as the last resort, to make inquiry in regard to the obtaining suitable persons to act as traveling agents of the society. The managers were encouraged to this by reading the annals of the British and Foreign Bible Society, which furnished ample proof of the efficacy of such a policy.

In 1822, agents were appointed by the board, who labored successfully in organizing auxiliaries in the District of Columbia, Delaware, Maryland, and North Carolina. Having thus before them a demonstration of the importance of such agencies, and following the example of their illustrious prototype, they determined on continuing them in the field.

An agent was appointed at this time to visit the Southern and Western States. In 1823 two more were appointed, one to labor in the North and East, and the other in the South and West.

Two were appointed the succeeding year, to labor in different places.

They were also reappointed in 1825.

The succeeding year four were appointed.

The importance of having agents who should devote their whole time exclusively to the work being no longer regarded by the board as problematical—their experience having demonstrated beyond all question that if they were evils they were necessary evils—from this time forward they were regularly appointed as the wants of the country seemed to demand, and the circumstances of the society would justify.

These agents are selected from the different denominations represented in the society, and are appointed by the agency committee, after having been previously recommended by the secretaries.

Specific instructions are given them for the direction of their movements, to which they are required faithfully to adhere. The following is an extract from those instructions:

"In entering on your agency, you will find that your main business is with auxiliary Bible societies; either the formation of new ones, or the reviving of those already formed. The appendix of the annual report will show you where societies now exist, and your map where they are still wanting. Most of the auxiliaries now formed embrace a single county, some nearly a whole state, and some a mere village or township; some have many members, others but few; some are much in debt for books, others a little, others none at all; some can every year make liberal donations, some can barely supply their own wants, and others stand in need of assistance. In visiting a society, therefore, your first business will be to learn its exact present condition. This can be done by calling on its officers, and then on ministers of the Gospel and other men of candor and intelligence connected with it. (In forming a new auxiliary, inquire whether it should be a county society, or one for a central village and vicinity, taking in several contiguous counties.)

"If the society is in debt for books, learn the reason *why* payment for them has not been made, and what the prospect is that they will be paid for hereafter. Where is the money to come from by which they are to be paid for? From branch societies, from annual subscriptions, congregational donations, or from returns for books sold on credit? Is the debt so great as to embarrass the society, and to prevent its ordering other books which are needed? If the parent society were to *cancel* a part of the debt due, would the auxiliary make a speedy effort and pay the other part? Or if the auxiliary were to receive a donation of books, could these be sold, and money thus be raised, and the *whole* debt paid? After judicious, thorough inquiry, try to inform us what wise arrangement can be made for the early settlement of the debt of each society owing us which you may visit.

"When the debt of each society visited is seen to, and provision made for its settlement, your next inquiry will be, what can be done toward exciting the same to new efforts in procuring and distributing Bibles? Many societies which supplied their destitute families six or eight years ago, have scarcely bought or distributed a Bible since. Such must again be surrounded with destitute households, and many more large families can have but one small Bible. Something effectual ought here to be done. The officers and managers of the auxiliaries should at once commence a *re-supply* of their districts, and in a systematic, thorough manner.

"When a new society is to be formed, you should previously visit different parts of the field to be included, and interest as many as possible by calls on individuals and families, and by small preliminary meetings; and then, by notices on the Sabbath and in the papers, fix the time and place for a public meeting. At this meeting state clearly and fully the objects and advantages of a Bible society; let a few other brief addresses be made; then read and adopt a Constitution, choose officers, and open a subscription on the spot. It is generally the best way to allow all subscribers of any sum to become members. When the society is formed, the secretary of the same should be instructed to give *immediate* notice of this fact to the parent society. He should give assurance that the sole object of the auxiliary is to circulate the Scriptures 'without note or comment,' and to pay over its 'surplus funds' to the parent society. He should give also the name and post-office address of the president, corresponding secretary, and treasurer, with their usual titles. Try to make the secretary of the auxiliary understand this, and make all the officers feel that the prosperity of the society depends mainly on *them.* Societies which die, usually die for want of work marked out by their overseers.

"Should there be some counties in the new settlements where no auxiliaries can yet be formed for want of materials, pains should be taken to induce some contiguous auxiliary to visit and supply the destitute in such places. Books should be solicited of the parent society, if necessary, for that purpose. A few energetic Christian men, on a given day or week, might take a quantity of Bibles, and go through and supply such a county, and the good done would be incalculable. This plan must often be adopted in the new settlements. Agents at the West and South are particularly requested to attend to this suggestion.

"In some populous counties you will find it advantageous to form branch societies in connection with large auxiliaries. These branches can be formed in townships or in congregations. Discretion should be used in forming them, as they are prone to languish and die unless there is a good number of acting individuals to sustain them. In some counties a few branches can *now* be formed, and the way left open for others to be formed a few years hence. Whenever they are formed, notice should be given to the secretary of the county auxiliary to which they belong, and *he* should forward the name of the secretary of each branch to the parent society, so that the monthly extracts may be sent to him. The annual meetings of the branches should occur a few weeks previous to the meeting of the county auxiliary, and should be attended by delegates from the latter, if possible.

"When the situation of a township or congregation will not justify the formation of a branch society, a *local committee* of *three* or *five* of the best individuals should be substituted in place, and which committee should meet often, collect funds, receive and distribute books, and make returns in the same manner as is done by a branch society. This committee will be more efficient for the present than the branch society, and will, in time, grow into such a society. In some places, perhaps a single active person should be appointed as a local agent, keeping a supply of books on hand, and making collections of money when practicable.

"Inquire always as you go through a county whether Sunday school children are supplied with the Bible or New Testament. Some county societies are placing one of these Testaments in the hands of every child in the county between eight and sixteen years of age, and our board wish *all* societies to do the same, according to a *resolution* of the American Bible Society three years since. Testaments can be had at six and a quarter cents, and Bibles at twenty-five cents for this purpose. When Sunday schools of any denomination are in want of Bibles or Testaments, they should apply to the Depository of the Bible Society for that region. If the local society is not *able* to purchase them, the secretary of the same should apply to the parent society for a grant.

"In some counties you should inquire what can be done toward raising funds for the general distribution of the Bible in our own and foreign countries. Can some specific amount be raised annually for this purpose? Are all the ministers within the bounds of the society life members of the American Bible Society? Can not some who are life members by payment of thirty dollars, be made life directors by payment of one hundred and twenty dollars more? Are there not some wealthy and benevolent laymen who will become life directors or life members? Aim, wherever you go, to give a *permanency* to all auxiliaries—to make them feel that they are to act from year to year. The wants of our own growing population will never cease, and we have several of our Indian tribes, Spanish America, Brazil, France, Spain, Greece, Turkey, Syria, Bombay, Ceylon, Siam, China, and the Sandwich Islands, where the Word of God is sought with a constantly increasing avidity. The managers need many thousand dollars this moment to aid foreign distribution, and ought to raise more and more every year for this object. No society must think of relaxing its efforts until the *world* is supplied with the Bible. Try to impress this truth *deeply* on every auxiliary. Missions are now so far advanced that they must, in the future, make greater and greater demands for means to print the new translations made.

"The managers are trying to establish a more permanent system of agencies than they have hitherto had. Their design is to have the whole country divided into districts, each containing one or more states, and to establish in each district a good agent. They design also to have an auxiliary society in each county, and have the anniversary of these auxiliaries occur in such successive order that the agent can attend them all. Try to prepare the way for such a system where you are located.

"You will frequently find auxiliaries which have funds on hand which they wish to remit to the parent society. If these funds are received by you to forward, very great pains should be taken to give us an early account of them, in a clear, business-like manner, so that we can be in *no doubt* as to what each dollar is for, and from whence it comes. Let us have names, dates, and post-office addresses, so that we can acknowledge all receipts correctly by private letter or through the Bible Society Record.

"It is required that every agent write once a month to the parent society. In doing this, you can *condense* your journal, and thus give us a view of your proceedings, of interesting incidents, good effects of the Bible and Bible societies, objections to the Bible cause, and kinds of opposition met with, so that parts of this journal can be published.

"It sometimes occurs that the publications of the society are not taken from the post-offices where they are sent, and yet no notice is given of an unwillingness to receive them. The committee wish the secretary of every auxiliary to be *urged* to give annual information on this subject; to inform us who do and who do not take the Record and Reports; and to inform us of deaths, and of removals to other places of such as are entitled to them.

"Inquiries are sometimes made whether it is the desire of the board that auxiliaries should *sell* Bibles and Testaments when furnished them gratuitously. The committee would say that such is the wish of the board, except in cases where the destitute are *unable* to buy. A purchased Bible is generally more valued and read than one which costs nothing. Moneys arising in this way should be used in *procuring* more books, or sent to the parent society as a donation to *make* others.

"Some auxiliaries sell their books, when purchased, at a much higher price than others. It is desirable that there should be *uniformity* in this respect, and a good rule is to sell them for cost and charges.

"It is sometimes asked whether auxiliaries ought to sell books to those who are not members. They are not bound, of course, to do so, but yet good would often be done by allowing those who will not become members to buy, as such kindness may perhaps lead them eventually to become members.

"While engaged in your agency you will frequently be called to preach, or make addresses on the Sabbath, and sometimes, perhaps, on common topics as well as on your special business. In all cases it is expected that you will be careful to avoid any of the peculiarities of denomination, and dwell on those great essential truths of religion in which all the evangelical unite. The Bible cause has no sectarian character, and its agents should give it none, either by their public speaking or conversation. All metaphysical, sectional, ecclesiastical, or political topics, which divide the opinions even of many good men, are to be avoided by those whose great business is to circulate the Word of God as it was received from heaven. Try to produce harmony, forbearance, and kindness among different denominations, by treating all who have the Christian spirit as members of the same great family, and expectants of the same inheritance in their Father's house on high. You can not feel too deeply the importance of your work, and the necessity of looking continually to the Great Author of the Bible for wisdom and strength. Without his aid you will do little to any valuable purpose; with his grace assisting, you can do all things well. Cherish habitually a modest, prudent, Christian spirit, which, with an entire devotedness to the business of your agency, will be the best recommendation both of yourself and your object among all the good people whom you may visit.

"With these suggestions, the committee would sincerely commend you to the guidance of our heavenly Father, praying that He would open the way, through your instrumentality, for the wide diffusion of the Holy Scriptures, which are able, through faith, to make men wise unto salvation.

"With affectionate regard, they subscribe themselves your obedient friends and brethren."

The above instructions from the Committee on Agencies are sent to every commissioned agent in the society's employ. In addition to what is here specified, agents are expected to visit each auxiliary society in the bounds of their respective fields once a year, and keep up a correspondence with them in relation to all matters pertaining to the work in which they are engaged.

The following list embraces the names of all the agents from 1820 to the present time, a period of twenty-nine years. The highest number employed at any one time was nineteen, and the lowest two. Some were in the employ of the society but a few months, others but one year, and others have been agents for a long time.

Rev. Richard Hall.
Dr. Samuel Robinson.
Rev. John M. Peck.
Dr. Nathaniel Dwight.
Rev. Jareb B. Waterbury.
Rev. Greenbury W. Ridgley.
Mr. Henry White.
Rev. Simeon Wilbur.
Rev. James C. Barnes.
Mr. Dennis M. Winston.
Mr. Samuel C. Jennings.
Rev. E. R. Fairchild.
Rev. George B. Davis.
Mr. Henry A. Rowland.
Mr. Samuel D. Blythe.
Rev. Herbert C. Thompson.
Rev. W. W. Stevenson.
Rev. Charles H. Weld.
Mr. Augustus Bagley.
Rev. Joseph P. Cunningham.
Rev. Thomas P. Green.
Rev. Reuben Taylor.
Rev. George Stacey.
Rev. William M. Stuart.
Rev. Solomon Hardy.
Rev. J. Lathrop.
Rev. M. Fairchild.
Rev. Samuel Hodge.
Rev. George Sheldon.
Rev. Mr. Gould.
Rev. P. W. Dowd.
Rev. Robert Tisdale.
Rev. J. P. Turney.
Rev. Eli Ball.
Rev. Mr. Wilcox.
Mr. Timothy Turner.
Rev. Mr. Patton.
Mr. W. H. Hadley.
Rev. Robert Piggot.
Rev. Neal Johnson.
Rev. James Williams.
Rev. Thomas R. Durfee.
Rev. Benjamin Chase.
Rev. T. A. Cornwall.
Rev. Sumner Mandeville.
Mr. Daniel Clark.
Rev. John S. Wilson.
Rev. Joel W. Newton.
Col. James M'Clung.
Rev. James B. Walker.
Rev. Joseph Lane.
Rev. Thomas Shepard.
Rev. Myron Tracy.
Mr. Philo Wright.
Rev. James R. Wetherby.
Rev. John Bartlett.
Rev. James M'Elroy.
Rev. James B. Shaw.
Rev. Francis Bowman.
Rev. Ira M. Easter.
Mr. Isaac W. Wheelwright, for Spanish America.
Mr. Joab Seely.
Mr. John C. Smith.
Rev. John Ford.
Rev. John S. Ebaugh.
Rev. Roswell Kimball.
Rev. William Vaughan.
Rev. Isaac Shook.
Rev. H. J. Kepler.
Damianos, a Greek priest, Athens, Greece.
Rev. Ward Childs.
Rev. John J. Aiken.
Rev. Francis Dighton.
Rev. Calvin N. Ransom.
Rev. William M'Kinney.
Rev. Simeon H. Calhoun, in the Levant.
Rev. John S. Mitchell.
Rev. Charles Macreading.
Rev. Hector Brownson.
Rev. Francis P. Goulding.
Rev. Sylvester Holmes.
Mr. Horace Hunt.
Rev. Jacob Shepherd.

Rev. John W. Powers.
Mr. Charles Hastings.
Rev. Stephen Peet.
Rev. E. W. Sehon.
Rev. C. M. F. Deems.
Rev. Benjamin Shipman.
Rev. Horace Spaulding.
Mr. A. B. Lewis.
Rev. Charles Fitch.
Rev. J. W. Dale.
Rev. C. G. Lee.
Rev. E. Jordan.
Rev. Mr. Mattison.
Rev. William Bacon.
Rev. John Lindsey.
Rev. Julius Field.
Dr. John H. Kain.
Rev. George H. Warner.
Virgil A. Bogue, Esq.
Rev. William Homes.
Rev. Anthony T. Scruggs.
Rev. Dr. Pierce.
Rev. Daniel Butler.
Rev. John Storrs.
Rev. Henry B. Pierpont.
Rev. John P. Knox.
Rev. Henry Colclazer.
Rev. Richard Bond.
Rev. J. S. Graves.
Rev. W. P. Strickland.
Rev. F. T. Mitchell.
Rev. Mr. Blodgett.
Rev. James V. Watson.
Rev. Henry W. Adams.
Rev. Calvin W. Wolcott.
Rev. Mr. Tooker.
Rev. Mr. Lore.
Rev. Aaron Wood.
Mr. L. S. Swezey.
Rev. John Poisal.
Rev. Mr. Jamieson.
Rev. Mr. Cochran.
Rev. Richard Killen.
Rev. J. A. Baughman.
Rev. H. S. C. Walker.
Rev. Thomas Stringfield.
Rev. J. S. Hughes.
Rev. C. Kent.
Mr. A. Lord.
Rev. E. H. Hatcher.
Rev. Mr. Goodenough.
Rev. A. R. Banks.
Rev. George West.
Rev. Mr. Norris, Mexico.
Rev. Mr. Duerielle.
Rev. James M'Mahon.
Rev. Benjamin Miller.
Rev. J. W. Parke.
Rev. W. H. Korkhill.
Rev. E. P. Jones.
Rev. H. J. Durbin.

CHAPTER XXXV.

LEGACIES.

One of the strongest evidences of the value placed upon the American Bible Society by Christians is its remembrance by many of the most devoted in the last hours of life. It has testimony from living witnesses in all parts of the world, Christian and heathen, and dying witnesses have given evidence of their belief of its importance and their attachment to it by the consecration of their property to the furtherance of its objects.

Legacies had been made during the first few years of the society's existence, from various individuals, of small amount, but not the less valued on that account. From the organization of the society up to 1821, there had been received into the treasury from these sources $2939 75.

The Hon. Elias Boudinot, LL.D., who had devoted his time, and talents, and influence in the support of the cause, at his death bequeathed to the society 589 acres of valuable land. Mr. John Withington also bequeathed $10,000.

In 1823, legacies were received to the amount of....	$610 00
In 1824, from Mr. Samuel Sheldon, of New York...	2,000 00
In 1825:	
From Mr. Matthew Benschoten, of New York........	2,000 00
From Mrs. Lydia Dixon........................	50 00
From Mr. Joseph Fletcher......................	25 00
In 1826:	
From Mrs. Campbell, of New Hampshire............	10 00
From Mr. Daniel Burger.........................	500 00
From Mr. James Thompson, Esq., deceased..........	1,000 00

From Dr. Elias Hawes	$1,000 00
In 1827 :	
From Othniel Smith, late of New York	500 00
From Mrs. Isabella Smith	30 00
From Mr. Thomas Henderson, of New Jersey	30 00
In 1828	1,910 00
In 1829	209 39
In 1830 :	
From the estate of John Fleetwood Marsh, of East Chester, N. Y., deceased	10,000 00
From that of John Withington, of New York, deceased	7,000 00
From a female friend to the Bible Society, late of Newark, N. J.	50 00
From Abel Burrit, late of New Haven, Conn.	40 00
From Olive Fowler, of Hartford, Conn.	20 00
From Martha Scott, late of Lexington District, S. C.	200 00
From Adam Wylie, Sen., late of Ohio	20 00
From Mary Herrick, late of Reading, Mass.	100 00
In 1831 :	
From Martin Thaxter, late of Worcester, deceased, $100 and interest	126 00
From Captain Thomas Punderson, late of New Haven, Conn., deceased, proceeds of sale of stock	40 00
From Cyrene Isaacs, late of Genoa, N. Y., deceased, by her executor, William Bradley	50 00
From Miss Sarah Greely, late of Hopkinton, N. H., to aid in sending the Word of Life to the poor and destitute in the western part of the United States	50 00
From John Taylor, Esq., of Albany, by his executor, Charles D. Cooper	300 00
From Miss Miranda Wright, of Westhampton, Mass., deceased, by Daniel Butler, Jun.	20 00
From Miss Belinda Clarkson, late of New York, deceased	100 00
From John Bartlett, late of New Ipswich, Mass., by Isaac Adams, executor	450 00
From Mrs. Hester Simpson, late of Wilkes county, Ga., by William and Robert Simpson, executors	30 00
From Josiah Penfield, late of Savannah, Ga., deceased, by his executor, Joseph Cummin	1,000 00
From William Semple, late of Pittsburgh, Penn., deceased, by his executor, William J. Semple	50 00
From Miss Thankful Moses, of Blandford, deceased, by her executor, Charles Hall, on account	500 00

In 1832:

From Miss Clarina Bacchus, late of Chillicothe, Ohio ..	$603 00
From Mrs. Mary Burnett, widow of James Burnett, of Newark, N. J.	50 00
From Edward M. Walker, deceased, by R. D. Silliman, acting executor	100 00
From Maria Merrick, late of North Brandford, Conn...	100 00
From Charles J. Jenkins, late of Jefferson county, Ga. .	25 00
From Daniel Clements, late of New Windsor, deceased, by his executors, John Clements and John Smith, of Cornwall, part of residuum of estate..............	500 00
From Miss Thankful Moses, late of Blandford, Mass., deceased, by her executor, Dr. Eli Hall, balance of $1000	652 00
From Edward Warren Rockwell, late of Hudson, N. Y., a child four years old...........................	1 26
From Thomas Hamilton, late of Kittaning, Penn., by James Hamilton, Esq........................	200 00
From Mrs. Elizabeth Tappan, of Poughkeepsie, N. Y., deceased, by P. C. Tappan, Esq.................	30 00
From Jonas Williams, late of New Windsor, deceased.	100 00
From Roxana Bishop, of New Haven, Conn., deceased.	30 00
From Colonel H. Rutgers, late of New York, deceased, by his executor, William B. Crosby, Esq...........	1,000 00
From William Smith, late of Troy, deceased	1,000 00
From Marinus Oudenard, late of Utica, N. Y., deceased, with interest	180 48

In 1833:

From Joseph Faulkner, late of Andover, Mass.........	200 00
From William W. Walmsley, late of Mexico, by James B. Thompson and George Savage, executors........	200 00
From John B. Lawrence, late of Salem, Mass., by Abel L. Pierson and Charles Lawrence, executors........	634 62
From George Paull, late of St. Clairsville, Ohio.......	100 00
From Miss Clarina Backus, late of Chillicothe, Ohio, second payment	301 50
From Miss Mary Hamilton, late of Carlisle, Penn.	100 00
From Miss Joanna Baker, late of Amherst, Mass.......	2 00
From Miss Mary Belknap, late of Boston, Mass., by her executors, John Belknap, A. E. Belknap, and J. Head	1,000 00
From Miss Clarina Backus, late of Chillicothe, Ohio, third payment................................	703 50
From John Vernon, late of Linton township, Coshocton county, Ohio	75 00

From Jacob Gilbert, late of South Salem, West Chester county, N. Y., per Josiah Gilbert, executor.........	$100 00
From Rebecca A. Sherman, late of New Haven, Conn.	50 50
From Deacon Levi Crosby, late of Lisbon, Conn., per Lyman Brewer, Esq...........................	50 00
From Mrs. Naomi Bridgden, late of Schenectady, N. Y., per N. B. Bassett............................	10 00
From William Thomas, late of South Carolina, William Dubose's one half, with interest..................	653 75
Another legacy	10 20
In 1834 :	
From Mrs. Louisa Pratt, late of Austerlitz, N. Y......	100 00
From Margaret Gray, late of Jaffray, Cheshire county, N. H..	209 00
From James Ralston, late of Chester county, Penn.....	60 00
From William Thomas, late of Cheraw, S. C., half of a legacy and interest...........................	653 28
From Gilbert S. Fowler, late of New York, deceased...	50 00
From Peter Paine, late of South Hartford, Washington county, N. Y., deceased.........................	12 50
From Mrs. Eliza H. Jones, late of Calcutta, deceased..	50 00
From Thames Wilcox, late of Bristol, Conn...........	575 00
From Frederic A. Graves, of Sunderland, Mass........	20 00
From Mrs. Maria Schuyler, deceased................	200 00
From Esther Turner, late of Newton, Bucks county, Penn., deceased...............................	250 00
From Mrs. Angelica Lane, late of Troy, N. Y., deceased	200 00
From Nathaniel Smith, late of Sunderland, Mass., dec'd.	500 00
From Mrs. Sarah Ingham, late of Saybrook, Conn., deceased	25 00
From Mr. Andrew M'Neely, late of Charlotte, N. C., deceased.......................................	50 00
From Eliza T. Wells, late of Philadelphia, deceased...	48 75
From Moses Cowan, late of Union Village, N. Y., in part	300 00
In 1835 :	
From Horton Strong, late of Augusta, Oneida county, N. Y.	10 00
From Mary R. Farrington, of do.	46
From Mrs. Margaret Saunders, late of Lansingburgh, N. Y..	50 00
From Thaddeus Northrop, late of Charlton, Saratoga county, N. Y., deceased.........................	473 44
From Mary Rowley, late of Galway, Saratoga county, N. Y., deceased.............................	15 00

From Nathaniel Smith, late of Sunderland, Mass......	$150 00
From Mrs. Sarah Willoughby, late of Washington county, Va., deceased....................................	20 00
From Wessell Van Schaick, late of Lansingburgh, N. Y., deceased..	250 00
From Peter Stryker, late of Flatbush, N. Y., deceased..	419 37
From Miss Clarina Backhus, late of Chillicothe, Ohio, deceased, on account..........................	255 49
From Mrs. Dorcas A. Bishop, late of Wilton, N. H., deceased..	425 00
From Isaac Waters, late of New Hartford, N. Y., deceased	100 00
From Mrs. Anne Woodward, late of Hartford, Vt., deceased..	30 00
From Hon. Josiah Rising, late of Rupert, Vt., deceased	100 00
From Moses Cowan, late of Union Village, N. Y., deceased	200 00
From John M'Lain, late of Brown county, Ohio......	100 00
From Horace D. Humphrey, late of Simsbury, Conn., deceased..	50 00
From Miss Sarah H. Nitherton, late of New Lexington, Mo., deceased..................................	5 00
From Mrs. Patience Moore, late of Marietta, Ohio, deceased..	50 00
From David W. Childs, late of Utica, N. Y., deceased..	500 00
From Levi and Amelia Tomlinson, late of Ohio.......	50 00
From John Mooney Mead, late of East Hartford, Conn., deceased..	2 00
From Miss Mary Allen, late of East Windsor, Conn., deceased..	300 00
From Samuel Howard, Jun., late of Benson, Vt.......	200 00
From Aaron Andrews, late of Ware, Mass., deceased..	50 00
From Isaac Van Horn, late of Zanesville, Ohio, deceased, first installment of $50........................	12 50
From Mrs. Catharine J. Andrews, late of Back Creek Church, N. C., deceased........................	5 00
From Joseph Yates, late of Fleming county, Ky., deceased	50 00
In 1836:	
From William C. Johnson, late of Burlington, Lawrence county, Ohio, and interest......................	205 00
From Miss Catharine Faulkener, late of Orange county, N. Y., deceased..............................	100 00
From a Friend, deceased........................	10 00
From James Nelson, late of Steubenville, Ohio........	100 00
From Mrs. Anne Powell, late of Liberty county, Geo...	25 00

From Isaac Warren, late of Charlestown, Mass.	$500 00
From Heman Averill, late of New York city	250 00
From Obadiah Thayer, of Wellsborough, Essex county, N. Y.	50 67
From Mrs. Jennette Bleakley, late of Wigton, Scotland	22 50
From Joseph Burr, late of Manchester, deceased, pecuniary legacy and interest, also stock, worth at par $8800	11,279 46
From Mrs. Anne Welch, late of New London, Conn.	2,123 21
From Hugh Kennedy, late of Hagerstown, Md.	1,000 00
From Samuel Bell, late of Preble county, Ohio	100 00
From John Flack, late of the city of New-York	500 00
From Lucy Adams, late of Charlestown, Mass.	10 00
From a young lady, deceased	6 00
From Mrs. Jerusha M. Ackerly, late of New York, deceased	200 00
From Normand Smith, Jun., late of Hartford, Conn.	800 00
From Mrs. Sarah A. Andrus, late of Madison, Conn., and interest	107 82
From Gilbert King, late of Newburgh, N. Y.	1,000 00
From Miss Mary Gilbert, late of South Salem, N. Y., deceased	200 00
In 1837:	
From Mrs. Anne Margaret Seyburt, late of Rome, N. Y.	100 00
From Deacon Elisha Dickinson, late of Hadley, Mass.	100 00
From Benjamin Tallmadge, late of Litchfield, Conn.	1,000 00
From Ferdinand Bailey, late of Scotchtown, N. Y.	325 00
From Joseph Burr, late of Manchester, Vt.	300 00
From Samuel Haynes, late of Prattsburgh, N. Y.	25 00
From William Ramage, late of St. Clairsville, Ohio	30 00
From Letitia Murphy, late of Churchtown, Penn.	10 00
From Miss Elizabeth A. D. Gardner, late of Charlestown, Mass.	7 00
From James Dunn, late of Belmont county, Ohio	30 00
From Normand Smith, Jun., late of Hartford, balance of legacy	200 00
From William Whitlock, late of New York city	500 00
From Stillman Jones, late of Boston, Mass.	274 05
From Joseph Burr, late of Manchester, Vt., 10 shares of Bank of America sold	1,000 00
From Mrs. Lydia Bassell, late of Lansingburgh, N. Y.	150 27
From Miss Fanny Greenough, late of Amherst, Mass.	50 00
In 1838:	
From Mrs. Grizzy Ross, late of Portland, Maine	50 00

From Mrs. Judge Wallace, late of Huntsville, Ala.....	$3 00
From Mrs. Caroline Averill, late of New York........	50 00
From Isaac Brewster, do. do. do............	500 00
From Rev. J. L. Pomeroy, late of Worthington, Mass...	1,500 00
From General Isaac Van Horne, late of Zanesville, Ohio	37 50
From Miss Lucy Ann Brown, late of Hadley, Mass....	150 00
From Elias Boudinot, LL.D., late of Burlington, N. J., proceeds of land sold..........................	2,027 00
From Miss Matilda Wright, late of New London, Conn.	50 00
From Miss Molly Shaw, late of Palmer, Mass.........	100 00
From Miss Julia Ann Maltby, late of Northford, Conn.	10 00
From Josiah Merlin, late of Jefferson, Tenn..........	5 00
From Polemna Smith, do. do. do...........	28 00
From Miss Jane Brice, late of Montgomery county, Ohio	20 00
From John Smith, late of Southport, N. Y.	100 00
From Rebecca B. Carpenter, of Rehoboth Village, Mass.	200 00
From Joseph Burr, late of Manchester, Vt., proceeds of stock sold..................................	7,800 00
From Peninah Hampton, late of Rahway, N. J.	50 00
From Stillman Jones, late of Boston, Mass.; balance....	661 66
From Mrs. Lydia Bassell, late of Lansingburgh, N. Y., balance	126 43
From Miss Martha Bernard, late of Highland county, Ohio......................................	10 00
In 1839:	
From John Salmon, late of Cincinnati, Ohio..........	427 97
From James Beekman, late of New York............	500 00
From Lydia S. M'Gaffey, late of N. Sandwich, N. H...	25 00
From Noah Bosworth, late of Halifax, Mass..........	196 50
From Mary Platt, late of Fishkill, N. Y.............	200 00
From Elias Boudinot, LL.D., late of Burlington, N. J., balance of proceeds of land sold..................	1,075 00
From Henry Gardner, late of Charlestown, Mass......	181 00
From Joseph Lathrop, late of New York.............	3,310 00
From Cyrus Sampson, a colored man, late of Kentucky, proceeds of land devised by him twenty years since, for the distribution of the Bible	97 87
From David D. Crane, late of Newark, N. J..........	50 00
From John Campbell, late of Piqua, Miami county, Ohio	62 00
From Lydia Bassell, late of Lansingburgh, N. Y.,.....	127 14
From Olive Perkins Kinsman, late of Warren, Ohio...	100 00
From Hetty Rice, late of Framingham, Mass.........	43 36
From Sarah Elizabeth Howe, late of Jaffrey, N. H. ...	200 00

In 1840:

From Rev. J. L. Pomeroy, late of West Springfield, Mass., on account	$1,500 00
From Eliza M. Hall, late of Wallingford, Conn.	100 00
From Joseph Lathrop, late of New York, avails of Hartford Bridge stock	321 00
From Mrs. Abijah Marshall, late of New York city	300 00
From Angus M'Niel, late of Richmond county, N. C.	50 00
From William Bryce, late of New York city, on account	112 00
From John W. Claxton, late of Philadelphia, interest on stock bequeathed by him	18 05
From Miss Martha Rogers, late of Hartford, Conn.	200 00
From Abel Drewry, late of Sangersfield, N. Y.	107 00
From Nathan Newell, late of Windsor, Me.	10 00
From Alexander M'Donald, late of Baltimore, Md.	500 00
From Normand Smith, Jun., late of Hartford, Conn.	250 00
From James Montgomery, late of Caswell county, N. C.	25 00
From Sewall B. Pratt, late of Bolton, N. Y.	25 00
From Hon. Jeremiah Nelson, late of Newburyport, Mass., on account	100 00
From Rev. J. L. Pomeroy, late of West Springfield, Mass.	500 00
From John Campbell, late of Miami county, Ohio	43 00
From Miss Polly Hubbard, late of York, Livingston county, N. Y.	25 00
From Mrs. Fally Taylor, late of East Bloomfield, N. Y.	2,000 00
From James Wilson, late of Champaign county, Ohio	10 00
From Timothy Allyn, late of West Springfield, Mass.	30 00
From John Shackford, late of Washington city	250 00
From John Galbraith, late of Steubenville, Ohio	438 22
From James Vance, late of Abingdon, Va.	42 00
From Asa Clarke, Jun., late of Sherburne, Mass.	10 00
From Mrs. Abigail Woods, late of Dunstable, Mass.	25 00
From Miss Anna Woodward, late of East Haddam, Conn.	50 00
From Mrs. Fanny R. Smith, late of New London, Conn.	100 00
From Mary E. Shepherd, late of Canandaigua, N. Y.	18 87
From Forster Allen, late of Manchester, Mass.	75 00

In 1841:

From Mrs. Rebecca Nickerson, New Bedford, Mass.	100 00
From John R. Smith, a soldier, late of Fort Towson	20 00
From William Smart, late of Gloucester county, Va.	250 00
From Ann E. Edgar, late of New London, Conn.	50 00
From Mrs. Hannah Gates, late of Waterford, Conn.	310 00
From William Kirkpatrick, late of Lancaster, Penn.	250 00

From Orson P. Wheeler, late of Charlotte, Vt.	$90 00
From Elizabeth Tuttle, late of Massachusetts	28 12
From Amos Tenney, late of Claremont, N. H.	50 00
From Polly A. Sterling, late of La Fayette, N. Y.	10 00
From Miss Mary Ann Brimmer, late of Boston, Mass.	5,000 00
From Mr. M'Ferson, late of Red Oak, Ohio	100 00
From Mrs. Dorothy Powers, late of Middletown, Conn.	30 00
From Mary Ann Belden, late of New York	10 00
From Normand Smith, Jun., late of Hartford, Conn., in part	556 00
From Miss Elizabeth Hotchkiss, late of Watertown, Conn.	75 00
In 1842:	
From Rev. J. L. Pomeroy, late of West Springfield, Mass., in part	700 00
From John Shackford, Esq., late of Washington City, balance	7,707 52
From Samuel Sheldon, late of Troy, N. Y.	117 50
From Elijah Comfort, late of Bridport, Vt.	3 67
From Moses A. Chapin, late of West Springfield, Mass.	100 00
From Mrs. Mary Ann Morgan, late of Stockbridge, Mass., one life member	30 00
From Thomas Crosby, late of Lee, Mass.	200 00
From John Caldwell, late of Morning Sun, Ohio	260 00
From Joseph F. Affolder, late of Newark, N. J., in part	200 00
From Elisha Hatch, late of Griswold, Conn.	30 00
From James Davidson, late of Stockbridge, Mass.	20 00
From William M'Farland, late of Worcester, Mass., in part	2,400 00
From Miss Freelove Collins, late of Westfield, Mass., in part	800 00
From Mrs. Christian Baker, late of Boston, Mass. (for dist.)	2,000 00
From Dr. Otis Spurr, late of Granville, N. Y.	5 00
From Dr. Henry W. Hornbeck, late of Montgomery, N. Y., in part	200 00
From Hon. Jeremiah Nelson, late of Newburyport, Mass., balance	604 00
From Miss Sarah Fletcher, late of Northbridge, Mass., in part	207 50
From Mrs. Jane Van Cortlandt, late of Newark, N. J.	500 00
From Dr. Henry W. Hornbeck, late of Montgomery, N. Y., dividend on stock	28 00
From Hannah E. Stirling, late of New Milford, Conn.	2 00

From Thankful Evans, Oakham, Mass.	$23 87
From Mrs. H. G. Powers, late of Phillipston, Mass.....	10 00
From Lewis Johnson	50 00
From Stephen Long, late of Honeybrook, Penn........	100 00
From Rev. Ebenezer Porter, D.D., late of Andover, Mass.	1,102 10
In 1843:	
From Julius Page, late of Binghampton, N. Y.........	500 00
From Lydia Boardman, late of Haverhill, Mass.......	50 00
From Ebenezer Smith, late of Schaghticoke, N. Y.....	10 00
From D. M. Beebe, late of Richmond, Mass..........	150 00
From Miss Elizabeth M. Mitchell, late of Norwich, Conn.	10 00
From Judith C. Upham, late of Rochester, N. H......	100 00
From Mrs. Rebecca Nickerson, late of Bedford, Mass., balance	121 08
From Esther H. Bullard, late of Holliston, Mass.......	1,000 00
From Matthew Stephenson, late of Leesburg, Tenn....	500 00
From Zenas P. Ives, late of Bristol, Conn............	150 00
From John Hopkins, late of North Hampton, Mass....	1,504 50
From Cyrus Williams, late of Stockbridge, Mass., one half for the blind	2,000 00
From Leffert Hagawout, late of Greenwich, N. J......	50 00
From Elisha Munson, late of New Haven, Conn......	100 00
From Lucy Fanning, late of Albion, N. Y., one life member	30 00
From John M'Donald, late of Pittsburgh, Penn.......	1,000 00
From Miss Lavinia A. Wilson, late of Marlborough, Mass.	25 00
From William Camp, late of Newark, N. J., in part...	229 69
From Deacon Samuel Galpin, late of Middletown, Conn.	5 00
From Joseph Battell, late of Norfolk, Conn...........	200 00
From Dyer White, late of New Haven, Conn., one life member	50 00
From Henry W. Delavan, late of Ballston Center, N. Y.	2,000 00
From Abial Cheney, late of Waterford, Vt...........	900 00
From Mrs. Lucy Grosvenor, late of Brookfield, Mass....	170 00
From John Caldwell, late of Morning Sun, Ohio......	240 00
From Emily A. Austin, late of Brooklyn, N. Y........	50 00
From Sarah Fletcher, late of Northbridge, Mass., in part	143 75
From Abigail A. Linsley, late of Northford, Conn.....	100 00
From W. M'Farland, late of Worcester, Mass., in part.	350 00
From Samuel B. Loud, late of South Weymouth, Mass., in part....................................	500 00
From Rev. J. L. Pomeroy, late of West Springfield, Mass., in part......	300 00

From Robert Gosman, late of Stuyvesant, N. Y.	$1,066 00
From Dr. Henry W. Hornbeck, late of Montgomery, N. Y., balance	883 00
In 1844:	
From Samuel B. Loud, late of South Weymouth, Mass., balance	500 00
From Dorothy Johnson, late of Cornwall, Conn.	54 50
From Abiah Chapin, late of Westfield, Mass.	50 00
From Cyrus Williams, late of Stockbridge, Mass., in part	1,122 62
From Hannah H. Perkins, late of Norwich, Conn.	50 00
From Sally Jewett, late of Hollis, N. H.	20 00
From John Campbell, late of Piqua, Ohio	160 00
From Dr. Jas. English, late of Monmouth county, N. J., balance	1,073 56
From Mrs. Anna Welsh, late of New London, Conn., balance	4,000 00
From D. Traphagen, late of Tewksbury, N. J.	100 00
From Normand Smith, Jun., late of Hartford, Conn., in part	500 00
From Olive A. Strong, late of Augusta, N. Y., three life members	90 00
From John A. Chamberlain, late of Dorchester, Mass.	1,000 00
From Miss Lucy Ann Whittlesey, late of Bunker Hill, Ill.	10 00
From Miss Freelove Collins, late of Westfield, Mass., in part	100 00
From Mrs. Abby Roff, late of Newark, N. J.	444 67
From Miss Sarah Fletcher, late of Northbridge, Mass., balance	147 50
From Wm. M'Farlan, late of Worcester, Mass., balance	250 00
From Miss Huldah Perley, late of Bedford, Mass.	100 00
From Phebe Osborn, late of Camillus, N. Y.	50 00
From Hon. Wm. Hampton, late of Piketon, Ohio, in part	340 00
From Nathaniel Smith, late of Flushing, N. Y.	1,070 73
From Thomas Gilham, late of Oglethorpe county, Geo.	62 50
From Daniel Bullard, late of Kingston, N. J.	25 00
From J. Sperry, late of Winchester, Va.	100 00
From Miss Emily A. Austin, late of Brooklyn, N. Y., balance	50 00
From Mrs. Sarah G. Bond, late of North Brookfield, Mass.	50 00
From Mrs. Abigail Cushing, late of Hanson, Mass.	10 00
From Andrew P. Hopper, late of Steubenville, Ohio	40 00
From Mrs. Elizabeth Nutt, late of Watervliet, N. Y.	100 00
From Joanna Stearns, late of Milford, Mass.	50 00

From Miss Emily J. Munson, late of East Bloomfield, N. Y.	$30 00
From Rev. J. L. Pomeroy, late of West Springfield, Mass., in part	1,765 00
From Andrew Anderson, late of Steubenville, Ohio	100 00
From Thomas Loomis, late of New Berlin, N. Y.	33 33
In 1845:	
From Mrs. Susan P. Root, late of Binghampton, N. Y., three life members	100 00
From Elizabeth Wylie, late of Sparta, Ill.	12 00
From Miss Emily A. Austin, late of Brooklyn, N. Y.	50 00
From James Goddard, late of Berlin, Mass.	100 00
From Henry C. Willard, late of Ashby, Mass.	14 06
From F. S. Key, late of Washington, D. C., in part	352 24
From John Morrison, late of New York	1,000 00
From Miss Nancy H. Roberts, late of Newark, N. J.	15 00
From Mrs. Jerusha Brockway, late of Hartford, Ohio	50 00
From Rev. Erastus Ripley, late of Meriden, Conn.	481 02
From Miss Temperance Bull, late of Essex, Conn.	150 00
From James C. Hanks, late of Elgin, Ill.	23 00
From Henry H. Wilson, late of Somerset county, N. J.	50 00
From Richard Carney, late of Portsmouth, Va.	1,000 00
From Mary Davenport, late of Little Compton, R. I.	78 07
From James Walker, late of Kingston, Tenn.	60 14
From Mrs. Emma Buckingham, late of Putnam, Ohio.	1,000 00
From Martha E. Watson, late of Warren, Mass.	50 06
From Rev. J. L. Pomeroy, late of West Springfield, Mass., in part	150 00
From Elizabeth Gibson, late of Auburn, N. Y.	50 00
From Rev. Josiah Chickering, late of Phillipston, Mass.	100 00
From Mrs. Rose Sikes, late of Springfield, N. Y.	4 00
From Miss Frances L. Hamner, late of Farmsville, Va.	10 00
From James Cox, late of Baltimore, Md., in part	333 00
From Joseph Affolder, late of Newark, N. J.	177 76
From Rebecca Baldwin, late of Waterbury, Conn.	30 00
From Mrs. Adeline W. Goff, late of Pulaski, Tenn.	20 00
From Henry Hurd, late of Starkey, N. Y., one life member	30 00
From Abby Roff, late of Newark, N. J., balance	282 06
From Robert Ormiston, late of Springfield, N. Y.	100 00
From Jerusha Reed, late of New Haven, Conn.	50 00
From Miss Rachel Bullard, late of Franklin, Mass.	5 00
From John Damon, late of Reading, Mass.	1,027 82
From Agnes Kemper, late of Madison county, Va.	20 00

From Cyrus Williams, late of Stockbridge, Mass., in part	$144 64
From Asa Fisher, late of Franklin, Mass.	750 00
From Elizabeth Jenkins, late of Rutland, Vt.	76 96
From Miss Sally Keyes, late of Westford, Mass.	25 00
From Ebenezer Elmer, late of Bridgeton, N. J	500 00
From Miles C. Brownell, late of Ovid, N. Y.	5 00
From Mrs. Rebecca Bell, late of Eutaw, Ala.	25 00
From Gen. John Francis, late of Royalton, Vt.	150 00
From Mrs. Sarah Watkins, late of Winhall, Vt.	3 00
From Thomas Gilham, late of Oglethorpe county, Ga., in part	68 75
From Mrs. Sarah Fitch, late of Westmoreland, N. Y.	2 00
From James M'Vean, late of Caledonia, Vt.	103 50
From Amzi Goddin, late of Louisville, Miss.	1,000 00
From Miss Lucretia Bliss, late of Springfield, Mass., three life members	190 40
From Mrs. Lucy H. Clark, late of Marlborough, Mass.	10 00
From Oliver Dickinson, late of Amherst, Mass.	700 00
From Elizabeth Reynolds, late of Pine Plains, N. Y.	50 00
In 1846:	
From Joseph Orr, late of Jefferson county, Ohio	20 00
From Sidney S. Mills, late of Gloversville, N. Y.	200 00
From Miss Elizabeth Hait, late of Connecticut Farms, N. J.	100 00
From John Fleetwood Marsh, late of West Chester county, N. Y., in part	26,000 00
From Samuel Sherman, late of Woodbury, Conn.	100 00
From John Campbell, late of Sidney, Ohio	36 00
From John Campbell, late of Piqua, Ohio	36 00
From Harmonia Allen, late of Sturbridge, Mass.	84 50
From Mrs. Harriet Stearns, late of Cornish, N. H., one life member	30 00
From Perez Marshall, late of Tolland, Mass.	261 02
From Elijah Sorter, late of Indianapolis, Ind.	20 00
Interest on Redo's legacy	7 00
From Volney Cook, late of Syracuse, N. Y., in part	142 86
From Stephen Soule, late of North Manlius, N. Y.	12 73
From Isaac Hine, late of Middlebury, Conn.	10 00
From Benjamin Swain, late of North Reading, Mass.	100 00
From James North, late of Bucks county, Penn., in part	2 47
From Judah Bement, late of Chenango county, N. Y., one life member	30 00
From Joseph Yates, late of St. Louis county, Mo.	50 00

From Mrs. Eunice King, late of Norwich, Conn., three life members	$90 00
From Alfred Holbrook, late of Byron, N. Y.	274 95
From Mrs. Phebe Pierson, late of Bridgeton, N. J.	100 00
From Eliza Funk, late of Franklin, Ohio	50 00
From James Worth, late of Bucks county, Penn.	409 28
From Mrs. Elizabeth P. Hornbeck, late of St. Andrew's, N. Y., in part	696 00
From Deacon Daniel Lang, late of Salem, Mass.	175 25
From Hon. Daniel Waldo, late of Worcester, Mass., for Asia, in part	7,288 00
From Mrs. Lois Ackley, late of Winchester, Conn., foreign distribution	396 26
From Elias Page, late of Marshall, N. Y.	145 20
From Mrs. Elizabeth Leaworthy, late of Camden, N. Y.	50 00
From Miss Sally Bodfish, late of Falmouth, Mass.	107 00
From Mrs. Roxana Davis, late of Greensborough, Vt.	10 00
From Elizabeth S. Garnsey, late of Clifton Park, N. Y., four life directors	600 00
From Levi Crocker, late of Clarkson, N. Y., in part	248 00
From Nehemiah Denton, late of Brooklyn, N. Y.	1,000 00
From Harvey Shepard, late of Toronto, U. C.	300 00
From Nathan Garnsey, late of Clifton Park, N. Y., in part	250 00
From Alexander M'Kee, late of Manchester, Conn., one life member	100 00
From Mrs. Jane Telfair, late of Hillsborough, Ohio	200 00
From Deacon Daniel Perry, late of Bristol, R. I.	10 00
From Deacon Gideon Burt, late of Long Meadow, Mass.	500 00
From Hon. David Read Evans, late of Winnsborough, S. C.	2,247 33
From Charles D. Betts, late of New York	1,000 00
From Hon. Charles Hunt, late of Gorham, Me., in part	62 50
From Mrs. Pamela Smith, late of Granby, Mass.	200 00
From Mrs. Eunice Averill, late of Hartford, Conn.	2,000 00
From Ebenezer H. Fowler, late of Northford, Conn.	500 00
From Dr. George R. Brown, late of Preble county, Ohio	100 00
From D. Finley, late of Saline county, Mo.	100 00
From Ephraim Chamberlain, late of Cambridgeport, Mass.	200 00
In 1847:	
From Ebenezer H. Fowler, late of Northford, Conn.	500 00
From Dr. George R. Brown, late of Preble county, Ohio	100 00
From D. Finley, late of Saline county, Mo.	100 00

From Ephraim Chamberlain, late of Cambridgeport, Mass.	$200 00
From Mrs. E. P. Hornbeck, late of St. Andrew's, N. Y., in part	813 00
From Miss Huldah Hunt, late of Seekonk, Mass.	100 00
From Hon. Daniel Waldo, late of Worcester, Mass., balance	2,772 00
From Heman Beebee, late of East Bloomfield, N. Y.	100 00
From Miss A. Forman, late of Newark, N. J.	35 00
From Stephen J. Bowles, late of Roxbury, Mass.	500 00
From Hannah Lang, late of Providence, R. I.	5 00
From Lois Ackley, late of Winchester Center, Conn., in part	136 47
From Levi Crocker, late of Clarkson, N. Y.	445 00
From Margaret M'Pherson, late of Broadalbin	175 00
From Mrs. Tamme Adams, late of Lee, Mass., in part	605 00
From Dr. Abishai Howard, late of Sturbridge, Mass.	50 00
From Maria M'Clellan, late of Baltimore, Md., in part	370 00
From John White, late of Meigs county, Ohio	50 00
From Judge Wm. Hampton, late of Pike county, Ohio, in part	200 00
From Sidney S. Mills, late of Gloversville, N. Y., in part	100 00
From Dr. Stuart (by Rev. E. Judson), late of Milan, Ohio	100 00
From James Weir, late of Greenville, Kentucky	1,000 00
From Mrs. Elizabeth Pool, late of New London, Conn.	50 00
From Judah Bement, late of Norwich, N. Y., one life member	30 00
From Cyrus Williams, late of Stockbridge, Mass.	294 83
From D. S. Minor, late of Woodbury, Conn.	50 00
From John Campbell, late of Piqua, Ohio	40 00
From David Edmiston, late of Ross county, Ohio	75 20
From Wm. Henderson, late of Warren county, Ohio	150 00
From Anderson Cone, late of Perry, Ohio	25 00
From Nathaniel Taylor, late of Little Compton, R. I.	310 02
From Mrs. Sarah Boardman, late of Haddam, Conn.	80 00
From Elizabeth S. Garnsey, late of Clifton Park, N. Y., balance	100 00
From Mrs. Dorothy Bissell, late of Lancaster, N. Y.	25 00
From Charlotte Bailey, late of Watertown, N. Y.	5 00
From Deacon Salmon Carter, late of Meriden, Conn.	400 00
From B. C. Wells, late of Stockbridge, Mass.	30 00
From Wm. David, late of Shawangunk, N. Y.	50 00
From Miss Nancy Hooper, late of Boston, Mass.	100 00

From Rev. A. A. Shannon, late of Shelbyville, Ky.....	$200 00
From Mrs. Electa Sage, late of Bolton, Mass..........	25 00
From Mrs. Martha A. True, late of Sutton, Mass......	25 00
From Wm. H. Fondey, late of Albany, N. Y.	100 00
From Mrs. Mary Hart, late of Candor, N. Y..........	18 00
From John Fleetwood Marsh, late of West Chester county, N. Y., in part...........................	5,000 00
From Nathan Garnsey, late of Clifton Park, N. Y.....	250 00
From Wm. B. Baird, late of Murfreesborough, Tenn....	57 87
From Dr. Samuel Smith, late of New York	26 00
From Charles Chamberlain, late of Homer, N. Y......	21 38
From Deacon Nathan Warren, late of Weston, Mass...	100 00
From Elijah P. Booth, late of Sauquoit, N. Y.........	50 00
From Rev. John C. March, late of Newbury, Mass. ...	100 00
From Owen Williams, late of New York	137 42
From Joseph Affolder, late of Newark, N. J., balance ..	39 26
From Mrs. Kinney, late of Cortlandt, N. Y.	10 00
From Mrs. Mary Ingle, late of Washington, D. C......	200 00
From Hepzibah Lawrence, late of Mason, N. H.......	152 32
From Elijah Waters, late of West Millbury, Mass.....	1,500 00
In 1848:	
From Francis S. Key, late of Washington, D. C., in part	142 85
From Hannah L. Murray, late of New York..........	1,000 00
From Mrs. Isabella M'Ninch, late of Chester District, S. C.....................................	560 29
From Samuel Perrine, late of Freehold, N. J..........	50 00
From Judah Bement, late of Norwich, N. Y..........	30 00
From John Guthrie, late of Rockbridge county, Va.....	100 00
From Miss Nancy Kendall, late of Worcester, Mass....	1,000 00
From Dr. James Corbit, late of Cantwell's Bridge, Del..	223 96
From Orrin Day, late of Catskill, N. Y., in part	120 00
From Sidney S. Mills, late of Gloversville, N. Y., in part	100 00
B. S. Car. Interest..............................	7 00
From Mrs. Tamme Adams, late of Lee, Mass., in part..	425 00
From Abraham D. Mead, late of Greenwich, Conn.....	500 00
From A. Coon, late of Perry, Ohio..................	75 00
From Amos Wright, late of Tallmadge, Ohio.........	23 12
From Deacon Israel Decker......................	10 00
From Miss Elizabeth Haywood, late of Boston, Mass...	100 00
From Rev. H. Smith, late of Bingham, Me...........	100 00
From Abigail Warner............................	32 50
From Wm. M'Caw, late of Fairhaven, Ohio..........	100 00
From Levi Crocker, late of Clarkson, N. Y...........	100 00

From Rev. Daniel Mansfield, late of Wenham, Mass. . .	$50 00
From Mrs. Susan C. Kellogg, late of New London, Conn.	250 00
From John Montgomery, late of Chester District, S. C. . .	50 00
From David Moore, late of Newark, Ohio	100 00
From Hon. Charles Hunt, late of Gorham, Me., in part.	125 00
From Dr. Amos C. Wright, late of Tallmadge, Ohio . . .	12 00
From Mrs. Mary Young, late of Newburyport, Mass. . . .	25 00
From Mrs. Clara B. Chappell, late of New London, Conn.	100 00
From Mary Roach, late of Salem, Mass.	30 97
From James Bryce, late of Israel township, Ohio, balance	500 00
From John R. Richardson, late of Albany, N. Y.	3,000 00
From John Fleetwood Marsh, late of West Chester county, N. Y., balance	8,790 19
From Volney Cook, late of Syracuse, N. Y.	71 30
From Heman Beebee, late of East Bloomfield, N. Y. . . .	100 00
From Isaac J. Baldwin, do. do. do.	100 00
From Mrs. Sophia N. Lewis, late of Brooklyn, N. Y. . .	300 00
From George Suckley, late of New York	100 00
From James M'Cawan, late of Bedford county, Tenn. . .	44 00
From James Roosevelt, late of New York	1,000 00
From J. Cox, late of Baltimore, Md.	100 00
From George N. White, late of Illinois	20 00
From Samuel Hitchcock, late of Bethany, Conn.	500 00
From Collin Reed, late of New York	5,000 00
From Miss Chloe Porter, late of Farmington, Conn. . . .	200 00
From Henry L. Webb, late of Albany, N. Y.	1,000 00
From William Tuttle, late of Newark, N. J.	200 00
From Sidney S. Mills, late of Gloversville, N. Y., balance	107 00
From Miss Catharine B. Patton, late of New York, in part	1,500 00
From Professor Solomon Stoddard, late of Middlebury College, Vt.	100 00
From Samuel B. Hotchkiss, late of New Haven, Conn., in part	233 55

CHAPTER XXXVI.

RECEIPTS OF SOCIETY.

The following table presents a view of the receipts of the American Bible Society from all sources, including sales of books, donations, legacies, life memberships and directorships, for each succeeding year from the first anniversary down to the present time, embracing a period of thirty-two years.

1817...	$35,877 46	1828...	$75,879 93	1839...	$95,128 26
1818...	36,564 30	1829...	143,184 33	1840...	97,355 09
1819...	53,223 94	1830...	170,067 55	1841...	118,860 41
1820...	41,361 97	1831...	163,537 86	1842...	134,357 08
1821...	47,009 20	1832...	129,059 00	1843...	126,448 77
1822...	40,682 34	1833...	85,362 95	1844...	154,440 05
1823...	52,021 75	1834...	88,600 82	1845...	166,652 00
1824...	42,416 95	1835...	100,944 38	1846...	197,367 98
1825...	49,693 08	1836...	104,899 45	1847...	205,063 23
1826...	56,115 47	1837...	90,578 89	1848...	254,377 18
1827...	65,192 88	1838...	85,676 83	Total,	$3,308,001 38

Among the receipts of the year 1839, one demands a special notice, viz., a donation of £1000 sterling ($4788 89) by James Douglass, Esq., of Cavers, Scotland, an individual whose purse unites with his able pen in spreading the knowledge of revealed truth. What imparts a peculiar interest to this donation is, that it came unsolicited, and when it was greatly wanted.

CHAPTER XXXVII.

BIBLE SOCIETY RECORD.

In 1819, the board, impressed with the belief that in proportion as the mind of the public became informed in regard to the nature and operations of the society, public feeling would be excited, and a corresponding activity produced in behalf of the Bible cause, deemed it important to issue a periodical. They accordingly directed the publication of a paper entitled "Quarterly Extracts."

The good effects of the measure were soon felt, and the board urged upon the members of the society the propriety of contributing, by their example and influence, to give this organ of the cause a wide circulation.

In 1821, the Quarterly was superseded by a "monthly" half sheet. In this the managers imitated the course pursued by the British and Foreign Bible Society.

The publication of a paper devoted to the interests of the society has been continued to the present day. It has, however, undergone some changes for the better. From a "monthly" it has become a semi-monthly, and its caption, which is embellished with an engraving of a large open Bible, emblematic of the universal diffusion of the Scriptures, is that of "*Bible Society Record.*"

It is in the royal octavo form, and contains from twelve to sixteen closely printed pages.

Its editor, the Rev. J. C. Brigham, D.D., is admirably well qualified for the post. For twenty-two years he has been associated with the society as corresponding secretary. Before his connection with the society he was extensively engaged in Bible distribution in South

America and Mexico, as the agent of the American Board of Foreign Missions. His extensive and thorough acquaintance with the operations of the society, both domestic and foreign, and his long experience combined, render him a most valuable acquisition to the Bible cause. He is a gentleman of liberal and enlarged views. His constant and unremitting devotion to the interests of an institution so truly catholic and benevolent in its character, are of such a nature as to produce the most happy effect upon his mind and heart, so that "sectional prejudices and sectarian jealousies" can find no room for admission. His Christian frankness and urbanity are just such as the friends of the Bible cause might expect from one whose relation to the society gives him the greatest influence in the management of its concerns.

The Bible Society Record, in addition to editorial matter, contains extracts from letters at home and abroad—reports from auxiliary societies in different parts of the country—also extracts from agents' letters, and from those of missionaries and other correspondents in foreign countries. The financial department of the Record is under the supervision of Joseph Hyde, Esq., the able and experienced General Agent and Treasurer of the society.

It furnishes a list of all contributions, and the amounts of donations and remittances for Bibles from the different auxiliaries—the names of all who are made life members or life directors—a notice of all new auxiliaries and all newly-appointed agents—the amount of sales effected through individuals or agents—returns from depositories—amount received from societies not auxiliary for Bibles—donations from societies not auxiliary—returns for books donated—con gregational collections—rules for correspondence—al', notices pertaining to the business of the society, &c.

It is issued gratuitously, and sent to the officers of all auxiliaries, to life directors, life members, agents, and a copy containing the acknowledgment of remittances from all donors. The Bible Record has been productive of much good in creating and keeping up an interest in the great cause, and is sought for with eagerness by all whose hearts are interested in the work of Bible distribution.

CHAPTER XXXVIII.

BIBLICAL LIBRARY.

THE society, very soon after its organization, laid the foundation for a library. The following by-law of the Board of Managers will serve to show the nature of that library: "There shall continue to be kept a library of the society, in which shall be placed and preserved all books not for sale belonging to the society, and all manuscripts and other interesting papers which the society, Board of Managers, or corresponding secretary may deem worthy of preservation. There shall also be placed in the library a copy of the first edition of every book published by the society, and a copy of every other edition thereof in which material alterations shall have been made in the stereotype plates."

Another object of the library was to collect, by donation or otherwise, valuable works on Biblical literature, particularly those of a philological and hermeneutical character, for purposes of translation and reference. Ministers of all denominations have access to this library for purposes of reference. The Biblical interchange kept up with the different Bible societies in the world has brought to its alcoves copies of all the versions which have been published, besides many manuscripts and rare and valuable documents from the different missionary stations in pagan lands receiving assistance from the society.

In addition to its philological and exegetical departments, embracing grammars, lexicons, and commentaries in the various languages, it has a fine collection of Patristic theology, &c.

The library has been increasing from year to year by donations, embracing several thousand of the most rare and valuable books.

It is, however, but the mere nucleus of what, in the providence of God, it is destined to be, and the managers hope that, among other objects of benefaction connected with the society, it will not be forgotten.

The following catalogue embraces a complete list of all the books in the library, received by donation or otherwise:

Biblical.

Biblia Polyglotta, Waltoni, 6 vols., folio, 1657.
Novum Testamentum Polyglotton, 2 vols., 1597.
Biblia Pentapla Polyglotta, 3 vols., 1711.
Aimara and Spanish Gospel of Luke, 1829.
Cherokee Gospel of Matthew, 1832.
Choctaw Gospels, 1831.
Chinese Scriptures (Morrison's), 21 parts.
" Testament, 3 setts, 1814.
" Pentateuch.
" Bible (Marshman's), 5 parts.
" Scripture Lessons, 3 parts.
" Specimens (Medhurst and others).
" New Testament, 1838.
" " " revised version, 1838.
Cingalese Testament, 1817.
Coptic and Arabic Psalter, 1826.
" " " Gospels, 1829.
Delaware Epistles of John, 1818.

Esquimaux Matthew, Mark, and Luke, 1813.
Eliot's Indian Bible, 1635.
Mohawk Gospel of John, 1804.
Mohegan Bible, 1685.
Seneca Sermon on the Mount, 1829.
Amharic Testament, 1829.
Arabic Bible, 1811.
Psalterium Scialac, Sionita, et Ar. Lat., 1614.
Arabic Bible, 1820.
" Testament, 1816.
" Psalter, 1819.
" Testaments, 1837.
Armenian Novum Testamentum, 1828.
Biblia Sacra, 3 copies, Armenian, 1805, 1814, and 1817.
Novum Testamentum, 1814.
Armeno-Turkish Testament, 1831.
Armenian Old and New Testament, 1837.
Four Gospels, Armenian, 1838.
New Testament, Armenian, 1838.
Assam Testament, 1819.
Bengalee Gospels of Matthew and John, 2 copies, 1819.
" Bible, 1818.
" Pentateuch, 1819.
" Psalms, 1826.
" four Gospels and Pentateuch, 1830.
" Bible, 1837.
" Pentateuch, 1838.
" Gospels, Acts, Romans, Corinthians, 1838.
Bohemian Bible, 1813.
Bullom and English Bible, 1816.
Burman Testament, 1832.
" Bible, 1834.
Calmuc Gospel of Matthew, 1815.
Carelian " " " 1820.
Carshun and Syriac Testament, 1824.
" Testament, 1827.
Bashmera Testament, 1837.
Danish Bible, 1633.
" " 1799.
" New Testament, 1814.
Biblia (Sextende Oplag.), 1819.
Biblia, 1829.
Biblia (Dutch), from 1603 to 1734, 14 versions.

Nieuwe Testament, 2 copies, 1734.
" " 1778.
Biblia, 2 copies, 1778.
Der Psalmen, 1778.
New Testament, Tyndal's version, 1526.
Bishops' Bible, 1575.
English Bibles, 103 different versions, from 1578 to 1849.
Wastne Testament, Dorpatian-Esthonian, 1815.
Psalterium Davidis Ethiopice, 1815.
Finnish New Testament, 1815.
Finnish Bible, 1817.
" New Testament, 1822.
La Sainte Bible et Nouveau Testament, from 1565 to 1849, in 9 different versions, 43 editions.
Gaelic Bible, 1807.
" New Testament, 1813.
" Bible, 1819.
Georgian New Testament, in ecclesiastical character, 1816.
" " " in civil character.
Die Bibel und das Neue Testament, in several versions and 24 editions, from 1531 to 1849.
Novum Testamentum Græcum, 2 vols., 1569.
" " Montani, interlin. interp., 2 vols., 1622.
" " Vater, 1824.
" " Tittman, 1824.
" " Griesbach, 1825.
" " Knapp, 1829.
Ancient and modern Greek New Testament, 7 copies, 1810.
" " " " " " folio, 1814.
" " " " " " 1817.
" " " " " " 1827.
" " " " " " Hilarion's, 2 copies, 1828.
Biblia Græca Latinæ, 1682.
Vetus Testamentum Græcum Vaticanum, 1683.
" " " Alexandrinum, 1821.
Psalterium Græcum cum New Testament, 2 copies, 1831.
Testimantitäk (New Testament in Greenland language), 1822.
Gujurattee New Testament, 2 copies, 1820.
Hanti Testament.
Harotee New Testament, 1821.
Hawaiian New Testament, 10 copies, 1832.
Biblia Hebraica, 1566.

Biblia Hebraica, marginal notes, 1607.
" " edition Simonis, 2 copies, 1766.
Hebrew New Testament, 1817.
Hebrew New Testament and Spanish Psalms, 1837.
Pentateuch in Hindee, 2 copies, 1812.
Isaiah " "
New Testament " " 1826.
Proverbs " " 1826.
Hindoostanee New Testament, 1819.
" and English Gospel of Matthew.
" Pentateuch, 1837.
" Old Testament, 1837.
" New " 1838.
" Proverbs.
" Isaiah.
" Genesis.
" Psalms.
" Matthew.
Icelandic Bible, 1813.
Irish Bible, Roman character, 1807.
Tiomna Nuadh, 1813.
An Biobla, Roman character, 1817.
Tiomna Nuadh (New Testament, Irish character), 1818.
An Biobla, Irish character, 1823.
Psalms in Irish.
Leabhuir an Tsean Tiomna, vernacular character, 1827.
Genesis in Irish, vernacular character.
Irish New Testament, 1830.
Javanese Testament, 2 copies.
" Gospel of John.
Il Nuovo Testamento, 2 copies, 1813.
" " Italiano, plates, 2 copies, 1816.
Italian New Testament, 1818.
La Sacra Biblia, 2 copies, 1819.
Italian and Latin Psalms, 1822.
Kashmeera Testament, 1821.
Laponian New Testament, 1755.
Biblia Sacra, 15 editions and 8 versions, from 1476 to 1849.
Lettonian New Testament, 1816.
Mahratta Gospel of Matthew and Acts, 1816.
Malay Bible (Elkitâb), Arabic character, 3 copies, 1817 to 1849.
" New Testament, Roman character, 2 copies, 1820 and 1831.

Mandjur Gospel of Matthew, 1822.
Manks Bible, 1819.
" Testament (Conaant Noa), 1815.
Moldavian New Testament, 2 copies, different dates, 1817.
Mongolian Scriptures, 1835.
Mooltanee New Testament, 2 copies, 1819.
Multan " "
Mordvinian Gospels, 1821.
Murat-hee New Testament, 2 copies, 1830.
Negro-English New Testament, 1829.
Oordoo Scriptures.
" Psalms.
" Isaiah.
" Proverbs.
Orissa Scriptures.
Persian Scriptures, 14 editions, in 6 versions, from 1815 to 1849.
Polish Bible, 2 copies, 1810 and 1822.
" New Testament, 1815.
Portuguese Scriptures, 4 editions, in 3 versions, from 1813 to 1823.
Punjabee New Testament, 1811.
Pushtoo " " 2 copies, 1818.
Revalian " " 2 versions, 1790, 1816.
Romanese Old Testament, 1818.
" New Testament, 1820.
Ancient and modern Russian Testament, 1822.
Psalter in modern Russian, 1822.
Samogitian New Testament, 1816.
Siamese Gospel of Luke.
" " Matthew.
" Acts, 1836.
" Ten Commandments.
Slavonian Bible, 2 copies.
" New Testament.
" " " modern Russian, 1822.
" Psalms, 1822.
Biblia Vulgata Latina en Espanol, 1794.
Spanish Testament, 2 copies, in 2 versions, 1817.
" Scriptures, 1823.
" Luke and Acts, 1823.
" New Testament (Amat's version), 1825.
Gospel of Luke in one of the Spanish dialects, 1835.
Swedish Bible, 2 copies, in 2 versions, 1812, 1828.
Novum Testamentum Syriacum, 1663.

Psalterium Syriacum, 1768.
Syriac New Testament, 1816.
Syriace Psalterium, 1822.
Carshûn and Syriac New Testament, 1824.
Syro-Chaldaic Gospels (Nestorian character), 1829.
Gospel of Luke in Otaheitan, 1820.
" Matthew and John in Taheitan, 1820.
Acts of the Apostles in Taheitan.
Oremburg Tartar Testament, 1820.
Telinga New Testament, 2 copies, 1818.
Tcheremisian Gospels, 1821.
Turkish New Testament, 1814.
Turco-Armenian Testament, 1819.
Turco-Greek Testament, 1825.
Turkish Bible, 1827.
Vikanera New Testament, 3 copies, 1820.
Y Bibl Cyssegr Lan a Llyfr Gweddi Gyffriedin, 7 editions, and 3 versions, from 1718 to 1849.
Moldavian New Testament.
Wallachian " "
Hebrew-Spanish Psalms, 2 copies.
Four Gospels, in ancient Armenian.
Biblia Sacra Vatabla, 2 vols., folio.
Douay New Testament.
French and Hebrew Pentateuch.
Hebrew Manuscript (Book of Esther).
Grebo Gospel of Matthew.
Acts of the Apostles in modern Greek.
Book of Genesis in Armeno-Turkish.
Psalms in Mongolian.
Acts of the Apostles in Tamul and English languages.
Genesis and Epistle of Timothy in Tamul.
Greco-Turkish Bible.
" " New Testament.
Ancient Armenian New Testament.
Spanish New Testament, by Valera, 1602.
" " " by Amat, 1837.
" Epistle to the Romans.
Clark's Bible, 1760.
Siamese Gospel of Mark.
Field's Bible, 1660.
Gospel of Luke and Acts in Hindoostanee.
Psalms in Arabic.

Pentateuch in Armeno-Turkish.
Gospel of Mark in Siamese.
Hawaiian Bible.
Spanish Bible, Cassindon de Regne, 1522.
Greek Testament, cum notis, 1739.
Old Testament in Tamul, 1839.
Ancient German Bible, 1661.
New Testament in Tamul.
Gospel of Mark, Luke, and Acts in Tamul, 7 copies.
" John in Hindoostanee, 6 copies.
Mongolian Scriptures.
New Testament in Chinese, complete in 2 vols.
Psalms in modern Armenian.
Hebrew-Spanish Pentateuch.
Armeno-Turkish Old Testament.
English folio Bible.
Armenian Testament, 1839.
Bengalee Testament.
" four Gospels and Acts, 1837.
" Genesis, 1840.
Hindoostanee Testament, 1840.
" four Gospels and Acts, 7 copies.
Sanscrit Testament, 1841.
" Psalms, 1840.
Siamese Gospel of Matthew.
Acts of the Apostles in Arabic, 1841.
Galatians in modern Syriac.
Gospels in Acra tongue.
Folio edition of Greek Testament, 1703.
Gospel of Matthew in Cherokee.
English black-letter Bible.
Bambas modern Greek Testament.
Greek and Latin New Testament, 1544.
Isaiah and Deuteronomy in Hindoostanee.
Deuteronomy and Daniel in Hindi.
Tamul Bible.
Hawaiian Bible.
Folio German Bible, 1765.
Hebrew Canticles.
Folio Latin Bible, 1509.
Psalms in Hindi.
Portuguese Bible, 4 copies.
" Testament, 4 copies.

Syriac New Testament, 1569.
Gospels in Chinese.
Old Testament in Chinese.
Gospel of Mark in Abenaquis language.
Wendish Bible, 1589.
Malay Bible, 2 vols., 1733.
Drury Testament, 1847.
Armeno-Turkish Old Testament, 2 vols.
Persian Old Testament.
" New Testament.
Tamul " "
Pentateuch in modern Armenian.
Syriac New Testament.
Latin Bible, 2 copies (rare).
Greek Testament, 1710.
Gospels in Spanish.
Quarto Protestant French Bible.
The Hexapla.
Kneeland's Greek and English Testament according to Griesbach.
John's Gospel in Sgau. Karen.
Père Amelot's New Testament, French, 1666.
Armeno-Turkish Old Testament, 2 vols.
Persian Old Testament.
Tamul New Testament.
Persian " "
Russian and English Testament.
Pentateuch in modern Armenian.
Syriac New Testament.
Dutch " " 2 copies.
Latin Bible, 2 copies (rare).
Græcum Novum Testamentum Variæ Lectiones, 1710.
Edinburgh copy of Bible, with copious references, 1796.
English octavo Bible, critical notes.
Four Evangelists, Spanish, copious notes.
Quarto Protestant French Bible, 1696.

Philological.

Castelli Lexicon Heptaglotton, 2 vols., 1669.
Cocceius's Hebrew Lexicon, 1714.
Schaaf Lexicon Syriacum, 1708.
Diccionario de la Academia Española, 1823.
Dictionnaire Français Armenian, 2 vols., 1812.
Judson's Burman and English Dictionary, 1826.

Adam's Dictionary of Hindee Language, 1829.
Hindee Grammar.
Grammar and Vocabulary of New Zealand Language, 1820.
Bengalee and English Vocabulary, 2 copies, 1810.
De Sacy's Grammaire Arabe, 2 copies, 1810.
Ludolph's Ethiopic Grammar, 2 copies, 1702.
Jones's Persian Grammar, 1828.
Palermo's Italian Grammar, 1777.
M'Curtin's Elements of Irish Language, 1728.
Neilson's Introduction to Irish Language, 1808.
Aucher's English-Armenian Grammar, 1817.
Donnegan's Greek Lexicon, 1835.
Morrison's Grammar of Chinese Language, 1815.
Johnson's Dictionary, 2 vols., 1819.
Negri's Modern Greek Grammar, 1828.
Oscanean's Armenian Grammar.
Cocceius's Hebrew Lexicon.
Sir William Jones's Persian Grammar.
Sharp on Greek Article.
Richardson's English Dictionary.
Newman's Spanish and English Dictionary.
Portuguese and English Dictionary.
Russian Grammar.
Gilchrist's Philosophical Etymology.
Low Dutch and English Dictionary.
Syriac Grammar.
Danish Grammar.
French and Portuguese Grammar.
Susoo Grammar.
Symonds on New Testament Translation.
Criticisms on Translations.
Grebo Dictionary.
Buxtorf's Lexicon in Hebrew and Chaldaic.
Rogers's French Dictionary.
Roy's Hebrew and English Dictionary.
Collins's Hebrew and Chaldaic Lexicon.
Syriac Lexicon.
Syriac Chrestomathy.
Polyglott Grammar of Ten Languages.
Hebrew and Chaldaic Lexicon in Commentary.
Grammar of the Moskito Language.
" " Santeax "
Portuguese Dictionary.

Russian and English Dictionary.
Parkhurst's and Frey's Hebrew Lexicon.
Webster's Octavo Dictionary.
Bush's Affinities of the Ancient British Language.
The Hierophant.
German and English Dictionary.
Walker's Rhetorical Grammar.
Greek and Latin New Testament Lexicon, 1635.
Russian and English Dictionary.

Theological, Historical, Biographical, etc.

Horne's Introduction to the Critical Study of the Bible.
Calvini Commentarii in Pauli Epistolas, 1557.
Works of the Early Christian Fathers in Greek and Latin, 26 vols., 1783.
Campbell on the Gospels.
Tromminius's Greek Concordance.
Caryl on Job, 1659.
Fulke's New Testament Annotations of Rheimish Translation, folio, 1617.
Dutch Annotations, 2 vols., 1657.
Enarrationes in Psalmos, 1619.
M'Ray's Translations and Interpretation, 1815.
Clark's Commentary, 6 vols., 1818.
Scott's " 6 vols., 1812.
Sharp's Harmony of the Prophets and Apostles, Lat., 1624.
Simon's Translation from Vulgate, 2 vols., 1730.
Newcombe's Historical View of Translations, 1792.
Lewis's History of Translations, 1739.
Turton on the Text of the English Bible.
Carpenter's Guide.
Life and Labors of Eliot, the Indian Missionary.
Clerical Guide.
Brief Exposition of the Minor Prophets.
Jones's Ecclesiastical History.
Owen's History of the British and Foreign Bible Society.
Loskiel's History of Moravian Missions.
Youth's Book of Natural Theology.
History of Josiah.
Vindication of the Sacred Books.
" of Miracles.
Objections to Hindooism.
Hindooism and Christianity contrasted.

Shastra Nermaga, or Hindoo Scriptures.
Essence of the Bible.
Memoir of Petamba Singli.
Reasons why not a Roman Catholic, in Syriac.
Memoirs of Lord Teignmouth.
Memorials of the Right Reverend Miles Coverdale.
Papal Rome as it is.
Oriental Customs.
Life of Christ.
Lives of the Apostles.
Cornelie a Lapide, Commentary on the Bible, 10 vols., fol.
Pilgrim's Progress, in modern Greek.
Life of Everts.
Reformation in Spain.
Debate on Baptism, by Campbell and Rice.
Essay on our Lord's Discourse at Capernaum.
Inquiry concerning True Religion, in Hindi.
La Russe y les Jesuites.
Protestant Memorial.
Antiquities of the Christian Church.
Annals of the English Bible.
Blunt's Coincidences of the Old and New Testaments, 2 copies.
Notices of distinguished Jewish Rabbis.
Broughton's Works.
Westminster Catechism, Hebrew.
Larger "
Ebaugh's Heavenly Incense.
Downame's Treatise on a Godly Life.
Adams's Explanation of the Christian Religion.
" Commentary on the Lord's Prayer.
" Jesus Christ, the only Deliverer.
Scripture Lessons, Spanish.
Collection of Sermons.
History of Christ.
Bush's Scripture Illustrations.
Wakefield's Version of the New Testament, 3 vols.
Francke's Guide to the Study of the Scriptures.
The Old Testament, without points.
Reprint of the Holy Scriptures, by Coverdale.
Critici Sacri, 6 vols.
Pradus on Ezekiel, 3 vols.
Nolan on the Greek Vulgate.
Todd's Vindication of English Translation.

Hared on the Psalms.
Essay on New Translation.
Berriman's Critical Dissertation.
Gell on Amendment of English Translation.
Brief Exegesis of the Parables, modern Greek.
Synopsis of Sacred History.
Summary of the Old Testament.
History of the Patriarch Abraham.
Chrysostom on the Scriptures.
" Commentary on the Epistle to the Romans.
Commentary on the Minor Prophets, Latin.
The Koran.
Foulke's Defense of the English Translation of the Scriptures.
Coray's Translation of the Epistles, with a Commentary.
Bickersteth's Scripture Help, Greek.
Hebrew Synagogue Service, with Hebrew Grammar and Notes.
Targums, Jewish.
Theological Definitions, Latin.

Miscellaneous.

Holme's Archæologia Americana.
Anderson's Observations and Greek Islands.
Memoirs of Mrs. Anna Judson.
History of the North American Indians.
Worcester's Universal Gazetteer, 2 vols.
Tanner's American Atlas.
Annual Reports of the American Bible Society from 1816 to 1849.
" " British and Foreign Bible Society from 1804 to 1849.
Annual Reports of the American Board of Commissioners for Foreign Missions from 1812 to 1849.
Stewart's Historical Anecdotes.
Dudley's Analysis of the System of the Bible Society.
Norris's Letter to the Earl of Liverpool.
Dealtry's Vindication of the Bible Society.
Norris on the Bible Society.
Work in Russian on ditto.
Compendium of the Bible.
Milner's Strictures on Marsh.
Publications of the New England Tract Society, 7 vols.
Book of Specimens of various Languages.
Brantley's and Winslow's Objections to Baptist Version.
New Testament for the Blind.

Tracts relating to Versions.
American Bible Society Controversy.
British and Foreign " "
Transactions of the College of Professional Teachers, Cincinnati.
Vindication of Baptists from the Charge of Bigotry.
Book of Mormon.
Eclectic Review.
Catalogue of the American Antiquarian Society.
Monthly Extracts.
Missionary Herald, 16 vols.
Quarterly Register of the American Education Society, 4 vols.
New York Observer, 2 vols.
Armenian Reader.
Repository of Useful Knowledge, 12 nos., Greek.
Christian Philanthropist.
Essay on the right Use of Property.
Biographical Dictionary.
Black's general Atlas.
Miscellaneous Volumes, 85, Dutch.
Divine Alphabet.
The First Catechism.
" Second "
A Jubilee Medal, 1717.
Mrs. Gardiner's Prose and Poems.
New York Bible Society's Reports.
Antiquities of the Christian Church.
Annual Report of the Committee on Patents.
Report of the Exploring Expedition to Oregon and California.
Congressional Documents.
Geographical Gazetteer.
Report of the Netherlands Bible Society.

CHAPTER XXXIX.

LIFE DIRECTORS AND LIFE MEMBERS.

The payment of one hundred and fifty dollars at one time constitutes a life director, and the payment of thirty dollars a life member.

The number of life directors is seven hundred, and the number of life members nine thousand two hundred and fifty-seven.

A director for life is privileged to attend and vote at all the meetings of the Board of Managers, and is entitled to receive annually, by making application at the Bible House any time during the year, five copies of the common Minion Bible.

The following extract from the twenty-sixth Report will show the motive which prompted the board to adopt the measure.

"The above regulation was adopted from a conviction that there are a multitude of individuals in the community—orphans, apprentices, servants, boatmen, stage-drivers, and others—who have no Bibles, and but few religious privileges, and who might, to some extent, be supplied by the method now proposed, for who will be so likely to scatter the sacred Volume among the needy as those who have shown such regard for that volume as to make themselves members and directors of the institution which furnishes it for distribution."

Many churches in different parts of the country have constituted their respective pastors directors and members for life. What tribute of respect and affection more appropriate for the flock to bestow, or more grateful to the pastor, who feeds it with the bread of life, than to receive such a tribute!

Of the thousands who sustain this interesting relation, the society expects much, and with confidence it looks to them for the support and advocacy of the great cause in which they are alike engaged, that the "light and truth" may be sent out to bless and save every land.

APPENDIX.

CORRESPONDENCE, ADDRESSES, &c.

Letters from the Hon. Elias Boudinot, President of the American Bible Society.

"BRETHREN AND FELLOW-LABORERS IN THE GOSPEL,

"Among the innumerable blessings of this life wherewith it hath pleased a gracious God to favor me, the permitting my union with you in those labors of love, which it is to be hoped will be made instrumental to the raising a monument to his glory, which may last till the recording angel shall announce to an astonished universe that '*it is finished*,' is one of the most dear to my heart.

"The consoling hope was once cherished that the unspeakable pleasure would, in one instance at least, have been afforded me, in the last decline of life, of meeting with you personally, to have testified my approbation of all your exertions in this glorious work. But a kind and merciful God, who knows all my deficiencies, has thought it best, in his infinite wisdom, to refuse this favor, in which dispensation of his all-wise Providence I do most sincerely acquiesce, firmly believing it will be most conducive to his own glory and the best interests of the institution committed to our care.

"I once thought I had much to communicate to you, but the extreme debility of both mind and body prevents my attempting it. Suffer me, however, as a last effort, however weak and feeble, to say a few words before I go hence.

"It is not vanity in me to say that I have labored hard and suffered much in this great cause, occasioned in some measure by a very low state of health; yet such has been the apparent interposition of an overruling Providence, that my faith and hope have never failed, even in the darkest days; and although there have been great temptations to despair of final success, yet have I been so strengthened with the assurance that it was a work of God, and that he would show his power and glory in bringing it to maturity in his own time and by his own means, that I had determined, in case of failure in the last attempt, to commence the great business at all events, with the aid of a few laymen who had testified their willingness to go all lengths with me. But no sooner had the work been brought to an issue, than the clouds began to disperse, and every one was obliged to say in his heart, '*This is the work of God.*'

"Thus, my beloved friends, hath God in his condescending grace appointed us to become his humble instruments in opening the eyes of the blind; in cheering the abodes of primeval darkness with the joyful sounds of redeeming love; in fulfilling the encouraging prophecy of the angel flying through the midst of heaven, having the everlasting Gospel in his hands, to preach to all nations, languages, tongues, and people on the earth.

"This, indeed, is an event devoutly to be wished, and most gratefully to be acknowledged. That such comparative worms of the dust should become fellow-workers with Christ in making the wilderness to blossom as a rose, and the nations of the earth to become the nations of our Lord and his Christ, is an honor in which the highest angels would rejoice. Is there, then, the least reason for fearing the great result? Shall any one be discouraged at the arduous prospect before us? By no means. Look at the disciples of our dearest Lord, and compare their relative situation when they beheld their blessed Master given up to the power of his enemies—condemned as a base malefactor—stretched on the cross, breathing out his precious life in a prayer in favor of his unrelenting persecutors—forsaken by all—every one fleeing to his own home, and one even repeatedly denying his Lord and Master, though forewarned of it but a few hours before!

"Realize their forlorn state when surrounding the risen Savior, hearkening to his invaluable instructions: he is suddenly parted from them, and carried up into heaven, and vanishes from their sight. It is true, they are commissioned to go forth and preach the Gospel to every creature—a Gospel in all its parts and each essential feature destructive of every religion on the face of the earth. This is to be preached to a world wholly absorbed in the works of the flesh; wholly inimical to the precepts of the meek and holy Jesus—a world in absolute possession of all temporal power and authority. All this is to be done by twelve poor, helpless, indigent, and illiterate fishermen, without power civil or ecclesiastical, friends, influence, riches, or rank to aid them in calling the public attention to their divine Master, who, though declared to be God as well as man, was crucified as a malefactor, being condemned by the known judicatories of their country. But will it be said that they had the personal assurance of their Almighty Savior for their encouragement and support against all the powers of earth and hell? Yes, my friends, they had; and a blessed support it was, and under it they withstood and overcame the world. And have you not equal, if not superior cause of trust and hope? Have you not all the promises made to them, with the advantage of their experience and success in the fulfillment of all that he said and did, beyond their most exaggerated expectations? Has your Savior lost his power and authority, or has he not given as much confidence and reliance on his continual presence and almighty arm to you as he ever did to his disciples of old? Is he not the same yesterday, to-day, and forever?

"As for my own part, I have been looking for greater opposition and causes of mortification than any that have yet appeared. I know the seductive power of the evil one, and the artful cunning of his devices. An opposition, indeed, has come from quarters whence we ought not to have expected it; indeed, it has been, as yet, too feeble to excite the fear or cool the zeal of God's people. But, brethren, we are all too well acquainted with the cunning and subtilty of the great enemy of the Gospel to suppose that he will thus early give up his designs. No; but as you have put on the armor of God, you must not put it off till you have obtained a complete, a decided victory. You must be guarded at all points. Woe be to them who shall be the cause of your trouble. Satan's principal endeavors will be to sow divisions among you: he will attack your union, by which you destroy his strong hold, in breaking down the walls of partition that have so long separated and wounded the Church of Christ. He will fear your apparent cordial love and esteem for each other. As long as real brotherly love shall continue and prevail among you, all the arts of the enemy of man's happiness may be defied. Guard well the weakest part of your citadel; forget not the solemn injunction of the captain of your salvation, '*By this shall all men know that ye are my disciples, if ye love one another.*' Stand on your guard; let no argument persuade you; let no vain alarm of danger to your interests intimidate you. Greater is he who is for you than he who is against you. I do know, and have carefully attended to your probable progress. You have an arduous, but a glorious work and labor of love before you: this will necessarily engage all your powers and all your spare time; but look to the great recompense of reward. That you are striving for eternity, not only for yourselves, but for a world lying in sin, who may, at the great day of account, be found surrounding the throne of the Eternal with hallelujahs and thanksgiving, that you were the cause of their coming to the knowledge of the Gospel. Forget not that your Lord and Master has all power given to him, both in heaven and on earth; that under his guardian care—that under the banner of his cross, you are to go forth and complete the triumphs of redeeming love.

"Once more suffer me to beseech you to promote love and harmony in your society as your strong bond of union. God is love. Love is the fulfillment of the law. Let it become a common proverb, 'See how these members of the American Bible Society love one another, though consisting of every denomination of Christians among us.' Let a motto be written in letters of gold on the most prominent part of your hall of deliberation, '*By this shall all men know ye are my disciples, if ye love one another.*' If this, then, is the great characteristic mark of discipleship with Christ, who will refuse to wear the badge as the most desirable trait in his character? The second advent of the Savior is comparatively near—the harbingers of his approach begin to appear. Hear the language of Jesus himself: 'For the Son of Man shall come in the glory of his Father, with his angels; and then shall he reward every man according to his works. Hereafter ye shall see the Son of Man sitting on the right hand of power, and coming in the clouds of heaven with power and great glory.' St. Paul commendeth the Thessalonians for their faith Godward, and waiting for his Son from heaven. 'For this we say unto you, by the words of the Lord, If we believe that Jesus died and rose again, even so (as certainly) they also who sleep in Jesus will God bring with him, for this we say unto you, by the word of the Lord, that the Lord himself shall descend from heaven with a shout, with the voice of the Archangel, and the dead in Christ shall rise first.' I rejoice with you, that to accomplish this glorious end, to hasten this blessed event, and to become fellow-workers with God, we are assisting in laying the foundation for spreading the Gospel throughout the habitable globe, that the earth may be covered with the knowledge of God as the waters cover the seas, when we may all sit down with Abraham, Isaac, and Jacob in the kingdom of our Lord.

"And now, brethren, beloved in the Lord, I commit you to the grace of that God who hath preserved my life to my seventy-eighth year as a living monument of his sparing mercy and goodness, to witness your zeal, activity, and perseverance in his service. May the broad hand of the Almighty cover you; may his Holy Spirit guide, direct, and influence you in all your deliberations and undertakings, and make you burning and shining lights in his Israel. And when the great Shepherd of the sheepfold shall call in his ancient people, the Jews, from the four quarters of the world, may you be found among the number of those who shall be made kings and priests to God.

"And now, my beloved friends and brethren, suffer me to leave you, under the pleasing expectation that we shall meet again, to unite in that song of everlasting praise that shall proceed from the trump of the archangel, when he shall sound the glorious anthem of hallelujah! hallelujah! hallelujah! for the Lord God Omnipotent reigneth.

"'*Soli Dei Gloria et Honor.*'

"ELIAS BOUDINOT, President.

"*To the Board of Managers of the Amer. Bible Society.*
"BURLINGTON, 5*th May*, 1817."

BURLINGTON, *June* 5, 1816.

"REV. AND DEAR SIR,

"I have the honor of acknowledging the receipt of your favor of the 1st instant, officially announcing my election to the chair of the American Bible Society. In expressing my grateful acceptance of this undeserved compliment (after trusting to the gracious influence of Almighty God), my confidence is in the aid and assistance of my worthy colleagues, by which alone I can entertain a hope of being useful in so very respectable a body, engaged in this all-important undertaking. I am not ashamed to confess that I accept of the appointment of President of the American Bible Society as the greatest honor that could have been conferred on me this side of the grave.

"I am so convinced that the whole of this business is the work of God himself, by his Holy Spirit, that, even hoping against hope, I am encouraged to press on through good report and evil report, to accomplish his will on earth as it is in heaven.

"So apparent is the hand of God in thus disposing the hearts of so many men, so diversified in their sentiments as to religious matters of minor importance, and uniting them as a band of brothers in this grand object, that even infidels are compelled to say it is the work of the Lord, and it is wonderful in our eyes! In vain is the opposition of man: as well might he attempt to arrest 'the arm of Omnipotence, or fix a barrier around the throne of God.' Having this confidence, let us go on, and we shall prosper. I can say no more: my feeble frame and exhausted spirit scarcely suffer me, lying in my bed, to dictate language sufficiently efficient to represent my deep sense of the polite attention of your honorable body. All I can add is, that should it please a sovereign God to suffer me to meet my faithful fellow-laborers in the Gospel vineyard, I will most cordially endeavor to make up, in unwearied attention and industry, what may be deficient in the mind and understanding.

"Accept of my acknowledgment of the polite manner in which you have made the communication.

"I am, reverend and dear sir, with esteem,

"Your humble and obedient servant,

"ELIAS BOUDINOT.

"Rev. Dr. ROMEYN, *Sec. for Dom. Corres. of the Amer. Bib. Soc.*"

Letter from the Secretary of the British and Foreign Bible Society.

"BRIGHTON, *August* 3, 1816.

"MY DEAR SIR,

"The Committee of the British and Foreign Bible Society have instructed me to offer you their warmest congratulations on the event of the formation of the American Bible Society; an event which they consider as truly auspicious, and pregnant with consequences most advantageous to the promotion of that great work in which the American brethren and themselves are mutually engaged.

"To these congratulations our committee have added a grant of £500; and they trust that both will be accepted as indications and pledges of that friendly disposition which it is their desire to cultivate and manifest toward every class and description of their transatlantic fellow-laborers.

"The crisis at which the American Bible Society has been formed, and the cordial unanimity which has reigned throughout all the proceedings which led to its establishment, encourage the most sanguine hopes of its proving, in the hand of God, a powerful auxiliary in the confederate warfare which is now carrying on against ignorance and sin. May those hopes be realized, and may new trophies be added, through its instrumentality, to those triumphs which have already been reaped by the arms of our common Redeemer.

"I am, my dear sir, very faithfully yours,

"John Owen,

"Secretary to the British and Foreign Bible Society.

"Dr. Boudinot, *President of the American Bible Society.*"

Letter from Prince Galitzin, President of the Russian Bible Society.

"Sir,

"Your letter of the 23d May, a. c. (anno currente), containing information of the establishment of the American Bible Society, was duly received by me, and brought to the knowledge of the Committee of the Russian Bible Society at their first meeting.

"The information of such an event as the forming a national Bible institution for the United States of America, for the purpose of promoting the circulation of the Holy Scriptures, not only at home, but also in other countries, whether Christian, Mohammedan, or pagan, was certainly of a nature to produce the most joyful feelings in the breasts of all who take a sincere part in this great and salutary cause. It is with peculiar pleasure that we saw thus a new step made toward hastening forward that happy period, when the knowledge of the Word of Life will become universal glory to Him who deigns to inspire his people every where with the use of means for the spiritual welfare of the human race. The sphere of operation which the American Bible Society has prescribed to its activity is very extensive and important. We have perused with satisfaction the constitution and the address to their countrymen, and we are happy to see that the same principles animate our American fellow-laborers which lead us to the same important end. Thus, notwithstanding the distance which separates us, being approximated by the same spirit of unity and action, we reach you the right hand of fellowship from these remote parts, and unanimously engage to exert ourselves for the same cause of benevolence. Yes, sir, it will certainly be very agreeable for us to communicate mutually with your society about our proceedings and successes; and we shall always be ready to take a most hearty interest in all that belongs to your work, which is the work of charity, even the work of God.

"We have not failed to forward some of the copies of your proceedings and Constitution you have sent us to some of our branch societies, in order to make them acquainted with your benevolent institution, and, in return, we have felt ourselves obliged to communicate to you some small publications of what was done in this country for the same salutary cause of disseminating the Holy Scriptures. We will thus mutually learn what our merciful Savior has done and is doing in both countries.

"Before I conclude, permit me, sir, to express to you the feelings of the most sincere and true esteem, with which I have the honor to be, sir, your most obedient and devoted servant,

(Signed) "PRINCE ALEXANDER GALITZIN,
"President of the Russian Bible Society.

"ST. PETERSBURG, *November* 30, 1816."

Letter from the Secretaries of the Hamburg and Altona Bible Societies.

"We have learned with great satisfaction, from the publications which have reached us, that the loud voice of the friends of the Bible in America has demanded and produced a union of the interests of all the provincial societies, by the establishment of a national Bible Society.

"We can not better express our joy at this event than by a request to be made acquainted, through the medium of your printed reports, with the results of your endeavors to diffuse the pure Word of God throughout the wide dominions of the states of North America.

"However great the distance at which we live from each other, we feel ourselves associated with you in the blessed vocation of offering those revered documents, upon which the faith of all Christians rests, to such of the children of men as do not possess them, and of thereby leading them to a nearer and fruitful knowledge of our Holy Redeemer, Jesus Christ, who 'of God is made, unto all that believe on him, wisdom, and righteousness, and sanctification, and redemption.' To glorify the name of Christ be, therefore, the aim of our exertions; exertions which can not fail to receive the approbation and blessing of God, even though but few evidences of it should be seen in this life.

"We send you, along with this epistle, twelve copies of our report for this year, to be distributed among your provincial societies, and by this act commence an intercourse and connection with you which we desire to render as extensive as we can. You will undoubtedly be able to make it as instructive to us as it will be interesting, by the rich fund of experience which your activity will supply. How much will you discover favorable to the advancement of our design! and, on the other hand, how many difficulties will you encounter! A wise application of the former, and a careful consideration of the latter, can not but yield valuable information to us, who have scarcely yet begun to mature our plan of operation.

"With joyful aspirations, we look forward with you to that day when 'the earth shall be full of the knowledge of the Lord, as the waters cover the sea;' when 'there shall be one fold and one shepherd,' and when all differences among Christians shall end in the worship of God and his Anointed, in spirit and in truth.

"May the head of his church, the Lord Jesus Christ, who knows all the true members of the same, of whatever name or people they may be, exceeding abundantly increase their number by smiling upon the labors of Bible societies in all parts of the world; thereby marking them out and lifting them up for a sign of the times, to which the nations shall look and praise him.

"Do not misconstrue it as presumption that we address you in our own language. There are among you many who were formerly inhabitants of Germany, and still speak German; and these will be our interpreters. We shall, on our part, thankfully receive your answer in the English language, with which we are acquainted, as soon as it shall be agreeable to you to honor us with the same.

"Please to accept the assurance of our inmost veneration.

"John Daniel Runge,
"J. H. Mutzenbecker,
"Gilbert Van Der Smissen."

Extract from an Address of Prince Galitzin.

"Our pious emperor, though at a distance from Russia laboring for the good of nations, yet always present with all that is calculated to promote the welfare of his people and of mankind, has in these circumstances given us a new token of his regard to the work of the Bible Society, for he has granted the same privileges to promote its correspondence that are enjoyed by the different departments of government themselves—*not only the privilege of sending all letters free from postage, but also of* SENDING BIBLES BY POST, TO ANY PART OF THE EMPIRE, FREE FROM CHARGE."—*12th Report, Appen.*, p. 18.

Letter from one of the Secretaries of the Prot. Bible Society, Paris.

"SIR, AND VERY HONORED BROTHER IN JESUS CHRIST,

"It is with a real pleasure that I find myself charged by the committee to inform the society of which you are the secretary of the formation in this place of a Bible Society, under the name of *The Protestant Bible Society of Paris*, and to testify its regret at not having done it sooner. We send by this conveyance to your committee twelve copies of our first report and two of our regulations. You will have the goodness to present them to it as a feeble mark of our esteem, and of our desire to fraternize with it. You will see there, sir, that the Bible Society of Paris is founded on the same principles and with the same views with those which have preceded it in the same career.

"To recall to those who forget it the good news of salvation, the news of God manifesting himself in the flesh, and dying upon a cross to save sinful man, and thus to shed abroad light where all was darkness, morality where all was corruption, life where was nothing but death, by putting into the hands of all the glorious Gospel of God the Savior—that divine word from the Lord himself, and to the efficacy of which alone are promised all the miracles of grace. Such is the object which is proposed by the Bible Society of Paris. And, thanks to the succors and to the blessings from on high, she has reason to applaud her first step.

"The American Bible Society will learn with pleasure, and with gratitude to Him who is the cause, and to whom alone belongs the glory, that this fine France, so richly endowed of God, awakens at last from her long lethargy with respect to religion, and participates with the rest of the known world the inestimable benefits of Bible societies, and that she will join her prayers to those of all true Christians, that the Lord would please to bless and to accomplish his work, and to call to the knowledge of Jesus Christ, by the reading of his Word, so many millions of immortal souls, which are all languishing far from him who is *the way, the truth, and the life*, and by whom alone they can be saved.

"Accept, sir, and very honored brother, and render acceptable to your committee, the fraternal salutations of ours, and its wishes that the Lord would be pleased to crown your efforts always with new success, and enable you to obtain the sole recompense to which you attach any value, that of conducting captive souls to the obedience of our Lord Jesus Christ.

"The grace of our Lord Jesus Christ, and the love of God, and the communion of the Holy Ghost, be with you and with us. Amen.

"Your very humble servant and brother in Christ,

"J. MONOD *the Son*."

Extract of a Letter from the Hon. Bushrod Washington.

"I had the pleasure to receive your esteemed favor of the 8th ult., together with a Bible from American stereotype plates, for which I return to the managers of the American Bible Society my grateful acknowledgments.

"As to the execution of the work, it merits the highest commendation. Although my sight is not good, I read it with great ease; much more so, and with less fatigue to the eye, than print of the same size in most other books. As to its freedom from typographical errors, I can form no just opinion, having only had time to read a few chapters; I have no doubt, however, of its accuracy.

"You do me but justice, kind sir, in imputing to me the most favorable opinion of the design and operation of the national Bible institution."

Letter from the Honorable the Secretary of the Navy.

"*Nov.* 15, 1820.

"I have the honor to acknowledge the receipt of your letter of the 17th October last, in behalf of the Standing Committee of the American Bible Society, evincing their Christian and benevolent intentions of supplying the navy with copies of the Scriptures, for the use and benefit of the seamen employed in the public service.

"I request you to present to the committee my thanks for their liberal views in this instance.

"Upon a full consideration of the subject, and believing it to be the intention of the committee to extend the knowledge of the Gospel equally to all, I have thought proper to suggest that the first supply should be equal to the whole number of seamen and petty officers actually employed, which is about three thousand five hundred; the number which may be required annually afterward, to supply losses or deficiencies, will probably not exceed three hundred.

"If the above number should be considered too great in the first supply, it may be reduced at the discretion of the committee.

"I should wish to have the Bibles deposited with the several commandants of navy yards, in the proportion hereafter mentioned, by whom they will be distributed to each ship when equipped for service. Proper regulations will be established, and the commanding officers required to report annually the number disposed of, and the number that may be wanted, and the information shall be communicated to the committee in such manner as they shall request.

"I have the honor to be, with very great respect, sir, your most obedient servant, SMITH THOMPSON."

Tribute of Affection from the Board of Managers of the American Bible Society to the Memory of their deceased President.

"The Board of Managers of the American Bible Society, while, in common with their fellow-citizens, they sensibly feel the loss which the Christian community has sustained in the removal, by death, of the Hon. ELIAS BOUDINOT, of one of its most valuable members, have reason more especially to lament that which their institution has suffered, in being deprived of its venerated president.

"When the managers carry back their recollection to the period which preceded the formation of this society, and review the laborious and persevering efforts of Dr. Boudinot to accomplish the interesting object; when they consider the noble example of beneficence which he soon afterward presented, in the generous donation of ten thousand dollars to its treasury, and of one thousand dollars since toward the erection of a depository; the unremitting interest which, under the pressure of acute bodily suffering and the infirmities of advanced age, he continued ever afterward to evince in its concerns; his great exertion, notwithstanding the personal inconvenience and pain to which it subjected him, to attend its stated anniversaries; the dignity and amiableness with which he fulfilled the duties of the chair; and the pious and affectionate counsels supplied by his official communications, they deeply deplore the chasm that has been made in their body by this afflicting bereavement.

"To the will of an all-wise Providence it becomes them to feel unfeigned submission, and to accompany this act of duty with the expression of their grateful acknowledgments to a merciful God for his goodness, in prolonging beyond the ordinary measure of human life that of their illustrious patron, in permitting him to witness the rapid growth and prosperity of the cherished object of his affections, in conveying to his heart the consolations of that blessed book which he had made the standard of his faith and the rule of his conduct, and in enabling him to close a well-spent life with the full hope, through the merits of his Savior, of a blissful immortality beyond the grave. The Board of Managers would not only derive from these cheering recollections consolation for their loss, but incitement to an increased measure of exertion in that work which so engrossed the affections of their lamented president; and, while they are diligently employed in diffusing abroad the Word of Life, encouragement in seeking to realize for themselves its inestimable benefits.

"With the mourning daughter of their deceased friend, for so many years the partaker of his joys and sorrows, the companion of his journeys, and his amiable assistant in well-doing, the members of this board sincerely sympathize, and respectfully transmit to her this feeble expression of their feelings toward her venerable parent, as evidence of the affection with which they wish to embalm his memory, and the sincerity with which they condole with her under the bereavement she has experienced."

Letter from the President of the British and Foreign Bible Society.

"*Dec.* 17, 1821.

"GENTLEMEN,

"In full accordance with the feelings of the Committee of the British and Foreign Bible Society, I now discharge the melancholy duty of communicating the expression of their sympathy and condolence to their American brethren and fellow-laborers on the loss which they have sustained in the lamented death of their most venerable and respected president.

"On such an event, they can not but indulge the soothing reflection that the remembrance of departed worth will long retain its influence in promoting the interests of that holy religion which Dr. Boudinot so zealously cultivated, as well as the prosperity of that society which he so anxiously labored to advance.

"I have the honor to be, gentlemen, your most obedient humble servant, TEIGNMOUTH,

"President of the British and Foreign Bible Society."

Letter from the Librarian of the British and Foreign Bible Society.

"*Jan.* 31, 1823.

"SIR,

"The Committee of the British and Foreign Bible Society feel a pleasure in every opportunity of confirming the fraternal relation that exists between themselves and the American Bible Society, though the present occasion of correspondence is indeed a mournful one.

"I have to acknowledge the receipt of a letter from you of the 23d Nov., 1822, inclosing the resolution of your committee on occasion of the intelligence of the decease of our late secretary, the Rev. John Owen. The satisfaction that we experience from the testimonies of respect for our lamented friend, which are received from every quarter of the globe, is great and reasonable, and we draw consolation from the hope that in each of these distant regions there may be some few at least who shall one day arise and call him blessed for his labors, and shall be to him for a crown of rejoicing.

"The correspondence with the American Bible Society was one of the departments of office in which Mr. Owen took much delight. His discerning mind saw clearly that the identity of our aims, and the singleness and simplicity of our object, afforded the surest bond of union; and his warm feelings exulted in the thought that a British and an American institution should march hand in hand together, to propagate the sacred truths of that religion, in defense of which their common fathers had resisted even unto blood, and he trusted that they would go forth endued with power from on high, conquering and to conquer. But he has been taken off in the midst of his years, and all his thoughts and his projects sleep with him, for a season at least, in the tomb.

"You are not unacquainted, sir, with the feelings attendant upon such a loss as that which we have sustained. We have not forgotten the late venerable head of your society, who so short a time since was gathered unto his fathers. He, too, was lamented by many who had never seen or known him in his life, but who joined in sympathy with the friends who had experienced more immediately his loss, and could better appreciate his worth. To the feelings of our friends, both in London and in Paris, on that occasion, I can bear testimony from personal observation.

"May these losses tend to excite in us all that spirit which you so well express, that we may reflect that with us also 'the time is short,' and it behooves us, therefore, to work while it is day, for that night is coming upon us wherein no man can work.

"I remain, sir, yours, with great respect and esteem,

"THOMAS PELL PLATT."

Address of the Hon. John Jay, President of the American Bible Society.

"GENTLEMEN,

"We have the satisfaction of again observing, that by the blessing of Providence on the zeal of our fellow-citizens, and on the fidelity, diligence, and prudence with which our affairs are conducted, they continue in a state of progressive improvement. The pleasure we derive from it is not a little increased by the consideration that we are transmitting essential benefits to multitudes in various regions; and that the value and important consequences of these benefits extend and will endure beyond the limits of time. By so doing we render obedience to the commandment by which He who 'made of one blood all nations of men,' and established a fraternal relation between the individuals of the human race, hath made it their duty to love and be kind to one another.

"We know that a great proportion of mankind are ignorant of the revealed will of God, and that they have strong claims to the sympathy and compassion which we, who are favored with it, feel and are manifesting for them. To the most sagacious among the heathen it must appear wonderful and inexplicable that such a vicious, suffering being as man should have proceeded in such a condition from the hands of his Creator. Having obscure and confused ideas of a future state, and unable to ascertain how far justice may yield to mercy, or mercy to justice, they live and die (as our heathen ancestors did) involved in darkness and perplexities.

"By conveying the Bible to people thus circumstanced, we certainly do them a most interesting act of kindness. We thereby enable them to learn that man was originally created and placed in a state of happiness, but, becoming disobedient, was subjected to the degradation and evils which he and his posterity have since experienced. The Bible will also inform them that our gracious Creator has provided for us a Redeemer, in whom all the nations of the earth should be blessed—that this Redeemer has made atonement 'for the sins of the whole world,' and thereby reconciling the divine justice with the divine mercy, has opened a way for our redemption and salvation; and that these inestimable benefits are of the free gift and grace of God, not of our deserving, nor in our power to deserve. The Bible will also animate them with many explicit and consoling assurances of the divine mercy to our fallen race, and with repeated invitations to accept the offers of pardon and reconciliation. The truth of these facts and the sincerity of these assurances being unquestionable, they can not fail to promote the happiness of those by whom they are gratefully received, and of those by whom they are benevolently communicated.

"We have also the satisfaction of observing that the condition of the Church continues to improve. When, at certain periods subsequent to the Reformation, discordant opinions on ecclesiastical subjects began to prevail, they produced disputes and asperities which prompted those who embraced the same peculiar opinions to form themselves into distinct associations or sects. Those sects not only permitted Christian fraternity with each other to be impaired by coldness, reserve, and distrust, but also, on the occurrence of certain occasions, proceeded to alternate and culpable acts of oppression. Even their endeavors to increase the number of Christians were often too intimately connected with a desire to increase the number of their adherents, and hence they became more solicitous to repress competition than to encourage reciprocal respect and good will.

"These prejudices, however, have gradually been giving way to more laudable feelings. By the progress of civilization and useful knowledge, many individuals became better qualified to distinguish truth from error, and the diffusion of their reasonings among the people enabled them to judge and to act with less risk of committing mistakes. Since the rights of man and the just limits of authority in church and state have been more generally and clearly understood, the Church has been less disturbed by that zeal which 'is not according to knowledge,' and liberal sentiments and tolerant principles are constantly enlarging the sphere of their influence.

"To the advantages which the Church has derived from the improved state of society, may be added those which are resulting from the institution of Bible societies. With whatever degree of tenacity any of the sects may adhere to their respective peculiarities, they all concur in opinion respecting the Bible, and the propriety of extensively distributing it without note or comment. They therefore readily become members of Bible societies, and in that capacity freely co-operate. Their frequent meetings and consultations produce an intercourse which affords them numerous opportunities of forming just estimates of one another, and of perceiving that prepossessions are not always well founded. This intercourse is rendered the more efficient by the great and increasing number of clerical members from dissimilar denominations. Convinced by observation and experience that persons of great worth and piety are attached to sects different from their own, the duties of their vocation and their respectable characters naturally incline them to recommend and encourage Christian friendliness.

"It is well known that both cathedrals and meeting-houses have heretofore exhibited individuals who have been universally and justly celebrated as real and useful Christians; and it is also well known that at present not a few, under similar circumstances and of similar characters, deserve the like esteem and commendation. As *real* Christians are made so by Him without whom we 'can do nothing,' it is equally certain that he receives them into his family, and that in *his* family mutual love and uninterrupted concord never cease to prevail. There is no reason to believe or suppose that this family will be divided into separate classes, and that separate apartments in the mansions of bliss will be allotted to them according to the different sects from which they had proceeded.

"These truths and considerations direct our attention to the *new* commandment of our Savior, that his disciples 'do love one another:' although an anterior commandment required that, 'as we had opportunity,' we should 'do good unto all men,' yet this *new* one makes it our duty to do so 'especially to the household of faith.' In the early ages of the Church, Christians were highly distinguished by their obedience to it, and it is to be regretted that the conduct of too many of their successors has, in this respect, been less worthy of imitation.

"Our days are becoming more and more favored and distinguished by new and unexpected accessions of strength to the cause of Christianity. A zeal unknown to many preceding ages has recently pervaded almost every Christian country, and occasioned the establishment of institutions well calculated to diffuse the knowledge and impress the precepts of the Gospel both at home and abroad. The number and diversity of these institutions, their concurrent tendency to promote these purposes, and the multitudes who are cordially giving them aid and support, are so extraordinary, and so little analogous to the dictates of human propensities and passions, that no adequate cause can be assigned for them but the goodness, wisdom, and will of HIM who made and governs the world.

"We have reason to rejoice that such institutions have been so greatly multiplied and cherished in the United States, especially as a kind Providence has blessed us not only with peace and plenty, but also with the full and secure enjoyment of our civil and religious rights and privileges. Let us therefore persevere in our endeavors to promote the operation of these institutions, and to accelerate the attainment of their objects. Their unexampled rise, progress, and success in giving light to the heathen, and in rendering Christians more and more 'obedient to the faith,' apprise us that the great Captain of our salvation is going forth 'conquering and to conquer,' and is directing and employing these means and measures for that important purpose. They, therefore, who enlist in his service, have the highest encouragement to fulfill the duties assigned to their respective stations, for most certain it is that those of his followers who steadfastly and vigorously contribute to the furtherance and completion of his conquests, will also participate in the transcendent glories and blessings of his TRIUMPH."

Extract of a Letter from the Rev. John Summerfield, Liverpool.

"LIVERPOOL, *May* 21, 1823.

"It [the nineteenth annual meeting of the British and Foreign Bible Society] was the most imposing scene that ever my eyes beheld! nor do I look for a full realization of the feelings with which I was then possessed at any future period of my life, until I gaze with open face upon the 'general assembly and church of first-born which are written in heaven,' presided over by 'Jesus, the Mediator of the New Covenant,' and 'the head of all things to his church.'

"'O that with that celestial throng
We at his feet may fall!
Join in the everlasting song,
And crown him "Lord of all."'

"The inclosed document from Baron de Staël I hoped to have forwarded by you; but I now judge it my duty to transmit it, that you may be put in possession of the cordial recognition of my relation to the society, thus officially communicated."

Letter from the Baron de Staël, Secretary of the Protestant Bible Society, Paris.

"PARIS, *April* 20, 1823.

"SIR,

"I can not but consider it as a very fortunate circumstance in my life, that it should be my lot to express, in the name of the Paris Protestant Bible Society, the heartfelt satisfaction with which they were filled in seeing a deputy from the American Bible Society present at their annual meeting.

"The Rev. Mr. Summerfield was in every respect a fit representative—I would almost say a faithful image of that admirable country which rates the luxuriant vigor of a rising nation with the experience of old states. He will tell you, and we trust you will hear with satisfaction, that it has pleased God to bless our efforts with new success. Notwithstanding the sad difficulties we met in some instances, we have added to our numbers thirteen auxiliary or branch societies, and more than thirty Bible associations, sixteen of which have begun their work of piety and regeneration in the very center of the metropolis. The contributions from our auxiliary societies have increased fourfold; and the total amount of our receipts exceed, by 63,000 francs, the resources of last year. Such a result has surpassed our most sanguine expectations.

"Our excellent friend Mr. Wilder will soon revisit his native shores, and we can not sufficiently express how deeply his absence will be felt by all who witnessed his indefatigable zeal for the promotion of true Christianity in this country. But if any thing can lessen our regret, it is the confidence that Mr. Wilder's stay among his countrymen will lead to a more and more evangelical union between the good men on both sides of the Atlantic, and secure to us the continuance of your kindness and benevolence, than which no human reward can be a more welcome recompense for our feeble labors.

"With the highest regard and most fraternal attachment, we remain, sir, your most obedient humble servants,

"For the Committee, A. STAËL, Secretary."

Letter from the Rev. Dr. Morrison, Macao.

"MACAO, *Sept.* 1, 1823.

"SIR,

"In October, 1821, I received from you, in the name of the American Bible Society, an elegantly bound English Bible, and, at the same time, one for the Rev. Dr. Milne. On June 2, 1822, Dr. Milne departed this life. The American Bible Society's present remains, in memory of their father, in the possession of his four orphan children.

"I now send for the American Bible Society a copy of Morrison's and Milne's Chinese version of the Bible, bound together in the Chinese manner.

"This book is daily studied at the Anglo-Chinese college, and there, it is hoped, its contents will be gradually understood by the Chinese students. To circulate the sacred Scriptures in China extensively, in the present state of things, is not practicable; and the colonists in the Archipelago are so eager in the pursuit of gain, or the enjoyment of pleasure, they but seldom show much inclination to study divine revelation. But the friends of the Bible still persevere; and at Malacca, and other stations of the London Missionary Society in the Archipelago, copies of the Scriptures or particular books are distributed to Chinese and Cochin-Chinese who visit those places.

"May the Divine Author of the Bible, by his Holy Spirit, create a taste for his Holy Word among the millions who read the Chinese.

"The Chinese missionaries connected with us notice corrections and emendations of the version, and send them to the Anglo-Chinese college, where they are preserved, and, being approved, inserted in the original blocks.

"May the usefulness of the American Bible Society daily increase.

"I remain yours, &c., ROBERT MORRISON."

Extract of a Letter from the Foreign Secretary of the British and Foreign Bible Society.

"LONDON, *May* 17, 1826.

"We should have been glad to have seen a deputy from America in the midst of us; however, we had an individual who was with you last year, the Rev. Mr. Ellis, from the Sandwich Islands, whose information greatly cheered and delighted us. The extracts from your last printed report introduced into ours, and read, were received with much satisfaction, and particularly the statement of your university Bible societies. Dr. Philip, from Cape Town, gave us, as you will see in his speech, pleasing information about Africa; and a Col. Phipps and a Mr. Fox brought tidings of great joy from the East. The French baron, whose speech is also given, was the representative of the Paris Bible Society; and thus, from the four quarters of the world, we heard abundant information to make us thankful for the society's formation and past operations, and to encourage us for the future.

"Since the annual meeting we have heard of the cessation of the Burmese war. We have no concern in politics. The politicians of the earth, however, in accomplishing their own schemes, often open a door at which Christian workmen may enter; and we can not but hope that this is the case in this instance. Mr. Fox, in his address, mentioned that such is the veneration of the learned Burmese for the Pali language, that nothing written or printed in it will ever be destroyed. The New Testament in this language must be nearly printed at Colombo by this time, and will shortly be put into circulation, and this superstitious regard for their language may, perhaps, turn to good account. The Chinese Bible is gradually working its way, and we are in hopes that, by employing a person for the express purpose, an extensive circulation may take place in the course of the ensuing year. This measure has been urged upon us from different quarters, and has only been delayed by our not having met with a suitable person to undertake the work. Such an individual we have now presented to us, acquainted with the Chinese language, but our measures with reference to him are not yet matured. I have said nothing about South America; the letters from that country continue to evince the lamentable want of the Scriptures, and the readiness of multitudes to receive them. Mr. Armstrong, whom you know, is settled at Buenos Ayres, not as the direct agent, but still the zealous friend of the society. Another individual has presented himself to our notice as an agent, and will, I believe, shortly leave England for this very important sphere of labor.

"In the closing paragraph of our report I have ventured to write, 'On every side we hear the voice of God and see his hand;' and I trust that this is not the language of presumption. May we enter fully into the sentiment, and be excited to have zeal to give the Bible to others, and to more affection and obedience to the sacred volume ourselves.

"Present my kind regard to your fellow-laborers.

"Dear sir, yours faithfully,

"A. Brandram, Secretary."

Letter from the President of the Swedish Bible Society.

"Gentlemen,

"The Swedish Bible Society, in consequence of the union and friendship which exist between the societies, has the honor of communicating their Twelfth Year's Report, from which the American Bible Society, certainly with pleasure, will see the progress which the society here has made during the course of the last year.

"It is with the liveliest interest the committee here received the intelligence of the increasing support and circulation which the Bible receives within the circle of the society's operations in America.

"The exchange of what we in common experience of the blessing of the Most High upon our weak efforts to effect the good work that God has established, constitutes the greatest joy and encouragement for all that are engaged in the circulation of the Scriptures, to go on with unremitting diligence with what has been begun, offering up the most earnest prayers to the Author of the Scriptures that he would take under his special care all our exertions for the good cause.

"The committee begs leave to assure the American Bible Society of its unalterable attachment and highest esteem.

"M. ROSENBLAD,
"President of Swedish Bible Society.

"STOCKHOLM, *4th May*, 1827."

Proceedings of the British and Foreign Bible Society.

"At a meeting of the Committee of the British and Foreign Bible Society, held 2d of June, 1828, the Right Hon. Lord Bexley, V. P., in the chair.

"Read a letter from the Rev. Dr. Milnor, secretary to the American Bible Society, dated New York, April 15, 1828, communicating three resolutions passed by the Board of Managers. The first explicitly declares that the principles on which the society was established exclude the circulation of the Apocrypha; the second directs the plates of the Spanish Bible (the only one to which the Apocrypha was attached by that Society) to be altered, so as to exclude the apocryphal books; and the third resolution orders that those books shall be removed from all the Spanish Bibles remaining in the depository before any more copies are issued.

"*Resolved*, That this committee receive the above communication with much satisfaction.

"(Extract from the Minutes.)
"JOHN JACKSON, Assistant Foreign Secretary."

"BRITISH AND FOREIGN BIBLE SOCIETY, *June* 20, 1828.

"REV. DR. MILNOR.—MY DEAR FRIEND,

"It has been my usual practice, at this period of the year, to write you at some length an account of our annual meeting. I would gladly adhere to the custom were it really in my power, but I have so much upon my hands that my time will not admit it.

"I received both your letters by Mr. Patton. I am sorry that he arrived too late for our anniversary. America was, however, very ably represented by the Rev. B. Allen, from Philadelphia.

"We rejoice much in the increase of your exertions and in your prosperity, and I would add also, as a matter of some considerable importance, in the determination which you have come to as a society, and to which the resolution I transmit to you refers. I can not but indulge the hope that the united voice of our respective societies will produce an effect. Though I myself resisted the adoption of the views now taken, I am perfectly satisfied, and can with the utmost cordiality endeavor to carry them into effect. In doing this we meet with much encouragement, though we are not without our hinderances.

"Mr. Patton, in examining the Bibles provided by our society, saw, or fancied he saw, a degree of superiority in them to those furnished by yours, and he therefore has requested that we would present you with some specimens. I need not say how much pleasure it gave our committee to show you this little token of the very sincere regard we entertain for you. They are offered in the true spirit of those lines, which I quote from memory,

"'Si quid novisti rectius istis
Candidus imperti. Si non his utere mecum.'

"Accept my kindest regards for yourself and fellow-laborers, and believe me yours very sincerely,

"A. Brandram, Secretary."

Letter to the Rev. J. C. Brigham, D.D., Corresponding Secretary of the American Bible Society, from the Rev. Mr. Temple, Malta.

"Malta, *Feb.* 18, 1833.

"My dear Brother,

"Your kind letter of Oct. 22d reached me some weeks since, bearing the agreeable intelligence that you have completed plates for printing the New Testament in modern Greek. I rejoice that you have done this, and still more do I rejoice in the prospect of your being able to meet all the demands of the missionaries from our country for the sacred Scriptures, for distribution at the various stations, and in the wide fields where they are laboring.

"This is as it should be; for surely every friend of the American Bible Society must wish to see its influence extended, and still extending far beyond the utmost bounds of the everlasting hills of his native land. I most devoutly hope it will very soon deserve, if it does not assume, the name of the American and Foreign Bible Society. It should be, and I trust it soon will be, the noble and virtuous emulation of all our pious and benevolent countrymen to scatter around the entire globe that divinely-inspired Volume, to whose influence, far more than to all other causes, our favored country owes its enviable rank among the nations of the world.

"Our Armenian Bishop Carabet will have finished, within another week, the translation of the Old Testament into the Armeno-Turkish language, should his life and health be spared him. I know not at present what arrangements may be deemed expedient in executing the printing of this translation. I should wish it to be done, if possible, by the American Bible Society. The whole must undergo a thorough revision before it can be put to the press, wherever it may be printed.

"Whenever your edition of the Greek New Testament is completed, I should anticipate many useful and important results should you send a good, trusty, and active agent into Greece and the Levant for the purpose of putting them into circulation. Some difficulties would doubtless be encountered in such an enterprise, and considerable items of expense must, of course, be incurred; but then an interest would be awakened at home on this subject, I should hope, that would more than justify such a measure. The British and Foreign Bible Society has, as you know, for a long time employed an agent in the Levant, and the good thus accomplished is very great. For myself, I should rejoice to learn that you have resolved to send an agent to encourage our Christian brethren in these countries, and to co-operate with them in reopening the wells of salvation, which have been stopped up for so many ages by the modern Philistines. The astonishing changes and revolutions in these countries within the last few years, and, more than all, within the last year, by the victorious troops of the modern Pharaoh of Egypt, have very greatly increased the facilities for giving free course to the Word of God. May these facilities increase till every obstacle is taken out of the way.

"I bless God that your life has been spared while the overflowing scourge has passed through your city and swept a multitude to the grave. Dear brother, my whole heart says, The Lord Jesus Christ be with your spirit, and with the spirit of all who are associated with you in the great work of diffusing the holy oracles.

"With much affection, very truly yours,

"D. TEMPLE."

Communication of the Rev. Wm. S. Plumer, D.D., of Virginia, in relation to the supplying of the world with the Scriptures in a short period.

"*To the respected Board of Managers of the American Bible Society:*

"GENTLEMEN,

"Knowing your great zeal and readiness in the immeasurable work in which you have engaged, and not doubting but my communication of recent date has ere this time been submitted to your venerable body, and feeling that some thoughts naturally consequent upon those of my communication of the present month are called for, I resume my pen to address you. In my late communication, I transmitted copies of several resolutions unanimously passed by different and widely-separated bodies of men, and also copies of other testimonies in favor of a resolution to supply the accessible reading and willing population of the earth, within a definite period, with the Word of Life. In my present communication I desire to show that such a work can be done, and that without any miracle, or any impoverishing of the world, or any large portion of it. I know the amount of money called for will not be a small sum, and yet I know that there is more money and property in one street of your city, or in two streets of Philadelphia, than would accomplish the work. If hundreds of thousands *sound* high, let it be remembered that one horse-race in the United States cost not less than $300,000, and that one nobleman in England has an annual income of £300,000 sterling. The interest on the national debt of great Britain is £40,000,000 per annum. So that we have large sums of real wealth presented to us, turn where we will. And shall such noble causes as your own be forever compelled to add up a few scores of thousands per annum, and no more, while even a horse-race gets hundreds of thousands? I trust not. Even from the foregoing statement, it is obviously not absurd, at the first thought, to speak of the plan as possible. But let us proceed a step further. The population of the earth may, for our present purposes, be estimated at 800,000,000. This calculation is 100,000,000 larger than many make. Allowing five persons to a family, there are then 160,000,000 families. But not less than 30,000,000 of these families are already supplied. This leaves 130,000,000 families destitute of the Bible. On an average, Bibles cost one dollar each. Then we want $130,000,000. We propose to get this sum, say in twenty years. Can it be done? In order to raise $130,000,000 in twenty years, we must raise $6,500,000 per annum for twenty years. Can this be done? There are believed to be in the world not less than 20,000,000 of truly pious persons. Can they not each raise 32½ cents per annum; and will they not do it? If they can, and will, we shall have the $6,500,000 per annum.

"But a large part of those to whom the Bible is sent are willing to pay for it. The British and Foreign Bible Society aim to distribute few copies of the Scriptures gratuitously. Suppose, then, that one third of the Bibles sent out by Bible societies shall be sold; then we want in twenty years *only* $86,000,000, or $4,333,333 per annum. This sum, divided among the 20,000,000 of pious people, gives to each one about 21⅝ cents. This would not be a burdensome contribution.

"But, then, just in proportion as the Bible cause in the hands of Bible societies goes forward, just in the same proportion does private capital prepare, and private enterprise scatter the Bible. All *experience* is in favor of this assertion. It was said, indeed, that Bible societies would injure private booksellers; but all experience disproves the assertion. 'One house,' said Dr. M'Auley, at your last anniversary, 'one house, in the space of a few months, sold 12,000 Bibles here in the United States.' I am credibly informed that another house, having several branches, sold in fourteen months, in the United States, $40,000 worth of German Bibles. Indeed, dear as stereotype plates are, one of your own body, who is acquainted with such business, told me that the founders could scarcely furnish stereotype plates for the Bible as fast as publishers of that holy book called for them. This is the state of things in America. How was it before the existence of Bible Societies? Why, in 1782, Robert Aitken, having obtained a long preamble and resolution from the Congress of the United States, setting forth the difficulties of printing the Bible in the United States, and pledging the national treasury for a certain amount, ventured to publish an edition of the Holy Scriptures; and now almost any little bookseller who chooses may, without any serious risk, have a large and handsome edition of the Bible printed, without having a single copy pledged before the work is published. So much for the state of things in this nation.

"Similar facts might easily be gathered respecting other parts of Christendom. The number, not less than the neatness, of the Bibles published at the Oxford press alone is truly amazing. Private enterprise may be relied on, then, to circulate one third of the whole number of copies of the Scriptures which are sent out among the nations, so that we only want $43,333,333, in twenty years, for gratuitous distribution. Or we want $2,166,666 per annum, being about 10 cents and 8 mills per annum for every pious person on earth. And can not this be had? Tell the tale to the world—the Christian world, and see if it can not be had. You will have the goodness to observe that nothing is here said of the certain reduction that will occur in the cost of paper, type, and the whole business of preparing books for use and circulation. That a further reduction must take place, I presume none will doubt.

"The foregoing estimate also goes on the supposition that every family on earth is accessible to Bible agents, is willing to receive and able to read the Scriptures. This, however, is by no means the case, nor have we the assurance that such will be the case within twenty years.

"Moreover, the Bible cause has thousands and tens of thousands of liberal and decided friends who do not even profess to be pious, and do not, therefore, make a part of the 20,000,000 of persons named in this calculation; so that we may boldly say, less than 10 cents annually from every hopefully pious man on earth will do the work in twenty years.

"But, throwing aside all abatements, supposing that Bible societies have to do the whole work alone, and are not able to sell a single Bible, even then all the money that will be necessary will be, from each hopefully pious man, if paid at one time, not $1000, nor $100, nor $50, nor $10, but merely $6 50. Give this, and the work is done. Respecting money, therefore, there can be no difficulty, except such as shall originate in a criminal and high degree of cupidity, selfishness, and sloth, so glaring as that the Christian world must just stand and have her face covered with a burning shame, or reform and come up to the work.

"The foregoing statements have been made, not for the purpose of showing *how* the work *will* be done, but *that* it *can* be done. None but a foolish man would ever think of actually raising funds in such a method from the Christian *world*. Nor are such arguments suited to the purpose of raising money; but they are *intended* merely to show to a calculating mind the entire practicability of the work, provided those who can be aroused shall engage in the plan. The real way in which the thing *will* be done will be by *some* giving all they are worth to have the work done. A *few* have already done this. Pass the river, and cut down the bridge, and *many* will do it. Many, also, who will not give all, will yet give some, perhaps as much as duty to their dependents will permit. The agent for Virginia has often told individuals to withhold their hands, to refrain, because they would distress themselves. Again, many would in their last wills remember this cause. It has been remembered in this way already out of Virginia, yes, and in Virginia. Children and poor people will forego even lawful gratifications to forward the work. A little girl in Virginia proposed to eat no butter for a month, that she might get twenty-five cents to make her an annual member of a little Female Bible Society. As the agent was pleading the cause of the dying world in one of the upper counties, a poor woman said to her husband, 'I have fifty cents saved to buy coffee with. It is hid in such a place. Go home and get it, and make haste back, lest the good man be gone. I will do without coffee a little while longer, until these people get the Gospel among them.' The truth is, the treasury of the Lord is the hearts of his people; get them rightly affected, and they will give all to a good object, if necessary. Many such things occur all over this land every year, and their occurrence increases in frequency every year. The money, therefore, can be had.

"The next question touching the feasibility of this plan relates to translations. On this subject it is easy, perhaps it would be best (it was in the original resolution, on the doctrine of which I received the letters which you have published) to frame a resolution so as not to pledge yourselves in the work of translation further than may be found practicable on a fair experiment. So that, on the subject of translations, there is not need of very much inquiry at present, in order to learn what our duty is. Estimating the population of the earth at 800,000,000, one fourth of the whole number live in Christian countries, and have translations of the Bible in their own languages. Two hundred millions are then furnished with translations. Not less than 350,000,000 of people *read*, if any, the language into which Drs. Milne and Morrison have translated the Scriptures. Five hundred and fifty millions are then provided for. The many translations prepared by the Baptists and others in the East will certainly supply at least an additional 100,000,000. We have then 650,000,000 provided for. The residue of 150,000,000, or three sixteenths of the whole, have the Scriptures to some such extent as follows: There are the Arabic Scriptures for 10,000,000; the Persian for 8,000,000; that for Asiatic Siberia (now in the press), not less than 20,000,000; the Turkish, Armeno-Turkish, and Armenian, not less than 12,000,000; leaving not quite 100,000,000 without any translation in their own language. But then not a few of them, as several of the Indian tribes, &c., are able, to some extent, to read some language into which the Bible is translated. Some other abatements are to be made; so that there are probably not more than 70 or 80,000,000 without a translation, and perhaps not 50,000,000, who have a written or printed language, without such translation in part or in whole. So that we may hope, that before the great body of these people shall be fairly accessible to agents, we will have either translations, or translators prepared to enter on the work of translation. But, as was said, no resolution passed by any Bible Society, contemplating the supply of the nations generally, need exceed the limits fixed by translations already made or soon to be made.

"The third point, to which I offer but *few* remarks, is the subject of agencies. Can agents be had to do the work? I suppose they can be had. There are men in abundance, many of whom would love to be employed in such a work. And it would require by no means as *many* agents as some would suppose. *One* efficient agent can himself, and alone, supply a considerable kingdom in the space of twenty years. Just see what one man has done in the north of Europe, and indeed all around the Baltic. I refer to Dr. Patterson. We have also had some voluntary agencies undertaken in the United States, which have brought about equally remarkable results. Suppose Gutzlaff shall live twenty years, and China continue even as accessible as it is now, and the books be furnished in any number he may desire, how many hundreds of thousands of copies would he distribute? Or furnish a less daring and more quiet, but equally worthy man, who was at your last anniversary, Rev. D. O. Allen, of Bombay, with as many Bibles as he can dispose of during the rest of his life, if he shall live but ten years, and what wonders would he effect! This man hastened home from the United States, intending to spend the rest of his days engaged in good part in this blessed work. Besides, it is found altogether practicable, and, of course, expedient, to employ in very successful agencies other persons than those who are reared in Christian countries. There are converts to Christianity already sufficiently numerous in Burmah to supply that empire in far less than twenty years, unless I am utterly erroneous in my calculations, and in this I think I can not be mistaken.

"So much for the feasibility of the plan, rendered probable by what we can *see* and *count*. These are not, however, the estimates of any thing more than cold and casual calculation. The estimates of Christian love and holy confidence in God are far higher, and are the only foundation on which much has ever been done, or ever will be done. The estimates of faith are the only basis on which we are justified in acting in the affairs of our royal Master, Jesus Christ. On this subject I say nothing further at present, not doubting but the faith of your respected body is much stronger than my own, and also intending to make another communication shortly on this great subject."

Dissolution of the Methodist Bible Society.

Previous to the year 1836 the Methodist Episcopal Church had a Bible Society of its own. To this society, from time to time, the American Bible Society made liberal donations for the gratuitous supply of destitute families and Sabbath schools.

At the General Conference of the year above named, held in the city of Cincinnati, a resolution was passed dissolving the Methodist Bible Society, and merging it into the American Bible Society.

The different Conferences, by resolutions and otherwise, yielded a cordial assent to this measure, and the co-operation of the Church in a very short time became general. At each annual convocation resolutions are passed making it the duty of every traveling preacher to take up collections in their respective churches in aid of the funds of the national society.

Extract from a Discourse on the Death of John Nitchie, Esq., Treasurer of the American Bible Society.

"The large and discriminating mind of Mr. Nitchie was richly stored with the treasures of information and thought. His education was originally thorough and solid; he had a great thirst for knowledge; his opportunities were uncommonly good, and his experience and observation were extensive; and these, connected with his various reading—particularly upon religious subjects, and, most of all, of the Bible—furnished him with a fund of important information altogether rarely to be met with. His knowledge of the Scriptures—particularly his critical acquaintance with the original language of the New Testament—was probably more minute, accurate, and extensive than that of almost any other individual, layman or clergyman, in our community. In addition to his ordinary reading of the Bible—which he daily practiced—the close attention which he was called to pay to it, during the nineteen years that he was in the service of the American Bible Society, in examining and correcting their publications, had almost copied it entire upon the tablet of his memory. And this fund of information contributed, in an eminent degree, to impart that value to his character which his acquaintances were ever ready to award to him. In all the relations and associations of life, he was the more highly esteemed because always instructive.

"Another interesting trait in our friend's character was almost an excess of modesty, combined with his excellent talents and great store of knowledge. His self-diffidence and humble estimate of his own powers approached toward a fault, and no doubt sometimes kept him back from imparting instruction in public, for which he was well qualified. His acquaintances know how averse he was to doing any thing that might be interpreted into an assertion of superiority; how readily, in the discharge of his duties, he condescended to the humblest walks of life; how disposed he was to defer to brethren who were, in many respects, his inferiors; and with what amiable meekness he would place himself to listen at the feet of one who could make no pretensions to equality with him in ability and acquirements. These were characteristics of his mind, which endeared him very much to the hearts of his associates and friends.

"But the time would fail us to remark on all that in him we esteemed and admired. We are most concerned with his religious character. We have said already that Mr. Nitchie professed religion at about twenty-three or twenty-four years of age; and as he died at fifty-four, he lived something more than thirty years a member of the Christian Church. From the universal testimony of those who knew him during the early part of his Christian life, and from the fact that he was chosen to sustain important offices in the Church, and that a most responsible station was confided to him in connection with the American Bible Society, it is evident he was early known as a consistent, decided, and devoted Christian. Such was the tenor of his whole life. To those, however, who were favored with a long and intimate acquaintance with him, it appears that the growth of his piety was much the most rapid within the last eight or ten years. In particular, during that precious revival of religion in 1831, his piety received an impulse which it never lost. His Christian feelings were then kindled up to a flame; with all his powers he was engaged in the work of the Lord in the South Reformed Dutch Church. It is thought that he accomplished more than any other layman in that church at that time; and, in the hand of God, he was made the means of bringing many from darkness into marvelous light. And, as we said, that spirit he never lost—that season he never forgot—but spake of it frequently with tender interest while he lived; and from that time his piety became ascendant, and the love of souls seemed to be the ruling passion of his heart. Shortly after the season alluded to, he became connected with the Allen Street Church, but he continued to manifest the same characteristic zeal and devotedness.

"He was eminently a lover of revivals, and delighted to dwell in the midst of their solemn and impressive scenes. Nothing caused his countenance to glow, and his bosom to heave with such emotion, as to know that the Lord was pouring out his Spirit. Many in that church can bear witness to the untiring faithfulness with which he labored in such scenes there; to the manner in which he visited inquiring souls, from house to house; the pains and patience with which he opened to them the plan of salvation, and the affecting pathos with which he besought them to be reconciled to God. The meeting which, during seasons of revival, was regularly appointed in that church, to converse with those who were the subjects of the Spirit's striving, was a place of his delight, and one which, to him, seemed to have in it something of the sweetness of heaven. In his faithful attendance upon it he was a bright example. If in health, the stroke of the bell was not more true in calling us together than the tread of his foot when the time arrived. He excelled in the treatment of souls. His discriminating mind, his great knowledge of the Scriptures, his deep religious experience, his condescending manners and tender flow of feeling, qualified him for it, and gave him great influence with them; and the seals of his labors in this interesting department of Christian duty are not a few. Under God, he turned many to righteousness.

"One other department of his useful labors was the Bible class. In this he was constantly engaged through many years of his life. His habit was to meet his class regularly twice every Sabbath; and here he applied his extensive biblical resources with great effect. He could shed light upon many portions of Scripture where common instructors would be utterly at a loss. He was faithful and successful; and from no other source, no larger, did the communion of the church receive so frequent accessions as from his Bible class.

"It now remains that we give some account of his last illness and death. His intercourse with his friends, during his sickness, was strictly characteristic and affectionate. He expressed a lively interest in them all, and requited their attentions with the warmest acknowledgments.

On various occasions his solicitude was manifested for his family, the church with which he was connected, for particular individuals, and the interests of the Church at large. As his strength failed, and the prospect of his recovery became more uncertain, his thoughts dwelt more on death and eternity; and when speaking on these subjects, he uniformly expressed an entire and cordial acquiescence in the Divine will, and high satisfaction that whatever took place, in respect to him, it would not be the result of blind, undesigning chance, but be ordered by infinite wisdom and goodness. His Christian hope was never obscured at all, but, as often as the inquiry was made, he said he enjoyed the light of God's countenance, and his soul was at peace. A few days before his death, when the hope of his recovery grew faint, he desired an interview with his late pastor. That interview was an interesting one, and in substance as follows: He said that, in view of the increasing uncertainty whether he should recover, he wished to examine his hope, and see whether it were well founded or not; and for this reason he had requested the conversation. He was asked if this desire arose from any darkness of mind, or any reason he had to fear his hope was not good. He answered, there was no change in that respect; but that he viewed himself as probably approaching a very solemn hour, and that he should be remiss in his duty to himself if he did not re-examine his title to the kingdom of heaven. On being told that this was proper, and that it was a matter of gratification that there was no other reason for his doing it, he proceeded, and with a mind perfectly collected and clear, gave his views of the way of salvation through Christ, and the reasons he had for believing himself interested in it. He said that all within himself appeared worthless and polluted; he had no confidence in any thing he had ever done; he viewed himself as a poor helpless sinner, and, if saved, must be saved by grace only; but that he looked upon the blood of Christ as having power to cleanse from all sin; his hope was wholly in him; that he felt sure he hated sin and loved holiness, and longed after nothing so much as spotless purity, an unvarying conformity to the Divine image. After having said much more of similar import, he ceased; and it was stated to him, that if such were his views and such his experience, there could be no room for mistake; that there was no Savior but Christ—no other object for the sinner's faith; and that, if his trust was in HIM, his anchor-hold was firm; and that it seemed to be his duty and privilege to rest secure, and let no temptation awaken a suspicion or excite a trouble in his soul about his safety. In this he acquiesced, and added, '*My faith* STANDS, *not in the word of man, but in the Word of God.*' And it is believed that from that time he never expressed anxiety about himself, but calmly, and with heavenly resignation, awaited the Divine will.

"Two days before the termination of his earthly trials—apprehending that the event might be sooner than it was—his medical attendants advised that he be informed that they had done what they could, that he was in the hands of the Lord alone, and that, if he had any thing to do, or wished to say any thing to his friends, it might be expedient not to delay. This communication was plainly and affectionately made to him. He listened to it with serious attention, and without any apparent increase of emotion; and after it was made, as was usual for him, he expressed his thankfulness that it had been done. He was asked if it had surprised him at all; he answered, it had not. Then, after pausing a few moments, as if engaged in prayer, he called the members of his family severally to him, and when they were all together, in the most feeling terms he addressed them to the following effect: 'My children, you here see what remains of your father. Now that I am dying, I wish to leave behind me my testimony that I die in the faith of that Gospel by which I have professed to live; and though my failings have been many, I have endeavored, in accordance with the Gospel, to bring you up in the nurture and admonition of the Lord. If I know what religion is, it is simply this: we are all sinners, and therefore without hope in ourselves; but God has laid help for us upon one that is mighty to save; he has sent his only and well-beloved Son into the world, that through his death we might have life. And "other foundation can no man lay than that is laid, which is Jesus Christ;" "for there is none other name given under heaven, among men, whereby we must be saved." Embrace this Savior, and you are safe. Do it now, while you have a day of mercy, and while you enjoy health and strength; for I assure you that sickness is a bad time to seek an interest in Christ—a sick bed is no good place to make preparation for death.' He then most tenderly charged them 'to be faithful to each other and to their *dear* mother, who had been like a ministering angel to him during his sickness;' and in closing, in a truly sublime manner elevating his eyes, he said, '*I* KNOW *that if my earthly house of this tabernacle were dissolved, I have a building of God, a house not made with hands, eternal in the heavens.*'"

Address of the President, Hon. John Cotton Smith.

"MY RESPECTED FRIENDS,

"There are few occasions more impressive than the annual meetings of this society; for no institution of human origin can be more sacred in its object, or more benign in its influence on the happiness and the hopes of men. To be constituted almoners of God's richest gift to our race; to be enabled by his bounty to offer the wandering and lost pilgrim a sure guide to his final home, cheering his way thither with the purest joys and the brightest anticipations, is a privilege and a distinction for which we should render our most humble and grateful adoration. In view of the Divine beneficence toward the American people, it would become them to adopt the language of the shepherd-king of Israel, when contemplating his elevation from the sheepfold to a throne, 'What am I, O Lord God, and what is my house, that thou hast brought me hitherto!' Who, at the period of our revolution, and some of us have a distinct remembrance of its soul-stirring scenes, who, I repeat, could have imagined that this young country, then bleeding at every pore, would so soon not only attain to her present height of worldly greatness, but would also exhibit the phenomenon of sending the Bible to the Old World! yea, of sending the light of divine truth to the region whence it first emanated, the sacred ground where the Redeemer revealed his mission of love and sealed it with his blood! to countries visited and taught by his apostles; to Persia and India, and those far-distant islands, where the transforming power of this wonderful book is at the present moment exciting universal astonishment! Nor have our aborigines, and Africa, and even civilized Europe, been wholly overlooked in this broad scheme of Christian philanthropy. If a review of these transactions may justly produce a virtuous exultation, we must look for its legitimate effect in corresponding exertions to meet the multiplied appeals to our benevolence from these and other destitute portions of the globe. The increasing demand for the Holy Scriptures affords exhilarating evidence of the successful progress of truth, and of the zeal and faithfulness of the excellent men who are employed in its promulgation. To us these soldiers of the cross confidently look for their spiritual armor, for that mysterious WORD which is at once 'the sword of the Spirit' and 'the balm' of heavenly consolation. Shall they look in vain? Shall their drafts upon your board be dishonored? Will the friends of the Bible faint and tire in its cause? Never, while there shall be found on earth one desolate heart to ask for the Word of Life, or one empty hand extended to receive it!

"In furtherance of the enterprise in which we are engaged, your Board of Managers have rendered an essential service by a careful collation of their authorized copy of the sacred text with a *fac simile* of our unrivaled version, as it came from the hands of the translators, and with numerous intervening copies of different dates in the society's library. The task was arduous, but the gentlemen who achieved it felt themselves abundantly rewarded by the high gratification of finding no material departure from the genuine copy—nothing more, indeed, than discrepancies in punctuation, and other particulars equally unimportant. With augmented confidence, therefore, have the board recommended the English version as the model to all who, under our auspices, are translating the Bible into other languages. Nor have they scrupled to give their unqualified sanction to the course pursued by our translators in adopting, or, as it is called, *transferring* the original word wherever an equivalent term can not be found in the foreign tongue. And a perfect coincidence of this kind can scarcely be expected in any supposable case. It certainly did not exist between the two most copious and polished languages of pagan antiquity. The Greek and Latin tongues reciprocated transfers in repeated instances. When the early Christian fathers rendered the original Greek of the New Testament into Latin, they found it necessary to adopt and *Latinize* the most important of the identical words which, from the same necessity, were subsequently adopted and *Anglicized* by our translators. On the other hand, when the Roman laws were translated into Greek for the use of the Oriental empire, the learned jurists of the imperial courts employed in that service found many cases in which the whole Greek vocabulary was utterly inadequate to a just expression of the meaning of the original. What was to be done? Without hesitation, and 'without regard to Attic elegance,' they transferred the original term itself, barely giving to the Latin word the sonorous termination of their own more musical language. And what course can be more unexceptionable? What more equitable, especially in cases where a diversity of construction may possibly arise? What thanks are due to a superintending Providence for thus allowing a perfect freedom of interpretation to every section of the Christian Church!

"But in extending our views to distant nations, let us not lose sight of our own. From the rapid increase of our native population, as well as from foreign accessions, many families in almost every part of our country must now be destitute of a Bible. To whom shall this important department be confided? If our American youth generally would emulate the noble spirit of the young men in this city, the work, we have reason to believe, might be speedily accomplished. It is worthy of particular notice, that, of numerous auxiliaries, if many have equaled, no one has exceeded the 'Young Men's Bible Society' here in generous and wisely-directed measures to promote the great objects of the parent institution. This is, indeed, to 'remember their Creator' in its appropriate and most affecting sense, in a way to insure blessings not less invaluable to themselves than to the recipients of their bounty. It is cheering to observe that the youth of some other cities are copying, with commendable zeal, this bright example. Should it be followed throughout the republic, who can estimate its auspicious bearing on the destinies of this nation! With what transport would the dying patriot resign his country into the hands of a generation who shall have consecrated the morning of life to so glorious a purpose!

"While with grateful hearts we recognize the smiles of Heaven upon the operations of the board during the past year, we deeply feel the afflictive dispensations of a holy Providence in removing by death the vice-presidents Bolton and Van Rensselaer since the last anniversary. The former, a highly respected citizen, had sustained the office from the first organization of the society; and, after his removal from Georgia to this city, he was punctual in his attendance at the Board of Managers, where his faithful services will be long and affectionately remembered. The gentleman last named has left testimonials of his worth too numerous and distinguished to require the tribute of my humble eulogy. Still, it is due to private friendship to say, that from the commencement of our acquaintance in early youth to his lamented departure, I have regarded his career with unmingled admiration. Who, in truth, has not admired the proofs of his cultivated and well-balanced mind, his superiority to the blandishments of fortune, the dignified simplicity of his demeanor, his elevated and straight-forward course as a statesman, his humble and exemplary walk as a Christian, the monuments, on all sides, of his public munificence, and, what is more, the gentle flow of that heaven-born charity which, with the silence of the dew, he shed on the cottage of the widow and the fatherless, and upon 'him that had no helper!' Surely his record and his reward are on high!

"During the same period, also, we have been called to mourn the demise of the venerable Boyd, an active and useful member of the board from its earliest establishment, and whose virtuous life has afforded a well-founded hope of a blessed immortality. Would that I might here have closed this sad obituary; but we who have beheld in the late president of the Wesleyan University the steadfast friend and patron of this society, and have felt the power of his eloquence at our annual celebrations, must be indulged in the expression of unfeigned sorrow at the early termination of his valuable life; a life eminently devoted to the advancement of religion and sound learning—in a word, to the best and highest interests of his fellow-men. Short as has been his pilgrimage, lasting will be the memorials of his extended usefulness; and although his voice shall no more be heard with delight in an earthly temple, we trust it is attuned to more exalted strains in the paradise above.

"Since such, my brethren and friends, are the consolations under sore bereavements which are derived from the precious volume we profess to circulate, let our sympathies be alive to the dark and hopeless condition of the many millions of the human race upon whom the Sun of Righteousness has never risen with healing in his beams."

Sketch of the Life of General Van Rensselaer, by Dr. Vermilye.

"The Hon. Stephen Van Rensselaer was the lineal descendant of one of our oldest families, who, at the earliest settlement of the country, obtained from the Dutch government the grant of the manor of Rensselaerwyck, which was subsequently confirmed, under the English, by letters patent from James II., in 1685, and again in 1704, during the reign of Queen Anne. He was born in the city of New York, on the first day of November, 1764, and, consequently, was in his 75th year at the time of his decease.

"He received the rudiments of his education first at a day school in this city, and then at Elizabethtown, N. J. He was afterward at the Kingston Academy, where commenced his acquaintance with the lamented Abraham Van Vechten, which ripened into a warm, confiding intimacy, and survived in all its strength until the recent death of his friend. From the academy, he was placed by his mother, ever anxious for his religious welfare, under the charge of the Rev. Dr. Witherspoon, whom he accompanied on horseback from this place to Princeton, part of the distance with an escort provided by General Washington, by whom they had been hospitably entertained at West Point. After a year or two of preparatory study, he entered Nassau Hall, but subsequently removed to Cambridge, where he graduated in 1782. His public career commenced in 1789, when he was chosen to the Assembly of this state. He was next in the Senate, and in 1795, at the age of thirty-one, became its presiding officer in the capacity of lieutenant governor, which station he held for six years. From 1800 to 1820 he was frequently in the Assembly; was a member of two different state conventions, called to explain and revise the Constitution; and for several years occupied a seat in the Congress of the United States. He was among the earliest and most ardent friends of internal improvements throughout the state. In 1810 he was appointed one of the State Commissioners, and for the last fourteen years of his life was President of the Canal Board. He was, at the same time, the Chancellor of the University of New York.

"He was a man of remarkable *humility*, connected with a striking *simplicity* in all his tastes and habits. The 'ornament of a meek and quiet spirit' seemed to shed its mild and softened light over his whole person, and appeared in all the intercourse of life. There were no arts to attract observation, there was not the slightest assertion of superiority, no elaboration of manners; nor could there be detected the smallest propensity to exact deference to his rank or will, which, however, all most cheerfully paid to his goodness. Indeed, any thing like pride, or haughtiness, or ostentation, in regard to himself or any thing pertaining to him, he was the farthest from manifesting, and evidently from feeling, of any human being I have ever known. Born to an almost princely inheritance, while he observed what seemed to be required from his affluence and station, he was yet moderate and even self-denying in personal indulgence. At the same time, the record of his liberality, a liberality amounting almost to profusion, may be read throughout the land, in the many churches of different denominations, in the institutions of learning of various kinds, in works of public utility, and on the lists of our various benevolent and religious societies he has aided. Of many of these last, he was among the very foremost to suggest the plans, and the most ready to supply the means. An enumeration of those with which he has long stood in honored and useful connection would embrace not only the most prominent, but a large share of the whole ; for so well was his disposition known, that he was always remembered when any appeal was to be made to the public. Nor did his benevolence stop here, but diffused itself abroad, descending by a thousand silent streams to the firesides of the poor and destitute.

"'He had a tear for pity, and a hand
Open as day for melting charity.'

And even to the last this hallowed flame burned brightly. He felt the force of the Savior's words, 'The poor ye have always with you.' Within two days of his decease, and while confined to his sick chamber, he sent for his agent, and said to him, 'It is very cold ! How the poor must suffer ! Go round and see if there are any that want, and give them what they need.' It was like the good old man. And while a whole community utters its loud lament, from the widow and fatherless, in the habitations of indigence and sorrow, among the children of bereavement and wo, many a silent tear will fall, sacred to the memory of Stephen Van Rensselaer.

"He became a professor of religion in connection with this church, on the second day of May, 1787, and for more than fifty years has he exemplified its doctrines. The views of truth he adopted were those usually denominated Calvinistic. Though there was no tendency to speculation, and nothing disputatious in the maintenance of his opinions—though, indeed, his mind revolted from every thing of the kind, and he regarded the confusions and conflicts such a temper has engendered with the utmost pain—yet experience, reflection, and a constantly increasing intimacy with his Bible had served to confirm his sentiments, to which he uniformly adhered with full conviction. Of the entire depravity of his nature, his utter unworthiness, he was fully persuaded. While he regarded his last severe visitations as fatherly inflictions, sent in mercy to his soul, and even demanding his gratitude, and would often say with deep emotion, 'I thank thee, Lord, for weaning me from the world!' 'Oh! how shall I be sufficiently grateful!' while he evinced the most submissive patience in his suffering old age, and not a murmur was heard to escape his lips, but with a sweet confidence in God he would employ the expression, 'Not my will, but thine be done,' yet he also felt them to be deserved by him as a sinner.

"He had been for a long period, and continued almost to the hour of his departure, an attentive and diligent *reader of the Bible.* That blessed volume was often in his hand, and thus became graven on his heart. So uniform was his habit in this respect, that a member of his family has remarked to me, 'He read his Bible more regularly and constantly than any person I ever knew. He was accustomed to read it early in the morning, and by candle-light in the winter, for an hour or two at a time. Not a year passed that his Bible was not read through.' In his sick chamber it was his constant companion.

"His death answered with a singular correspondence to the tenor of his life. He had long stood ready. With patriarchal simplicity, he observed, but a few days previously, as if anticipating the event to be near at hand, 'I wish I might once more gather all my children around me, to bless them before I die, and tell them how good God has been to me.' That wish was denied, but his name and his virtues remain to bless them.

"On the morning of the day on which he was taken to his rest, he had read from 'Jay's Exercises,' according to his custom, a meditation on death, and had marked the book for his Sabbath morning's devotion, at a beautiful description of the bliss of heaven, from the passage, 'The inhabitant shall not say, I am sick.' Instead of reading, he was permitted to go and enjoy the reality. He expired suddenly on Saturday afternoon, January 26. Having been seized with coughing, he rose to obtain some relief, and the difficulty seeming to increase, he said to a son who was with him, 'Can this be dying?' He regained his chair, and while his family collected round and were hanging over him, his spirit was released so quietly that the moment was unperceived by them."

Letter from the Hon. John Quincy Adams.

"WASHINGTON, *May* 3, 1832.

"DEAR SIR,

"I have received your letter of the 28th ult., inviting my attendance at the anniversary meeting of the American Bible Society on the 10th instant, at New York.

"I regret that my engagements here will not admit of my compliance with this invitation; but I pray you to assure the society of the sincerity with which I have sympathized with their affliction in the loss of two of their most distinguished members, the late president, Colonel Richard Varick, and his venerable associate of the revolutionary war, Colonel Robert Troup.

"I offer also to the society my cordial congratulation upon their prosperous condition and prospects, and upon the choice of the eminent citizen whom they have elected as the successor of Colonel Varick.

"I am, with great respect, dear sir, your friend and fellow-citizen,

"J. Q. Adams."

Letter from J. J. Gurney, of the Society of Friends.

"Philadelphia, *4th month, 23d,* 1839.

"Dear Friend,

"I hope I shall not have put thee to inconvenience by not having before answered thy obliging letter, but the pressure on my time and mind of our late yearly meeting here must plead my excuse.

"As far as I can look forward in such matters, I have reason to believe that, at the time of your approaching anniversary of the Bible Society, my religious engagements will be occupying me at a long distance from New York, so that it will not be in my power to be present with you on that occasion. I do, however, feel deeply interested in the objects of the society, and heartily crave its continued and increased prosperity. I hope the committee will accept $100 as a token of my attachment to the cause.

"And am thy sincere friend, J. J. Gurney."

Letter from Bishop Waugh.

"Baltimore, *March* 6, 1841.

"*Rev. Messrs. J. C. Brigham and E. S. Janes :*

"Brethren,

"In August last I received your communication requesting me to act as the delegate of the American Bible Society, to present it to the Annual Conferences of the Methodist Episcopal Church falling under my immediate oversight the past year. Such were the engrossing duties of my visitation to these Conferences, that I could not allow myself formally to accept the additional trust of your appointment. But, considering the importance and value of your noble institution as a powerful agency in the conversion of the world to God, it afforded the greatest pleasure to present its claims to the most favorable regards of my fellow-laborers in the Christian ministry. I did, therefore, introduce it to the notice of the Rock River, Illinois, Missouri, Arkansas, and Texas Conferences. It is gratifying to me to be able to say that these Conferences manifested a deep interest in the prosperity of the American Bible Society, and with entire unanimity adopted resolutions expressive of their high regard for it. I can not but hope, reverend brethren, it will be found that the interest felt will be showed as well in action as in profession. In Texas, a country of great prospective importance, there had been formed an independent Bible society previously to the organization of the Texas Conference. One of the resolutions of this Conference requested that society to become auxiliary to the American Bible Society, and I entertain no doubt that this will be done. Although, for the present, most of the section of our country through which my route passed may exhibit only a moderate action on this Christian enterprise, yet the day is not far distant when its bearing will be lofty and commanding. The Valley of the Mississippi will never prove recreant to this fundamental principle, 'That the Bible, and the Bible only, is the religion of the Protestant.' I am persuaded, also, that Texas will, in due time, be found assuming her proper place in the great cause of Protestant Christianity, as she is now doing in the cause of civil and political independence. Accept, brethren, the expression of my ardent desire that your excellent institution may prosper more and more, until the whole earth shall have been enlightened and converted to God through Jesus Christ.

"Respectfully and affectionately, B. WAUGH."

Letter from the Hon. John M'Lean.

"WASHINGTON, *March* 9, 1846.

"DEAR SIR,

"Your letter of the 6th instant, informing me that the Board of Managers of the American Bible Society have elected me as their President, has been received. I feel most sensibly this distinguished evidence of the respect and confidence of the board, which was as unexpected as it was unmerited.

"Separated as this Bible association is from all sectarian principles and aims, and extended as its means and operations have become, it is a most powerful agent for good.

"The eminent individuals who have presided over the institution have contributed to give it a permanency and success which insure its rapid advance for the future. The identification of my name with so noble an enterprise could add nothing to its character or usefulness; and I therefore feel the less reluctance in saying that my public duties, in regard to the time and place of their performance, are incompatible with those which appertain to the presidency of the society.

"My Circuit Courts, which I am required to attend in four states, commence in May, annually, and engage my time, with short intervals, up to the period when I am obliged to leave the West to attend the Supreme Court at Washington.

"You will perceive, therefore, that it will not be in my power to attend the meetings of the society, and that the office, under such circumstances, if accepted, would be merely nominal.

"I beg, therefore, most respectfully to decline the appointment, and to ask the board, through you, to accept of my profound gratitude for the honor they have done me.

"With great respect, I am, dear sir, your obedient servant,

"JOHN M'LEAN.

"Rev. J. C. BRIGHAM, D.D., *Corres. Sec. of the Amer. Bible Soc.*"

Death of Count Ver Huell.

"PARIS, *November* 28, 1845.

"*To the President of the American Bible Society, N. Y.*:

"MR. PRESIDENT,

"We are called upon to perform a mournful duty in announcing to you the serious loss which our society has sustained in the demise, on the 29th ultimo, of our worthy president, Count Vice Admiral Ver Huell, at an advanced age. You are aware with what devotion he committed himself, for many of his latter years, to the cause of religion, a cause which he served because he loved it, and desired ardently to see spread throughout the world what he had experienced of its power in his own heart.

"After we had lost our first president in the person of the learned Stapfer, our society felt itself happy, in 1840, in being able to call Admiral Ver Huell to be his successor. He said himself of his predecessor, in rendering homage to his memory at a public meeting of the society which was called, 'We know, alas! that our friend is gone; we know that he is already with his Savior in the celestial country.' These words we are able to-day to repeat with confidence in relation to him who then uttered them, and it is consoling to repeat them in connection with our great loss.

"Admiral Ver Huell felt a lively sympathy in the great and generous operations of Bible societies abroad, and particularly in that over which you are called to preside. More than once, on public occasions, he spoke of it, and rendered to it that tribute of respect which is due. Permit us to say in this place, if our society has lost a worthy president, yours has lost in him a true friend. And while we would not anticipate too confidently their views, we are persuaded your honorable board will in a measure share with us in the loss, and sympathize with us in our grief.

"Please accept, Mr. President, the assurance of our high consideration.

"For the Committee, COUNT JULES DE LABORDE."

Note.—The president of the American Bible Society, Governor Smith, to whom the above letter was directed, expired on the 7th of December, while the above letter was on its way.

Co-operation of the Methodist Episcopal Church South.

"Rev. Dr. Pierce, from the committee to whom the subject had been referred, made the following report, which was unanimously adopted, and ordered to be printed.

"The committee to whom the claims of the American Bible Society were referred beg leave to report,

"That this noble institution commends itself to the confidence and liberal support of the Church and country, whether we regard the benevolence of the design, the fidelity of its management, or the success of its operations. The committee can not enumerate all the reasons which justify our countenance and co-operation, or, indeed, elaborate the details of any, but will present three considerations, in their judgment ample both as to authority and encouragement.

"First, the unremitted efforts of the society to place a copy of the Holy Bible in the hands of every man, woman, and child in our own country, in the shortest time possible, demands our concurrence in so vast a work. This design has been zealously carried out by the parent association through its auxiliaries, and by its own direct action, which, like the heart in the animal economy, is the great propelling power, producing and promoting a healthful circulation. The obligation to become co-laborers in this enterprise of supplying all classes of our rapidly increasing population with the Scriptures of truth can be measured only by the value of the Bible in a government where vice tends to destroy the only life-preserving element in its structure, and virtue to nourish and perpetuate it.

"This vital principle is morality, religion—that religion which derives its existence from God, and finds the rule of its faith and practice in the inspired Volume. It should never be forgotten by an American citizen that there is not, perhaps, in the wide world, another nation made up of so great a variety of human beings as may be found in these United States.

"The ports of our country are open for free admission of emigrants from all parts of the earth. No jealous or watchful policy of political quarantine has ever authorized or delayed the entrance of the stranger and foreigner among us. This state of things must introduce into our midst an evil leaven, for which government can provide no antidote. For when a man steps upon our shores, he intrenches himself behind the Constitution and laws of the land, and triumphantly asserts his freedom of opinion. And if he has his mind and prejudices trained, in politics and religion, to the belief of doctrines, the adoption of which in this land would lead to the defense of the wildest agrarianism on the one hand, or the most diabolical atheism on the other, our people have no alternative but to stand by, mournfully gazing upon the work of dilapidation, or to forestall this disastrous agency by impregnating the public mind with the truth of revelation.

"It must be apparent to every reflecting mind, that while the knowledge of the Bible is salutary under any form of civil government, it is indispensable to the purity and perpetuity of our own. And by how much less the laws of the land may interfere to prevent the sad effects of a misguided and abused freedom, by so much more it is our duty and interest to encourage the circulation of the Holy Scriptures among all classes of our citizens.

"The restraints which a belief of the threatened judgments of Heaven impose upon man in the civil, social, and moral relations of life, are neither few nor feeble, albeit they may not be effectual for regeneration and salvation. To the Bible, then, and the strong moral suasion which may be drawn from its momentous truths, must we go, and upon their modifying, restraining, and purifying influence we rely for the salvation of our country—for the nation's safety is to be found in the nation's purity.

"The claims of the American Bible Society are vindicated, and ought to be endeared to every lover of 'the sincere milk of the Word,' by that constitutional law which restricts the work of publication to the *Bible without note or comment*, and by the faithfulness with which they have adhered to this avowed purpose; for, while it may be admitted that some inaccuracies are to be found in the English version commonly used, it may be doubted whether an entire new translation would not multiply rather than diminish errors. The plenary inspiration of the sacred writers would become a useless benefit to the world if modern criticism were allowed to mutilate the present venerable version, under the vain pretense of amendment, or accommodation to the fastidious caviler.

"Indeed, it seems to us that if, in a few instances, King James's translators had transferred rather than translated a word, it must have been because the simple translation of that particular word into a specific, definite term, would have incurred the danger of leading the mind into a greater error than could follow upon a transfer of that word to the English language; for by such transfer is to be understood merely using the letters of our own alphabet in place of the Greek, in bringing that word into an English edition of the Old and New Testament.

"If the above view is correct, it will be seen at once how much the

American Bible Society did for the cause of truth and justice when they refused to yield to the solicitation of a large and respectable Church to admit such a translation of a word as would narrow down the mind of a people in a foreign mission to a specific mode of baptism. No other reason could have operated upon the translators when they simply *Anglicized* the Greek word from which we derive our notions of Christian baptism, than that a translation would have reduced a religious *act* to a religious *mode*, contrary to the analogy of faith. To give the Holy Scriptures any sectarian bearing by a new translation of them, or even a simple doctrinal term, would be both unwise and injurious: unwise, because a denomination seeking to give authority to their particular views by changing any word in the present authorized version would only admit that such views are not well sustained without the change; injurious, because it would mar the unity of the word, unsettle the foundations of confidence, and afford to infidelity the benefit of denying, on plausible grounds, the purity of the Bible as a divine rule of faith and practice.

"Finally, your committee would offer as a reason why the American Bible Society should be liberally patronized, the very low price to which they have reduced Bibles and Testaments, and, consequently, the almost illimitable good they have enabled the benevolent to do at a very small cost. For twenty-five cents a donor may put an entire copy of the Bible into the hands of the forlorn and ignorant poor, and for six and a quarter cents give to some hapless orphan the New Testament of our Lord and Savior Jesus Christ. To the wisdom and zeal of this association is the country indebted for the present low prices at which Bibles of the finest material and workmanship may be obtained, but especially of such quality and price that the poor, yet not utterly destitute, may purchase.

"It is, in truth, too manifest to be denied, and too precious to be forgotten, that the price to which the blessed volume has been reduced has put thousands of copies into circulation which else had slumbered upon the shelves of book-stores unbought and unread. Nor will it be doubted that the simple reading of 'the law and the testimony' has been the instrumentality by which many have been brought to God and salvation. 'Every man,' saith Christ, 'that hath heard and hath learned of the Father, cometh unto me.'

"The entrance of the Divine Word giveth light. It hath a voice, too, to awaken and to charm, and as that voice peals in thunder along the solitude of a soul made dreary by the desolations of sin, conscience aroused echoes back the sound, till the guilty man, trembling, abashed and penitent, cries in the fullness of his grief, 'What shall I do to be saved?' and then the still small voice whispers, 'Come unto me, all ye that labor and are heavy laden, and I will give you rest.' Christ our Savior died to redeem us to God out of every kindred, and tongue, and people; and the love of Christ should constrain us to do 'as much as in us is' to give to all earth's ransomed millions the only book, in this world of books, which pours the light of heaven upon the pathway of man, to his tomb and his eternity. Your committee offer the following resolutions for adoption:

"*Resolved*, By the delegates of the Annual Conferences of the Methodist Episcopal Church South, in General Conference assembled, that we will heartily co-operate with the American Bible Society in the glorious work of giving the Bible to the whole world without delay.

"*Resolved*, That we will earnestly recommend the American Bible Society to all our people, and urge them to a more liberal support of the noble enterprise.

"*Resolved*, That we believe the destitution of Bibles in our own states and territories is much greater than is generally supposed, and that the only plan of supply that will remove this great evil from among us is the one now practiced of carrying the Scriptures to every family, and knowing that all are supplied.

"*Resolved*, That we recommend to all our Conference districts, circuits, and stations, to aid in every way they can the speedy supply of the whole American people.

"Respectfully submitted, L. PIERCE, Chairman.

"PETERSBURG, *May* 20, 1846."

Address of the Hon. Theodore Frelinghuysen, LL.D., President of the American Bible Society.

"By the good providence of God we are permitted to celebrate the thirty-second anniversary of the American Bible Society. Ever since its institution the world has been assuming new relations, and undergone many and great changes; and the past year, perhaps, more than any before, has been full of exciting and fearful interest. Events have followed each other that will form an instructive chapter in the history of mankind. Death has multiplied his victims from among illustrious names. War has rung his doleful notes through our valleys, and waked up the deadly passions of depraved nature. And nearer still in time, revolution has shaken the thrones of the mighty, and struck an appalling apprehension in the heart of every earthly potentate. It has made them feel, as they never did before, how frail are the foundations of power, and how vain the securities of political sagacity and forecast.

"Amid all these momentous developments of Divine Providence, we may take refuge in the Bible. This not only prepares expectation for these overturnings, but consoles us, by the promised fruits of them all, in the certain accomplishment of God's gracious and glorious purposes, whether by works of mercy or of dreadful righteousness.

"He sits at the head of these threatening floods, and on a throne whose dominions neither earth nor the powers of darkness can disturb. Happy for us that in the Word of God, the true exponent of his counsels, we may learn, and cause others to know how nations and men can best secure a defense against the assaults of violence, and best prepare for the inroads of change and decay. And while these commotions have dealt so much of lamentation and woe, yet they will open the way for the wider circulation of the Scriptures, and spread more rapidly and extensively over the earth the only influences that can bring good out of these convulsions, and happily direct and compose the spirit that has caused them.

"It is a free spirit that works beneath these political upheavings, deep, constant, and unquenchable. Power may for a long time cramp and stifle it, but can not long repress it. Its struggles are fearful, but they will at last triumph. And that same spirit will claim the right to look into God's Word for itself.

"The Bible will be an open volume whenever the rights of man, as a rational and accountable being, are asserted and enjoyed. Let him come to feel, with an enlightened conviction, that he must answer for himself in the judgment of the great day, and he will search the Scriptures with deep and anxious earnestness, and all the more resolvedly should any question his privilege or attempt to interrupt its exercise.

"Nations contending for freedom are in the pursuit of truth in one of its most interesting forms. They have learned that man's immortal nature is created, endowed, and designed for nobler ends than to become the mere tool of ambition and the make-weight of power. And the Bible in almost every page vindicates this exalted destiny, and labors to fix the deep conviction that man is born for liberty—the liberty of *truth* and of *law*.

"As the belief enters and forms within him, he rises in the scale of existence—rises in his own estimation, not vain-gloriously, but the solemn consideration that he has within him a being for bliss or woe beyond measure and without end, exalts, while it subdues and humbles him; his soul expands to the thoughts of his destiny; and as he looks through the great scheme of redemption, and strives to gauge the price paid for his ransom, his free spirit swells from the chains that have bound it, and oppression, in all its forms, trembles before the demonstrations of his deliverance.

"We stop not to look into the philosophy of the process, but we rejoice in the relation, and bless God for the close and constant connection between civil and religious liberty—all history illustrates and confirms it. Those communities enjoy the largest share of the one, are the best protected in their rights, and the most secure in their possessions, that faithfully cultivate and cherish the spirit and principles of the other.

"Let us, then, amid the crumbling of thrones and the tumults of the people, take the consolation of the Word of God, and there learn how the wildest uproar of the political elements holds relation to the certain fulfillment of his purposes, and final encouragement to animate us in this blessed Bible agency, ordained of God to heal the woes and to pacify the strifes that distress the nations."

Death of the Hon. John Quincy Adams.

"The committee appointed to prepare a suitable minute to be entered on the records of this board, on the occasion of the death of the Hon. John Quincy Adams, respectfully report, and recommend the adoption of the following resolutions:

"*Resolved*, That the board enter upon their minutes the lamented death of John Quincy Adams, a vice-president of this society since the second year of its organization, who departed this life at the Capitol, in the city of Washington, on the twenty-third day of February, one thousand eight hundred and forty-eight.

"*Resolved*, That while the several state Legislatures in session have vied with each other, and with the general government, in rendering homage to the memory of the illustrious patriot and statesman, who for more than half a century has borne so conspicuous a part in our national history, it is the grateful duty of this board to dwell upon other relations and features of his accomplished character. A man of the purest morals, he was the ardent friend of the Bible, esteeming it as the source of all civil and religious liberty, as well as of individual happiness. He was a diligent student of the Word of God. It was the delight of his great and discriminating mind to be daily refreshed at this fountain of Divine wisdom; and it is our deliberate judgment, that not only the stern integrity of his private life, but his widely-extended influence as a ruler and legislator, an advocate of human rights, a patriot and philanthropist, is to be attributed to his long and intimate familiarity with the eternal laws of truth, love, and righteousness which are revealed in the Holy Scriptures.

"*Resolved*, That we recognize the good hand of God in qualifying our departed friend for the enlarged sphere of usefulness in the world, which he occupied with surpassing ability; that we tender our sympathies to his bereaved family, and that these resolutions be communicated to his widow and surviving son.

"HORACE HOLDEN, WM. ADAMS, WM. H. ASPINWALL.

"*April* 6, 1848."

To the above it may be added, that while this distinguished officer was prevented by public duties from attending the annual meetings of the society, his frequent communications expressing his regret that he could not attend, and his gratification in the growth and usefulness of the institution, showed how deeply he participated in all that pertained to its welfare.

Notices of the Death of the Rev. Noah Levings, D.D., late Financial Secretary of the Society.

" Since the last meeting of the Board of Managers, intelligence has been received of the death of the Rev. Noah Levings, D.D., financial secretary of the American Bible Society, at Cincinnati, Ohio, on the 9th of January. Highly appreciating, and entertaining a grateful remembrance of his Christian and ministerial character, and most particularly of his assiduous and successful labors in the cause of the society, the Board of Managers deem it appropriate to take a brief notice of his life and death.

" Dr. Levings was born in Westmoreland, Cheshire county, N. H., on the 29th of September, 1796. At the age of sixteen he removed with his parents to the city of Troy, in this state. He there became the subject of renewing grace under the ministry of the Rev. Laban Clarke, of the Methodist Episcopal Church, and was brought to entertain the hope of the Gospel in 1815. On the 20th of December, 1817, he was licensed to preach; and in May, 1818, he was received into the New York Annual Conference. The estimation in which he was held by his brethren appears from the appointments he received and filled. He was twice stationed in Troy, once in Schenectady, once in New Haven, once in Brooklyn, twice in Albany, and twice in New York. He was twice elected a delegate to the General Conference, the highest judicatory in the Methodist Episcopal Church. He received the honorary degree of doctor of divinity; but his highest honor arose from the instrumentality with which he was owned by the Head of the Church in the conversion of hundreds 'from darkness to light, and from Satan to God.'

" In June, 1844, he was chosen financial secretary of the American Bible Society, to succeed Bishop Janes. The fidelity with which he discharged the duties of this important office is well known to the board. He has, with diligence, acceptableness, and efficiency, labored during the course of his official service; has visited different parts of our extended country, and succeeded in exciting greater interest and increased efforts in the Bible cause. He left on a Southern tour, on behalf of the society, on the 11th of October last, and visited the Tennessee, Memphis, and Mississippi Conferences of the Methodist Episcopal Church South. During this tour he traveled nearly four thousand miles, preached eighteen sermons, and delivered nine addresses. On a portion of this route he was subject to much inconvenience, the weather being stormy and the roads bad. During the latter part of November he was taken ill; but, obtaining temporary relief, he went forward till he arrived at Natchez, where he preached his last sermon, in the Presbyterian Church, on the 24th of December. Thence he took passage, on the steam-boat Memphis, for Cincinnati. He was eight days upon the boat, severely afflicted, without medical counsel, and almost without attention. The cholera was on board, and Dr. Levings was suffered to lie unnoticed, except by a single individual. At Cincinnati he was taken to the house of his friend, Dr. Burton. In his last sickness he enjoyed peace of mind. Passages in his diary exhibit his deep devotedness, and his conviction that his departure was at hand. On the Sabbath evening preceding his death, being asked if he felt a firm faith in Christ, he answered, 'Oh, yes; the Lord Jesus is the strength of my heart, and my portion forever.' On one occasion, while sitting up, a Bible was placed, by his kind host, in such a position as to support his head, and enable him to breathe more freely. Fixing his eye on the Bible, he exclaimed, '*O thou blessed book! lamp to my feet, and light to my path! thou guide of my youth, directory of my manhood, and support of my declining years! how cheerless would this world be, were it not for thy divine revelations and Christian experience!*' After his will was signed, he said, 'Thank God! one foot is in Jordan, and I shall soon cross over.' Bishop Morris arrived in town, and visited him in the afternoon before his death. 'Thank God,' said he, 'that I am permitted to see your face in the flesh once more. I am not able to converse much, but can still say, Glory to God!' The bishop asked him if he had any message to send to his brethren of the New York Conference. 'Tell them,' said he, 'that I die in the hope of the Gospel. Tell them I have an unshaken confidence in the atoning sacrifice of the Lord Jesus Christ as the foundation, and the only foundation, of my hope of eternal life. Relying on that foundation, all before me is light, and joyful, and glorious.'

"With this brief reference to the life and death of Dr. Levings, the Board of Managers adopt the following resolutions:

"*Resolved*, That this board have received with deep regret the intelligence of the death of the Rev. Noah Levings, D.D., financial secretary of the American Bible Society, at Cincinnati, on the 9th of January last. While they deplore the loss which the Church of Christ and the American Bible Society have sustained by his removal to the 'rest which remaineth for the people of God,' they hold in grateful remembrance his Christian character and life, now sealed by a peaceful and blessed death, and appreciate his diligent and efficient services as secretary of the society.

"*Resolved*, That a copy of this statement and resolution be transmitted to the widow and family of Dr. Levings, with the expression of the sympathy of this board with them in their bereavement, and of their prayers that they may richly enjoy the influence and consolation of that precious Word of God, the truths of which were so dear to him in life and death, which were the theme of his Christian ministry, and for the diffusion of which he devoted the last years of his life as secretary of the American Bible Society."

The Young Men's Bible Society of Cincinnati, within whose limits this officer closed his life, paid a just and feeling tribute to his memory, as will be seen by the following letter and resolutions:

"CINCINNATI, *January* 13, 1849.

"*To the Cor. Sec. Am. Bible Soc., N. Y.:*

"DEAR SIR,

"In accordance with the directions of the Board of Managers of the Young Men's Bible Society of Cincinnati, it is my painful duty to transmit to you the accompanying resolutions, occasioned by the death of the Rev. Noah Levings, D.D., which occurred in this city on the evening of the 9th instant.

"Deeply do I regret that my first official act, as corresponding secretary of this society, should be the communication of intelligence of so sad a nature.

"In your report, presented in May, 1845, you announced the commencement of Dr. Levings's labors as the financial secretary of your board, bespeaking for him the cordial co-operations of the auxiliary societies; in answer to that appeal, we announce to you that God has closed by death those labors, and return to you his lifeless remains.

"Permit me to add my personal sympathy, to that expressed by the board, with you in the loss your society has sustained, and also with the bereaved family of the deceased, to whom you will have the kindness to send one of the copies of the resolutions inclosed.

"Very respectfully, your obedient servant,

"R. W. BURNETT, Cor. Sec. Y. M. B. S."

"YOUNG MEN'S BIBLE SOCIETY ROOMS, CINCINNATI, *Jan.* 10, 1849.

"At a special meeting of the Board of Managers of the Young Men's Bible Society of Cincinnati, held this day, the following resolutions were unanimously adopted, viz.:

"*Whereas* it has pleased Almighty God to remove by death from our midst the Rev. Noah Levings, D.D., financial secretary of the

American Bible Society, a venerable minister of God, whose praise is in all the churches, and one whose life was deeply and laboriously devoted to the cause of the Bible; and who, in the prosecution of this noble work, has fallen a victim to death, far from his home and friends, in a land of strangers; and whereas, in this event, this board can not but feel a deep and mournful interets, therefore

"*Resolved*, That we deeply deplore, in this sad dispensation, the loss which is sustained by the American Bible Society in the death of one who, so far as human instrumentality is concerned, proved himself to be one of its brightest ornaments and most efficient supports.

"*Resolved*, That in the severe bereavement which has thus unexpectedly fallen upon the family of our deceased brother, we sincerely offer in their behalf our prayers to God, whose wise but inscrutable providence has taken him away; and for ourselves, and in behalf of every lover of the Bible, we proffer them our Christian condolence.

"*Resolved*, That this board meet at the Bible room to-morrow morning at the published hour, and proceed thence to attend the funeral services of the deceased at Wesley Chapel, in this city.

"*Resolved*, That copies of the foregoing resolutions be forwarded to the family of the deceased and to the parent board.

"(Signed) E. M. GREGORY, Pres.
"WM. RANKIN, Sec. *pro. tem.*"

Notices of the Death of Alexander Henry, Esq., Peter G. Stuyvesant, Esq., and John Aspinwall, Esq.

"Among the vice-presidents deceased since the last anniversary, Alexander Henry, Esq., of Philadelphia, is the first to be noticed. His death, peaceful and full of hope, occurred on the 18th of August last. Being a resident of another city, he was able to have but little personal intercourse with the board. To some of the members, however, he was well known, and all were well aware of his elevated and pure character as a man of business and as a Christian in the city and region where his lot was cast. His interest in this society was evinced not only by his conversation and occasional letters, but by generous contributions, which were sure to come, unsolicited, at least once a year. The memory of such a man is precious.

"But three days subsequent to the death of Mr. Henry occurred that of another vice-president, Peter G. Stuyvesant, Esq., of New York. The death of this officer, from the circumstance of his residence in this city, his long connection with the board, oftentimes its presiding officer, together with his frequent and liberal benefactions, and with the suddenness of his removal, occasioned a shock which all here associated have deeply felt. A committee was appointed, consisting of the Hon.

Theodore Frelinghuysen, the Hon. William Jay, with the Rev. Dr. De Witt, to prepare a suitable notice of the loss which had been sustained, and to communicate the sympathies of the board to the family of the deceased.

"In the month of October the managers were called to part with one of their own number, John Aspinwall, Esq., who, by his long and faithful services, and his kind, unassuming deportment, had gained the affections of all his associates."

ANNIVERSARIES—ADDRESSES.

The annual meetings of the society are held in the city of New York, on the second Thursday in May.

The exercises consist in reading a portion of the Holy Scriptures, prayer, the annual address by the president, report of the treasurer, report of the corresponding secretary, and addresses by persons appointed by the Anniversary Committee for that purpose.

In 1843 the society held a semi-annual meeting at Cincinnati, Ohio. The chair was occupied by the Hon. John M'Lean, of the Supreme Court of the United States. Addresses were delivered by the Rev. Drs. Spring, Beecher, and Tomlinson, and by the Rev. William Jackson.

In 1844 a similar meeting was held at Washington City. The chair was occupied by the Hon. J. Q. Adams, the first vice-president, assisted by Judge M'Lean and the Hon. Robert P. Dunlap. Addresses were delivered by the Rev. Mr. Berry, of Georgetown, D. C., the Hon. Mr. Howard, of Indiana, the Rev. Dr. Tyng, of Philadelphia, and Dr. Cox, of Brooklyn, L. I.

In 1845 another semi-annual meeting was held at Richmond, Virginia, in the hall of the General Assembly. His Excellency Governor M'Dowell presided, and made the opening address. Other addresses were delivered by ministers and laymen of the different denominations, and also by the corresponding secretary, Dr. Brigham.

One of the same description was subsequently held at Raleigh, North Carolina. The meeting was held in the House of Commons, many members of which were in attendance. The Hon. Judge Cameron, one of the earliest vice-presidents of the parent society, occupied the chair. Addresses were made by the presiding officer, by the Hon. Judge Potter, by Ex-governor Swain, and by Dr. Brigham, corresponding secretary.

The following addresses and extracts have been taken from the many which, from time to time, have been delivered at the anniversaries. They have been selected on account of the topics discussed; and as we could not publish all, we have, without any reference whatever to exclusive merit, selected these. The addresses which have been delivered at the different anniversaries are all of a high order, and no institution in the world has enjoyed the advocacy of more distinguished or talented men.

The Use of the Scriptures as a Reading Book in Schools. By the Rev. Robert J. Breckinridge, D.D.

Mr. Breckinridge observed that "there are certain great principles, certain fundamental ideas, which always are, and necessarily must be assumed as true, and even indisputable, in every enterprise, system, and organization which can exist among men. If it were not so, all progress would be impossible; and the commonest attempts to perform the most pressing duties might lead only to contention and embarrassment.

"Thus, in the very fact of our organization as a society for the printing and distribution of the Scriptures, we have assumed as undeniable the great truths that the Bible is a divine revelation from God, that it is given for the whole human race, that it is most fit to be received by all, and that it is perfectly adapted to produce its intended effects; nay, more, that it is our duty to make efforts for the multiplication, the dissemination, and the general reception of these Scriptures among men, and that our present form of action is one proper and wise mode of performing this sacred obligation. But even beyond this, we have, from the beginning, firmly advanced other great axioms of our system; for we have agreed that this noble version shall be the only English translation which we, as a body, will print and circulate; and that in every case, but especially in this, we will neither add nor permit note or comment on the sacred text. These principles constitute this society a Bible Society, in opposition to the notion of its being a society for making commentaries, glosses, or other like things; they distinguish it as a Christian Bible Society, in contradistinction from all schemes that would make it virtually Jewish, by limiting its action to the Old Testament, or something little better, in restricting it chiefly or entirely to the New; and they equally mark it out as a Bible Society of Reformed Christians, carrying out their distinctive views and faith in clear distinction from the papistical doctrines touching the great questions, What is the Word of God? and how, to whom, and for what purposes should it be distributed?

"It had been happy, both in other lands and in our own, if the friends of this great cause had always clearly marked these obvious truths, and respected the distinctions which flow from them. It will be useful to us, now that we are about to take a step in advance, and commit ourselves and this institution to a new principle, or, at least, to a new and most important aspect of certain principles not heretofore so fully developed, to keep steadily in our view the great truths from which we start, that our warrant and full justification may be ever before our eyes; for that the successful prosecution of our work, and the openings which Providence spreads successively before our advancing steps, should require us to acknowledge these additional truths, or force upon us new aspects of duty, is what has again and again occurred to us, and what will hereafter occur, in proportion as we are attentive to God's dealings, and faithful to them. I understand the resolution which has been this moment adopted, in regard to the duty imposed on distributers of the Bible to secure, if possible, its faithful perusal also, to cover a case very much of this kind. And still more clearly, the one I stand here to advocate has this great advantage, that while it fully accords with the whole objects and principles of the society, it opens a vast and newly-unexplored field for its exertions. It is the beginning, as I trust, of a national effort, the first expression of a national purpose to restore in youth the dissevered connection between piety and knowledge, between God and the first search of childhood after mental treasures.

"Perhaps the most striking aspect of my duty is, that its performance should ever have been needful, but especially in this country, and at the present moment. From the beginning of time till a period very near to us, and among the entire race of man, except only reformed Christians of these latter days, the general principle remotely occupying the base of this subject has been cordially and universally received and acted on as of paramount importance. Every people, without exception, has thought it necessary to teach its religion to its children, as the very basis of all other knowledge; and every nation that has been sufficiently advanced to have a written religion, and places for the regular instruction of youth in knowledge, has made the national religion a national study in childhood. The sacred books of all heathen nations have been known of all who knew any thing whatever. The pages of the Koran, in every age and country, have been the first study of every follower of the false prophet. The very highest literature of all antiquity is thoroughly impregnated with the popular religion, so that every Greek and Roman youth was made a scholar and a pagan by the self-same process. The Hebrew parent, by the most express command of God, made his child from its very birth, by every outward mark and every inward accomplishment—at home, by the wayside, in the school, in the sanctuary, in the halls of justice, on the field of battle, and upon the throne itself, thoroughly and intensely a Hebrew. The early Christian Church was in no degree less assiduous in the same devotedness to the exact and universal religious instruction of the young. Every corrupt and apostate sect which has forsaken or renounced our divine Redeemer—and most conspicuously those who have most thoroughly and openly rejected the Bible—has instilled each its own peculiar heresies by every means, not excluding their schools, into the minds of their children. The leaders of the glorious reformation of the sixteenth century, and for two centuries and more, all their true followers, received as from God the solemn duty of the public as well as private instruction of the young in the Word of Life. The illustrious spirit of Luther, as he drew near his rest, in a review of his literary labors, rejoiced the most in this, that he had written his book *De Servo Arbitrio* against Erasmus, and had prepared his small catechism—a performance which, like the similar one of his immortal fellow-laborer, John Calvin, remains, each, after the lapse of three hundred years, respectively the symbol of churches, states, and races. Nay, until a period so little remote that many who hear me can recall it, the school-house and the church stood side by side throughout our country, and the Bible and the Catechism constituted in both the basis of perpetual instruction.

"It is not my present duty to trace the causes and the manner of the exclusion of the Bible from our schools. It is sufficient to indicate, as the chiefest, the spirit of popery which every where suppresses the Word of God; the spirit of indifferentism, which treats it with total slight; and the spirit of infidelity, which openly rejects it. Other causes, less obvious, have no doubt conspired in the production of the same fatal result; among which are perhaps to be ranked as of no small importance, the excessive multiplication of school-books of inferior quality, a proportionate increase of incompetent and unworthy teachers, and a general disposition to prostitute to unworthy ends that part of the education of youth which could be turned to immediate profit. Nor can it be denied that the system of Sabbath-school instruction, so valuable in itself, has been at least an occasion for this great evil; that the public has been allowed—it may be, even induced to consider the moral instruction thus imparted a sufficient substitute for that formerly given in the week-day schools, if not, indeed, for that before received under the paternal roof.

"A general review of the efforts which have been made in our day to restore the Bible to the schools would occupy far too much time to be now attempted; although this, like the mode of its exclusion, is a portion of this great subject full of interest and importance. It may be sufficient to state in passing, that the minds of Christians over the whole world have been for some years deeply pondering *this matter*. Christian Protestant churches generally throughout Europe have made a more steadfast resistance than ourselves to the exclusion of the Bible from the course of general education, and are therefore, in this respect, generally in a better condition than ourselves. In England there is no school system of sufficient extent to deserve the name of national, but the institution which has the oversight of what are called the national schools has introduced the Scriptures into them. The schools of Scotland, so far as they have been under the care of the national church of that kingdom, remain on their ancient model. In Ireland, a systematic attempt was recently made by a committee of the British House of Commons, which, in 1825, '26, and '27, carefully investigated the whole subject of Irish education, with a view to provide a general and thorough system of popular instruction. The result is given in nine reports, which, together, contain considerably more than three thousand printed pages in folio; and the sum of all is, that the most ignorant and illiterate of all civilized states absolutely repudiated, by the high dignitaries of the papal church, every system of public, nay, even of gratuitous instruction, which should not, as a starting point, reject the Bible and admit the dogmas of popery. As it regards our own country, the only successful effort of a general kind with which I am acquainted had been lately made in the state of Maryland, where the admirable society which I represent this day are now in the midst of an attempt, which has been attended with the most cheering success. In the course of that movement, two facts, of great importance in themselves, and strongly illustrative of the past and present spirit of the country, have been fully established. The first is, that the public mind is more thoroughly prepared for this great reform, and all the sources of public influence and authority much more accessible in regard to it, than the most sanguine had supposed; that is, God has prepared the work to our hands before we had faith and zeal to undertake it. The second fact is, that the more pretending the schools are, the more completely is God excluded from them, and the more decided is the opposition to the introduction of the Bible, while many of the humbler sort have all along kept the Scriptures in them; that is, the richer sort of our people in this, as in many other respects, have been among the most of all indifferent to God and removed from our evangelical influence. It is an item in this hasty outline too significant and too pleasing to be omitted, that all our Christian missionaries, it is believed without exception, have made the Bible the principal class-book in every school established by them.

"Let me now present in a more direct form some of the great considerations which decide our duty on the subject before us. In doing this, I shall separate such as more particularly regard the *individual* aspect of the question from those which may be considered as pertaining more properly to its *social* character. And in presenting both views, the occasion admonishes me rather to make suggestions than to attempt an argument.

"It may be observed, then, as the first axiom of every *individual* consideration of this subject, that religion is the most imperative necessity of the human soul. No people have ever been without the elements of a regular system of religious faith; nor can as many single persons be computed in any age or nation who are destitute of the religious sentiment, as there can be of persons destitute of reason, of speech, of a perfect human form. So that man is as essentially a religious as he is a rational, a speaking, or even a defined being at all. It is equally indubitable that this necessity of the soul is developed as early as any other want of it; and it is evolved with a steadiness and intensity equal to any other. Upon what other principle are we to account for the horrible excesses and the inconceivable follies of the human race in connection with this solemn and all-pervading sentiment of our spiritual dependence, this ever-pressing sense of our spiritual necessities? And what conceivable excuse can be pleaded for not providing for this necessity from the first moment of its development? for not directing this sentiment by an instruction as ceaseless as its own activity? for not sustaining and molding this confiding and absorbing impulse by the power and the wisdom which God has made manifest to this very end?

"Let it be further considered that there are but two possible foundations, upon one or other of which all religion must repose. One is *authority*, the other *conviction*. The former, professing to emanate from the throne of God, and to be perpetuated in a manner always supernatural, sustains its pretensions by unceasing miracles, and appears before men only to state its claims and receive unqualified obedience to its behests. To hear, to believe, and to obey, are in its view the sole duties of mankind; while to reason, to investigate, to compare, to analyze, are all alike rebellious against its sacred character. On the other hand, the religion of conviction, recognizing God as its author, and the present blessedness and eternal glory of man as its immediate ends, throws open the heart, the mind, and the conscience to its sweet and ennobling influences. It appeals constantly to the understanding; it pleads for nothing more earnestly than for the most ample, thorough, and mature consideration; it asks for dominion over the affections, the conscience, the intellect, only when that dominion shall have been conceded by a willing, an enlightened, a convinced spirit. This is our religion. This Bible is at once its sacred repository and the great instrument of its propagation. Why, then, shall we withdraw it from the very seats of knowledge? Why withhold it from the active and inquiring spirit of childhood? Our religion is based on knowledge, founded in liberty, approved by conscience. Let us act as if we felt this to be true.

"In the general education of youth, we commit a great mistake as to what education really is; and in deciding who are educated, fall into a fatal error. To omit in education all moral training, is to train imperfectly for time and not at all for eternity. It is, indeed, to neglect the man himself and train some of his inferior powers. No man is or can be educated whose moral faculties have not been adequately trained; and if they have been mistaught, he has been enslaved, not educated; degraded, not enlightened. Now it so happens that among us the case is so presented, by reason of a thousand concurring circumstances, that no adequate moral instruction can be furnished generally in our public schools unless the Bible itself be put into the hands of the pupils; so that we are shut up to the necessity of rejecting from public education all true discipline and instruction of the better and more urgent part of our being, or of using for those purposes the best, and greatest, and fittest of means, the teacher of all teachers, the very Word of God himself. Blessed alternative, which forces a people, panting to be taught, to remain in ignorance or learn of God!

"For if we restrict our views of education so narrowly as to embrace in its scope only that which is purely mental, no absurdity can be more audacious than to reject the Bible even from such a plan. Is it of use to know what we are, what we can be, what we have been? to know how we can be and achieve whatever is most excellent? Is it a part of instruction to set before us the highest exhibitions of whatever is great and striking in the past? the greatness of virtue, the greatness of passion, of achievement, of effort, of transcendent civilization, of unparalleled crime? Well, what is the Bible? It is, among other things, the record, the safest, often the only record, of the largest, the longest, the most striking part of the history of genius, of knowledge, of sublime adventure, of all glorious success; yea, of man himself! It is the text-book out of which to unriddle the great mystery of God's providence in the government of the world! The greatest of all poets, philosophers, orators, moralists, lawgivers, rulers, and conquerors who have adorned these long annals which cover two thirds of the whole duration of human existence here below—these are the men who have written this book! It contains their legacy of wisdom and instruction to generations of generations; a legacy so vast and so enduring, that one single man, and he the beginner of the book, has bestowed, in a few brief pages, the elements of civilization, of organized society, of law, of morals, and of religion, upon every age that has succeeded him, and stamped the impress of his mind upon the whole human race! Why, this book, which is the sum and substance of all literature more ancient than the Greek, is the substratum also of whatever exists in our modern tongues! The two great Protestant translations of the Bible, the

Germanic and our own, formed, in truth, the two languages ; and they reign over them still when centuries have passed, the highest classic respectively in each. In sober verity, this book is not only the book of God, but also the book of the human race, so that to reject it is at once to be separate from the Lord and from enlightened man.

" Let us turn for a moment to the *social* aspect of this question. As there are but two principles on which religion can repose, so, also, there are but two on which the social state can be perpetuated among men. Organized society, in any supportable or even possible form, can be sustained only in one of two modes. The *first* method limits the numbers who take part in the public authority or control to those who are presumed to be capable of these functions, increasing or reducing the amount as experience shall suggest or necessity enforce. Upon this principle the great bulk of human institutions have been constructed ; and so simple is it, and so deeply seated in the nature of the case, that the mass of mankind have been generally unable or unwilling (and the distinction is immaterial to the argument) to prevent their own disfranchisement, and to arrest the tendency of power to accumulate in a few, often in a single will. We can not be too profoundly sensible that, in the long run, power not only should not, but can not be exercised by those unfit to wield it ; and that all attempts to violate this necessity entail the destruction of society itself. The *second* method proceeds on the assumption that the whole society is endowed with this capacity ; and that, in the particular case, all are, or all can be, prepared to take part in every exercise of public authority. It is on this second principle that all our political institutions are founded. Our great republic, and all our free and sovereign commonwealths, have been frankly periled upon this great and stirring truth, that man is capable of self-government. Not man every where, for history would contradict us. Not man imbruted and demoralized, for our previous reasonings show this to be absurd. Not man generally, embracing women and children, idiots and slaves, for this subverts the very order of nature. But generally the truth, that man, enlightened, civilized, and free, is the safest depository of all ultimate authority, and the wisest dispenser of so much as the exigences of society require to be parceled out for common use. If this be not true, our country is undone. If it be true, the people must nevertheless be sustained in that condition which we call enlightened, civilized, and free.

" But I believe no reflecting man will hesitate to admit that, of all influences which affect the character, the prosperity, the duration, the glory, and the usefulness of nations, moral influences are incomparably the most controlling. And of that immense class of influences which might, in a large sense, be called moral, the most important and enduring are, beyond all doubt, those which are strictly religious. Is it too much to assert that the influence of a national religion is greater upon national character than all other influences combined? Is it going too far to declare that the destinies of states have been more deeply affected by their religious faith than by all other circumstances? The very history of mankind is essentially and chiefly a history of religious ideas and religious developments. The great intellects of all ages have comprehended this truth; and though they differed about what religion is or should be, yet they felt and saw that, to the world, it is in fact every thing. In every nation, before these latter days of scoffing, the entire mass of men, though they saw not, felt the same truth; and hence the vehement opposition in them all to every change in their national faith. The sentiment uttered on this platform to-day by the chief magistrate of this commonwealth (Governor Seward, of New York), 'that without the Bible this republic would never have existed,' is as just as it is emphatic; and I solemnly insist upon this inference from that truth, that without the Bible this republic can not continue; for the general principle contended for has a most peculiar application to ourselves. Our institutions belong to an advanced condition of society; they can be sustained only by a community whose moral condition is as peculiar and as advanced as their social system. This Bible contains the religion of this nation. This Bible, which alone is able to prepare our children for virtuous and enlightened liberty, which contains the sanction of our Creator to the principles of our polity, and throws the sacredness of religion around the simple, upright, humane, and free spirit of our institutions; this Bible, which is of value to us equal to the value of liberty and independence, merely because it contains our religion, and which has, besides, this inappreciable worth, that its religion is true and divine, and the only religion that is either the one or the other; this Bible, which will perpetuate our glory, if that can be done at all, and if it can not, will prepare our posterity to be and to do, in the midst of all calamities, whatever becomes the worthy descendants of our glorious ancestors—this treasure of all treasures we dishonor and defile by a deliberate act of national rejection!

"No truth is more clearly established by the whole course of history than that there is a wise and holy providence continually exerted over the nations of the earth. They rise, and flourish, and pass away, under the eye and by the purpose of Him who, in the development of his sublime proposals, will not allow them to abide in strength which would be used to his dishonor; and who, in pity to suffering man, will not permit the principles of evil to consolidate their force, and accumulate, through successive ages, irresistible means to do wrong. Without the blessing and favor of God, no nation can stand, no people endure.

Alas! how multiplied and how sad are the evidences of this truth; and how copiously has he taught us that his blessing is to be expected only by the grateful and the obedient; that his favor is bestowed only as we walk in the ways directed by himself, and toward the ends which he proposes in his all-pervading goodness. But the revelation of his will is contained most plainly, if not alone, in this blessed Volume, which we dishonor by a great public act; and the promises of his favor and protection are written in those pages which he has so urged, persuaded, commanded us to make the light of life in every condition, every age, every relation, and every office through which his providence may guide us. Oh, blessed is that people whose God is the Lord!

"It is not to be supposed that such an event as the exclusion of the Word of God from popular education could extensively occur or continue for a considerable time without furnishing for itself many pretexts by which even good men might be beguiled, nor that such a calamity could be removed without serious resistance from many quarters. Several objections to the restoration of the Scriptures to the schools are so often urged by persons deserving to be heard, that it seems necessary briefly to state and answer them.

"Among these, the most frequent, perhaps, are urged against the Scriptures themselves, which, it is alleged, are, in many particulars, far above the comprehension of children and youth, and which are, moreover, so often disfigured by a certain plainness of expression as to be unsuitable for promiscuous or even public reading before the young. To this the first reply may well be, that God who created us, and who perfectly knows us, has judged otherwise; and that he made the Volume of his Word such as we have it, and has added the most express and emphatic commands that it be early, constantly, publicly, promiscuously read. To all this he has joined the most precise assurances that exact obedience to this precept will have no other tendency than to make us wise and pure here below, and blessed beyond conception forever; that all manner of intercourse with him, and all communion with his holy Word, are most pure and most profitable; and that all contrary suppositions are highly offensive to him, and full of dishonor to his infinite being. As a second reply, it may be stated with equal truth, that all experience proves the objection to be entirely mistaken; for of all mankind, the wisest, the purest, the best were selected to write this sacred Volume; and in all ages, the objectors themselves shall say if this has not been eminently the character of those who have the earliest, the most thoroughly, and the most sincerely pondered, mastered, imbibed, and rejoiced in its precious contents. But, as a final answer, it is to be considered, that if the objection have any weight, it will be not only against the early and promiscuous study of the Bible, but also, in a fundamental manner, first against the Christian religion itself, and, secondly, against all religion whatsoever, as being in itself too obscure for profitable study, and too immodest for public statement; for there are multitudes of truths which adult years do not unravel more than the simplicity of childhood—yea, of truths which are the most vital in Christianity. And as religion in its largest sense, if it be true and profitable at all, must teach us what God is and what he requires of us, it is manifest that an immense portion of it, treating of God, must be more or less inscrutable, and revealed merely as truths to be believed, while still larger portions, treating of duties, of sins, and of divine sanctions touching both, must be always subject to such cavils as that now confuted.

"A second objection, which seems to be urged out of a spirit of amiable solicitude for the Bible itself, would exclude it from the course of systematic education lest a too great familiarity with it in early life should disparage religion itself in our subsequent regards. This conceit is founded in total ignorance of the human heart, and they who utter it overlook one of the firmest and most unalterable laws of our moral being. The objects which we cherish most fondly and most steadfastly are those which first occupied our early and ardent thoughts. The spirit cherishes a kind of immortal gratitude for that which made it first acquainted with itself, and revealed to it all its strength. Our earliest associations are our most enduring ones. Our first friendships are not only our sweetest, but, as one by one they fail and pass away, we learn with surprised grief that they are friendships which can not be replaced. We make new friends, valued, dear, perhaps even more deserving; but, alas! they are those we trusted first in childhood, not those whose images grew into the substance of our hearts. The deepest feelings of the human breast have been linked by God, in adamantine fetters, with the strong impressions and vivid remembrances of our early years. The objects of that period are the sacred objects of life, and the heart will not endure to have the meanest of them invested with less than the costliest of its treasures. O that we could bind the early and tender affections of the whole people to the name of Christ, to the throne of God! O that this fatal familiarity with divine truth were the universal heritage of the children of our country!

"There are those who make it a third objection to restoring the Bible to the schools, that we have reason to dread great strifes and permanent division among the friends of education, if not of religion itself, by pursuing this enterprise. It is to be feared that many who call themselves the friends of education are totally opposed to all religious influence either in the school or the community; and there is too much reason to suppose that plans are already extensively matured, whose success will exclude forever all moral instruction from the course of popular education. This branch of this great subject needs, and must receive, first or last, a thorough sifting. But this is not the occasion. I will at present merely say, that manifestly there can be no union of effort between those friends of education who exclude from their system all moral training, and those who make conscience of taking the Bible to school with them; and the sooner the question is made between them at the bar of the public, the better for the country; for the question involved is no less than this, Whether the education of a religious people shall be subjected to an infidel or a Christian control? As it relates to the true friends of the Bible, there can be no cause nor even occasion of strife here. If there be one single point in which all true Christians can unite, it surely is this, that the Word of God should be given to the human race, and be received by it. Or, if this may not be, it is the strongest possible proof that there must be some inherent or some providential hinderance to all united action among those who are earnestly contending for the same general object. This I do not believe. We shall find the Christians of this country united, not divided by the present proposition; which, while it may separate the friends of the Bible more widely from its enemies, will bind them more firmly to each other. For the rest, strifes and divisions are the price we pay for all that is precious in a sinful world. They can be nowhere better met than under the shadow of the cross; no standard is more worthy to endure them under than the banner of divine truth; no object can be set before us for which we might better suffer them than the charter of salvation.

"Beloved brethren, friends of the Bible and of the Lord Jesus, this is the instrument which God himself has provided with which to subdue the earth unto himself, and triumph over sin and hell. Nothing can stand before a weapon whose edge has been tempered in heaven. It is our part to use this great weapon of our sacred warfare, this sword of the Spirit of God, which we know to be, through him, mighty to pull down every strong hold of iniquity; to use it as men who combat not with flesh and blood, but with principalities and powers; yea, as men who fight the good fight of faith under the eye and guidance of Him who has long ago openly triumphed over our stoutest enemies, and led captivity itself captive.

"And why should doubts arise in our minds, or our faith or courage for a moment fail us? What has not the past witnessed? What victories of grace and redeeming love has it not recorded? Let long history repeat. Time would utterly fail us to speak of the triumphs of this blessed Volume in great antiquity; its triumphs while it was itself incomplete; the triumphs of all, even its smallest parts, each adding trophy upon trophy as proofs of its own title to be added to the portions that had come from the skies before it. How glorious was its career throughout all the East—the great Shemite age—the early manhood of the world! Then, in the mighty transition age of the Greeks—Egypt and Asia surrendering civilization to Europe—Shem transferring the golden scepter to Japhet—the light of the world only chased away the night before the advancing radiance of the light from above! Then came the mighty Cæsars, victorious over all besides; and they and Rome itself, subdued by three centuries of meek endurance and uncomplaining martyrdom, sat down also at the feet of Jesus! Its next trophies came from fierce barbarians, subdued by empires and by armies rather than by single men; invading millions, the shadow of whose banners obscured the Roman world, as they descended like successive floods, overwhelming every seat of civilization; savages who, but for the Bible, had sealed the doom of man. Greater, perhaps, than all the past, its achievements during the long night of the Middle Ages—that time and times, and the dividing of time, when all open sacrifice of praise seemed lost, and the weeping and bleeding church sat desolate in the great moral wilderness, listening in silence to the only voice that dared speak truth or utter comfort. Here is that voice, meek but undismayed, as in those centuries of despair. Here are those witnesses, ready to speak, and die, and live again, as when the gloomiest sackcloth covered them. But God heard their testimony when man was deaf to their entreaties; and God restored again, as from the dead, his persecuted and corrupted Church. The Reformation was, in the strictest sense, accomplished by the Bible; and its greats fruits were the restoration of the Bible, with its knowledge, liberty, and righteousness, to man. Similar were the fruits of what men strangely call the great rebellion of England, but which was, in fact, a rebellion *to* God and *against* iniquity; which has, until now, exerted so great an influence over all the interests of the human race; and in the midst, and by the means, and through the agents and influences of which, the Bible had its Golden Age in England. And, last of all, among ourselves, amid all the blessings we enjoy, and all the efforts we are making, what Christian does not admit that all are the fruits of the blessed Word of God—of that Word believed, obeyed, received into our hearts, and held forth in our lives?

"And all these great successes which the past records, all these victories which our eyes behold, are proofs to us, as from God himself, of what we might still achieve by the same living Word. Let us not fear—let us not faint. Give us but the Word of God, and scope to spread and teach it—all else is sure. Let darkness revisit the earth; let error, ignorance, and superstition return; let the defeated enemies of truth and light come forth and rule; set up your tyrants in the state, your bigots over the Church; establish falsehood by the law; corrupt the ministers of truth, and burn once more its martyrs at the stake. Do this and more. Twice already, since Jesus bled, has it been done throughout the earth—yea, done for long and bloody ages. And yet again we look that such things shall be, for so God speaks. What then? Give us but the Bible, and we will purge your priesthood, dethrone your tyrants, defeat your bigots, put shame on error, and make again the martyr's blood the Church's seed! Give us the Bible—the Bible without note or comment—the Bible as God gave it, and we will, with this alone, by God's indwelling grace, defy death and hell, and for the third time conquer the world for Christ!"

"The Rev. Dr. Milnor, after a complimentary notice of the speech of Mr. Breckenridge, presented the society the following excellent letter from Mr. Greenleaf, professor of law in the University of Cambridge, Mass., which, aside from its own excellence, was such a happy illustration and confirmation of the views just presented, that he could not deny himself the pleasure of reading it at large.

"'Cambridge, *May* 4, 1839.

"'Rev. and dear Sir,

"'I can hardly express the regret I feel at being again deprived of the privilege of attending the ensuing anniversary of our beloved society; but the necessary absence of my colleague in the law department of our university renders it unavoidable. I particularly wished to have urged on the society the importance of new effort to introduce the Bible into *all* our common schools throughout the land. Having myself been early acquainted with such a school, where the Bible was the principal reading-book, I have seen something of its influence on boys up to their riper years; and the observations of subsequent life have deepened the conviction of my mind, that if our institutions are to be perpetuated, it will be only through a wide and general diffusion of the principles inculcated in the Word of God. The Bible is the only faithful picture of real life—the only true history of man—the only unvarnished narrative of his sins, and of the just retributions of his holy Sovereign. It is the only historical book which gives a true account of the human family in all its relations and its motives of conduct. Man falsifies his own history; God has written it with the pen of truth. Its fidelity is evinced in the fact that it has never become obsolete. The man delineated in the Bible is the man of every age of the world, from the creation to our own days, and will be such to the end of time. And if it is important to man to learn the moral nature of his race, and to learn it early, let him be taught it in his youth among the rudiments of his education, from the fountain of all truth—the Bible.

"'It has been well observed by one of our most gifted men, that to seek to make children become good citizens without the aid, and sanctions, and light of religion, is to cultivate the branches and neglect the root. They can be made such only by the early inculcation of the radical principle of all good citizenship, the fear of God and the habit of filial obedience to his commands. It is a great inconsistency to "leave them to decide for themselves till maturity" in this important matter, while, with better reason, we decide for them, during the immaturity of the judgment, in all things else. Man is a confiding being, constituted, by his Creator, to believe implicitly during the entire period of his inability to judge for himself. In infancy he takes every thing upon trust; and of this condition of his mind we avail ourselves in every part of his education. The system of education itself is based upon it, and is conducted upon this principle, changed, by degrees, only as the disposition to universal and implicit confidence gradually decays, and is succeeded by the power of ripened intellect. If the mind is not subdued and enslaved by the inculcation of mathematical truth, which in childhood is as much received upon trust as any other, neither will it be by the inculcation of the truths of religion and good morals. Indeed, the mind can not be kept free from all impressions on this subject. The education of children is far from being confined to school, or even to the fireside. All with whom the child is permitted to associate contribute their share to the formation of his moral character; but it is only in the school, and under the paternal roof, that the hostile influences of the world can be successfully met and counteracted. We can not begin too early to teach our children the truths of the Christian religion, nor pursue it too long. There is in the Bible enough that the weakest can comprehend, and enough for the grapplings of the strongest mind.

"'The present state of Europe and America furnishes another and strong argument for increased effort in the religious and moral education of children. Public opinion in both countries is in a state of revolution, and great changes are in progress. There is not only a struggle between despotism and liberty, but another controversy going on between the liberty of good government and extreme licentiousness; and yet another between the cause of Christ and the enemies of his cross and of his religion. From these causes, deriving, as they do, great force from the tide of European emigration to our shores, the character of our population is unstable, and deep and important changes are almost daily proposed in our institutions. The conservative energy on which these must depend for safety, will be mainly in the virtue of our immediate successors; and this is to be created and preserved only by their religious education. They may be trained in the love of God and his law; and to this end his law must be early set before them, day by day, in the common schools. If we would have them imbibe correct principles, we must lead them daily to the fountain of all truth. Our country is a Christian country. The Christian religion is acknowledged, more or less directly, as that of the people, in the laws and usages of every state in the Union. Our religion, as Protestants, is that of "the Bible, the whole Bible, and nothing but the Bible." If we would have good rulers, we must have good electors; for our rulers receive their public character at the ballot-boxes, and represent, in official conduct, the principles and character of their constituents. This character will be determined by the influence impressed in youth, and perhaps no influences bear more strongly upon youth than those of the books they read. It is easy, on this ground, to account for the opposition of the enemies of religion to the use of the Bible as a school-book; and this opposition of a sagacious enemy should lead us the more strenuously to urge its adoption in all the common schools of the country.

"'It is no new experiment that I would urge, for it has been already tried with the most beneficial results. The fathers of our Revolution were trained in common schools, with the Bible for their principal, and, generally, their sole reading-book. We confess our own degeneracy from the high standard of those pure patriots; but wherein has our education differed from theirs, except that we have discarded the Bible from common schools? In other nations the like results are seen. In Iceland, for example, though they have no common schools, their children are carefully instructed in the Bible, it being almost their only book; and among no people are its precepts more familiarly referred to, or more conscientiously regarded.

"'I might add, that the possession of a common faith, and an engagement in united and common effort for its propagation, by means of the Bible, may prove to be among the most efficacious of means for the prevention of war. The great body of Christians thus engaged at this time in this great work can not be without influence in their respective nations. Children who have been taught God's Word from the Bibles of strangers, will not easily be induced, in maturer age, to make war upon their benefactors. When Sweden was compelled by Napoleon to declare war against England, and a form of prayer for the success of their arms was sent to the several churches, the Dalecarlians refused to read it, saying it was a *mistake;* for the English, who had sent them bread in their famine, and *Bibles* too, *could not* be their enemies!

"'But I must stop somewhere; and the only apology I can offer for writing this much is, that I write from a full heart, and to a fellow-Christian. If my absence from the anniversary should leave the cause with one advocate the less, pray submit these views to some fellow-laborer, and ask him, in his own way, to advocate them, if approved,

"'I remain, dear sir, affectionately yours.

"'SIMON GREENLEAF.'"

The Facilities for the Circulation of the Scriptures in all Languages. By the Rev. Dr. Newton, England.

Mr. Newton said, "I feel that, were we convened for any other purpose, as a stranger in your city and country, something in the form of an apology might well be expected of me; but I am free to confess that, where the Bible is concerned, I feel a sort of instinctive dislike to apologies. Have we not one Master? and can we not engage in one cause together, seeing we are all brethren? Where the Bible is in question, I like not the idea of stranger; I know not that the vocabulary of the British and Foreign or the American Bible Society furnishes a word to express the idea of *stranger*—strangers and foreigners we are not. We are not strangers to the Bible nor the Bible cause. No, we are not strangers, not even foreigners, 'but fellow-citizens with the saints and the household of faith.' A distinguished individual, an invalid, who was very fond of music, asked his daughter to play a favorite air, and while he listened, and observed the tears flow from the eyes of his wife and daughters, he exclaimed, 'I am surrounded with an atmosphere of affection.' Sir, I think we may adopt that language here to-day, and that in a higher sense, and say, We are surrounded with an 'atmosphere of affection'—undying affection—which will live when these bodies go down to the dust, and continue to eternity.

"It is asserted by this great society that the Bible is a divine book, and that the religion it unfolds is from Heaven, and not of men, and that this revelation is duly attested and authenticated. The Bible is based on the rock of eternal truth. It stands like the cerulean arch, and can not be overturned.

"It is also asserted that it is not only a divine book, but the best of books. Indirectly it is asserted, that if it comes from God, it must be worthy of God; it must be suited to his purposes, and to the circumstances of those for whom it is designed; and this we find to be the fact. And why do we give it that distinctive appellation? Because the Bible is THE BOOK, it being the foundation of all other books which are worthy the attention of men. As says an old writer, 'The Bible has not only God for its author, but truth for its matter, and salvation for its end.' I remember an anecdote of George III., when an author presented him for consideration an apology for the Bible. After examining it, he said, 'I like the book, but not the title; the Bible needs no apology.'

"It is also asserted by this great society that the Bible is adapted to its end. A contrary opinion would be an impeachment of its Author, as though he had caused a book to be given for the use of man which was not adapted to his necessities. The Bible is adapted to *all* the ends for which it is designed. I remember the words of an eminent saint of a past age: 'I am as an arrow flying through the air; a spirit come from God, and must return to God. A few moments I have on earth, to be seen no more. I want to learn one thing, the way to heaven. I hear God has caused this to be written in a book. Give me that book.' I am one of those who hold that the Scriptures contain all that is necessary to salvation. You, or I, or any one might put forth a book on any given subject, and might obtain readers; but some readers might not see the force of my arguments, and others might question my authority. But it is otherwise with that book; for wherever that book is found, there is its Author; and wherever that book is carefully and seriously examined, there is the Spirit that dictated it, to assist him that reads, to shine upon the word, and to shine into his heart. In the north of Britain a very worthy individual called on her minister to let him know that she had received the knowledge of the truth. He invited her into his study, and very kindly inquired how she had been awakened, and under what sermon it was. 'Sermon!' said she; 'is it the sermon ye're asking about? It was not the sermon at all, but the text, "God so loved the world, that he sent his only-begotten Son into the world, that whosoever believeth in him might not perish, but have everlasting life."'

"There are advantages to be derived from this book sufficient to justify you in giving it the widest circulation. I want not to put the light under a bushel, but to set it up on high, that it may give light to the whole world. If there is a remedy for disease, let all the diseased of our race know where it is. If there is a supply of food, let all the famishing come. If there is living water, let us do all we can to open channels in every direction, that all the thirsty may drink."

After some remarks upon circulating the Bible without note or comment, he said, "Whatever there is of my creed in the Bible (for I would not have any thing even of my own creed circulated which is not in the Bible), whatever there is of my creed in the Bible, that goes wherever the Bible is circulated. But you can not circulate the Bible without note or comment. But what is the comment? Here is an example: In the Bible we read, 'Behold how good and how pleasant it is for brethren to dwell together in unity!' Behold the comment; where is there a better than we now see? But that has not gone far enough. David was only able to say this in respect to *brethren*. That was *Jewish;* for in the Jewish synagogues you never see any but brethren—

there are no *sisters* there; but we can say, 'Behold how good and how pleasant it is for brethren and *sisters* to dwell together in unity.' Again, the Bible says, 'Love thy neighbor as thyself.' Behold the precious comment. Who is my neighbor? Not the man who lives next door to me, but the man who needs my help. Here we are showing our love to our neighbor, by endeavoring to extend to him one of heaven's choicest gifts. And I trust that on this great anniversary occasion you will always have such precious notes. Another word: this society is not hostile to any other Christian society. Reference has been made to not a few of them to-day. That reverend brother from India—I rejoice to meet him here, and to hear the testimony of that brother; for I have a brother whom he doubtless knows, a brother of the Wesleyan connection, in that section of the world where he labors."

Mr. Meigs.—"Yes, I know him, and thirty of your dear brethren, and we labor together in unity."

Mr. Newton.—"Thank you; there's another *comment.* I like to connect the Missionary and Bible societies together. They have taken root in the same soil, and have been watered by the same hand; and they bear the same kind of fruit. One branch does not envy the other, but they grow up and commingle their branches together to strengthen each other. If your great society be employed in sending forth this book, and the missionary society in translating and circulating it, it is all one work. When you give your book to the native, and, as he is reading, the missionary begins at that Scripture and preaches Jesus to him, he receives the truth and goes on his way rejoicing.

"Now, as already intimated, I have just come from England, and already I have traveled over five or six hundred miles of your territory. I have been greatly delighted. I have seen what a little while ago was an unbroken wilderness turned into a fruitful field, with cities and villages teeming with a busy population. I thought, as I was coming from Philadelphia, 'What is this great Bible Society?' And I thought it might be compared to a great moral engine for cultivating the moral soil; and in how many instances has the wilderness already been seen to blossom with the loveliness and fragrance of the rose! And when I approached your city, I inquired again, 'What is this great Bible Society?' And I said, it is a stately vessel, well built, of good materials, well manned; and with so venerable a man as yourself at the helm, I think no one can have any fears as to her making a good voyage—a vessel richly freighted; and though your ship, as well as ours of the British and Foreign Society, has had to pass through the straits, she has always got safely through, and now she is under full sail, conveying her cargo to the nations of the earth.

"She has sometimes to encounter great opposition; but this only occasions the vessel to appear to better advantage as she moves gracefully and majestically along. She has touched at various ports. The breeze of opposition has only served to keep the streamers flying, to let the world know that she is there. She is going on her way—she has taken in her cargo; and I pray that she may have a most prosperous voyage, and that often the spectator may hear the sound going up from her, 'All's well!'

"And now I have to tell you I have just been on an excursion to the City of Washington; and I was there fortunate enough to find an eagle's nest—a golden eagle's nest; and I found ten half-grown eagles in said eagle's nest; and the owner of the nest said I might take them and give them to you; and I pledge myself that there is not a broker in the city that will not give you fifty dollars for the ten half-grown, half-fledged eagles—from a member of the Wesleyan Episcopal Church of the City of Washington."

The Circulation of the entire Bible. By the Rev. Thomas Brainerd.

Mr. Brainerd said "he concurred in the sentiment already expressed, that the Bible, the *whole* Bible, should be circulated. The resolution called upon him, especially, to remonstrate against a usage, now said to be too prevalent, of separating the Old Testament from the New, because the New Testament could be circulated at less expense than the whole Bible. None will contend that the New Testament *alone* ought in no case to be printed and diffused.

"When the circumstances of the case preclude the circulation of the whole Bible, let us give a part. To the famished traveler half a loaf is better than none; while it is still true that a whole loaf is better than half. What we oppose is the practice of holding back a part of the sacred Volume from those to whom the whole *might* be given. We are not to consult a false economy, and organize our arrangements for giving *only* the New Testament to our fellow-men. If any societies have acted on this principle, they would do well to remember,

"1. That it is not in accordance with the *plan of God.* While they give the Old Testament last, or never, God gave it first to our race. We know not why He, who could throw moral light into the world with noontide radiance, ordained that the breaking dawn should brighten gradually into the perfect day. But so it was. It is not for us to say that light accumulated gradually is not best adapted to honor God in the sanctification of men.

"2. The practice in question is opposed to the philosophy of human nature. The opinion may be questioned, but it is the settled opinion of the speaker, that nearly all children who ever gain a relish for reading the Bible, are first attracted to it by the simple and touching narratives, the marvelous incidents, the scenes of tender pathos and chivalrous adventure recorded in the Old Testament. Constituted as children are, the Old Testament is the dimly lighted but attractive vestibule which leads to the radiant temple of Gospel truth.

"3. The practice in question is peculiarly ill adapted to meet the wants of the Oriental world. In manners, customs, and political institutions, Oriental nations are now substantially the same as three thousand years ago. The Old Testament is arrayed in a rich Oriental costume. Its bold metaphors, its high-wrought poetry, its adaptation to the enthusiastic temperament of Eastern nations, commend it as a pioneer of the Gospels. Let us not withhold a part of the Bible so providentially fitted to attract the attention and charm the hearts of the heathen world.

"4. The practice of suppressing, or negligently circulating the Old Testament, is rebuked by *the nature* of the Bible. The Old Testament has its hundred fingers pointing to the New. The New Testament is built, not only on the foundations of the apostles, but of the *prophets*. To give the Bible its highest moral influence, we must not separate truths to which God has given such interesting relations.

"5. To withhold the Old Testament is perilous to the salvation of souls. Not because the New Testament fails to reveal a safe rule of duty and a precious salvation by the cross, but because man is spiritually blinded, is the *whole* Bible indispensable. The more defective the moral vision, the more necessary is clear, concentrated, steady light over the pathway of man. Can the sweet strains of David be shut out from the human ear, can the voice of prophecy be hushed to silence, without peril to the interests of the soul?

"5. To withhold the Old Testament when it might be given, is opposed to the *fundamental principles* of the Bible Society. We are to give the Bible, not only without note or comment, but without mutilation. We are to distribute the Word of Life, not in fragments, but as God gave it to us, in all the soberness of its history, the tenderness of its promises, and the symmetry of its doctrines.

"7. It is bad economy of time and money to distribute the Bible in fragments. We are compelled to investigate the wants of the world, overcome a reluctance to receive the Word of God, and bear the book to every man's door.

"When these agencies are all in requisition, and in their nature adequate to supply families with the *whole* Bible, shall we be so stinted in charity as to give but one part of the blessed book? When, with so little additional sacrifice, we can confer the whole Bible (Heaven's own agent of moral renovation) upon the ignorant and wayward, shall we hold back a part of the treasure?

"We have but one generation with whom our march is made to eternity. Shall we grudge the means requisite to give the Bible, unmutilated, to our fellow-pilgrims?

"The Bible contains the literature of heaven—of eternity. It is destined to survive in human hearts every other book, and command the ultimate veneration and obedience of the world.

"When Sir Walter Scott returned, a trembling invalid, from Italy, to die in his native land, the sight of his 'sweet home' so invigorated his spirits that some hope was cherished that he might recover. But he soon relapsed. He found that he must die. Addressing his son-in-law, he said, 'Bring me *a book*.' 'What book?' replied Lockhart. 'Can you ask,' said the expiring genius, whose fascinating novels have charmed the world, but have no balm for death—'can you ask what book? there is but *one*.'

"No, there is but *one* book that God has *given* to us; let us *give* that *one book unmutilated to the world*."

Bible Destitution, a Reason for increased Circulation. By the Rev. S. H. Tyng. D.D.

Dr. Tyng proceeded to say, that "the first point here noticed was the immense *destitution* which still exists. In 1830 the society attempted the enterprise of supplying every family in the United States with a copy of the Bible; and it believed that this had been accomplished, when, in one enterprise, half a million of copies had been sent abroad to disseminate light and knowledge, and comfort and peace. And yet, when their periodical examination was made, more or less generally, it was found that there was still a destitution, most alarming in its impression upon the mind and exciting to the most ardent efforts for its supply. He need hardly refer to the West. He would go back to the most populous, and intelligent, and cultivated portions of the land. In the very scenes where exists the greatest light there is still found a most surprising destitution of the sacred Scriptures. In the northern counties of Massachusetts, in Norfolk and Middlesex, and even in Plymouth, standing full in sight of the modern Athens of the land—in sight of that majestic and venerable institution of learning dedicated by its motto, *Christo et Ecclesiæ*, to Christ and the Church—in the midst of these counties have been found fifteen hundred families utterly destitute of a copy of the sacred Word. In Plymouth county, the very field where our forefathers placed their feet—I say *our*, for I yield to no man in the flowing of the Pilgrim blood in my veins—where the very rock still stands on which they first knelt in prayer to the God of the Bible, in that very county were found five hundred families destitute of a single copy of the Word of God.

"Now, sir, if old Massachusetts, my native state, which has exerted so great and so noble an influence over the rest of the Union—which has done so much to influence and adorn the councils of the nation, to magnify her Senate, to give dignity to her bench, and to elevate the national character—if old Massachusetts is not able, with her concentrated wealth, her indomitable energy, which has built up a system of rail-roads reaching in every direction, drawing to her bosom the resources of every region, until they have become so many *blood-suckers* fastened and fattening upon other states—if she, the center of so much power, and possessed of such abundant means, can not maintain herself in the possession of the Scriptures, but in her central counties so large a portion of her population have not a copy of the sacred Word, what are we to expect when, following that best class of our pioneers, the Methodist preachers, we enter upon the new and wide-spread regions of the Western world? The whole land in which we dwell needs a re-exploration and supply; and it will again require a distribution of another half million of copies of the Scriptures in the United States before we can say that there are as many Bibles as families upon our soil. We are brought into a condition requiring us to look at the fact as it stands before us. We must look upon it with the feelings of one who sees that there is pressing need to do something, and who brings a strong will to the work. We must look upon it, not with a speculative glance, but with the feeling of a man who has a note to pay at a distinctly marked and well-remembered hour, and default in which incarcerates him, not in walls of stone, but in the iron bonds of conscience forfeited and privileges abused. We must make it a matter of conscience to meet this emergency, or God will soon be disregarded by the people, and his system of truth put under the shadow of neglect and carelessness by us.

"In looking at this destitution, we can not separate from it the remarkable growth of the population of the country—a growth of more than 500,000 per annum, and 100,000 of this number immigrants from the Old World. Now we are told that this society can furnish 6000 copies of the Scriptures in five days. But we have a vast weekly addition to our population from one source, and they of a class that especially need to be supplied with the Holy Scriptures. Why, sir, we are trying to sweeten, not a bitter fountain only, but a mighty river, which is continually flowing down upon us like the vast Mississippi, with all its waters, and something, I fear, of its mud, carrying desolation in its track, and scarcely leaving a trace of cultivation behind. More than one half, at least, of these immigrants are Roman Catholics—persons who, we may safely say, have not the Bible, because they are not permitted to possess it. But we are to regard no decrees that prohibit the use of the Word of God. God gave it to man, and man has not the right to take it from him. God has given man the right to read it, to understand it, and to apply it; and that any man or body of men shall say to us that they only have authority to interpret it, and that its truths shall be in their keeping, under lock and key, is an arrogant assumption not to be countenanced—it is a trespass upon the rights of man, and is not to be endured, but is to be resisted with the sternest determination that Christian feeling and peace will allow. And here I am compelled to throw in a qualification. I can not give, even by silence, my consent to the doctrine which has been held upon this platform, that the Bible ever warrants us to shed the blood of our fellow-men, even in defense of its sacred truth. I believe in the independence which it teaches; but it is that of Luther's reply when all Germany, Saxony, and Hesse exclaimed, 'Why not draw the sword?' I believe with him that man's surest road to success in teaching the things of God is to work with the sword of the Spirit, which is the Word of God, and remembering that he that useth the sword shall perish by the sword. I will use no sword that will cause men to perish in my warfare.

"But looking at this immense evil, for we can call it nothing else, we must not yield or abandon it. We are responsible for their souls, and for them must we labor. No man living—no council in the world, shall interfere to prevent us from laboring for their enlightenment, for no man living has a right to live in spiritual darkness and error, to shut himself up from God's sun shining all around him, to cast away the privileges with which God has surrounded him. The soul of man we have no right to despise or esteem of little worth; and while the Bible, and not the authority of man, or the decrees of councils and of senates, is the sole instrument of spiritual light, the sole charter of human hope, the sole ground of eternal life, it is not in man to throw it from him and not become a rebel. We are compelled to urge it upon him, to force it upon his attention; and if after seven visits he should still refuse, we are to make the eighth, and press it upon him still. When we look at that portion of this immigration which comes from Ireland—and once when I expressed my sympathy for Ireland on an occasion like this, I was called in question for the stand I had taken; but I feel no disregard for Ireland. I never knew a feeling of contempt for Ireland. I honor its spirit—I have lived in imagination among its hills and valleys, and have felt the wrongs done to its hardy peasantry. But I feel that there is other than Catholic blood in Ireland—other sons than those of Rome, and other hearts besides those which are bleeding under English tyranny, or the priestly tithes of an Established Church. There is a Protestant body in Ireland who are pushed to the wall, and the time may not be distant when we shall hear that torrents of the blood of oppressors shall have deluged the fields of the green isle. From Ireland, and from the mountains and vales of Switzerland and Germany they come—a multitude that no man can number. They come Bibleless; shall we leave them Bibleless here? The responsibility of their supply rests upon us. Their condition is a new argument for increasing our efforts; nay, it is a command from Heaven that we may not disregard—a decree of Divine Providence—an expression of the Divine will, and we have not the right as Christians—as American Christians we may not withhold from them that book without which they perish.

"Now, while there is this destitution even in our own land, there is an intense excitement of *desire* upon the subject throughout the world. There has been no year before when your agents have had such a demand upon them as during that which has just closed. Demands pour in upon the board in such a way as to show that God is hastening forward the time for the universal diffusion of his light and his truth. We are approaching those rapids which anticipate the cataract. We are drawing near the time when multitudes of minds are awakened at once into the most anxious concern for some path of peace, some refuge of hope. They come in from the most distant parts of our territory. Month after month do they awaken solicitude in view of the fact that we are straitened in our means of supply. While some reject it, others are reaching—are panting in their eagerness to receive it. And they are willing not only to take it, but to pay for it, so far as their utmost means will allow. Permit me to call your attention to some facts concerning the progress of the cause at Manchester, in England, as an instance of what has occurred elsewhere, and as a type of what is occurring every where. The Manchester Auxiliary Bible Society had for about thirty-four years sold and circulated annually about 5000 copies: last year, up to September, the demand had increased to 15,000 or 16,000. The committee were astonished at this threefold demand. But this was only the droppings before the shower. In the months of October and November alone, there were 20,000 additional copies distributed, chiefly on sale. And this great increase had been effected by the young persons in the mills, junior clerks in counting-houses, &c. They had become the agents in circulating the Word of God. At the latest accounts the work was still going on, and spreading itself like the waves of the sea, in evidence of the secret energy with which the Bible wins its way in the manifestation of the Spirit, and diffusing light and glory into the hearts and minds of men. In this connection I may call your attention to the testimony of Bishop Sumner, of Chester, a man whose publications have been widely circulated from this city under the sanction of high official persons, and who has been considered by many a type of a party to which I should not wish to be understood to belong. This gentleman, in writing to the agent, says that he has been requested to hand in a donation of £500, to be entered as from an octogenarian friend. He expresses further his determination to sustain the society in its crisis, and his thankfulness at being permitted to co-operate in so good a cause. And shall I err in walking in the path of that holy and dignified man? No! no! I will take up his song and exclaim, How highly am I honored in being permitted to aid in so good a cause! I feel that I am doing my Master's work while I plead the cause and further the interest of the American Bible Society. I have nailed my flag to the mast in this cause, and never shall it be hauled down. I view it as the work of God, and it is not the right of any man to gainsay the principles on which it is founded, or the work which it accomplishes. I can not find it within my conscience to withhold my co-operation in its efforts. From the first day until this day, and in time to come, my heart is with it. The day is hastening when the men who have clung to this cause will be the truly honored. The interests in which we are engaged are imperishable, and the time will come when men who now look with jealousy upon this society will be glad to shelter themselves under an influence which is felt to be good, only good, and good forever.

"In looking abroad upon this spiritual destitution, the direct and only method of its supply is by giving them the Bible. That is the only method. I do not mean to undervalue other instrumentalities; but every thing connected with the Bible, except its sacred truth, is but an instrument thereto. Give me that, and I view all other things —the Church and the clergy—but as its binding, as the means and instruments of its conveyance. For this were churches made, and for this alone was the ministry established. I agree most heartily with the gentleman from Virginia, 'Stick to the ministry while, and only while, they stick to the Bible.' The right to have the Bible, to interpret the Bible, and to apply its truth, is not the right of the Church nor the clergy. It is the right of every individual. The Comforter is not promised to the Church nor the clergy, but to every believing soul. And I hold that each individual soul has the *unqualified* right to read, and interpret, and apply the Bible for himself. It is my Pilgrim blood that has made me now Episcopalian. It is the very independence which brought our fathers to Plymouth Rock, that brought me under the shelter of that kind of hierarchy which, in the corruptions of its power, those men rejected, and against which they rebelled; and I honor them for that rejection. I would have rebelled, and rejected it myself. And should similar oppression and similar corruption arise even nearer home, I would follow the Puritans and the Scotch in resisting its power; but I would imitate the Puritans in seeking a refuge in the wilderness, rather than the Scotch in taking up the sword in my own defense. In this spirit we are bound to follow out this work. We must respect and regard the right of every man to have the Bible. What are the great contests now going on in the world but contests between the Bible and something which men would force us to accept in its stead? At what do all the anti-Christian organizations of the day aim, but to deprive us of the Bible, and lead us to take what they offer us in its room? The Socialists, the Fourierites, the infidels of every class, would take from me my Bible, and throw me upon passions, and appetites, and interests which nothing but the Word of God can give me power to control. And shall I abandon this sure guide and accept of their proffered substitute? Shall I leave the light and the glory of God, and go down to dig and delve with self, and sin, and Satan, beneath the sod? Shall I leave the lofty heights of the empyrean, the seat of God's ineffable glory, and stoop to commune with the powers of darkness and of hell? I hold the whole system to be a perfect incarnation of Satan in its influence. Its purposes are base, and its principles, which I am sorry to see some respectable booksellers and publishers keep upon their shelves, involve nothing but moral pestilence and death to be dealt out to man.

"There is another class who would take the Bible from me, and give me in its place the dogmas of the Church of Rome. Now, sir, I hold, that if any man is infallible, I am infallible myself. If I am to submit to the mere opinions of any mere man, it shall be the man who lives within my own breast. I will be bound by no man's infallibility. But I will take the Bible for myself, and ask assistance from that source where all have the promises of guidance and direction. But there is still another form of hostility to the Bible—sacred in its origin, but baneful in its results. It is that which seeks to block it up in catechisms, and forms, and creeds, and plans of man's device. I will take the creeds of my own church on the ground which that church decides, so far as to me they are in accordance with the sacred Scriptures, and no farther. The connection between the Bible and the men who immediately succeeded the period of inspiration is between infallible and fallible. However I may reverence the men, I can acknowledge no authority in them beyond the Word of God. There is no shelving shore from revelation to later periods of the Church. The junction is like the elevated pier in the full tide of the ocean; no man shall throw me overboard, no man shall tempt me overboard, nor will I go to sea with any man, or any class of men, without that sure and infallible compass, the Word of God, and by that and that alone shall my bark be directed. (Loud applause.) I care nothing for this applause—I am not a man to be moved or governed by it. And yet I shall probably be assailed ere long as having come here on purpose to obtain it. I do not court it, nor do I care for it. I freely approve and adopt the sentiment of Daniel Webster, who, when asked by his brother how he could face unmoved such a sea of heads as stood gazing at him, answered, 'Why, brother, I always take them to be a garden full of cabbage-heads.' That is the noble independence of a man who speaks for himself, who utters his own mind, without stopping to ask whether others will agree or disagree. What is it to me that those whom I address may deny or denounce the truth which I speak? Why should I shape my thoughts and words to meet the wishes of my fellow-men for the few brief moments we have to live, when I am on my way to a heavenly kingdom, where all will unite and dwell in the harmony of the sons of God?

"The Bible is itself supreme. It does not need a ministry to interpret it—it does not tolerate a ministry to stand upon its ground. Every one, the highest and the lowest, the poorest cottage girl who sits by her door and knows nothing but the truth as it is in Christ—

'A truth the brilliant Frenchman never knew'—

must read it for herself, and interpret it for herself, and is as truly responsible for the manner in which she applies its truths as the most learned of its readers. When I go to that book, God speaks to me. I need no succession—I go at once to the fountain-head. It is not man that speaks. It is God who speaks; and he speaks to me as if there were but one single Bible on the earth, and that Bible an angel had come down and bound upon my bosom. It is *my* Bible. It was written for me. It is the voice of God holding communion with my own soul, and never will I forfeit my right to commune with God. Nor is that communion to be held before councils, or in open temples, or in the presence of sects and of priests, and through the intervention of others. It is an act to be transacted in the most secret sanctuary of the Lord. No sects, no priestly interference can be admitted. It is an affair between God and my soul; and as Abraham bid the young men abide with the ass at the foot of the mountain, so will I ascend, and go to meet God alone upon the top. I wish my views upon this point, thrown out as they are before this large assembly, to be stated clearly and to be distinctly understood, and the press may proclaim them to the world as those of a man who speaks for himself, and not under the constraints of creeds or the impositions of men. That book is the book of God; and when I go out and commune with it, I hold communion with my God. I am Moses, just come down from the burning mountain, his face shining with joy and the glory of God. I am Isaiah, and have come from the golden courts where the seraphim and cherubim shout hallelujah to the Lord God of Hosts. I am Paul, and have seen the third heavens opened, and can tell what is uttered there, and have seen glories ineffable which no tongue can tell nor imagination conceive. I am John, and have laid my head upon the Master's bosom, and have caught, warm with his breath, the very whispers of the sweet counsels which he has breathed into my ear. It is not from any intervention or interpretation of man that it derives its power. God gave it to me. He made it, and he has preserved it. Nor does the fact that he transmitted it for centuries through the agency of unclean birds, as Elijah was fed by the ravens of the valley, change its character. It is still bread and food for all the world.

"And now, as I am called to speak for this society, I can speak with confidence and determination. We are brought to this crisis, when the work must either go on or be given up. On every side, need, desire, suffering, pressing want meet our view, and we this day, to an extent we have little power to calculate, hold the key of supply. Brethren, will you work in this cause? Not speak, nor think, nor feel—but will you work? We are to save this land for Christ in this generation in which we live, or we are to lose it forever. We are to carry out the work now, or lose the chance of settling the question who shall have dominion over it. If each one of the thousands gathered here from widely-distant sections of the land will go away resolved to double his exertions and contributions in the cause, we shall carry out the plan, and 750,000 apostles and prophets will be sent out into the length and breadth of the land in which we dwell."

The Bible the great Moral Renovator of our Race. By the Hon. B. F. Butler.

Mr. Butler expressed his high sense of the benevolence and grandeur of the effort to which their attention had been invited, and his concurrence in the views presented to the meeting in the eloquent and truly Christian appeal which had just been made to them. The beneficent effects of true religion on the interests of society, as well as its efficacy in saving the souls of men, had been portrayed with great felicity and distinctness; and the obligations and motives which should prompt to a general diffusion of the sacred Volume had been enforced upon the consciences of those present in a most impressive manner.

Mr. B. said, "I will not attempt to enlarge on either of those topics; but it might be well to state two or three of the reasons which induced the friends of the Bible to rely upon the universal circulation and reception of that blessed book, not only as the appointed means of evangelizing the nations, but as the true and only method by which the barbarous were to be civilized, the ignorant enlightened, the vicious reformed, and the miserable of all countries improved in their condition. This consideration, if clearly established, would not only increase the zeal of the professed believer, but commend the effort now before us to the approbation and support of every benevolent and well-regulated mind.

"It is only necessary," said Mr. B., "to cast a hasty glance over the surface of our country, to see that it is filled with individual, social, and public evils, which are the fruitful sources of an incalculable amount of suffering and crime. But if such be our own condition, how much worse is that of the great majority of Christian nations? And who can adequately describe the abominations of heathenism, or the degradation and misery of those who are subject to its sway? It was but natural that such a state of things should excite the sympathies of benevolent men; and it was honorable to the age in which we live, that this feeling was stronger and more general than it had ever been at any former period. Men of all classes and pursuits, in every part of Christendom, were proposing schemes to meliorate the condition of their own communities, and for the civilization and improvement of the rest of mankind. These schemes naturally took their complexion from the feelings and pursuits of their authors. The mere politician tells us that the object may be accomplished by wise and paternal institutions of government, and by the faithful administration of their various functions. And surely no one—in our country at least—would underrate the value of such institutions. But all experience has shown that human legislation can only reach a small part of the ills to which the individual members of every community are liable, and that unless the mass of the community are sufficiently instructed to be capable of self-government, the wisest institutions will fail of their object, and soon fall into decay. And therefore we are told, that to well-adapted schemes of government there must be added thorough education of the people, by the means of primary schools, academies, and other institutions; the general diffusion of useful knowledge by a free press; the cultivation of the sciences; and the general improvement of the intellectual faculties. But, although education and knowledge ought ever to be cherished, as sources of abundant and incalculable good, yet, in numerous instances, it has been found that vicious practices and sentiments, and much individual and social misery, might coexist with the cultivation of knowledge, with the arts of refined and elegant society. In view of this fact, the political economist advances another step, and insists upon the indispensable necessity of such arrangements as will check the growth of pauperism and crime, and promote the certain acquisition and the advantageous distribution of national wealth.

"That immense good may be effected by the adoption of judicious economical arrangements, and that many improvements in this respect are indispensable to the well-being of the most enlightened nations, is not to be doubted. But the most perfect system of political economy will still fall short of reaching the sources of the general evil. This truth is so deeply impressed on the hearts of those amiable and exemplary men whose morality possesses every claim to the epithet of Christian, except that it does not flow from 'repentance toward God' and 'faith in our Lord Jesus Christ,' that they are earnest in their endeavors to inculcate the precepts and enforce the practice of a pure and operative morality. They feel and know that virtue is indispensable to individual happiness and public prosperity, and they would therefore make all men sober and orderly, industrious and upright. In all this they think and act wisely; but, unfortunately, they do not wield an instrumentality powerful enough to accomplish their benevolent designs; for here, again, we have the testimony of experience, which has shown that only a small portion of mankind can be induced to yield obedience to any system of morals which does not proceed from, and is not sanctioned by, a supernatural authority. All systems merely human are so deficient in the sanctions which accompany them, that many of those who adopt them feel themselves at liberty to violate, at pleasure, their most solemn injunctions. This was the case with many celebrated teachers among the Stoics—the most rigid moralists of pagan antiquity—and the same thing has been exemplified in the lives of some of the most eloquent expositors of natural religion among the moderns.

"Now the reason of all this is perfectly familiar to every experienced and well-instructed Christian who takes his philosophy from the Bible. He is informed, and he believes, 'that out of the *heart* are the issues of life,' and he therefore traces all moral action to that capacious source. He is further informed, and he feels and knows it to be true, that 'the *heart* is deceitful above all things, and desperately wicked;' and because it is so, he understands the reason of the authoritative declaration, that from within, out of the *heart*, 'proceed evil thoughts,' and all the abominations 'that defile the man,' and make him at once the victim and the author of sorrows, suffering, and crime. To reach the origin of these evils, and, so far as our present condition will permit, to banish them from the world, the Christian knows some remedy must be found which shall reach and purify the heart; and he also knows that the sincere and vivid apprehension of the Christian faith is the only thing that can accomplish this necessary result. But though, for this reason, he regards all the mere human instrumentalities recommended by statesmen, lovers of learning and science, economists, and moral philosophers, as inadequate, yet he does not reject any one of them. He would employ them all; but to each and to all he would superadd the Gospel of Christ, the 'wisdom of God;' and 'the power of God,' and the knowledge that the practical reception of this system is indispensable to complete success, makes even the humblest Christian to be 'wiser than his enemies,' and to 'understand more' than the most erudite 'teachers' of a barren philosophy.

"Not that the general prevalence of Christianity would banish poverty or sickness, suffering or sorrow, from the earth. The poor we have always with us; the ordinary ills of life are incident to our present state, and the Christian is not exempt from them. On the contrary, he is exposed to many peculiar trials, and in matters personal to himself is seldom free from anxiety and disquietude. But the universal adoption and practice of our religion would dry up many sources of misery; and by promoting the love and fear of God, peace, virtue, and benevolence, and giving a new impulse and a proper direction to the intellectual faculties, and to all the arts and improvements of social life, would insure to humanity the highest happiness of which it is susceptible. And though many trials would still remain to be encountered, it needs no argument to show that the blessedness of heaven will constitute an overflowing indemnity for all the sufferings of life. He is *truly* happy, whatever may be his temporal condition, who can call God his father, in the full assurance of faith and hope. And amid all his trials, and conflicts, and doubts, the feeblest Christian is still comparatively happy, because cheered by the hope—faint and humble though it be—that the hour is coming when he shall be delivered from 'this body of sin and death,' and in the vision of his Redeemer, and by a never-ending progression in knowledge and virtue, approximate to the perfection and felicity of angels.

"I will mention another reason why the friends of the Bible consider its dissemination as the most powerful instrument which can be employed for the reformation and improvement of the human race. Not only does it inculcate, with sanctions of highest import, a system of the purest morality, but in the person and character of our blessed Savior it exhibits a tangible illustration of that system. In him we have set before us what, till the publication of the Gospel, the world had never seen—a model of feeling and action, adapted to all times, places, and circumstances, and combining so much of wisdom, benevolence, and holiness that none can fathom its sublimity, and yet presented in a form so simple that even a child may be made to understand, and taught to love it. This idea is thus happily expressed in a favorite hymn:

"'My dear Redeemer, and my Lord,
I *read* my duty in thy Word;
But in thy *life* the law appears,
Drawn out in *living characters*.'

"And what is more, though none can equal, all can *imitate* the perfections displayed in the story of his life. The strictness and fervor of his devotions—the justice, meekness, and benevolence of his conduct, may be imitated by the humblest of his followers; and each of them is bound to make the effort to do so. Those who truly embrace the Gospel will assuredly make such an effort; and on those who do not thus receive it, this living exemplification of perfect virtue will yet produce a much greater influence than any merely perceptive code, however useful or complete. Many men who have never believed in Jesus Christ as the 'Lamb of God who taketh away the sin of the world,' have yet been attracted by the simplicity and loveliness of his character, as drawn by the evangelists, to the practice of benevolence and virtue. With a view to even such an influence as this, the universal dissemination of the Bible deserves the support of every well-wisher to the happiness of mankind.

"Independently of the reasons which have been assigned, and of the predictions and promises contained in the Word of God, there are abundant grounds, in the former experience of the world, for believing that the universal diffusion of the Bible will actually produce the most blessed effects on the temporal condition and prospects of all nations. We know, from authentic history, what the state of Europe was at the promulgation of Christianity, and we can see for ourselves what it has become under the influence of that religion. We can see, also, what is our own state; and when we compare those portions of our country which have enjoyed for the longest period, and in largest abundance, the blessings of the Gospel, with districts less favored in this respect, we see something of the moral power of the Bible.

"But, after all, the great argument to be urged upon a Christian audience, on an occasion like the present, is that to be derived from the fact that the Bible is the word of eternal life, and that a great majority of the human family are yet followers of the false prophet, or worshipers of idols. The duty of sending them the Bible is palpable and pressing. It is also a most encouraging circumstance that the channels of intercourse between Christian and Mohammedan countries are every day increasing; and as for heathenism, its old systems are evidently tottering, and as no new one has been established since the Christian era, there is reason to hope that none will hereafter come into existence. Above all, China, Burmah, and all the East, are not only ready, but eager to receive the oracles of God. Whether this anxious, this increasing demand, is to be met in the spirit of her Master, is now the only question to be decided by the Church. It can not be treated with indifference without stifling the most generous emotions of the heart—without denying our allegiance to Him who has bought us with a price, even with his own most precious blood. Would to God we could awake to the true importance, the heavenly grandeur of this work! The world is full of combinations for the acquisition of wealth, and authority, and honor, and myriads of our race are giving themselves up to such pursuits. But here is an object in comparison with which wealth is but dross, and earth's highest honors an empty bubble! an object to inflame the ambition, not merely of men, but of angelic hosts, for it involves the conversion of a world—the glory of the eternal! Doubtless all of us are constantly engaged in labors and pursuits, the remembrance of which will impart no pleasure in the hour of death. But the proceedings of to-night, if with proper motives we have participated in them, will plant no thorn in our dying pillow. If any thing connected with the recollection of this meeting shall then inspire us with regret, it will be that we felt and contributed so little for an object so stupendous and sublime. Let it, then, be our study to give it our warmest prayers, our utmost efforts; and not only our prayers and efforts, but the aid of a holy life. With such a life on the part of every Christian, added to well-directed efforts, and the present generation may see not only the accomplishment of the great work now proposed, but even greater wonders in the results it will have produced. The Word of God, distributed among all the nations, and possessed by every family on the globe, can not return to Him that sent it, void: it will—it *must* accomplish the purpose for which it was designed!"

Demand for the Scriptures in Foreign Countries. By the Rev. Dr. Bethune.

"Among the pleasing aspects of these hallowed meetings," observed Dr. Bethune, "one of the most pleasing is the spirit of holy Christian courage with which they seem to be animated. I have never witnessed a finer exemplification of the spirit of the text, 'Be careful for nothing; but in all things, with thanksgiving, let your requests be made known unto God.' We have been quite too accustomed to complaint and lamentation. The people of God have been gathered together to be scolded and depressed by the story of failures and deficiencies; and the goodness of Heaven has been almost impeached by the scantiness of our praise. We have too often forgotten the clause 'with thanksgiving.' But now another spirit animates us; the accents of encouragement and the tones of hope are given forth by all societies.

"There is, I say, the spirit of Christian courage. There are many things in the aspects of the times and the condition of the world which might alarm any but a Christian. But with the Word of the Lord in our hands, and its promises engraven upon our hearts, we have no right or occasion to fear. Confidence in God is the source of holy boldness. Luther was filled with it when he drew forth this Word from the dust and forgetfulness of ages, and lifted it up for the healing of the nations in the face of men and devils. I love this spirit—I love it always, but especially now. At one time we stood aghast at the violence of party strife; at another, at the corruption of political intrigues; and again, at the extravagances of false zeal and the prevalence of false sentiment. The Church, even, has adopted the dialect of fear, and turned pale at the perils which seem to hang menacingly over her. But I envy not the man who, with the history of this country before him—with the brightening aspects of the present by the side of the deficiencies of the past—can withhold the expression of gratitude for success, or suppress confidence for the future. True, we are not perfect; we are sinners, and the fellow-citizens of sinners. The rulers are sinners, and they who elect them; and all that could be desired is not and will not be attained. But, amid all the evils of our times, there is a spirit of religion abroad in the land. The spirit of our fathers is not fled. And as long as the Bible is kept among us—so long as it is made as free as the air—it will not depart. With this Bible in our hands, and its promises our inheritance, I will not fear for our country or the world.

"There have been fears that, as infidelity was increasing and becoming even more rampant, our common schools would be deprived of the Bible and of the influences of religion. There has been too much public—not too much private—expression of apprehension of such a result. There will be no more likely way to bring it round than by proclaiming our fear of its occurrence. But the fear is perfectly idle, because teachers and parents, patrons and friends, are, and will be, too much inclined to religion, and too sensible of the great benefits which the Bible confers. But what if infidelity should banish the Bible from the school-house? so long as the people read, they will be open to the influence of the Bible. I would unite with the rankest skeptics or errorists to circulate spelling-books, if I could do no more, because in the wake of the spelling-book the Bible will follow; and if, six days of the seven, they shut out the Bible, the influence of the seventh would show the folly of their attempt to destroy it.

"I am not afraid of infidels, or the pope, or of tyrants, but I *am* afraid of the devil. While we rely upon the weaponry of the truth, and have the pledges of Omnipotence for our defense, we need not fear; but we *may* fear that we shall be seduced from that trust to confidence in other means. It is an old saying, 'Every cock fights best on his own dunghill.' If we will go down to contend with the devil upon his own level, we shall be defeated; but, high upon the fortress of truth, our warfare shall be both safe and victorious.

"I am not afraid of Catholics. I can afford to be civil to them. I do hope that none of us shall exhibit a spirit of enmity or a disposition to interfere with the freest enjoyment of their rights. They have their rights; if I disregard them, I teach *them* the lesson of intolerance. We want no Church and State; we ask not, nay, we spurn the aid of the magistracy in our grapple with the Man of Sin. In an atmosphere loaded with the truths of the Bible, popery can not live. It can live nowhere but as it is nursed and strengthened in the lap of tyranny. It is a fact that the pope himself is bolstered up by Austrian bayonets. Eight thousand Austrians patroling the streets of Rome, is the secret of the stability of the papal throne. Take away these minions of tyranny, and I would not give sixpence for the old man's life, kind and amiable though he be. A deep and unconquerable hate lies in the hearts of the people. An eminent artist once remarked to me, 'Other nations have their tyrants, inflicting their oppressions in this life; but we are crushed by a tyranny which, not content with cruelties in this life, pursues us with the torments of another.' Give freedom to men's bodies, and their souls will assert their liberty.

"If perils have been thickening upon us, so have the means of resisting them here also augmented. It is within my own remembrance that Bibles could hardly be obtained in this country for distribution. My own father was in the habit of sending to England for copies for his own distribution, and there paying an exorbitant price for them—a price which would now procure three or four copies at your depository.

"The wisdom of the world looks with a cold and careless eye upon the operations of religious benevolence. But if that wisdom would be wise enough to look, it might discover in these operations as much to claim the respect of the philosopher as the affections of the Christian. At the formation of the British Bible Society, translations might have existed in fifty of the languages of the globe. Now they exist in more than one hundred and fifty. And whose is the achievement? Has it been done by your men of science—your *savans* at Paris or Berlin, London or Madrid? Is it the triumph of science? No; it is the triumph of the Gospel: religion has done it. And if all the contributions which missionary labor and Christian effort have made to the cause of science could be gathered together, the result would claim of the lover of science, and the mere philosopher, the homage of respect.

"An interesting and touching fact is brought to mind by the presence of this venerable stranger (Mar Yohannan), that the land to which the Bible owes its birth is calling to us to send it back again.

It is a thrilling thought, that the land upon whose acres the feet of Jesus once trod, where his disciples lived and labored, should be calling to us, in these ends of the earth, for the bread which it first produced. Whose heart can resist such a call from such a source! It seems like a petition to us, before the door is forever shut, 'Give us of your oil, for our lamps have gone out.' Yes, God has given us the oil; we obtained it through them, and they ask only for its return.

"But though in our efforts to distribute the Bible we act upon masses, that action can be induced only by the personal experience of its quickening and sanctifying influences. It is not by the power of these exciting scenes that we shall develop the spirit of Christian effort. Each must believe, and feel, and experience for himself. We must go personally, alone, and for ourselves, to the cross. We can not be animated, any more than we can be saved, by the piety of parents or the fidelity of others. If there be one here whose heart is cold to the claims of a dying world—if one can refuse to look upon the wide-swelling desolations around us, O! he may be sure that he has not had personal, close, and living communion with God. It is this which is needed, and without this the world will continue to perish in darkness and neglect.

"The spirit of the Bible—this is the animating principle, the power to save the world. And I can not conceal my delight to witness a tendency to recur to the Bible. The dust of neglect has been permitted to gather upon its cover; and I have trembled as one puny, paltry book after another has been substituted for the Bible, as guides, and manuals, and systems thrust between the soul of the inquirer and God. I have trembled to hear sermons in which Christ was not mentioned, and which could only be distinguished from Plato and Seneca by their inferiority. But the public appetite is no longer satisfied with your milk and water. It craves a healthier diet. It goes back to the old writers—to Leighton, whose every sentence is redolent with the odor of Christ—to men who, after the bustle of the Reformation, had the piety to sit down by the Bible and extract its sweetness to hoard up in hives, from which the busy Church of our day may feed while they go forth to bless the world.

"The day is coming when we shall be gathered to a mightier assembly than this. It will be one, the contemplation of which will give exquisite delight to Him who sitteth upon the throne. It will be one, the joy of whose salvation supported him under the dark apprehensions of the garden and the burden of the cross. Will it not be a joy to stand by the side of that throne, and to participate in that joy? Is it not a thing to be coveted and labored for, to enter into a happiness like this? But its price is labor. It can never be gained but by those who, animated by his spirit, have suffered with Christ, that they may be also glorified with him."

In closing his address, Dr. Bethune introduced the Nestorian Bishop Mar Yohannan to the audience, who rose in his full Oriental costume, and was addressed by the president as follows, holding in his hand a splendidly bound quarto Bible:

"REV. SIR,—In the name and behalf of the American Bible Society, I present you a copy of the English translation of the Holy Scriptures. Accept it, sir, as a testimony of our high respect for your character, and of our confidence in your zeal to promulgate the great truths which this precious volume reveals. May you long continue a blessing and an ornament to the Christian church, and finally receive from her glorious Head the benediction, 'Well done, good and faithful servant, enter thou into the joy of thy Lord.'"

On the first leaf was beautifully written the following: "A COPY OF THE HOLY BIBLE, PRESENTED BY THE AMERICAN BIBLE SOCIETY TO MAR YOHANNAN, BISHOP OF OOROOMIAH, PERSIA. 1842."

Looking at the Bible, the bishop replied in Syriac (translated by Mr. Perkins), "How beautifully and tastefully this Bible is bound; but that which it contains is far more beautiful and precious. The Scriptures are more precious than gold. I show you a book—the New Testament, which I have brought from my own country; how great is the contrast which it presents. I wish you to observe particularly how meanly it appears. But still it is the same precious Word. It was written 642 years ago, by the hand, on parchment. From ancient times a few copies of the Bible have been with our people; and it has been peculiarly precious to us, in giving us consolation and support under the severe oppressions which the Mohammedans have inflicted upon us; and kept us not only from their errors, but also from yielding to the wiles and seductions of Roman priests, who have swarmed our country.

"Among our population of 40,000, there are but six or eight copies of such Testaments as this. We ask of this Bible Society if they will not increase the number, and give the Bread of Life to these famishing people? Other nations also, as well as ours, are looking to you from that dark East, to give them the Bible. It is this which makes the great difference between this land and those.

"I heard with astonishment from the secretary, Mr. Brigham, the other day, that a thousand copies of the Bible could be printed by the society every day. How blessed would be the gift, if a few days' labor of this society could be given to my country; how soon it would become like America. We want the Bible more than any thing else. We are poor, but with this we should be rich. Will you not send the Bible to us?"

Unity and Catholicity of the Bible Cause. By Rev. S. Olin, D.D.

"No topic, Mr. President," said Dr. Olin, "could more perfectly harmonize with my feelings and most established principles, than the one assigned me by your Committee of Arrangements, and yet I must avow that I attempt the advocacy of it with unfeigned diffidence. Though nominally, and of warm affection, belonging to a profession addicted to public speaking, I have been long estranged from its active duties. Once only in my life, and that twenty years ago, have I ventured to ascend a platform, and I have not more than twice been a spectator of such exhibitions. How much the unavoidable deficiencies arising from these causes must disqualify me from doing justice to my theme, and contributing to the interest of this great occasion, will soon be made but too apparent, and I should certainly avoid the egotism of referring to considerations merely personal but for a painful and most embarrassing apprehension that the good cause may receive harm from my unskillful efforts to promote it. I can not be quite ignorant of the high objects of the American Bible Society, and of the general basis of union among the different Christian denominations who co-operate in this labor of love; but of those conventional rules, and tacit understandings and agreements which must of necessity exist, and constitute a kind of common law upon the platform, and in the administration of this most catholic institution, defining the subjects and limiting the range of discussion, admonishing the practical advocate of the liberties, the reserves, and the delicacies of the partnership—of all these I am profoundly and unavoidably ignorant. With the most ardent wish to say nothing that will not promote harmony and brotherly love, I am liable to trespass upon feelings which I would sedulously guard, and awaken suspicions which I would gladly allay. Let me begin, sir, by an earnest disclaimer of every word, thought, and intent incompatible with the largest, warmest charity, and the most ardent desire to win for the principles embraced in my resolution the favor of those who hear me.

"Little as I have known of the history and transactions of this society, I well remember the strong sensation created by its organization and by some of its earlier anniversaries. They seemed for the time to have developed new elements of Christian union and sympathy. The spirit of love which glowed so intensely here in the center, warmed to the distant circumference, and even in the remote position which I then occupied many pious hearts beat high with new-born hopes of the speedy advent of charity and brotherly kindness. I think, however, that these delightful impulses declined in vigor and nearly ceased with the novelty of the enterprise. The catholic spirit soon became chilled by contact with the sectarian—was lost in the collision of antagonist interests. The religious press and the pulpit fell back upon their own ground, and gradually resumed their customary tone. Hence the ardent professions, the brotherly greetings, and high resolves of the platform fell into discredit as stereotyped declarations—as fit topics to adorn a speech or a report, but of no further application, and as even designed only to serve the occasion. I freely confess my own skepticism in the matter; and one of the first articles I ever wrote for the press was a hot denunciation of the measures and policy of a state Bible society, auxiliary to the American Bible Society. I still think there was something to complain of in the proceedings of that society; but I have never ceased to regret an error which finds only an adequate apology in my too little experience and too much sectarianism. After this confession, I may perhaps be allowed to say that I was an advocate, obscure and feeble certainly, but yet one of the earliest and most zealous advocates for the dissolution of the Methodist Bible Society, and for union with this noble institution, where I trust in God we shall continue to labor and rejoice in harmony with our sister churches so long as there is a family on the wide earth that wants a Bible.

"Twenty years of observation, sir, have produced in my mind a deliberate conviction that the sorest evil which presses upon the American churches—the chiefest obstacle to their real progress in holiness and in usefulness—is the spirit of sectarianism; and that most pressing want, for which, as lovers of souls and the Savior, we are called on to provide, is that of a more pervading and warmer charity. It is in this view of the subject, and from a painful sense of the obstacles which are as yet in the way of any direct attempt toward the removal of the evil, that I attach great importance even to the partial and transient influences exerted by this catholic institution. As there is no other common ground for the congress of liberal Christians, this should be the more highly prized—the more sedulously guarded—should, I think, be kept open at all hazards. We should thank God for a day, or an hour in the year, hallowed by the presence and predominance of larger views and holier aspirations. It is good to inhale a higher, purer atmosphere, neither agitated by the din of controversy nor tainted with the breath of bigotry. It is really inspiring—it gratifies our better nature to stand in a clear light, even if it must be only for a brief moment, where the veriest hack and drudge of polemics would be ashamed to be seen with the badge of sect—where the poorest tool and bondman of party may deny for once that he calls any man master. For myself, I should desire to build my tabernacle here, and remain forever.

"But our business should rather be to get from the occasion a profitable lesson. May we not diffuse this spirit more widely, and retain it longer? Good will be done by even transient impulses. It is well to see religion in its beauty, if only once in a life-time; it gives us the *beau ideal* of the Gospel, and pious hearts will sometimes reproduce it amid less congenial scenes, as the true genius is likely to become a better artist for having obtained a single view of the Apollo Belvidere or the Transfiguration.

"But may we not secure more decisive and permanent benefits? Can we obtain no useful hint for practical uses? Whence the delightful emotions awakened by this inspiring scene? We have consecrated two or three hours to a consultation on the best means of sending the Word of God to the nations of the earth. We have lifted up a banner upon which there is only one word written—the Bible—and so dazzling is the glory that surrounds the magic device, that the blindest zealot could not add to it the shibboleth of his sect without feeling some dread of having added to himself the plagues of the Apocalypse. Who reads our glorious motto to-day without feeling his bosom swell with hope, and faith, and heavenly charity? It is like the brazen serpent which Moses lifted up in the wilderness. It sends forth upon all who look upon it a joyous tide of spiritual health; and he must not only be bitten with sectarianism, but far gone in his malady, whose case does not yield to the sovereign antidote. Now, sir, if this good banner which floats over our heads only for a holiday exhibition has power to inspire the most timid with courage, and to stir the spirit of the bold like the sound of a trumpet, what might we not expect if it were adopted universally, or generally, by those who go forth to battle in the name of the Lord? What if we could agree to nail it to the mast, to sink or conquer under its protection? Or what if all the tribes of our Israel would covenant together to adopt it as the common standard? No matter who leads the van. Let the truest soldier of Christ be our captain, only let our common flag be the pledge of harmony and co-operation. Let not Ephraim vex Judah, nor Judah envy Ephraim. It need impair no man's privileges, nor trespass upon any body's rights. Each shall enter into his appointed inheritance in the land of promise. Levi may keep the priesthood, and Judah wield the scepter. Zebulon may still dwell at the haven of the sea, and Issachar shall bow down between his burdens.

"No doubt valuable progress has been made by all our evangelical sects. They all have orthodoxy and vital piety, but they mutually repel each other and the world by dubious or belligerent manifestations. Each has loyalty in its heart and on its banners, but nothing is distinctly visible to those without but a bristling array of guards, and sentinels, and spies, and marauders, who keep the outposts, throng all the approaches, and disturb the vicinage. Our churches have, in this respect, no little resemblance to many English country-seats, as seen over high walls and tangled hedges, by travelers on the top of a stage-coach. There are splendid mansions, venerable oaks, green lawns, exquisite shrubbery and flowers; while every tree, and gate-post, and angle is labeled with terrific announcements that if any man so much as set his foot within this enchanted inclosure—if from all this floral opulence he pluck so much as a blue violet, or inhale a breath amid this wasted fragrance, all the dread penalties of the law shall be wreaked upon him; and that, in the mean time, the premises are thick set with man-traps and spring-guns, ready to anticipate the tardy movements of justice.

"One is perpetually reminded by our preposterous contests of the ill-concocted coalitions formed by the powers of Europe, in their feeble attempts to make head against the hydra of the French Revolution in its earlier stages. No sooner had they concluded an alliance, which the diplomatists chose to call triple, or quadruple, or holy, as was best adapted to the case, and issued a pompous manifesto, full of brave resolves, and of unanimous, undying wrath against the common enemy, than they straightway fell into a quarrel about the division of the British subsidy, or the proper interpretation of the treaty, or about some question of kingly dignity. *Cœlum ruat*, the sky might fall, but Austria would not abate a jot from her high hereditary claims as head of the empire, and regular successor to the powers of Charlemagne. Prussia was a young kingdom, but could afford to be arrogant on the score of her more efficient and adapted institutions, and her military reputation won by the great Frederic, and often at the expense of the proud Hapsburg. The smaller princes, meantime, had their own special interests and most sacred honors to take care of, and would by no means march against the French until they had clearly settled the order of precedence at a review or presentation day, and made all sure against irreverent omissions and curtailments in the matter of their very prolix, inharmonious titles. These were controversies not to be easily adjusted, and the parties litigant could seldom agree in any thing but contempt for the semi-barbarous Russians, who had scarcely exchanged their sheep-skin coats for regimentals, but always had a full share of the fighting to do. While the halting potentates were thus absorbed with the care of minor and selfish interests, the great captain, after a few weeks of noiseless preparation, bade his legions move from a hundred points, and with a precision and terrible efficiency, which his genius knew so well how to educe from harmonious counsels and central power, poured the tide of war upon their disturbed camp, annihilating at a stroke the threatening league, in which scores of princes and crowned heads had conspired his overthrow. History teaches us, in some of its most impressive lessons, that it was not till the sovereigns of Europe had been shamefully and repeatedly defeated, and had lost their capitals and their crowns, or held them by the sufferance of the conqueror, that they consented to learn the obvious truth which finally achieved for them a glorious deliverance.

"It may be, sir, that I over-estimate the mischief and the danger of our present position, but I reluctantly entertain the sentiment I have already expressed, that our divisions, jealousies, and rivalries constitute at this moment the greatest evil that afflicts the Church, and the greatest hinderance to the triumphs of the Gospel at home and abroad. The energies which ought to be consecrated to the world's salvation are exhausted on unworthy objects. The religious sentiment, which is more active and pervading than at any former period in the history of American Christianity, is lavished on trivial controversies, or frittered away in the vindication of petty claims and the conservation of petty interests. It has pleased God to lead us on to a crisis which, more than any that has occurred since the Savior's advent, demands the entire consecration of every church and every Christian to the holy work of carrying out his benevolent designs. By agencies which are only the more clearly divine because no man has been able to discern their source or progress, a thousand bolted doors are suddenly thrown open before us, and broad entrance proffered to the Gospel in every nation under heaven. Which of all our churches is ready to go forth to do the bidding of its Master? Which has not its heart and its hands already filled with domestic or neighborhood difficulties? Which is prepared to render a tithe of gratitude and duty to Christ? Who has a response for the Macedonian cry that comes on all the winds of heaven like peals of distant thunder? Who is ready-armed to rush over the Chinese wall, which has fallen down flat on the earth by an act of God, without so much as the blast of a ram's horn? These doubtless are serious questions, and they must have a serious answer, if not before, when inquisition shall be made for blood, and talents misimproved shall be found written in the same book with the deeds of positive enmity and open rebellion.

"But, sir, I am asked what all of this has to do with the Bible Society? I am entreated to point out the latent affinities which bring such topics into some reasonable alliance and propinquity with the proper business of this occasion. I rely for justification, sir, upon the nature of my subject and the goodness of my object. So manifold are its relations to all that is dear in our own most precious enjoyments and hopes, so urgent its claims on the Christian's heart and conscience, that it may well demand audience on all occasions. The grievous evils of sectarianism might well form the peroration, if not the theme, of all harangues. 'Delenda est Carthago' were a graceful conclusion of every discourse which is concerned for the progress of piety and the honor of the Redeemer. The interest which I advocate before men of all parties is a common interest, and not that of a clique or a corner. I stand, too, on high ground, where a feeble voice is likely to be heard by many, and may awaken some faint echoes. It is also neutral ground, and adapted, on that account, to protocols and overtures. But beyond all these considerations, and yet more to the point, the cause of Christian charity is identical with that of the Bible Society, and its wider diffusion must, to the same extent, open new fields of action and triumph for this noble institution, and produce new resources for the prosecution of its objects. I go farther, and freely declare, that the Bible Society is capable of achieving vastly more than it has yet done for this great melioration, and that to it we must chiefly look for all future progress. I believe it possesses elements and adaptations for doing good as yet in embryo, or but partially and indirectly developed. I know not who may agree with me in the sentiment, but I ascribe nearly all the improvements which, within these latter years, have beautified and enlarged the churches, to the benign influence of the Bible Society. True, the symptoms of better things had begun to appear before its institution, and it may be even true that it had its origin in the wants brought to light by the missionary movement. But if there were omens of good already, nothing efficient was done; little was attempted until the great work of giving God's Word to all the nations of the earth was fairly entered upon by the churches. It was a heaven-born idea, that of unchaining the Bible, and carrying it boldly up to every man's door and every man's conscience, and bidding him, as God bids him, read and judge, and abide the responsibility for himself. It was, perhaps, to be expected, that He who permits no duty to go unrewarded, should crown this high act of loyalty and faith with special tokens of his favor and approbation. And so it was, that as soon as the eyes of millions were turned with reverent and earnest gaze upon the revealed Word, light and grace were given them to 'read wondrous things out of God's law.' Great truths, that had lain unheeded and unseen ever since the day of Pentecost, suddenly blazed forth from the illuminated page. The unsealed book poured forth oracles upon the wondering ear of the rejoicing churches, and they started into action from their dream of ages. Then it was that they gathered the children of rich and poor into Sabbath schools, and called lisping infancy to the task of solving mysteries which had long proved an overmatch for giants of intellect and erudition. Then it was that they first mastered the import of that great saying of Jesus Christ, 'The field is the world.' We have all since written new articles in our creed, and we have all wondered, and we still wonder, that doctrines and duties, so plainly revealed and so often read, should have eluded our spiritual perception so perfectly that the wisest and the best among us hardly guessed at their existence. Henceforth, to the consummation of all things, the cause of missions, of Sunday schools, of the Bible, will be taken and deemed to be the cause of Christ, and respected accordingly by all who truly love him ; for the diffusion of Bibles at once insures progress and guarantees the permanence of all religious improvement. That most kind-hearted school of philosophers, which teaches the perfectibility of man and society, affirms that there can be no more decline in knowledge and the arts, now that the reproducing energies of the press can counterwork the devastations of a thousand Omars and the conflagration of a thousand Alexandrian libraries. So, thanks to the Bible Society, and to God's blessing upon it, we may confidently hope it will be with the progress of religious truth. The Gospel has appealed from councils to Sabbath schools. Its divine treasures of truth and life are committed to an innumerable company, each of whom shall stand up its faithful witness. We shall have no more dark ages in religion. What we get we shall keep, the best encouragement to get all we can.

"Now, sir, the Bible Society, which has done so much for us, can do a great deal more. Of the new truths and duties which it has developed, all are catholic and common to all the churches—not one is sectarian. It has thus evolved the nucleus of a universal creed, and developed a hint for its completion. We adopt reforms and religious improvements because God acknowledges them in his Word and providence. Suppose we should carry out this principle over the whole field of our practical theology. There are a few Gospel truths which, wherever they are faithfully inculcated, result in the production of evangelical piety, and without which, whatever else is taught, souls are not converted and sanctified. Justification by faith—redemption by the blood of Christ—sanctification by the Holy Spirit—these are the doctrines that save, that God owns and honors. They are the heroic remedies of the Gospel pharmacopœia, sufficient, and alone sufficient for the soul's maladies. And, thank God, they are the doctrines, by eminence, of all our evangelical churches. Go where you will, in town or country, in log meeting-houses or Gothic cathedrals, be the sermons or prayers read or extemporized, if the preacher be pious and faithful, no matter what his sect, his learning, or the grasp of his intellect, you shall listen to the same doctrines, a little diversified, it may be, in theological technology ; a little alloyed, it may be, by peculiarities of system ; but always, if there be no blinding influence present, nothing to be lost or won by proselytism, substantially the same doctrines, 'repentance toward God, and faith toward our Lord Jesus Christ.' Sir, I have wandered much in the length and breadth of this land, and heard men of all names and all varieties of education and intellect, and this is my testimony: Substantially, and in the main, they are one in faith. The few months which I was permitted to spend in the ministry in early life were much devoted to an immense congregation of slaves. I mingled freely in their religious meetings and exercises, and even they were one with the Church catholic in all the truths of the cross. Sad work they made of tropes and figures; reckless they were of the graces and artistic unities of discourse; but in all the matters of sore repentance of sin, and humble confession, and child-like faith in Jesus's blood, I never knew their betters. Sir, I have indicated a basis of union. These fundamental truths, without which all others are nothing worth, and with which no others can be essentially pernicious, these may be a creed for our charity—at least, they may be adopted as articles of peace.

"These are terms on which, as it seems to me, right-minded Christians may harmonize and co-operate, may live and love, without compromising any principle truly Christian, without damage to any interests worth preserving. They are not justly liable to the charge of latitudinarianism, for they are not proposed as the full expression of our faith, but only as a guide to our charity. Make as stringent as you please both the creed and the code by which a man is to measure his own conformity with the Divine mind and the Divine law, but do not demand of your neighbor that he follow with you, as well as cast out devils, as a condition of favor or fellowship. It is only in the light of this distinction that the stereotyped arguments about the infinite importance of keeping clear of even the smallest errors, and of embracing every Christian dogma in every body's mouth, are either true or tolerable. They teach sound doctrine in reference to my own obligation to study diligently, and embrace cordially, every word that proceedeth out of the mouth of God, but the essence of all uncharitableness and heterodoxy if intended to put a limitation upon my love and confidence toward my neighbor, the only purpose for which these stale commonplaces of sectarian bigotry are commonly used. I do not remember, for I was yet a child when I began to listen to them, but the memory of every one has store of such aphorisms. The sentiment often finds utterance in the form of a metaphysical abstraction, and affirms that in the matter of religion, itself the expression of the infinite Mind, the smallest truth is unspeakably important, and every mistake fearfully dangerous. It often bends and perverts the Word of God to its purpose, and argues, that if a beam completely darken the eye, a mote, also, is unfavorable to clear vision; that while none but madmen would essay to swallow a camel, a great philosopher may be choked by attempting to swallow a gnat. Men who aspire to logical precision in this matter affect scientific illustrations, and admonish us that 'the slightest divergence from a right line tends always to a perpetual and infinite departure;' as if the Divine operations obeyed mathematical laws; as if the compassions of Christ were not always looking after the lost, and bringing back the wanderer; as if the greatest miracles of grace were not often wrought in the heart while the head is far from having attained to completeness of orthodoxy. The captious polemic who, instead of rejoicing in the great truths of the Gospel, spends his days and sharpens his vision in microscopic observations on the small ones—who sees specks of war in the clearest sky, and reckons himself as good as idle when not plying his weapons, frequently and appropriately borrows his illustration from military tactics. He is guarding and defending the outworks of Christianity; an ingenious expedient, by which the citadel is not only kept from the danger, but from all the noise and dust of the fray—a figure of speech which goes the length of teaching this sage maxim in the science of war, that a good general who had the defense of New York committed to him, would not think much of manning the Narrows and filling the city with brave soldiers, but should take special care to have a squadron of gun-boats cruising off Key West, and keep up a furious cannonade on Cape Cod.

"But, sir, if under the auspices of the Bible and the Bible Society we may hope to find favor for these few and simple articles proposed for the furtherance of our charity and usefulness, it is interesting to inquire into what company they may bring us, with whom they are likely to ally us in fellowship and co-operation. It is obvious that the basis proposed is not wide enough to comprehend all. It is a Protestant basis. The Bible is to be the sole bond of union, and they who do not bow to it as the one and sole law for faith and virtue, probably will not desire more intimate relations with those between whom and themselves there exist differences so fundamental and irreconcilable.

"I say it, without the remotest wish to reflect upon any party, or to canvass their pretensions, that I do not see how men who believe that God has made the efficacy of the Gospel dependent on certain forms or prescribed channels of communications, can abate any thing from their sternest demand for strict conformity with their own views. If certain men are endowed with power or authority, in virtue of which the sacraments, in their hands, become the true and proper sacrifice for sin, and the appointed media for imparting pardon and holiness, then there is an end of all concession, and the want to be satisfied is that of absolute unity, and not of union. The only proper question is, Are we convinced by their arguments? If so, we may pass over to them, but on no terms can they pass over to us. As Protestants, we have answered that question already, and taken an appeal from traditions and hierarchies to the Word and the Spirit of God.

"I am equally unable to perceive any proper ground of union and co-operation between the evangelical sects and those who only recognize in the Gospel a pure system of morals, but deny its Divine transforming power. Such sects profit by strifes and divisions. They have no desire for union, and no need of it. Neither their creed nor their objects have any sympathies with the great reason that exists for union and charity among other denominations.

"That reason results and derives its chief importance and force from the spiritual character of the Christian dispensation. It has pleased God, in the plenitude of his wisdom and sovereignty, that the Holy Ghost should be the great and sole-sufficient agent in the saving operations of the Gospel, the Divine instrument on which all other instrumentalities do wholly and absolutely depend for success. This is a dogma which we are wont to acknowledge as a truth, and reverence as a mystery; but the time has come when we are called upon more fully to recognize it, and give to it wider scope, as a fact, as the great fact of practical Christianity. To this fundamental principle all our plans and arrangements must be accommodated, or they will prove powerless. Now we know well from God's Word, and from the well-observed phenomena of universal Christian experience, that all the sentiments, and tempers, and tendencies of sectarianism are the direct and proper antagonists of the great Sanctifier. They grieve and quench the Holy Spirit, and ultimately drive him away from the heart and the Church. This is the great evil produced by our unhallowed contests, in comparison with which all others are unworthy to be mentioned. It is, indeed, a sad thing to think of the vast amount of talent, and influence, and piety neutralized and lost to the common cause in our mutual contests and rivalries. It is heart-rending to look upon the hosts of sheer party-men who hang upon the skirts of all the churches—Presbyterians, or Churchmen, or Methodists—ever more interested in a controversy than in a revival—lovers of sect more than of the Savior—ready to follow any leader who will blow a trumpet and assume the offensive. These are the legitimate and bitter fruits of our strifes, but infinitely greater and more baleful are the latent influences, visible to none but God, and of which none but the Omniscient mind can gauge the magnitude of their mischief. The bitterness, the wrath, the resentments, the jealousies, the heart-burnings provoked by our controversies, are taken up into the general spirit of the Church, to poison the fountain of its joys and clip the wings of its faith. There are ministers—pious men, no doubt—in all our churches and sects, who infuse enough of the sectarian temper into their public teachings to keep down the tone of religion, and put to shame the spirit of charity around them. There are religious papers that from week to week send forth by tens of thousands their flying scrolls, each rife with the malignant elements of bigotry and wrath. A jest, a sneer, a biting sarcasm, perpetrated at the expense of charity, has awakened contempt for another denomination, or resentment for an insult offered his own, in the reader's heart, and ten thousand Christians come to the throne of grace with enfeebled energies and a wounded spirit. The agony of desire and the wrestling of faith are no more, and no fire falls from heaven to consume their offering. I sometimes almost doubt, after the contemplation of such evils, whether the religious periodical press be indeed, and upon the whole, a blessing to the Church, and whether any great progress can be expected in catholic charity and true piety under its auspices. Certain it is that this one instrument has transformed sectarian bigotry into a monster of such huge proportions, that while he pollutes the waters of the Atlantic with the tread of his feet, he can stretch out his long arm above the Alleganies, and drop poison into the sources of the Missouri.

"Still more injurious are the influences of the sectarian spirit upon the missionary enterprise, which is, indeed, but an expression of the abounding and overflowing piety of the churches. The malign agency is felt at home in neutralizing or diverting from Christian to party objects the intellectual and spiritual energies, by the right use of which it is God's will that the world should be converted; and on more than one foreign field has the ripening harvest, the growth of years of toil, and sacrifices, and tears, and prayers, been well-nigh blighted by its unholy interference. I know American missionaries, and I believe them to be among the holiest men of the age; yet they are but men, and their piety must partake of the character of that of the churches at home. The churches, in their present state, would not, probably, send them out without a pledge, tacit or avowed, that they should represent the peculiarities and prejudices which constitute our denominational badges and our themes of controversy. Sir, our missionary Christianity must be recalled, and remanded to Sabbath-school, and taught new lessons of brotherly love and catholic charity before it will prove equal to the conversion of the world.

"Allow me, sir, in conclusion, to say, that so far as the denomination which I have the honor to represent here to-day is concerned, I believe there is an observable advancement in the great melioration which I have attempted to advocate. A Methodist, sir, if a bigot at all, is one for pure love of the thing. It must be with him a sheer amateur business. I thank God, sir, we have no *essential* peculiarities. What we hold to be vital and most precious in religion, we hold in common with our brethren of other names. We hold nothing, we want nothing which ought to shut them out from our charities, nor, as we verily believe, which should exclude us from theirs. Do they prefer an episcopal organization and government? Every body knows we have no objection to that. Do they more rejoice in presbytery? We claim no higher office or dignity. Are they congregational? We would that all God's people were prophets. Do they use forms of prayer? We often do the same. Do they extemporize their devotions? Our common practice shows that we think this a no less excellent way. Do they use much or little water in baptism? So the Spirit preside over the sacrament—so the blessed auspices of Father, Son, and Holy Ghost be conciliated, it is all one to us whether the baptismal font be the ocean or a goblet.

"Sir, I am a sincere Methodist, and might be found ready, if there were occasion for it, to vindicate the doctrines or usages of my church; but, I repeat it, I know of nothing in either incompatible with the largest charity, and the most cordial co-operation with all who truly love the common Savior.

Inspiration of the Scriptures and their Sufficiency as a Rule of Faith. By the Rev. H. V. D. Johns, D.D.

Mr. Johns said "that the Council of Trent, at one of its sessions, declared that the traditions of the Romish Church as to ancient matters of faith and discipline were to be received with equal reverence as the sacred Scriptures, and that he who despised them should be accursed. A popish bishop is reported to have once said that they must bid farewell forever to the Scriptures; that they must no longer rest their faith upon the beggarly elements of inspiration, as they could then 'hear God speak'—presumed to mean thereby the pope. And Paul the Fifth, in a commentary upon one of the works of Fulgentius, says that 'this author stands too much upon the inspired Scriptures, which, if it be generally done, *will certainly ruin the Catholic faith;*' a remark so true, that if all in the books that have emanated from the Vatican were of equal validity, there would be much less reason to regret the vast volumes that have proceeded from that source.

"The sixth article of the Creed of the Church of England very correctly represents the opinions of the Protestant world concerning the Bible. There are two propositions, which, if clearly established, sufficiently vindicate the high claims of the Word of God as they are there set forth:

"1. The first is, that the inspired Volume—the Volume which professes to be the foundation of our faith—is genuine, authentic, and inspired; and that it is the only book which has ever been proved to be thus related to God above.

"2. The second is, that the Volume of our faith contains ample directions for our faith and practice, and claims to be a competent guide to everlasting salvation.

"These two propositions indicate the basis on which the language of the Church of England rests, and present the strength of their position in reply to the papal Church. It is not possible, within the limits of a discourse like the present, even if it properly belonged to the occasion, to enter upon the argument by which the first of these propositions is established. So abundantly has it been defended that it may now be deemed impregnable. It is beyond the reach of victorious assault. Nor is it necessary to go over the ground of this discussion. A bare reference to a few of the passages in the inspired Volume in which its claims are thus set forth will be all that can be attempted." Mr. Johns then referred to passages in St. Peter's Epistles, and in the writings of St. Paul, wherein the Scriptures are distinctly spoken of as the inspired oracles of God. "Luke gives us the reason for writing his epistle to Theophilus, that he might certainly know the things that had taken place. And to crown the whole, the Author of our salvation himself distinctly tells us to 'search the Scriptures, for in them ye think ye have the words of eternal life; and they are they which testify of me.' If these things could be said of the contents of the Old Testament, how much more true are they of the same blessed book when its pages have been still farther illumined by the light that shines upon them from the New?

"The supremacy of the pope impugns the supremacy of Christ. The charge that the Scriptures are insufficient for salvation impugns the truth of God. The allegation that the services of a priest are essential, affirms that the atonement of Christ is incomplete. These are three great errors worthy to rest on the triple crown of his holiness the pope. To deny these truths is to insult the blessed Trinity—the Father, Son, and Holy Ghost. The man who in our day denies the sufficiency of Revelation, seems to me to approach as nearly as is possible to the commission of the sin against the Holy Ghost. So stands the argument of the resolution I have presented.

"But the practical bearing of this doctrine is of high importance, and its results are in the keeping of history. The universal distribution of the Word of God sprung up as the natural child of the Reformation. And it is this, and this alone, which has given such extension and efficiency to the missionary operations of the day. It is this which has proved so powerful in resisting oppression, and in effecting the deliverance of the enslaved nations of the earth. It is this free and wide extension of the Word of God which has so diffused the blessings of education, and is carrying light and truth into the darkest corners of the world. The effects of the general study of the Bible may be clearly traced in history. We point to Ireland, and to Spain, and to South America, and ask you to contrast the condition of these Catholic lands with the Protestant nations of Great Britain, with those counties of Ireland where the Bible has been read, and with the whole continent of North America. Why are the people of Great Britain so bold and free in spirit, so vigorous in action, and so great in all they do? And why are their Anglo-American descendants still more bold, and elastic, and free than they? It is because those lands which rest beneath the shadow of the papal power have never been allowed this food for the immortal mind which our very nature craves, and which all the legends of saints or the mummeries of priests can never supply. Those lands, instead of Christ crucified, have given to them the crucifix; instead of God's Word, they have the everlasting sound of matins and the tinkling of the vesper bell. In Mexico every sixth man is said to be a mendicant or a robber. Shall this ever be the case with this our beloved land? Let the advocates of tradition put in their wedge here, and there may be ground for the apprehension. But so long as we keep our hold upon the Volume of our faith, and trust to it as the one great ennobling principle of practice and of faith, so long will the life-blood flow clearly and the pulsation beat high and strong through the heart of the American people."

The Importance of the "Written" Word. By the Rev. George B. Cheever, D.D.

Mr. Cheever commenced with a quotation from Bishop Hooper. "'I had rather follow the shadow of Christ,' said the noble reformer and martyr, Bishop Hooper, 'than the bodies of all the general councils or doctors since the death of Christ. It is mine opinion unto all the world, that the Scripture solely, and the apostles' church, is to be followed, and no man's authority, be he Augustine or Tertullian, Cherubim or Seraphim.' This is noble. What heart that loves the Bible does not respond to these noble sentiments? How admirably do they coincide with that beautiful image used by the apostle Peter, 'As new-born babes, desire the sincere milk of the Word, that ye may grow thereby.' Let the church of Christ be as an infant. How it clings to its mother's bosom! How it turns to the heart for nourishment! You can not allure it away by temptation. Let the Church come to the Word of God as a babe to its mother's milk. Is there aught else for it to feed upon? Will the crusts of philosophy, the miter, the book of discipline, the apostolical succession, the holy water, the sign of the cross, extreme unction, or a grand cathedral, nourish it? Will these things bring back a lost world from the death of sin to the life of holiness in Christ?

"The Bible Society seeks to make us all children. This is delightful; children in malice, children in our pure relish for the Word of God; but, for that very reason, in understanding, men! It carries us back to our mother's milk. This is blessed; for it sometimes seems as if the Church were wandering farther and farther from God's Word, from its purity, its simplicity, its experience. How do we need to be brought back to its homely but divine relish! The Romish Church, and they who symbolize and sympathize with her, will tell us that we need to be brought back to mother church; but this is not it. Our mother church herself, and we ourselves as a part of mother church, need to be brought back to God's Word. The discipline of severity and power which God made Luther and Bunyan pass through, beneath the fires of his Word, the Church needs collectively, and we individually; for of the Word of God, as a fire and a hammer, burning and beating in our hearts, we know little; and if we know little, the world knows less. Alas! we have used the Word of God rather as an external lamp than an inward fountain; and hence, amid great enterprise, our spiritual weakness and poverty, our mountains of speculation, but grains of experience.

"The Oriental churches, to which this resolution refers us, read as a solemn lesson. Would that God would make this country lay it to heart, amid the tide of Romanism that sweeps so harmoniously with our native inward current and disease of formalism. There was a time when these churches were seven golden candlesticks, and one like unto the Son of man walked in the midst of them, the seven stars in his right hand, his eyes as a flame of fire, his voice as the sound of many waters. The stars are fallen, the fire is gone out, the voice is hushed, the glory has departed, and darkness has settled down over some of the loveliest, the most Eden-like of earth's regions.

"Now, the history of this ruin is the history of the neglect of God's Word, and of the melancholy change of the ministry of Jesus Christ from a ministry of the bread of life into a ministry of forms, ordinances, gorgeous rituals, self-aggrandizement, and hierarchical splendor, power, unity, despotism. This was the fall of the Church spiritually, this exaltation of the idolatry of formalism. It began with the concealment and withdrawal of the Word of God out of notice. When the apostles died, the voice of living prophets having ceased, then began men to abandon the Word of God and worship tradition. Then they perverted the ministry of the Word into a priesthood of ordinances. Then the great sower of tares bestrode the field, and scattered his devilish seed broadcast. One superstition after another was adopted, till the very germs of truth seemed to have died out of existence. The seed sown shot up into a great harvest of heresies. In the absence of the Word of God, these grew from green blades and leaves into strong, overshadowing black oaks; and the world, like swine in autumn, were driven by the priests into the wilderness, to fatten on the acorns. For ages you could hear nothing in the world but the champing of swine in the wilderness of Romanism. Those nuts contained every thing but the sincere milk of the Word. Paul has given us their contents beforehand; the meat of 'philosophy, vain traditions, rudiments of the Word, ordinances, voluntary humilities, worshiping of angels, vain deceits, strong delusions, profane and old wives' fables, lies in hypocrisy, seducing spirits, doctrines of devils, questions and strifes of words.' There were Aristotle and Plato, and Abelard and Thomas Aquinas, and all the bitter, thorny, astringent fruits of the scholastic philosophy and learning of the Dark and Middle Ages, but neither Paul, nor Peter, nor John. There were Peter's keys and Peter's sword, but not Peter's epistles. Sword and keys mankind had in plenty to feed upon, and their teeth were ground to powder in the mastication; but Peter's 'sincere milk of the Word,' the priests would none of it themselves, and they kept it from the people.

"Now, what were some of the consequences by which we may take warning? for even with the Word of God in our hands, if we too neglect it, or overlay it with forms, or suffer it to be brought in bondage, there will be the same evils. Churches without Christians; the form of godliness without the power; the education, religion, and welfare of the people neglected; great hierarchies in which all evil passions, that out of the Church raged under their own names, in the Church were baptized into Christ's name. The ordinances of religion were turned into slavish and idolatrous superstitions, or made a set of sable chalices, in which an ungodly priesthood might administer to the people the anodyne of a deadly religious ignorance and insensibility. The Word of God was as if dead and buried, and its place supplied by the resurrection of a gilded, rotten Judaism and paganism. If, here and there, amid all this, solitary men lived, like Anselmo or Bernard, in an atmosphere of religious truth, these were like sepulchral lamps supplied with oil by stealth, and shining within damp walls upon dead men's bones and all uncleanness. D'Israeli, a man who will not be suspected of religious bigotry or uncharitableness, he even hazarded the assertion that it may be doubted if, in the time of the crusades, there was a single Christian in all Christendom.

"Now the cause of all this was the concealment of God's Word, and the despotism of a priesthood of ordinances. In the midst of all this the Reformation broke upon the world. It was simply the resuscitation, the reappearance of the Scriptures, and the change from a priesthood of ordinances into the ministry of God's Word. This is precisely what is needed now in those Oriental churches contemplated in this resolution. This is what is needed to make a second reformation from popery in lands where the light of the first reformation either did not penetrate, or was early extinguished. In regard to the Greek and Romish churches, I can speak from personal observation, having traveled in the midst of them, and witnessed their superstitions, from the extreme of the splendor and wealth of some, to the extreme of ignorance, poverty, and degradation. Almost every where there is profound ignorance of the Word of God; and, what is worse, a deep hostility against it. The system of Romanism especially is characterized by this the world over; and if it looks otherwise here or in England, it is only because of its proximity to Protestantism, and because it has to respect Protestant public opinion. In some respects, however, it does not even look different here. The burning of two hundred Bibles in New York tells the same story as an auto da fé of the Scriptures tells in Spain or in Asia Minor.

"Look into Borrow's Bible in Spain, a remarkable book, which indeed about every body has read, and you may learn how Romanism in 1838 hates the Word of God, even though the people would be glad tc get it. That resolute individual was imprisoned, was threatened with death, and the prime minister of Spain himself told him distinctly that the Church forbade the circulation of the Scriptures. I happened to be in Spain during some of those years in which Mr. Borrow was prosecuting his work, and from some little experience of my own in distributing the Bible, I know the truth of his descriptions. The priests preached against us in the Cathedral; one of the few sermons of the year was almost wholly given to this denunciation. They called us *Satanistas*, or the devil's emissaries. And yet these same priests, some of them, had the Word of God themselves. In the cell of one of them, who invited me to visit him, I found a magnificent edition of the Bible in Spanish, in huge folio volumes, with a grand commentary. I suppose we might have carried a shipload of these ponderous tomes into the country, and never a priest would have disturbed us; for what can the people do with such books? But when it comes to an edition of the Scriptures which the people can purchase and peruse, when the living Word without note or comment is offered to them, when its speaking fountains are set flowing and brought to every man's thirsty lips, then they cry Satanistas! Ave Marie! Satanistas! To the dungeon with him!

"So profound is the horror and aversion of the Word of God sometimes inspired among the people by these means, that the ordinary perusal of the Scriptures comes to be regarded absolutely as an act of impiety! In fact, it is only in Protestant countries that the Romanist ever pretended to put the Bible in the hands of the people; and whenever they have done it, they have taken care so to muzzle it that it may not speak against their system. Like soldiers compelled to abandon a citadel, they spike the guns before leaving them.

"When they can not keep the Bible from the people, they mingle its fountains with such ingredients that their own purposes are accomplished better than if the poison were administered by itself. The poison comes in the shape of a medicine, and the true medicine is effectually neutralized by poison.

"When I was a boy, and would eat fruit, my playmates used to tell me that if I swallowed the stones with my cherries they would not hurt me. The Romish Church acts upon this principle, and gives its children stones to swallow with the cherries, to keep the fruit of Divine truth from hurting the people. Turn to the 21st verse of the 11th chapter of the Epistle to the Hebrews, and read in their version how the holy patriarch Jacob, when he was dying, worshiped—the top of his staff! and there read a justification of all the idolatrous usages of the Church of Rome in the worship of images. This is one of the ingredients of deadly poison to the soul mingled with the fountains of Divine truth.

"Our blessed Lord once asked the Jews, 'If a son shall ask bread of any of you that is a father, will he give him a stone? Or if he ask a fish, will he for a fish give him a serpent? Or if he shall ask an egg, will he offer him a scorpion?' Yes! you see that this is possible; it is really practiced, this fearful cruelty; it is done systematically, done on principle, done even in regard to the life of the soul! I have only pointed out to you one of those serpents given instead of bread; the scorpion of idolatry, coiled in one of those eggs, and given to the people in a text of Scripture! In reference to such tampering with the Word of God, and such preaching, and such traditions, it may be said, in the language of one of the old prophets, that 'he that eateth of their eggs dieth, and that which is crushed breaketh out into a viper.'

"I might pursue this train of thought much more minutely, into the consideration of the Sabbath and the atonement turned into sin, superstition, and idolatry, by this same enshrinement and adoration of form and ordinance, to the exclusion of the written Word. What, let me ask, are the two grand sources of our education in religion, liberty, and happiness?

"The Word of God is the first; the spiritual and intellectual preaching of Divine truth on the Sabbath is the second. The spirit of Romanism would take them both away. In the absence of these two things, and the substitution of the despotism of a priesthood of ordinances, is to be read the history of almost all past evil in the Christian world. Take, then, your Bibles from your schools, erase their peculiar truths from your school-books, and let a priesthood of ceremonies and sacraments take place of the ministry, and the ruin of our country's religion and liberty is sure. The grand conflict in this country is to be for the supremacy of God's Word ; a conflict between faith and form ; between justification by faith and justification by ordinances. All external forms ought to proceed from an inward life, fed by the Word of God, or they are worthless.

"They must be the natural force, the springing vitality of God's Word in us, jutting from our hearts like a water-fountain, that, because it has run all the way under ground, springs into the air in beauty. Your magnificent fountains in your parks would cease to play, and would leave nothing but the marble fixtures, though they had the whole Croton River to play from, if you did not confine the water in an interior circulation. Just so our religious forms, if they be not the natural force of Divine truth that has circulated in the arteries of our spiritual being, are ready to become the miserable forms of idolatry. All flesh, saith Peter, is as grass, and the glory thereof as the flower of the grass. The grass withereth, and the flower thereof falleth away, but THE WORD OF THE LORD ENDURETH FOREVER. And this is that Word, which by the Bible Society is presented unto the world."

The Universal Adaptation of the Scriptures. By the Rev. Dr. Pierce, of Georgia.

"If," said Mr. Pierce, "the universal success of the Bible cause, the realization of the most sanguine wish of the most devoted adherent, depended upon the establishment of this truth, we might consume the hours of this anniversary in congratulatory addresses, and antedate the joys of a victory wide as the world, and stable as the pillars of heaven. If the propriety of the sentiment, the conviction of its justice and truth, were the pledge of a zeal as unwearied as its importance demands, and of an enterprise commensurate with its value, then, sir, you would have nothing now to do but to regulate your appropriations and direct your future movements. But, sir, human nature is made up of such contradictory impulses, that conscience is sometimes powerless where truth is clear, and the purest minds must needs be stirred by way of remembrance."

Mr. P. then proceeded to comment upon the following points: "That the Bible, after prolonged research, has been admitted to be divine by the consent of the master-minds of every age. Though the oldest book in the world, it is still ever new ; its leaves never wither, and its beauties never fail. In the palmiest days of persecution, when the spirit of despotism was abroad, and the leaves of truth were mutilated by the frauds of the impostor, even then it might be said of it as was said of the ruler's daughter, 'It is not dead, but sleepeth.'

"This element of perpetuity is proof not only of its truth, but of its wonderful adaptation to the wants and woes of human life. Though stretching, as it does, over a thousand years, and composed by men of various mental complexion, under as various circumstances, it is still the perfect realization of the idea of one mind. The dark gulf of futurity, over which poetry and philosophy hang with wearied wing, is lighted up by its rays; it attracts by no ingenious subtlety of argument, but all its teachings are perspicuous and popular. Lucid in its enunciation, the points of faith on which hang our hopes of heaven are covered with a flood of light. Through its columns the most gifted intellect may roam with profit, and before its revelation human reason stands rebuked, unable, perhaps, to believe, and afraid to doubt; and at the end of its pilgrimage, after the measure by which it shall test its own rectitude and consciousness, when that reason stands in doubt and despair, the great Teacher comes with the rule, 'If any man do my will, he shall know of the doctrine whether it be of God, or whether I speak of myself.'

"The Bible deals not in subtle analogies and cold abstractions, but in the healthful virtues of life; it comes home to the heart, and makes its truths the subject of consciousness, whereby we exclaim, 'That which was from the beginning, which we have heard, which we have seen with our eyes, which we have looked upon, and our hands have handled, of the Word of Life.' It commends itself to every man's conscience in the sight of God by the excellence of its law and the conclusiveness of its testimony, so that even human depravity, when it walks amid its precepts, is compelled, like the devils among the tombs, to acknowledge the purity of its morals and the holiness of its presence. The genealogy of its proof demonstrates it to be the same yesterday, to-day, and forever; the faith that justified righteous Abel, and whereby Enoch walked with God; the faith by which Abraham kept the covenant, the importunity by which Moses prevailed, and the penitential sighs of David, still attract the notice of heaven, and call down the blessing of God; the baptism of the Spirit still attends on the ministration of the Word; and though no cloven tongues of fire flame from the lips of proselytes, the heart still palpitates beneath the warm breathings of the Holy Ghost, before whose stately steppings the human reason falls in reverence, and the human fancy cowers in astonishment.

"In every age there have been men who have set themselves forth as teachers of wisdom, but they have divided their doctrines into parts for the schools and parts for the people, and imparted them to a company of select friends or pupils, whom they regarded, and who regarded themselves, as a privileged order. Occasionally these instructors may have done more; and for the sake of winning the temporary admiration of a fickle crowd, may have enhanced their reputation and deepened their sacred reverence by obscure enunciations of awful mysteries—enunciations which were calculated rather to stupefy the soul than to make the reason dawn. Disdainful distributers of what she fondly called the first elements of religion, Philosophy kindled her dim fires upon the peaks of human science, and left man covered with mist and darkness in the vales below. All other systems than this of the Bible have been founded on misconceptions of the wants of man, enriching time by despoiling eternity; they appeal to human reason, and exhibit, even when the majesty of mind is associated with them, an intellectual glory that stuns rather than instructs, and elicits an admiring wonder rather than the consent of the heart. But the Bible is adapted to all classes, ends, and states of men; and where it fails to save, it never fails to refine: the conviction of its truth is sustained by what man feels within him and sees without him; and however invisible its operations, and however difficult to trace its effects to their source, it still operates slowly and surely, and builds the monuments of its divinity by the moral changes it creates. Whatever skepticism may insinuate of its improbability, whatever malignity may coin of its worthless tendency, it is still the rejoicing of us all that the leaven is in the meal, and will surely penetrate the whole lump—that the mustard seed, the smallest of all seeds, is in the soil, and will shoot forth its trunk and its branches, and cover itself with foliage, in which the birds may nestle and take repose from the heat of the day. For the divinity of the record, for the truth of its testimony, for the defense of our calling, and the justification of our ministrations, we rely singly and solely upon the inherent energies of God in the book.

"There may be nothing in the operations of the Bible to attract the notice of the great world; but simplicity is nature's great law. The cloud that passes along without the pomp of thunder or lightning, pours from its generous bosom the gentle rain to gladden the earth, and makes the garden to smile and blossom. Philosophy, however, proposes herself as the regenerator of the race. Standing out at the base of human corruption, with her form but half revealed by the artificial glare about her, she talks to the victim who is wallowing in filth and uncleanness, about fate and necessity, and leaves the miserable wretch disconsolate in his lot, diseased in his fancy, and bankrupt in his hopes. But the Bible at one breath sweeps off the mists from this palpitating mass of festering rottenness, reveals the present and the future to the eye of the morally maimed and halt, and says to them, as unto the man at the pool, 'Arise, for thy redemption is near.'

"The Bible is a source of consolation in the calamities of life, and is equally adapted to the rich and the poor. But there are privations in the lot of the poor which make its teachings peculiarly necessary. The beams of the sun are never more grateful than when he bursts from the clouds and the storms; and, in like manner, the Bible is never more welcome than when its leaves come distributing consolation to the needy, the desolate, and the heart-stricken of earth. The primitive denunciation falls heavily upon the poor man; and when all other resources fail, where shall he look for consolation but to Him who cares for all—to Him who listens to the chirping of the lone sparrow upon the wintery hedges of the world, and sees the parched lily drooping with heat and blight? Fear not, then; for are ye not of much more value than many sparrows? It tells us that He feeds the ravens, and hears the young lions when they roar; and thus, when man is forsaken, and his house and his earthly fortunes left unto him desolate, it tells him that God, his friend, looks down from heaven, and careth for these things. In the course of my pastoral visitations, I lately called upon a widowed lady who had but recently buried a fond husband, and now had three or four children about her, dependent for their support upon her needle. As I entered the house, one of the little ones told me their mother had gone out for the morning. I passed on, and came to the habitation of an old lady who was without father, or mother, or near relation in the world, decrepit with years, and with a soul bowed down with often mourning; she was alone in the world, and her tenderest earthly affections reposed in the silence of the sepulcher. There I found also the first lady, who had left her home, lonely and depressed with sorrows and care, and had called on Mother Cox—such is the name of the aged servant of God—that she might gather strength and comfort from her communion. There sat those lone ones, widowed of earthly hopes—the one with a heart freshly scathed by the mysterious chastening of the wise God, and the other with gray hairs leaning upon the reed of faith, which that same God would not suffer to break and pierce her hand; and the latter, just tottering on the edge of her grave, was discoursing to the friendless Ruth, and leaning over the ever-bubbling well of salvation, and drawing the waters of life to quench the spiritual thirst of her young sister, and refresh her soul in its bitter wretchedness. It was there the divinity of the Gospel, healing wounds and elevating hopes, and encouraging to that patient endurance whereby we inherit the promises.

"It is the sin of the nations and the curse of the Church that we have never properly appreciated the Bible as we ought. It is the book of books for the priest and for the people, for the old and for the young. It should be the tenant of the academy as well as of the nursery, and ought to be incorporated in our course of education from the mother's knee to graduation in the highest universities in the land. Every thing is destined to fail unless the Bible be the fulcrum on which these levers revolve. Can such a book be read without an influence commensurate with its importance? As well might the flowers sleep when the spring winds its mellow horn to call them from their bed—as well might the mist linger upon the bosom of the lake when the sun beckons it to leave its dewy home. The Bible plants our feet amid that angel group which stood, with eager wing expectant, when the Spirit of God first hovered over the abyss of Chaos, and wraps us in praise for the new-born world, when the morning stars sang together for joy. The Bible builds for us the world when we were not, stretches our conceptions of the indefinite beyond the last orbit of astronomy, pacifies the moral discord of earth, reorganizes the dust of the sepulcher, and tells man heaven is his home and eternity his lifetime.

"What, sir, was the Reformation, but a resurrection of the Bible? Cloistered in the superstition of mediæval Rome for a thousand years, its moral rays had been intercepted, and the intellect of man, stricken at a blow from its pride of place, was shut within the dark walls of moral despair, and slept the sleep of death beneath its wizard spell. Opinion fled from the chambers of the heart, and left the mind to darkness and to change. But Luther evoked the Bible and its precepts from its prison-house, and the Word of God breathed the warm breath of life upon the valley of Vision and upon the sleeping Lethean sea. Intellect burst from the trance of ages, dashed aside the portals of her dark dungeon, felt the warm sunlight relax her stiffened limbs, forged her fetters into swords, and fought her way to freedom and to fame.

"The Bible, sir, is the guide of the erring and the reclaimer of the wandering; it heals the sick, consoles the dying, and purifies the living. If you would propagate Protestantism, circulate the Bible. Let the master give it to the pupil, the professor to his class, the father to his son, the mother to her daughter; place it in every hamlet in the land; then shall the love of God cover the earth, and the light of salvation overlay the land as the sunbeams of morning lie upon the mountains."

Union of Effort in the Bible Cause. By the Rev. Dr. De Witt.

Dr. De Witt said, "There is perfect Christian unity in heaven; there are gathered the redeemed from among different tribes, and kindred, and nations, and from different forms of religious association. They dwell in cloudless light, and walk in pure love, and in full holiness, and unwearied consecration. They have passed through the wilderness from the different encampments of Israel, and now they are gathered, not in tents, but in the temple made without hands, from which there is no going out. But the elements of this Christian unity are the elements of Christian character here on earth. The life of God, quickened in the renewed Israel, partakes of these elements, and thěre is a light that shineth here, the day-star in the heart of every Christian, growing brighter and brighter till the perfect day. It is as a pillar of cloud by day, and of fire by night, leading through all the mazes of the wilderness. Israel may have different tribes, but she has but one head, and she travels to one home. And nowhere is there to be found so strong a proof of this as when we come here with the Bible before us as the spring of hope and the rule of life. Acknowledging that Word as the sufficient rule of faith, all come together here, without regard to denominational differences. We have heard of family gatherings, after the members have been long scattered wide asunder; at some common call they have all been brought home, and around the father's fireside they have remembered that they belonged to one family. So is it with us. Widely scattered, we come together here in a hallowed family circle; we have one Father, one Savior, one Sanctifier; and there is the *one* book, the fountain of all life, and of all hope. This principle, then, stamps and proves the feasibility of this great enterprise. No Christian can fail to love it, and embrace it, and promote it. At our monthly meetings we have known no differences. The Bible alone was before us, and to that alone were our exertions directed. From that do we all drink life and hope, and truly has it been felt as the dew of Hermon falling upon us. In our own souls is the living witness. Is not here a practical demonstration of the feasibility of the work? Forty years ago the British and Foreign Bible Society was formed, springing from a simple proposition to supply a destitute region among the mountains of Wales. It was a mustard seed then; it is a vast, wide-spreading forest now. A small stone then, its base has widened, and its top reaches heavenward, and soon there shall be but one song on the earth, of grace, grace unto it. There has been but one name to this institution. The Bible alone has been the bond of union. We have been enabled to spread abroad this bread of life throughout the world. Some of the fathers of the institution have gone to rest. Places are vacant to-day which were once filled with those whom we delighted to meet in our midst. We miss him whose whole appearance commanded respect, who was a zealous laborer through its whole history; who did much by his Christian character and fidelity to establish and extend the influence of this society. It was the beautiful blending of the intellectual and the spiritual in his character that made him what he was, and enabled him to bring forth fruit even in his old age. He was conscientiously devoted to his own church, and in his departure a burning and shining light has gone from their midst; but we claim him as a member of this great body of Christ's church, and there is now a star in heaven that sheds light upon his hallowed memory. It was said by a celebrated minister, in speaking of the loss sustained by his departure, 'Never fear; you can spare one from the oar while the Master is at the helm.' The ship is now on her way; precious cargoes have been gathered; but much remains to be done. Let the bread of life, then, be scattered every where throughout the world."

Pacific Tendencies of the Bible. By the Rev. Dr. Parker.

Dr. Parker said "that he felt overwhelmed with the responsibility of speaking upon this topic at the present time, because, as all were aware, there were exciting circumstances connected with it, and because whatever was said there was spread, through the agency of the press, throughout the land and before the world. He was, however, glad of this, and especially glad that the secular press might now be regarded as the friend of the Bible Society, and as willing and glad to lend its aid in the glorious work of that society freely, zealously, and without pay. The subject of this resolution necessarily involved some allusion to the present condition of the country; and he wished to speak of it as delicately as possible, and yet with the utmost frankness as to his real views and opinions. The country had been invaded, and was now at war. This we must all deplore. We might, too, deem it an unnecessary, as well as a lamentable result. If he could have had his way, a different result would have been sought. But when the executive department of our government has had its way, and now that it has involved our country in hostilities, he felt bound to stand forth before the world as the friend of the executive, and he should do so just as freely and just as firmly as if he had not voted for Henry Clay. He would not imitate, for he did not respect, the spirit of the half-grown boys who set up for politicians, and talk censoriously of men in high places, and denounce all their acts, and vilify their characters and their conduct. Upon preliminary steps he might doubt and differ from them in opinion; but when the government has acted—when the shield has been lifted and the sword drawn, then he should appear as the friend of the government. If he did not think well of its measures, you, said he, shall not know it—the world shall not know it, from any thing I may say, directly at least.

"He did not doubt that the Bible was to extend the influence of pacific principles; but he did not believe that this was its only influence. He honored the sentiments of those who were opposed to war in every case. He believed they were guided by heavenly principles;

but he thought they did not exercise their intellects sufficiently, when they expected that the Bible was to put an end to war in any other way than by doing away with the *necessity* of war. He did not believe that the legitimate influence of the Bible was to make states and nations pusillanimous and mean. He did not believe that the sword was always taken in vain, or with God's displeasure.

"The Bible, he thought, promoted peace in two ways: by producing a high intelligence and independence of character—the necessary elements of wisdom and bravery essential for self-protection; and by causing a holy gentleness, a spirit of conscientiousness, which will not allow men to resort to force even for self-protection, except in the last resort, for the defense of order and of law, and for preserving a free course for the progress of Christian truth. The Bible always has made men pacific, but it has likewise always made them equally independent and determined in the maintenance of right. Think of the influence and the conduct of your Puritan ancestors. And who were the men of the Scottish Reformation? Why, John Knox was a veritable Andrew Jackson in fearlessness, every where and always; but this spirit was blended in him with great gentleness, and conscientiousness, and loyalty. Dr. P. said he was very much interested lately in reading an account of a lovely and interesting woman, the wife of John Welsh and the daughter of John Knox. Welsh had been banished by King James for his boldness and independence. He went to France, and labored for a time among the Huguenots; but his health failed, and he sailed to London, where he sought permission to return to Scotland. His application was in vain. But his wife sought an interview with the king. She told him that her husband wished to return to Scotland, from which he had been banished; that he would do no harm; and that even if his sentiments were wrong (which she denied), he could do no injury, for he was too near the gates of death. The king, being struck by her bearing, asked whose daughter she was. She said, the daughter of John Knox. 'The daughter of John Knox,' said he, 'married to John Welsh! No; the devil never made such a match.' 'Very likely,' said she; 'for, please your majesty, *we never speered his advice.*' Here was independence, as well as courage and gentleness. That is the spirit which the Bible produces. That is the spirit which makes this race of ours so formidable in iron energy, in strength, independence, and bravery. The Bible is pacific in its influence by elevating the character—by making those upon whom it acts brave to maintain the right, and wise in devising the means to do so. War can be justified only as a temporary evil—only as the least of two evils; and the pacific principles of the Bible provide a perfect way, where no evil need be chosen. That alone is the best and the perfect method. The resort to force has a great show of strength. Its armies, its ordnance, its prancing cavalry, and standards trailed in blood, and prisoners led in triumph—all this is grand and imposing, and the foolish and thoughtless world say, here is the power, here is the best way to put down wrong. They forget that this may create the necessity for doing the same work over again. But God's method is final, and in the end far more powerful. It is silent and quiet in its operation. All his universe moves on without as much friction as the finest chronometer ever made exhibits. And so is it with the principles of religion. The kingdom of God cometh not by observation. None but thoughtful souls can see the power. And yet it is the mightiest of all powers. When the Bible Society produces its thousand copies of the Bible a day, men hear or think but little of it, and know nothing of its results. But its millions of Bibles are educating millions of souls, and it takes several generations to show its full results. The mass know not that such a work is going forward. It excites comparatively no opposition —none, indeed, but of the far-seeing spiritual organization which has its center in Rome. That society, when it hears our reports, knows the meaning of them. Their language comes like that of the great city of the old world. It proclaims to their ears that *Rome must perish*. Yes, she shall perish, but not by violence. She shall perish of consumption and decrepitude. Her death is involved in the quiet operations of this society. It will be brought about by raising a spirit that will not brook her domination. Rome will find the Bible has taught Protestants to be independent while they are pacific; to resist her encroachments while it seeks the good of all the earth.

"The influence of the Bible, too, produces a more *permanent* peace than any other agency. The effects of the arts on ancient nations is seen to have been fleeting. The halls which once resounded with melody and glittered with beauty now hear the hissing of the serpent, and the long grass grows on the very hearth-stones of the ancient palaces. The works of art have perished; the very ashes of their authors have been scattered to the winds. Whatever conquests the Bible gains, it keeps. It was not so, indeed, until the invention of printing. But now its influence is handed down from one generation to another, and so it never dies. All sentiments and principles have a power to propagate and preserve themselves. The Jews have always preserved their clannish feeling of nationality. So, too, the sentiments awakened by the Reformation in regard to liberty of thought and the right to read the Bible have lived ever since, and will always live. They have become the ruling principles of that race. They have fired the hearts of freemen with a determination to resist tyranny even unto death. And now this new sentiment in favor of distributing the Scriptures is acquiring power, and is becoming deeper and still more deeply fixed in the hearts of the people. This whole land is demanding an open Bible, and will defy the world to take it from them; and this sentiment will be transmitted to the remotest generations. That is God's system, shadowed out in his providence and in the progress of events. And when the Bible shall exert its legitimate influence over all the land, there will be two reasons why even the enemies of the Bible must keep the peace: the first is, because Bible men *love* them; and in the second place, they will put them in irons if they oppose the free circulation of the truth of God. There will then be power as well as gentleness in the feeling of the Christian world; and never will they allow their rights to be wrenched away. The Bible brings a freedom strong to maintain itself and to aid others; a freedom which will as soon contend for the rights of the strangers who come among us as for those of others."

Address of the Rev. Mr. Bridel, of Paris.

The Rev. Mr. Bridel said, the Bible society which he represented proposed for its special object to supply every Catholic family in France with a copy of the Word of God. He said there were two proofs of the effect of its labors: 1st. The religious impression it had produced in France; and, 2d. The bitter opposition it has awakened. He gave passages from the pastoral letters of the archbishops in France, stigmatizing the movements of the colporteurs and Bible agents as venal and corrupting, to show how different is the temper of the French archbishops from that of the Archbishop of Canterbury, to whom Dr. Tyng had alluded. He spoke of the encouragements held out to the friends of the Bible now to labor with renewed energy in the cause, and of the especial claims which France had upon America, as a sister republic, for aid in this great work. France was now a republic; but she was young; she lacked experience; she had not the knowledge of the Bible which she needed. But where it was possessed it was faithfully studied and used. America must instruct France. The French Bible Society had been in successful operation until the recent political movements had brought a commercial crisis upon France, which had reduced to poverty some of the wealthiest friends of the society, and had thus stopped its resources and crippled its hands, just at the very time when there was the greatest and best opportunity for laboring in the cause of truth. Like a younger sister, France now appeals to America to give her the instruction she has herself acquired.

Demands of France upon our Sympathy and Aid in the Circulation of the Scriptures in that Country. By the Rev. Dr. Kirk.

Mr. Kirk said "that every person who has attended the meetings of the week must have discovered a peculiar tone, a peculiar impression. We are living at an unusual period. The voice of God is speaking through his providence in solemn, awful, and encouraging tones. We have heard all the while the rolling of his awful chariot wheels. It is his hand that sways the nations. He has caused the great ground-swell which men can not resist. Men can not meet under such circumstances without peculiar feelings, and all whom we have heard have evinced the same deep under-current. His own heart had been full of it. It appeared to him that these anniversaries, in expressing the views of the Church on the great movements of the age, did a great and a good work. There have been various meetings to sympathize with France. The one in Boston was a miserable failure, one of the flattest he had ever seen, and that because they had dragged in the miserable questions of socialism, and had forgotten the great movements of the providence of God. The movement was the result of no plan; it was the work of God. We may still be only in the first day of French creation; man may not yet have come up; but there is one that can bring him up from the brutality to which Rome has brought him. God is in human events, and we now may and must recognize this great fact. All our hopes for the future must be fixed on him. This is a day for earnest and for constant prayer. Let man sink to his own nothingness, and let God clothe himself in power and in majesty.

"He would simply say, that in regard to France, we must give a *practical* sympathy for her. We must show the amount of our sympathy with France. She has not been a practical nation. Yet her race is a noble people, and has a great mission. But now they are not practical men. It is for us to show the result of what can be *done.* We of the Bible Society sympathize with the revolution, and we put it down in the shape of 50,000 francs to send to France. That is the practical work we ought to do. When shall we begin to show the nations of Europe that we are a people that will give our money—that we are not a dollar-loving people? We have been misunderstood. We have been obliged to earn our dollars; but we have learned from the Bible that, having freely received, we must freely give. We are acting for God, and we must give out his property to help our brethren in France. There would be a great moral lesson imparted by this conduct. But our conduct must not only be practical, but *religious.* We must tell France that there is her hope. Voltaire said that, in the nineteenth century, there would not be found a man of intelligence who would look at the Bible, except as an old curiosity; and now he had been told that the very room in which Voltaire penned that sentence is piled up to the ceiling with Bibles, to be distributed all through France! Within that book lies the charter of every hope of every soul that will survive the wreck of death. It shows the High-priest offering up incense for our souls. We love it more than life, and if all our gold were piled in heaps, we should say, 'More precious is it than gold—yea, than much fine gold.' It is the daily use we make of it that makes it so precious to us. It is that on which we lean and in which we trust. The idea that this society shall to-day tell France what we think of that book, can not fail to produce a good effect."

THE END.

RECOMMENDATIONS.

From the Rev. Lyman Beecher, D.D., President of the Lane Theological Seminary, Cincinnati.

"I have examined the contents of the 'History of the American Bible Society,' comprehending all the variety of topics which belong to it, and regard it as an invaluable work due to posterity and the world, and as executed with fidelity and ability both in research and execution."

From the Rev. Thomas J. Biggs, D.D., President of Woodward College, Cin.

"I regret that my other engagements have allowed me to examine cursorily only your manuscript of the 'History of the Origin and Progress of the American Bible Society.' The circumstance of my having been present at its formation enables me to vouch for the truthful statements which you have so lucidly furnished in your history. Its subsequent successful progress you have presented felicitously in ample documentary testimony, confirmed by American missionary enterprise co-operating with that honored society throughout our land and throughout the world.

"In furnishing this History of the American Bible Society, you have, in my judgment, rendered important service to the Christian cause. The result, I trust, will prove that 'your labor has not been in vain in the Lord.'"

From the Right Reverend Charles P. M'Ilvaine, D.D., Bishop of the Protestant Episcopal Church, Ohio.

"I had great pleasure in inspecting the plan and execution of your 'History of the American Bible Society.' You have fallen upon a most interesting subject, which brings into its connection a great variety of important information, such as deserves the use you have made of it. So great and wonderful a work as that which Bible societies have, under God, effected, is indeed a fit subject for the pen of the historian, and the part which our own society has had the honor of taking in that work you have done well thus laboriously to record. From what you have permitted me to see of your work, I can not but feel assured that it will be highly interesting and useful, and I trust you will reap your reward in the advancement of the great cause to which your labors are devoted. May the Lord continue eminently to prosper the distribution of the Scriptures, and send his blessing upon all who are engaged in that work."

From the Rev. Stephen H. Tyng, D.D., Rector of St. George's Church in the City of New York.

"I have examined, with great satisfaction and delight, a considerable portion of the manuscript of the Rev. Mr. Strickland's History of the American Bible Society. I have been astonished at the amount of patient labor through which the author must have passed in compiling it, and extremely gratified with the result and character of his efforts, as far as I have had opportunity to examine the work. It is a most desirable, and will be a most useful publication. Among future monuments of the true greatness of our country, this history will stand as most important authority, and a witness of high esteem and value. I earnestly hope the work will meet with the circulation and encouragement among the friends of the Gospel in our land which it deserves."

From the Rev. Thomas H. Stockton.

"I am greatly pleased to learn that you are about to publish a 'History of the American Bible Society.' There is no history out of the Bible so interesting to me as that which is immediately connected with the Bible. I would regard a complete history of the Bible as the most valuable literary production in the world —except the Bible itself. It is enough to say in relation to your work, that I am satisfied it will be eminently attractive and useful. May the Lord sanctify it to the advancement of Bible supremacy."

From the Honorable John M'Lean, one of the Justices of the Supreme Court of the United States.

"It is no common approbation of a work to ask ourselves the question, on reading it, why it has not before been written and published? This implies a conviction that society has a deep interest in the subject, and that it is discussed with a clear and comprehensive method. Short as has been the lapse of time since the formation of the American Bible Society, yet its progress has been so wonderful, that in looking into your book the above idea will be suggested to every reader.

"We have heard much of interest respecting the society at its anniversaries, but how few are acquainted with its history. You lay before the reader, from the most authentic sources, its formation, its instrumentalities, its extension and effects, in a manner so clear and attractive as to encourage the hopes and increase the efforts of its friends. Whether we consider man as a social being, possessing moral susceptibilities which may lead to happiness or misery in this life, as they shall be improved or abused, or as an immortal being, there is no book so essential to his felicity as the Bible. And its dissemination at home and abroad, through the efforts of the Bible Society, in my judgment, is the great agency through which all nations may become civilized and Christianized.

"To record the achievements of this mighty progress is to write a record of events for the world, which must, more or less, sooner or later, influence its destiny."

From the Rev. Gardiner Spring, D.D.

"The 'History of the American Bible Society,' by Mr. Strickland, is a work of humble pretensions, but of great value; valuable for the facts it embodies, and for the order and simplicity of style in which they are presented. To the friends of the Bible, and especially to the advocates of the Bible cause, it furnishes a volume rich in matter, and in manner interesting and impressive."

From the Rev. Edmund S. Janes, D.D., Bishop of the Methodist Episcopal Church.

"Having read a part of the proof sheets of the 'History of the American Bible Society,' and acquainted myself with the general plan and design of the work, I take pleasure in commending it to the public. In my judgment, its publication will subserve the cause of Christianity by directing attention to one of the most powerful agencies ever employed in its promulgation. No one can read your 'History of the American Bible Society' with candor, without being convinced of the great efficiency and immense importance of that institution. This conviction must secure to it increased favor and patronage, and thus augment its power for good.

"The work will also be useful in furnishing clergymen and other advocates of the Bible cause with such incidents and statistical information as will afford them essential aid in their efforts.

"In my opinion, the volume is what its title imports, and is, in all respects, worthy of general patronage. I hope it will be extensively circulated."

From the Rev. Thomas A. Morris, D.D., Bishop of the Methodist Episcopal Church.

"Having read the first seven chapters of your 'History of the American Bible Society,' and the captions of the forthcoming ones, I take pleasure in expressing the opinion that it will be a valuable work, and one of interest both in matter and style to the friends of the Bible cause generally. That your effort to impart information on the subject may be abundantly successful, is the sincere wish of,

"Yours, respectfully and fraternally, THOMAS A. MORRIS."

From the Rev. J. P. Durbin, D.D., Philadelphia.

"I have carefully considered the contents of the History of the American Bible Society, prepared by the Rev. W. P. Strickland, and am satisfied that it is worthy of public confidence and patronage. It is a matter of surprise that such a work had not been projected before, and a cause of thankfulness that it has been so well planned and so ably executed by Mr. Strickland. Its general circulation will give increased interest in the Bible cause, and increased confidence to the friends of the Bible."

From the Rev. Samuel W. Fisher, D.D.

"It gives me great pleasure to commend to the Christian public the 'History of the American Bible Society' by the Rev. William P. Strickland. A glance at the table of contents will sufficiently evince the diversified and important character of the work; while an actual perusal of it will excite surprise at the immense extent and deeply interesting nature of the field it covers. This noble institution, among the grandest of all those benevolent associations peculiar to this age, is interlocked with several of them, like lofty trees whose roots and branches ramify through each other. The history of one, indeed, often is, in a great measure, that of the others; to unfold the doings of the Bible Society is to give in brief the leading facts of more than one other institution. This is especially true of our Foreign Missionary Board, to which the society has liberally ministered; and by the combined result of its generosity, and the learned labors of the missionaries, is the Word of God made vernacular to all nations. To the Christian, who loves to trace out the providence of God in its ministrations of mercy to men; to the philanthropist, who recognizes in the Bible the best instrument for the elevation of the race; to the pastor, who is often at a loss for the statistics which are here presented, and to whom the history of the Church in all its various operations is of unspeakable value, this book will commend itself as a thesaurus of well-arranged facts and interesting historical notices, valuable in themselves, and worthy to be transmitted in this compact form to the generations of the future."

From the Rev. Charles Elliott, D.D.

"I have examined the contents of a very interesting and instructive volume, comprising a history of the Bible Society and its operations by the Rev. W. P. Strickland, prepared with great care and with becoming fidelity and ability. I consider it a great desideratum on the topics on which it treats, and I am certain it will be read very generally by all the lovers of the Bible."

From the Rev. Robert Baird, D.D., of New York.

"I have read enough of Mr. Strickland's 'History of the American Bible Society' to be satisfied that it is an excellent work, containing a mass of most valuable and interesting information, and written in a spirit eminently *catholic* and *Biblical.* While it will be valuable to those who, in future times, will desire to trace to their sources the streams of benevolence which now bless the earth, it will be read with great profit by thousands of our own day."

SECOND EDITION.

THANKFULNESS—A NARRATIVE.

By the REV. CHARLES B. TAYLER, M.A.,
Rector of Otley, Suffolk.

Foolscap. 6s. 6d.

"'In every thing give thanks.' This vital duty of sincere Christianity is beautifully enforced by Mr. Tayler in the delightful volume before us. . . . The great charm of the work is its unforced piety."—*John Bull.*

"We heartily recommend this interesting narrative to our readers."—*Christian Lady's Magazine.*

"The Diary refers to the past century, and the visits to the old Catholic mansion, with its hiding places, may be justly cited as an example of pictorial power."—*Athenæum.*

"This little volume now before us is one that calls forth our warmest approbation."—*Morning Chronicle.*

THE HILL DIFFICULTY,

AND OTHER ALLEGORIES,

By DR. CHEEVER, Author of "Wanderings of a Pilgrim," &c. &c.

Foolscap, price 3s. 6d.

PESTALOZZIAN INSTRUCTION.

THE QUARTERLY EDUCATIONAL MAGAZINE,

And Record of the Home and Colonial School Society,

For 1848-1849. 2 vols. 8vo. 12s.

THE HARMONY OF EDUCATION,

DESIGNED TO ASSIST THOSE ENGAGED IN TEACHING.

"The object is to advocate a system of education carried on with reference to the development of individual character and the harmonious cultivation of conscience, reason, and imagination. Many interesting educational questions are discussed in a Christian and sensible manner." —*Christian Lady's Magazine.*

Foolscap 8vo., cloth, 3s. 6d.

SERMONS FOR FAMILY READING.

By the REV. W. SHORT, A.M.

Rector of St. George the Martyr, Queen-sq.; Prebendary of Salisbury; and Chaplain to His Grace the Duke of Buccleuch.

1 vol. 8vo, 10s. 6d.

BENJAMIN FRANKLIN;

AN AUTOBIOGRAPHY;

WITH A NARRATIVE OF HIS PUBLIC LIFE AND SERVICES.

By the REV. HASTINGS WELD.

With many Illustrations. 8vo., price 14s.

"When we state this book is illustrated to our liking, we mean the statement to convey high praise."—*Athenæum.*

"Altogether we consider this to be an exemplary sample of interesting biography, replete with entertainment and utility; farther we will not enter into this his "illustrated" and illustrious life,—but content us with cordially recommending it to our readers as a production which cannot fail to satisfy every taste, and be perused with great advantage by every class."—*Literary Gazette.*

BY THE REV. J. H. MERLE D'AUBIGNÉ, Author of the "History of the Reformation."

THE CONFESSION OF THE NAME OF CHRIST

IN THE SIXTEENTH AND SEVENTEENTH CENTURIES.

Translated from the French. Foolscap 8vo, 1s. 6d. cloth.

THE SWISS FAMILY ROBINSON,

OR, ADVENTURES OF A FATHER AND MOTHER AND FOUR SONS ON A DESERT ISLAND.

With Explanatory Notes and Illustrations. *Second Series.* 12mo. 6s.

By the HON. AND REV. BAPTIST W. NOEL, M.A.,—THE

CHRISTIAN'S FAITH, HOPE, & JOY,

Being the Substance of Twelve Sermons preached at St. John's Chapel, Bedford Row, during Lent 1848.

FROM NOTES BY ONE OF THE CONGREGATION.

18mo, cloth, 1s. 6d.

BY THE SAME AUTHOR,

THE MESSIAH,—FIVE SERMONS

[On "His name shall be called Wonderful, Counsellor, Mighty God, Everlasting Father, Prince of Peace."—*Isaiah* ix, 6.

18mo, cloth, 1s. 6d.

A COMPANION TO THE BOOK OF COMMON PRAYER.

BY A MEMBER OF THE CHURCH OF ENGLAND.

Foolscap 8vo, cloth, 1s.

Upham's Life of Faith:

Embracing some of the Scriptural Principles or Doctrines of Faith, the Power or Effect of Faith in the Regulation of Man's Inward Nature, and the Relation of Faith to the Divine Guidance. 12mo, Muslin, $1 00.

Upham's Life of Madame Adorna;

Including some leading Facts and Traits in her Religious Experience. Together with Explanations and Remarks, tending to illustrate the Doctrine of Holiness. 12mo, Muslin, 50 cents; Muslin, gilt edges, 60 cents.

Upham's Life of Madame Guyon.

The Life and Religious Opinions and Experience of Madame Guyon: together with some Account of the Personal History and Religious Opinions of Archbishop Fenelon. 2 vols. 12mo, Muslin, $2 00.

Upham's Principles of the Interior or Hidden Life.

Designed particularly for the Consideration of those who are seeking Assurance of Faith and Perfect Love. 12mo, Muslin, $1 00.

Sacred Meditations.

By P. L. U. 48mo, Muslin, gilt edges, 31¼ cents.

Thankfulness.

A Narrative. Comprising Passages from the Diary of the Rev. Allan Temple. By the Rev. C. B. Tayler. 12mo, Paper, 37½ cents; Muslin, 50 cents.

Book of Common Prayer:

Elegantly printed, according to the revised Standard adopted by the General Convention, in the following varieties of binding and size:

Standard 4to. A splendid volume, suitable for the desk. Turkey Morocco, gilt edges, $10 00.

Standard 8vo. From the same stereotype plates as the preceding. Sheep extra, $2 00; Calf extra, $2 50; Turkey Morocco, gilt edges, $5 00.

Royal 8vo. Hewet's Illustrated Edition. Turkey Morocco, gilt edges, $6 00.

Medium 8vo. Double Columns. Sheep extra, $1 25; Turkey Morocco, gilt edges, $4 00.

12mo, Sheep extra, 62½ cents; Roan extra, 75 cents; Turkey Morocco, gilt edges, $1 75.

18mo, Roan or Sheep extra, 75 cents; Calf or Turkey Morocco, gilt edges, $1 75.

24mo, Sheep extra, 35 cents; Roan extra, 40 cents; Calf or Turkey Morocco, gilt edges, $1 25.

32mo, Roan or Sheep extra, 40 cents; Calf or Turkey Morocco, gilt edges, $1 25.

Pearl, Roan or Sheep extra, 40 cents; Pocket-book form, gilt edges, $1 00; Calf or Turkey Morocco, gilt edges, $1 25.

Summerfield's Sermons,

And Sketches of Sermons. With an Introduction by Rev. T. E. Bond, M.D. 8vo, Muslin, $1 75.

Spencer's Greek New Testament.

With English Notes, critical, philological, and exegetical Indexes, &c. 12mo, Muslin, $1 25; Sheep extra, $1 40.

Barnes's Notes on the Gospels,
Explanatory and Practical. Designed for Bible Classes and Sunday Schools. With an Index, a Chronological Table, Tables of Weights, &c. Map. 2 vols. 12mo, Muslin, $1 50.

Barnes's Notes on the Acts of the Apostles,
Explanatory and Practical. Designed for Bible Classes and Sunday Schools. With a Map. 12mo, Muslin, 75 cents.

Barnes's Notes on the Epistle to the Romans,
Explanatory and Practical. Designed for Bible Classes and Sunday Schools. 12mo, Muslin, 75 cents.

Barnes's Notes on the First Epistle to the Corinthians, Explanatory and Practical. Designed for Bible Classes and Sunday Schools. 12mo, Muslin, 75 cents.

Barnes's Notes on the Second Epistle to the Corinthians, and the Epistle to the Galatians, Explanatory and Practical Designed for Bible Classes and Sunday Schools. 12mo, Muslin, 75 cents.

Barnes's Notes on the Epistles to the Ephesians, the Philippians, and the Colossians, Explanatory and Practical. Designed for Bible Classes and Sunday Schools. 12mo, Muslin, 75 cents.

Barnes's Notes on the Epistles to the Thessalonians, Timothy, Titus, and Philemon, Explanatory and Practical. Designed for Bible Classes and Sunday Schools. 12mo, Muslin, 75 cents.

Barnes's Notes on the Epistle to the Hebrews,
Explanatory and Practical. Designed for Bible Classes and Sunday Schools. 12mo, Muslin, 75 cents.

Barnes's Notes on the General Epistles of James, Peter, John, and Jude, Explanatory and Practical. Designed for Bible Classes and Sunday Schools. 12mo, Muslin, 75 cents.

Barnes's Questions on Matthew.
For Bible Classes and Sunday Schools. 18mo, Muslin, 15 cents.

Barnes's Questions on Mark and Luke.
For Bible Classes and Sunday Schools. 18mo, Muslin, 15 cents.

Barnes's Questions on John.
For Bible Classes and Sunday Schools. 18mo, Muslin, 15 cents.

Barnes's Questions on the Acts of the Apostles.
For Bible Classes and Sunday Schools. 18mo, Muslin, 15 cents.

Barnes's Questions on the Epistle to the Romans.
For Bible Classes and Sunday Schools. 18mo, Muslin, 15 cents.

Barnes's Questions on the First Epistle to the Corinthians. Designed for Bible Classes and Sunday Schools. 18mo, Muslin, 15 cents.

Barnes's Questions on the Epistle to the Hebrews.
For Bible Classes and Sunday Schools. 18mo, Muslin, 15 cents.

Neal's History of the Puritans;

Or, Protestant Non-conformists; from the Reformation in 1517 to the Revolution in 1688; comprising an Account of their Principles, their Attempts for a further Reformation in the Church, their Sufferings, and the Lives and Characters of their most considerable Divines. Reprinted from the Text of Dr. Toulmin's Edition: with his Life of the Author, and Account of his Writings. Revised, corrected, and enlarged, with additional Notes, by JOHN O. CHOULES, D.D. Embellished with Nine Portraits on Steel. 2 vols. 8vo, Muslin, $3 50; Sheep extra, $4 00.

Abercrombie's Miscellaneous Essays.

Consisting of the Harmony of Christian Faith and Christian Character; the Culture and Discipline of the Mind; Think on these Things; the Contest and the Armor; the Messiah as an Example. 18mo, Muslin, 37½ cents.

Jarvis's Chronological Introduction to Church History:

being a new Inquiry into the true Dates of the Birth and Death of our Lord and Savior Jesus Christ; and containing an original Harmony of the four Gospels, now first arranged in the Order of Time. 8vo, Muslin, $3 00.

Butler's Analogy of Religion,

Natural and Revealed, to the Constitution and Course of Nature. To which are added two brief Dissertations: of Personal Identity—of the Nature of Virtue. With a Preface by Bishop HALIFAX. 18mo, half Bound, 37½ cents.

Hawks's History of the Protestant Episcopal

Church in Virginia: being a Narrative of Events connected with its Rise and Progress. With the Journals of the Conventions in Virginia. 8vo, Muslin, $1 75.

Jay's Morning and Evening Exercises for the Closet,

for every Day in the Year. With Portrait. 8vo, Muslin, $1 25; half Morocco, $1 50.

Jay's complete Works:

Comprising his Sermons; Family Discourses; Morning and Evening Exercises for every Day in the Year; Family Prayers; Lectures; Lives of Cornelius Winter and John Clark, &c. Author's enlarged Edition, revised. 3 vols. 8vo, Muslin, $5 00; Sheep extra, $5 50.

Saurin's Sermons.

Translated by the Rev. ROBERT ROBINSON, the Rev. HENRY HUNTER, and the Rev. JOSEPH SUTCLIFFE. A new Edition, with additional Sermons. Revised and corrected by the Rev. SAMUEL BURDER. With a Preface, by the Rev. J. P. K. HENSHAW. With a Portrait. 2 vols. 8vo, Sheep extra, $3 75.

Lewis's Platonic Theology.

Plato against the Atheists; or, the Tenth Book of the Dialogue on Laws, with critical Notes and extended Dissertations on some of the main Points of the Platonic Philosophy and Theology, especially as compared with the Holy Scriptures. 12mo, Muslin, $1 50.

Protestant Jesuitism.

By a Protestant. 12mo, Muslin, 90 cents.

Noel's Essay on the Union of Church and State.

12mo, Muslin, $1 25.

Gieseler's Compendium of Ecclesiastical History.

From the Fourth Edinburgh Edition, revised and amended. Translated from the German by Samuel Davidson, LL.D. 8vo.

The Sacred Philosophy of the Seasons.

Illustrating the Perfections of God in the Phenomena of the Year. By Rev. Henry Duncan, D.D. With important Additions, and some Modifications to adapt it to American Readers, by F. W. P. Greenwood, D.D. 4 vols. 12mo, Muslin, $3 00.

Theology Explained and Defended,

In a Series of Sermons. By T. Dwight, LL.D. With a Memoir of the Life of the Author. With a Portrait. 4 vols. 8vo, Muslin, $6 00; Sheep extra, $6 50.

Waddington's History of the Church,

From the earliest Ages to the Reformation. 8vo, Muslin, $1 75.

Brown's Dictionary of the Holy Bible.

Containing an Historical Account of the Persons; a Geographical and Historical Account of the Places; a Literal, Critical, and Systematical Description of other Objects, whether Natural, Artificial, Civil, Religious, or Military; and an Explanation of the appellative Terms mentioned in the Old and New Testaments: the whole comprising whatever important is known concerning the Antiquities of the Hebrew Nation and Church of God; forming a Sacred Commentary, a Body of Scripture History, Chronology, and Divinity; and serving in a great measure as a Concordance to the Holy Bible. With the Author's last Additions and Corrections, and further enlarged and corrected by his Sons. Also, a Life of the Author, and an Essay on the Evidence of Christianity. 8vo, Sheep extra, $1 75.

Brown's Pocket Concordance to the Holy Bible.

32mo, Roan, 37½ cents.

Hunter's Sacred Biography;

Or, the History of the Patriarchs. To which is added the History of Deborah, Ruth, and Hannah, and also the History of Jesus Christ. 8vo, Muslin, $1 75.

Milman's History of Christianity,

From the Birth of Christ to the Abolition of Paganism in the Roman Empire. With Notes, &c., by James Murdock, D.D. 8vo, Muslin, $1 90.

Milman's History of the Jews,

From the earliest Period to the present Time. With Maps and Engravings. 3 vols. 18mo, Muslin, $1 20.

The Old and New Testaments Connected,

In the History of the Jews and Neighboring Nations, from the Declension of the Kingdoms of Israel and Judah to the Time of Christ. By Humphrey Prideaux, D.D. To which is prefixed, the Life of the Author, containing some Letters which he wrote in Defense and Illustration of certain Parts of his Connections. Illustrated with Maps and Plates. 2 vols. 8vo, Sheep extra, $3 75.

Lord's Exposition of the Apocalypse.

8vo, Muslin, $2 00.

Turner's Sacred History of the World,

Attempted to be Philosophically considered, in a Series of Letters to a Son. 3 vols. 18mo, Muslin, $1 35.

Vol. I. considers the Creation and System of the Earth, and of its Vegetable and Animal Races, and Material Laws, and Formation of Mankind.

Vol. II., the Divine Economy in its special Relation to Mankind, and in the Deluge, and the History of Human Affairs.

Vol. III., the Provisions for the Perpetuation and Support of the Human Race, the Divine System of our Social Combinations, and the Supernatural History of the World.

The Incarnation;

Or, Pictures of the Virgin and her Son. By Rev. C. Beecher. With an introductory Essay, by Mrs. Harriet Beecher Stowe. 18mo, Muslin, 50 cents.

Paley's Evidences of Christianity.

A View of the Evidences of Christianity. 18mo, half Roan, 37½ cents.

Paley's Natural Theology.

With illustrative Notes, &c., by Lord Brougham and Sir C. Bell, and preliminary Observations and Notes, by Alonzo Potter, D.D. With Engravings. 2 vols. 18mo, Muslin, 90 cents.

Paley's Natural Theology.

A new Edition, from large Type, edited by D. E. Bartlett. Copiously Illustrated, and a Life and Portrait of the Author. 2 vols. 12mo, Muslin, $1 50.

Neander's Life of Jesus Christ:

In its Historical Connection and its Historical Development. Translated from the Fourth German Edition, by Professors M'Clintock and Blumenthal. 8vo, Muslin, $2 00; Sheep extra, $2 25.

The Land of Israel,

According to the Covenant with Abraham, with Isaac, and with Jacob. By A. Keith, D.D. With Plates. 12mo, Muslin, $1 25.

Evidence of Prophecy.

Evidence of the Truth of the Christian Religion, derived from the literal Fulfillment of Prophecy; particularly as illustrated by the History of the Jews, and by the Discoveries of recent Travelers. By A. Keith, D.D. 12mo, Muslin, 60 cents.

Demonstration of Christianity.

Demonstration of the Truth of the Christian Religion. By A. Keith, D.D. With Engravings. 12mo, Muslin, $1 37½.

The Mysteries Opened;

Or, Scriptural Views of Preaching and the Sacraments, as distinguished from certain Theories concerning Baptismal Regeneration and the Real Presence. By Rev. J. S. Stone. 12mo, Muslin, $1 00.

The True Believer;

His Character, Duty, and Privileges, elucidated in a Series of Discourses. By Rev. Asa Mahan. 18mo, Muslin, 50 cents.

The Novitiate;

Or, a Year among the English Jesuits: a Personal Narrative. With an Essay on the Constitutions, the Confessional Morality, and History of the Jesuits. By ANDREW STEINMETZ. 18mo, Muslin, 50 cents.

Duer's Speech,

Delivered in the Convention of the P. E. Church of the Diocese of New York, on Friday, the 29th of Sept., 1843, in support of the Resolutions offered by Judge Oakley. 8vo, Paper, 12½ cents.

Biblical Legends of the Mussulmans.

The Bible, the Koran, and the Talmud. Compiled from Arabic Sources, and compared with Jewish Traditions. By Dr. G. WEIL. 12mo, Muslin, 50 cents.

Scripture Illustrated,

By interesting Facts, Incidents, and Anecdotes. By Rev. C. FIELD. With Introduction, by Rev. J. TODD, D.D. 18mo, Muslin, 50 cents; Roan, 60 cents.

Mosheim's Ecclesiastical History,

Ancient and Modern; in which the Rise, Progress, and Variation of Church Power are considered in their Connection with the State of Learning and Philosophy, and the Political History of Europe during that Period. Translated, with Notes, &c., by A. MACLAINE, D.D. A new Edition, continued to 1826, by CHARLES COOTE, LL.D. 2 vols. 8vo, Sheep extra, $3 50.

Turner's Essay on our Lord's Discourse at Capernaum,

recorded in the Sixth Chapter of St. John. 12mo, Muslin, 75 cents.

The Heart Delineated in its State by Nature, and

as renewed by Grace. By the Rev. HUGH SMITH, D.D. 18mo, Muslin, 45 cents.

Smedley's History of the Reformation in France.

Portrait. 3 vols. 18mo, Muslin, $1 40.

Gleig's History of the Bible.

With a Map. 2 vols. 18mo, Muslin, 80 cents.

Zion's Songster;

Or, a Collection of Hymns and Spiritual Songs, usually Sung at Camp-meetings, and also at Revivals of Religion. Compiled by the Rev. THOMAS MASON. 32mo, Sheep, 25 cents.

D'Aubigné's Discourses and Essays.

Translated from the French, by CHARLES W. BAIRD. With an Introduction, by the Rev. Dr. BAIRD. 12mo, Muslin, 75 cents.

Sunday Evenings.

Comprising Scripture Stories. With Engravings. 3 vols. 18mo, Muslin, 93¾ cents.

Beauties of the Bible:

Selected from the Old and New Testaments, with various Remarks and brief Dissertations. Designed for the Use of Schools and the Improvement of Youth. By EZRA SAMPSON. 18mo, Muslin, 50 cents.

Luther and the Lutheran Reformation.

By Rev. John Scott. With Portraits. 2 vols. 18mo, Muslin, $1 00.

The Comforter;

Or, Consolations for Mourners. 12mo, Muslin, 45 cents.

Parker's Invitations to True Happiness,

And Motives for becoming a Christian. 18mo, Muslin, 37½ cents.

Evidences of Christianity,

In their External or Historical Division. By the Rt. Rev. Bishop M'Ilvaine, D.D. 12mo, Muslin, $1 00.

M'Ilvaine's Charge.

A Charge delivered to the Clergy of the Diocese of Ohio, at the 26th Annual Convention of the same. 8vo, Paper, 12½ cents.

Christianity independent of the Civil Government.

By Archbishop Whately. 12mo, Muslin, 90 cents.

Uncle Philip's Evidences of Christianity;

Or, Conversations with the Children about the Truth of the Christian Religion. 18mo, Muslin, 35 cents.

Help to Faith;

Or, a Summary of the Evidences of the Genuineness, Authenticity, Credibility, and Divine Authority of the Holy Scriptures. By Rev. Peter P. Sandford. 12mo, Sheep, 75 cents.

Pusey's Sermon.

The Holy Eucharist a Comfort to the Penitent: a Sermon delivered before the University of Oxford. 8vo, Paper, 6¼ cents.

Life of Christ,

In the Words of the Evangelists. A complete Harmony of the Gospel History of our Savior. For the Use of Young Persons. Illustrated by 30 fine Engravings by Adams from Designs by Chapman and others. 16mo, Paper, 62½ cents; Muslin, 75 cents.

Colton's Thoughts on the Religious State of the

Country, with Reasons for preferring Episcopacy. 12mo, Muslin, 60 cents.

John Ronge, the Holy Coat of Treves, and the new

German-Catholic Church. 18mo, Paper, 25 cents; Muslin, 37½ cents.

The Consistency of the whole Scheme of Revelation

with Itself and with Human Reason. By Philip N. Shuttleworth. 18mo, Muslin, 45 cents.

Persecutions of Popery:

Historical Narratives of the most remarkable Persecutions occasioned by the Intolerance of the Church of Rome. By F. Shoberl. 8vo, Paper, 25 cents.

The Reformers before the Reformation.

The Fifteenth Century. John Huss and the Council of Constance. By Emile De Bonnechose. Translated from the French, by Campbell Mackenzie, B.A. An Introduction to D'Aubigné's "History of the Reformation." 8vo, Paper, 50 cents.

Blair's Sermons.

To which is prefixed the Life and Character of the Author, by J. Finlayson, D.D. 8vo, Muslin, $1 50.

The Sufferings of Christ.

By a Layman. 12mo, Muslin, 50 cents.

Bunyan's Pilgrim's Progress.

With a Life of Bunyan, by Robert Southey, LL.D. Illustrated with 50 Engravings, by J. A. Adams. 12mo, Paper, 50 cents; Muslin, 75 cents.

Josephus's complete Works.

A new Translation, by the Rev. R. Traill, D.D. With Notes, explanatory Essays, &c., by Rev. Isaac Taylor. With numerous Engravings. Publishing in Numbers, at 25 cents each.

Jost's History of the Jews,

From the Times of the Maccabees to the present Day. Translated from the German, by J. H. Hopkins, Jun., M.A. (In press.)

Pise's Letters to Ada.

18mo, Muslin, 45 cents.

Lives of the Apostles and early Martyrs of the

Church. Engravings. 18mo, Muslin, 25 cents.

The Days of Queen Mary.

With Engravings. 12mo, Paper, 25 cents.

Bishop Hopkins's Humble but Earnest Address to

the Bishops, Clergy, and Laity of the Protestant Episcopal Church in the United States, on the Tolerating among our Ministry the Doctrines of the Church of Rome. 8vo, Paper, 12½ cents.

Malan's Inquiry.

Can I Join the Church of Rome while my Rule of Faith is the Bible? An Inquiry presented to the Conscience of the Christian Reader. Translated from the Second French Edition. 8vo, Paper, 25 cents.

Smith and Anthon's Statement of Facts.

The True Issue for the True Churchman; a Statement of Facts in relation to the recent Ordination in St. Stephen's Church, New York. 8vo, Paper, 12½ cents.

The True Churchman Warned against the Errors

of the Time. Edited, with Notes, by the Rev. Henry Anthon, D.D. 8vo, Paper, 12½ cents.

The True Issue Sustained;

Or, an Exhibit of the Views and Spirit of the Episcopal Press in relation to the recent Ordination in St. Stephen's Church, New York. Compiled by a Member of the Protestant Episcopal Church in the Diocese of New York. 8vo, Paper, 12½ cents.

No Church without a Bishop;

Or, the Controversy between the Rev. Drs. Potts and Wainwright. With a Preface by the latter, and an Introduction and Notes by an Anti-Sectarian. 8vo, Paper, 25 cents.

Harper's New Catalogue.

A NEW DESCRIPTIVE CATALOGUE OF HARPER & BROTHERS' PUBLICATIONS, embracing the most recent of their issues, is now ready for distribution, and may be obtained gratuitously on application to the publishers personally, or by letter, post-paid.

The attention of gentlemen, in town or country, designing to form Libraries or enrich their literary collections, is respectfully invited to this Catalogue, which will be found to comprise a large proportion of the standard and most esteemed works in English Literature—COMPREHENDING ABOUT TWO THOUSAND VOLUMES—which are offered in most instances at less than one half the cost of similar productions in England.

To Librarians and others connected with Colleges, Schools, etc., who may not have access to a reliable guide in forming the true estimate of literary productions, it is believed the present Catalogue will prove especially valuable as a manual of reference.

To prevent disappointment, it is suggested that, whenever books can not be obtained through any bookseller or local agent, applications with remittance should be addressed direct to the Publishers, which will be promptly attended to.

82 *Cliff Street, New York.*

www.ingramcontent.com/pod-product-compliance
Lightning Source LLC
LaVergne TN
LVHW020913110826
845150LV00004B/658
9781425556921